FEMINIST PERSPECTIVES ON PUBLIC LAW

Cavendish
Publishing

FEMINIST PERSPECTIVES ON PUBLIC LAW

Edited by

Susan Millns
Lecturer in Law,
University of Kent at Canterbury

and

Noel Whitty
Lecturer in Law,
Keele University

Cavendish
Publishing
Limited

London • Sydney

First published in Great Britain 1999 by Cavendish Publishing Limited,
The Glass House, Wharton Street, London WC1X 9PX, United Kingdom
Telephone: + 44 (0) 171 278 8000   Facsimile: + 44 (0) 171 278 8080
E-mail: info@cavendishpublishing.com
Visit our Home Page on http://www.cavendishpublishing.com

Feminist perspectives on public law
1. Public law
I. Millns, S II. Whitty, Noel
342.4'1

ISBN 1 85941 480 X

Printed and bound in Great Britain

SERIES EDITORS' PREFACE

Public law has proven peculiarly resistant to feminist analysis. Other subjects have at least benefited from the development of a 'ghetto', a place where feminist insights are acknowledged and investigated in the margins, with the hope of their being moved into more central focus. This has been the case, for example, within Health Care law, where the relevance of feminist scholarship on reproductive issues has increasingly been acknowledged, and in employment law, where feminist work on sex discrimination and maternity rights has now become crucial. The same is not true for public law.

This is surely not because the subject matter of public law holds little of interest to feminists. Concepts of democracy, sovereignty, participation, citizenship and rights have been central to a wide range of feminist scholarship. Equally, feminist work has played an increasingly important role in work on political theory. But this vibrant body of work has hardly rippled the surface of the legal academy. It has had little impact, for instance, on the work undertaken by many European Union lawyers and, even when and where such work exists, it has failed to infiltrate mainstream public law theory, which has maintained an almost blinkered loyalty to the tradition of Dicey.

As such, we are particularly excited to welcome this new contribution to the *Feminist Perspectives* Series. This storming of one of the most impenetrable of law subjects takes the series into the very heart of the mainstream law curriculum. The volume's unique combination of public law and feminist scholarship strikes a new note and one which is long overdue. Its contextualisation of the key public law concepts within gendered power relations, and the new feminist perspectives which it offers on the key institutions of government, open up an important new space for critique and dialogue amongst public law scholars. More radically than this, the volume fundamentally questions the sustainability of public law scholarship as currently constructed.

The volume is also particularly timely because we are in a period of substantial constitutional change. The possibility of transfer of political power to Scotland, Wales and Northern Ireland seems ever more real; major changes are underway in the protection of human rights; and important developments are possible in systems of representation. This provides both the perfect moment and the perfect momentum for feminists to seize the political stage. All of these changes raise profound choices regarding how we wish to organise our society. It is essential that a plurality of voices be heard in debating them. Without a proper understanding of the gender context within which our governmental institutions operate, and the gendered nature of the way certain key concepts are deployed, there can be no adequate understanding of the nature of public law. This collection offers new ways of thinking about public law – ways which are experimental and exciting and which ultimately offer the promise of a more inclusive understanding. Above all, this volume offers a reminder that, whilst public law may appear to be a discipline which looks ever backwards to our histories and traditions, it is also a subject with a future. Feminist theory has a good deal to contribute to this future, and this collection is a sure step in that direction.

As ever, we wish to acknowledge with thanks the ongoing support of our colleagues at Keele and Kent Universities, and the enthusiasm of our editor, Jo Reddy, at Cavendish.

Anne Bottomley and Sally Sheldon

ACKNOWLEDGMENTS

This collection arises from a one day workshop on 'Feminist Perspectives on Public Law' held at Keele University in May 1998. We would like to thank all the speakers at the workshop, together with members of the audience for taking the time out of their busy schedules to attend and generously participate in the discussions on the papers.

Our special thanks go also to Lara McMurtry for her amazing efficiency and competence in compiling the index and bibliography of the collection, and to Jo Reddy at Cavendish for her relentless enthusiasm and unstinting patience.

Finally, we would like to acknowledge the generous support given by our colleagues in the Law Departments at Keele University and the University of Kent. More specifically, working under the guidance of the series editors, Anne Bottomley and Sally Sheldon, has proven to be both an intellectually challenging and extremely pleasurable experience. We hope that we have done justice to their unfailing faith in the merits of a public law addition to the *Feminist Perspectives* series.

Susan Millns and Noel Whitty

CONTRIBUTORS

Davina Cooper is a member of Keele University Law Department. In the mid-1980s, she was an active new urban left London councillor. Since then, she has written in the areas of feminist political theory, local government, education and religion. Her publications include *Sexing the City: Lesbian and Gay Politics Within the Activist State* (1994), *Power in Struggle: Feminism, Sexuality and the State* (1995) and *Governing Out of Order: Space, Law and the Politics of Belonging* (1998).

Adam Gearey is a lecturer in law at Birkbeck College. His most recent publications include 'The Bible, law and liberation', in *Current Legal Problems* (1999), 'Outlaw blues: law in the lyrics of Bob Dylan', in the *Cardozo Law Review* (1999) and 'Stephen Dedalus' magic words: law and death between James Joyce and Pierre Legendre', in Manderson, D, *Courting Death: The Legal Constitution of Mortality* (1999). He is presently researching a book on law and aesthetics.

CJ Harvey is a lecturer at the Centre for International and Comparative Human Rights Law, School of Law, Queen's University Belfast. He has written extensively on refugee and asylum law and is presently completing a book on the subject. He has recently been working on the public law implications of the Northern Ireland peace process. He is on the editorial board of the *Journal of Civil Liberties* and is a member of the Public Law Subject Section Panel of the SPTL.

Elizabeth Kingdom is a senior lecturer in sociology at the University of Liverpool. She publishes on the legal politics of rights discourse and on the legality of cohabitation contracts. She is the author of *What's Wrong with Rights?: Problems for Feminist Politics of Law* (1991). She is Deputy Editor of *Res Publica* and an Associate Editor of *Social and Legal Studies*.

Angus McDonald teaches philosophy of law/critical legal studies and constitutional/public law at Staffordshire University. His research interests are in these areas, with particular emphasis on a postmodern philosophy of constitutionality and the theory of the public sphere. He has published articles on these topics and on the situationists and theories of urbanism.

Clare McGlynn is a lecturer in law at the University of Newcastle upon Tyne, having previously taught at the University of Durham. She has written widely in the fields of European Community law, anti-discrimination law, and gender and the legal profession. She is author of *The Woman Lawyer: Making the Difference* (1998) and editor of *Legal Feminisms: Theory and Practice* (1998).

Susan Millns is a lecturer in law at the University of Kent and has published in the areas of European and comparative public law and law and gender. She is co-author (with Jo Bridgeman) of *Feminist Perspectives on Law: Law's Engagement with the Female Body* (1998) and co-editor (also with Jo Bridgeman) of *Law and Body Politics: Regulating the Female Body* (1995). She is on the editorial board of *Feminist Legal Studies*.

Thérèse Murphy teaches law at the University of Nottingham. She writes primarily in the area of feminist legal theory. Her chapter developed from work funded by the Fulbright Commission. She is the author of 'Health confidentiality in the age of talk', in Sheldon, S and Thomson, M (eds), *Feminist Perspectives on Health Care Law* (1998).

Michael Thomson is a lecturer in the Department of Law at Keele University. He has published widely in the areas of health care law, gender and sexuality, and law and literature. He is the author of *Reproducing Narrative: Gender, Reproduction and Law* (1998), and the co-editor (with Sally Sheldon) of *Feminist Perspectives on Health Care Law* (1998). He is on the editorial board of *Res Publica*.

Noel Whitty teaches public law, law and society, and health care law at Keele University. He is co-author of *Teaching Human Rights* (1999) and he is the author of '"In a perfect world": feminism and health care resource allocation', in Sheldon, S and Thomson, M (eds), *Feminist Perspectives on Health Care Law* (1998).

CONTENTS

TABLE OF CASES

TABLE OF ABBREVIATIONS

AC	Appeal Cases
All ER	All England Reports
CJLS	Canadian Journal of Law and Society
CMLR	Common Market Law Reports
CSP	Critical Social Policy
EHRR	European Human Rights Reports
EJST	European Journal of Social Theory
EL Rev	European Law Review
FLS	Feminist Legal Studies
FR	Feminist Review
Harv L Rev	Harvard Law Review
HLR	Housing Law Reports
HRQ	Human Rights Quarterly
ICLQ	International and Comparative Law Quarterly
ICR	Industrial Compensation Reports
JLS	Journal of Law and Society
JSWFL	Journal of Social Welfare and Family Law
LGR	Local Government Reports
LRB	London Review of Books
LS	Legal Studies
LQR	Law Quarterly Review
MLR	Modern Law Review
NLJ	New Law Journal
NLR	New Left Review
OJLS	Oxford Journal of Legal Studies

PL	Public Law
QB	Queen's Bench
RP	Radical Philosophy
SLS	Social and Legal Studies
Stan L Rev	Stanford Law Review
Web JCLI	Web Journal of Current Legal Issues
WLR	Weekly Law Reports
YBEL	Yearbook of European Law

CHAPTER 1

PUBLIC LAW AND FEMINISM[1]

Susan Millns and Noel Whitty

INTRODUCTION

Feminism is characterised by a focus on gender as a central organising principle of social life; an emphasis on the concept of power and the ways that it affects social relations; and an unwavering commitment to progressive social change.[2] Feminist approaches generally reject universalist claims or accounts of the abstracted self. They ask questions about subject and standpoint, and try to recognise the situated nature of people's lives. They also acknowledge and explore the structural factors which contribute to the void between legal and substantive equality, crossing disciplinary boundaries and traversing conventional divides.

So, why should feminists be interested in public law, or public law in feminism? These are the questions we try to answer in this collection. Basically, our argument is that '[i]nsights from feminist theory now offer the means to interrogate all aspects of modern public law and policy'.[3] At least three opportunities are immediately apparent. First, working outside the disciplines of public law and politics, feminists have developed critiques of core, but essentially contested, concepts of public law. These include citizenship, power, the public/private divide, sovereignty, relationality, authority and the rule of law.[4] Secondly, feminist theory has been committed not just to critiquing but also to 're-visioning' the political, seeking to provide a normative framework for just relationships between the state and civil society.[5] Thirdly, feminism has recently faced a crisis similar to the one bubbling in contemporary public law. Feminists are familiar with loss of

---

1   Our thanks to Davina Cooper, Thérèse Murphy and Ray Cocks for their comments on this chapter.

2   See Gelsthorpe, L, 'Feminism and criminology', in Maguire, M, Morgan, R and Reiner, R (eds), *The Oxford Handbook of Criminology*, 1997, Oxford: Clarendon, p 529, for an account of a similar 'convergence of interests between feminism and criminology in some quarters, and thus scope for positive dialogue'.

3   See Harvey, Chapter 10, this volume, p 212.

4   See, eg, Hirschman, N and Di Stefano, C (eds), *Revisioning the Political: Feminist Reconstructions of Traditional Concepts in Western Political Theory*, 1996, Oxford: Westview.

5   See, generally, Smart, C, *Feminism and the Power of Law*, 1989, London: Routledge; and Lacey, N, *Unspeakable Subjects: Feminist Essays in Legal and Social Theory*, 1998, Oxford: Hart.

certainty and widespread disorientation, and may be able to help public law think through its current problems.

We want to emphasise from the outset that this volume does not aim to write a feminist account of public law. As its title indicates, and as each chapter clearly demonstrates, it is important to speak of a variety of feminist perspectives on public law. The contributors draw from various strands of feminist theory and political practice in order to critique and re-vision aspects of public law. The volume as a whole reflects the diverse (often inter-disciplinary) foundations of feminist theorising, as well as its grounding in real (and often marginalised) experiences. Strands of liberal, cultural, communitarian, materialist, Foucauldian, radical, Habermasian, postmodern and poststructural feminist theories are all represented in this collection.[6]

We hope that this eclectic feminist methodology and intellectual hybridity will make apparent that what *should* constitute the core concepts, values and functions of public law is contested territory. Moreover, we believe that this is precisely why feminist theory offers such potential to public lawyers.

THE FRACTURING OF PUBLIC LAW

Public law and public law scholarship is fracturing badly. The doctrinal tradition familiar to generations of law students[7] – perhaps best exemplified in the *Constitutional and Administrative Law* textbook by Wade and Bradley[8] – is slowly being undermined by a growing 'new public law' scholarship. As Morison and Livingstone point out in their innovative and wide ranging critique of British constitutionalism, the 'series of comfortable ideas handed down from Blackstone to Bagehot to Dicey'[9] are now woefully inadequate tools for understanding the nature and exercise of power in the UK today:

> Even now, the main textbook tradition operates within the parameters set within a different age. A glance down the contents page of any of the main textbooks will reveal a world where the exercise of power is more or less neatly within the collection of institutions that the accidents of a long history have thrown up ... In the United Kingdom, Parliament still appears at the top

---

6   See, generally, Davies, M, *Asking the Law Question*, 1994, Sydney: Law Book; Barrett, M and Phillips, A (eds), *Destabilising Theory: Contemporary Feminist Debates*, 1992, Cambridge: Polity; Brooks, A, *Postfeminisms: Feminism, Cultural Theory and Cultural Forms*, 1997, London: Routledge; and Robson, R, *Sappho Goes to Law School: Fragments in Lesbian Legal Theory*, 1998, New York: Columbia UP.

7   See, generally, Sugarman, D, 'Legal theory, the common law mind and the making of the textbook tradition', in Twining, W (ed), *Legal Theory and Common Law*, 1986, Oxford: Basil Blackwell, pp 26–61.

8   Bradley, AW and Ewing, KD, *Constitutional and Administrative Law*, 12th edn, 1997, Harlow: Longman.

9   Morison, J and Livingstone, S, *Reshaping Public Power: Northern Ireland and the British Constitutional Crisis*, 1995, London: Sweet & Maxwell, p 1.

of this hierarchy of institutions, as if somehow it and the Crown operate a monopoly of public power. The privatisation of public power and the internationalisation of national authority that have radically altered the constitution in the last 20 or so years seem strangely absent in the mainstream of constitutional writing.[10]

This is no new criticism of public law and public lawyers. In 1986, Lewis pointed out that, traditional treatments of public law are 'on the whole, pretty baffling in terms of the presuppositions on which they are based ... [and] the intellectual strategy to be adopted in seeking to map out or chart an anatomy of some unspoken version of constitutionality'.[11] Furthermore, the influence of Dicey, 'the high priest of orthodox constitutional theory', has been so pervasive – for example, in relation to the constitutional law textbook, the obsession with sovereignty, and the conservative ideology – that 'we seem incapable of recognising any work which predates Dicey; it is as though he invented the subject'.[12] Allied to these criticisms is the traditional discomfort that surrounds the parameters of the subject itself; as evidenced by the protracted intellectual journey from 'constitutional law' to 'constitutional and administrative law' to 'public law' – with 'civil liberties', 'European law' and 'human rights' variously added to the mix along the way.

The 'new public law' scholarship has added to these traditional criticisms in significant ways, in large part stimulated by the limited conceptions of power and the state in public law theory. We can identify at least four main areas of concern.

The re-invention of government

First, the complacency of some public (or, as subject boundaries remain, administrative) lawyers in the face of the radical changes in public administration instigated by the Thatcher (and successive) governments has been criticised. Clinging to outmoded concepts of state power and parliamentary controls, the traditionalists appear to have convinced themselves that orthodox constitutionalism is still capable of accommodating the shifts in the mode of governance in the UK. Remarkably, successive editions of textbooks follow earlier formats, saying little, or nothing very critical, about far reaching government policies such as the privatisation of utilities, deregulation, contracting-out of services, or the creation of new

---

10 *Op cit*, fn 9, Morison and Livingstone, p 6 (note omitted).

11 Lewis, N, 'Public law and legal theory', in *op cit*, fn 7, Twining, p 100. See, also, Prosser, T, 'Towards a critical public law' (1982) 9 JLS 1; and 'Journey without maps' [1993] PL 346.

12 Loughlin, M, *Public Law and Political Theory*, 1992, Oxford: Clarendon, p 140.

executive agencies and quangos.[13] Even though the structures of UK government have been radically altered – with public power transferred and dissipated beyond the reach of traditional political and judicial controls – orthodox constitutionalism either avoids the issue or adopts a purely descriptive tone[14] As Sedley confirms:

> It was during the 1980s, while practitioners, judges and academics were congratulating themselves on the approach of a comprehensive system of public law, that politics throughout the common law world set about dismantling the very structures of which public law had assumed the continued existence. With the systematic dispersal of the sites of power beyond the confines of what we had learned to recognise as the State, the old certainties of public law are no longer there.[15]

While the textbook account of the proper parameters of administrative law still retains some of its intransigence, increasingly, the work of authors such as Harlow and Rawlings,[16] Harden,[17] Galligan,[18] Graham and Prosser,[19] Scott[20] and Taggart[21] provide alternative accounts of constitutionalism and regulation from a variety of different perspectives. As this legal scholarship on the 're-invention' of government and its empirical realities becomes more influential in the law curriculum, the traditional atheoretical artifice of a court-centered, rule based system of administrative law will become even more shaky. However, as Morison argues, merely updating the textbook tradition to include the new structures and methods of government in the UK will not be adequate. There is a need for mainstream public lawyers to broaden their horizons well beyond the legal literature to writings in public administration, and social and political theory. Without such a shift, the task of contemporary public law will remain unfulfilled: that is, to recognise 'the multiple levels

---

13   See Le Sueur, A and Sunkin, M, *Public Law*, 1997, London: Longman, for an attempt to reorientate the structure and focus of the public law textbook.

14   See, eg, Wade, H and Forysth, C, *Administrative Law*, 7th edn, 1994, Oxford: Clarendon.

15   Sedley, S, 'Foreword', in Taggart, M (ed), *The Province of Administrative Law*, 1997, Oxford: Hart.

16   Harlow, C and Rawlings, R, *Law and Administration*, 1997, London: Butterworths; Harlow, C, 'Changing the mindset: the place of theory in English administrative law' (1994) 14 OJLS 419; and Harlow, C, 'Back to basics: reinventing administrative law' [1997] PL 245.

17   Harden, I, *The Contracting State*, 1992, Buckingham: OU Press.

18   Galligan, D (ed), *A Reader on Administrative Law*, 1996, Oxford: OUP; and 'Judicial review and the textbook writers' (1992) 12 OJLS 2.

19   Graham, C and Prosser, T, *Privatising Public Enterprises: Constitutions, the State and Regulation in Comparative Perspective*, 1991, Oxford: Clarendon; and Prosser, T, *Law and the Regulators*, 1997, Oxford: Clarendon.

20   Barron, A and Scott, C, 'The Citizen's Charter programme' (1992) 55 MLR 535; and Loughlin, M and Scott, C, 'The regulatory State', in Dunleavy, P, Gamble, A, Holliday, I and Peele, G (eds), *Developments in British Politics*, 1997, London: Macmillan, p 205.

21   *Op cit*, fn 15, Taggart.

where governance now takes place, claiming these as legitimate areas for constitutional control, and developing a legal technology for constraining and shaping public power as it now operates'.[22]

Evolving European constitutionalism

A second main theme of critical public law scholarship in recent years has been the effects of external forces now operating on the traditional UK nation state, in particular, European integration. Perhaps, more than any other issue, the perverse annual ritual of teaching first year law students whether 'parliamentary sovereignty remains intact' since the European Communities Act 1972 best exposes the inadequacy of the British constitutional tradition in coping with supranational developments.[23] Even though the supremacy of European law is unambiguous – as is European law scholarship on the topic – no issue seems to excite the interest of traditional constitutional lawyers more than reflection on whether Dicey's views are reconcilable with membership of the European Union. As Weiler highlights, it is the work of authors like MacCormick that should be central and not peripheral to the teaching of public (and European) law:

> We have witnessed in recent years the emergence of a new academic discourse which attempts to rethink the very way in which classical constitutionalism was conceptualized. For me, the most powerful and influential voice is that of MacCormick in his trilogy, 'Beyond the sovereign State'; 'Sovereignty, democracy and subsidiarity'; and 'Liberalism, nationalism and the post-sovereign State'. Here is a discourse which understands the impossibilities of the old constitutional discourse, in a polity and a society in which the key social and political concepts on which classical constitutionalism was premised have lost their meaning.[24]

However, it is not just in relation to state sovereignty that the failings of public law are laid bare. As Ward argues, in general, 'European law has emerged as the least contextual and thus least intellectually focused study in the law school curriculum'.[25] The dominant constitutional law textbook tradition

---

22 Morison, J 'The case against constitutional reform?' (1998) 25 JLS 510, p 526. For an overview of administrative law theory, see Leyland, P and Woods, T, 'Public law history and theory', in *Administrative Law Facing the Future: Old Constraints and New Horizons*, 1997, London: Blackstone, pp 374–449.

23 See, generally, Wade, H, 'What has happened to the sovereignty of Parliament?' (1991) 107 LQR 1; Craig, P, 'Sovereignty of the United Kingdom Parliament after *Factortame*' (1991) 11 YBEL 221; and the discussion in Hunt, M, *Using Human Rights Law in English Courts*, 1998, Oxford: Hart, pp 44–126.

24 Weiler, J, *The Constitution of Europe*, 1999, Cambridge: CUP, pp 233–34. See, also, Harden, I, 'The constitution of the European Union' [1995] PL 609; and Allott, P, 'The crisis of European constitutionalism: reflections on the revolution in Europe' (1997) 34 CMLR 439.

25 Ward, I, *A Critical Introduction to European Law*, 1996, London: Butterworths, p 1.

must share the blame for this outcome, along with the relentlessly black letter, court focused approach of the first textbooks on European Community law.[26] Only with the growth in European Union legal studies in recent years, as evidenced by the contributions in Shaw and More's collection,[27] has scholarship on the European project developed a critical and interdisciplinary character. Needless to say, this work has impacted only sporadically on the teaching and literature of public law. Even where a concept such as citizenship is raised for discussion, the richness (and obvious relevance) of writings on European Union citizenship are largely ignored or downplayed in public law texts.[28]

The new orthodoxy of constitutional reform

A third contemporary theme of public law scholarship is the 'constitutional reform' movement, especially in relation to discovering or promoting a human rights basis to public law.[29] Throughout the 1980s, and certainly since the election of the New Labour Government in 1997, the conviction of mainstream public lawyers that a 'modernisation' programme is the remedy for British constitutionalism (Northern Ireland, as usual, is unmentioned) has solidified.[30] New public law texts now faithfully cite official documents, such as *Rights Brought Home: The Human Rights Bill*[31] or *Scotland's Parliament*,[32] without any attempt to retheorise the dominant tradition of parliamentary sovereignty or locate the project in broader historical, political and social contexts.[33]

This remarkably rapid replacement of one orthodoxy with another has received little critical comment. In his acclaimed text, *Using Human Rights Law in English Courts*,[34] Hunt demolishes Diceyan accounts of parliamentary sovereignty while mapping the tortuous and contradictory paths along which

---

26 See, generally, Shaw, J, 'European Union legal studies in crisis? Towards a new dynamic' (1996) 16 OJLS 321.

27 See, eg, Shaw, J and More, G (eds), *New Legal Dynamics of European Union*, 1995, Oxford: Clarendon; Armstrong, K and Shaw, J (eds), 'Integrating law' (1998) 36 Journal of Common Market Studies (Special Edition); and Armstrong, K and Bulmer, S, *The Governance of the Single Market*, 1998: Manchester: Manchester UP.

28 For a comprehensive account, see Shaw, J, 'The interpretation of European Union citizenship' (1998) 61 MLR 293.

29 See, eg, Institute for Public Policy Research, *A Written Constitution for the United Kingdom*, 1993, London: Mansell; and *A British Bill of Rights*, 1996, London: IPPR.

30 See, eg, Beatson, J, Forsyth, C and Hare, I (eds), *Constitutional Reform in the United Kingdom: Practice and Principles*, 1998, Oxford: Hart.

31 1997, Cm 3782.

32 1997, Cm 3658.

33 See, eg, Oliver, D and Drewry, G (eds), *The Law and Parliament*, 1998, London: Butterworths, pp 174–91 and 192–200.

34 *Op cit*, fn 23, Hunt.

judges have asserted a legal basis for the articulation of human rights norms. For judges who view the common law as the 'constitutional bedrock' of the UK, an 'interpretive obligation' to give effect to the commitments of international treaties (such as the European Convention on Human Rights) is now available as a judicial tool.[35] A different strand of critical opinion, led by Ewing, is wary of increasing judicial power and clings to the Westminster model of representative and responsible government:

> [By] ensuring that legal sovereignty continues to rest with Parliament, the government has retrieved the first constitutional principle of democratic socialism, and overcome one of the principal concerns about incorporation of the [European Convention on Human Rights].[36]

Yet, this scholarship does not fully address the *political* enterprise of legal elites reconstructing the foundation of constitutionalism on the once alien bedrock of positive rights. Loughlin has placed the 'hazardous' nature of the exercise in context:

> At the level of legal practice, the liberal normativist objective – of trying to reinvent the traditions of the common law in a rationalistic light and of substituting a modern for the ancient conception of the rule of law as the foundation of our constitutional tradition – remains far from being realised. At the level of political thought, their programme for constitutional reform has achieved a degree of intellectual consensus only by fudging the issues. At this level, the ambiguity is most clearly expressed in the tension between negative and positive conceptions of liberty.[37]

Apart from this intellectual fudge, the actual mechanics of controlling power in a UK state that is now subject to complex external relationships (such as European integration and globalisation), and to internal changes in the practices of government (centralising power in Downing Street, diffusing power to satellite agencies, creating new devolved parliaments) – remain unaddressed by the liberal reformist tradition.[38] For example, in her valuable study of administrative law and its impact on British immigration practices, Sterett highlights one central failing in mainstream debates on constitutional reform:

> Constitutionalism has been perceived as a question of imposing limits on what state institutions can do to people. The courts then are discussed as though they are not part of the state, and whether they can hold the rest of the state to

---

35 *Op cit*, fn 23, Hunt, p xi. For judicial confirmation, see *R v Secretary of State for the Home Department ex p McQuillan* [1995] 4 All ER 400, p 422 (*per* Sedley J). Contrast this view with Waite LJ's remark that 'cases depend on their own facts and render generalisations – tempting though they may be to the legal or social analyst – wholly out of place': *Re T (a minor)* [1997] 1 All ER 906, p 917.

36 Ewing, K 'The Human Rights Act and parliamentary democracy' (1999) 62 MLR 79.

37 *Op cit*, fn 12, Loughlin, p 228. See, also, Loughlin, M, *Rights Discourse and Public Law Thought in the UK*, 1997, Warwick: University of Warwick Legal Research Institute.

38 *Op cit*, fn 9, Morison and Livingstone, pp 35–88.

prohibitions becomes the central question. The discussion has attended in part to protection of individuals, but the individuals most likely to rely on judicial review in Britain, immigrants, have not often been addressed as part of constitutionalist accountability. Discussion has instead addressed the core political issue in Britain, the control of central government. It has not been conceived as a question of reorganization of the State but instead how to place legal limits on the central State.[39]

Another major failing of mainstream public law discourse lies in its understanding of human rights. The range of scholarship that addresses the social, economic and political dimensions of rights discourse continues to be ignored, as (mostly Dworkin inspired)[40] internal analyses of competing rights dominate.[41] Typically, human rights provisions are subjected to an interpretive process that never reveals the power relations inherent in their creation and interpretation,[42] nor addresses the role of law in constructing national and cultural identities. Furthermore, the relationship between human rights law and social change, whether progressive or regressive, is left out of most public law accounts.[43] In contrast, the critical and inter-disciplinary work of authors such as Brown,[44] Herman[45] and Stychin,[46] exploring the potential and pitfalls of rights discourse in Canadian, US and Australian legal cultures remains ignored. For example, Bakan's critique of the Canadian Charter of Rights may offer valuable pointers for public lawyers in the UK, as they embark on litigation under the Human Rights Act:

> I argue ... that the Charter, and particularly its failure to advance social justice, must be explained in relation to the specific conditions in which it operates. All political institutions, including the Charter and rights, are necessarily constrained in their operation by the wider social system that they are established to govern. That is why it is necessary to be sceptical of both Charter

---

39 Sterett, S, *Creating Constitutionalism? The Politics of Legal Expertise and Administrative Law in England and Wales*, 1997, Ann Arbor: Michigan UP, p 8.

40 See, eg, Dworkin, R, *Taking Rights Seriously*, 1977, Mass, MA: Harvard UP.

41 Compare, eg, Harris, D, O'Boyle, M and Warbrick, C, *Law of the European Convention on Human Rights*, 1995, London: Butterworths, with Steiner, H and Alston, P, *International Human Rights in Context: Law, Politics, Morals*, 1996, Oxford: Clarendon.

42 See Bell, C, Buss, D, Mansell, W, Millns, S and Whitty, N, *Teaching Human Rights*, 1999, Warwick: National Centre for Legal Education; and Williams, P, *The Alchemy of Race and Rights*, 1991, London: Harvard UP.

43 The literature is vast but see, eg, Abel, R, *Politics by Other Means: Law in the Struggle Against Apartheid 1980–1994*, 1995, London: Routledge; Bogart, W, *Courts and Country: The Limits of Litigation and the Political and Social Life of Canada*, 1994, Toronto: OUP; and Dixon, D, *Law in Policing: Legal Regulation and Police Practices*, 1997, Oxford: Clarendon.

44 Brown, W, *States of Injury: Power and Freedom in Late Modernity*, 1995, Princeton: Princeton UP.

45 Herman, D, *Rights of Passage: Struggles for Lesbian and Gay Equality*, 1994, Toronto: Toronto UP; and 'The good, the bad and the smugly: perspectives on the Canadian Charter of Rights and Freedoms' (1994) 14 OJLS 589.

46 Stychin, C, *Law's Desire: Sexuality and the Limits of Justice*, 1995, London: Routledge; and *A Nation By Rights: National Cultures, Sexual Identity Politics and the Discourse of Rights*, 1998, Philadelphia: Temple UP.

optimism and pessimism when they are based on allegedly essential features of the Charter or rights. The emancipatory and egalitarian potential of the Charter ultimately depends on the social and historical circumstances surrounding its use.[47]

The search for public law values

The fourth main theme of public law scholarship, intersecting with all the other themes, is the search for values. While much attention is still directed towards institutional reforms, there is an increasing desire to root UK constitutional structures and processes in a more explicit set of democratic values. As Morison and Livingstone argue '[o]nly a shift to a focus on the values which the constitution is designed to espouse can help us to guide the development of new forms of public power ...'.[48] The work of authors such as Craig,[49] McAuslan,[50] Allan,[51] Lewis,[52] Oliver[53] and Feldman[54] can be viewed as part of this ongoing project. Most obviously, the Bill of Rights movement has been to the forefront in articulating the need for a human rights foundation in UK law, albeit predominantly derived from the civil and political rights character of the European Convention on Human Rights.[55] The participation of the UK in the European Community, and now European Union, has also exerted its influence on the search for public law values. Indeed, some argue that the complex ideals that drive the project of European integration – supranationalism, mobilisation, legitimacy, the free market, citizenship, subsidiarity and so on[56] – have had a most profound impact.

Nevertheless, much of the public law debate on values still remains trapped within a Westminster/liberal state mindset and anchored to a common law history. A constitutional and administrative law tradition that long scorned the recognition of positive legal rights and that boasted

---

47 Bakan, J, *Just Words: Constitutional Rights and Social Wrongs*, 1997, Toronto: Toronto UP, p 9.

48 *Op cit*, fn 9, Morison and Livingstone, p 220.

49 Craig, P, *Public Law and Democracy in the United Kingdom and the United States of America*, 1990, Oxford: Clarendon.

50 McAuslan, P, 'Public choice and public law' (1988) 51 MLR 687.

51 Allan, T, *Law, Liberty and Justice: The Legal Foundations of British Constitutionalism*, 1993, Oxford: Clarendon.

52 Lewis, N, *Choice and the Legal Order: Rising Above Politics*, 1996, London: Butterworths.

53 Oliver, D, 'Common values in public and private law and the public/private divide' [1997] PL 630.

54 Feldman, D, 'Public law values in the House of Lords' (1990) 106 LQR 246.

55 See, generally, Sedley, S, 'Human rights: a twenty first century agenda' [1995] PL 386.

56 *Op cit*, fn 24, Weiler, pp 238–63; *op cit*, fn 25, Ward, pp 138–72; and Alston, P and Weiler, J, 'An "ever closer Union" in need of a human rights policy: the European Union and human rights' (1999) Jean Monnet Papers: http://www.law.harvard.edu/Programs/JeanMonnet/.

'typically, English law fastens, not upon principles but upon remedies'[57] leaves a lasting mark.[58] When public lawyers now appeal to 'values' without recognising the changed political and constitutional landscape, or without moving beyond an exclusively internal legal discourse, it may be a limited exercise.[59] Concepts such as democracy, participation, transparency, subsidiarity, proportionality, rights, autonomy, equality, social justice and power should be the core concerns of public law, but they do require an interdisciplinary critique.

Just as importantly, the extraordinary depoliticisation of the debate about values – as if state authorities, social movements, interest groups and individuals do not struggle over the definition and promotion of competing values – needs to be problematised. Discourses about values, as with public law generally, cannot be other than ideological. As Weeks argues:

> ... values have shot to the top of the political agenda on both left and right ... Value debates are about taking sides, about placing yourself in a tradition or traditions of arguments extending through time which necessarily conflict at many points with other traditions, other values. We can rightly require that the debates are conducted dialogically and democratically – that seems to me an absolute prerequisite of argument in a pluralist world.[60]

FEMINISM, POLITICS AND PUBLIC LAW

In 1995, Loughlin concluded his survey of 25 years of public law scholarship by noting how a changing legal and political culture has provoked 'innovation':

> Innovation in public law scholarship has mainly been a response to uncertainty and disorientation; it is a product of the attempt to continue work in public law without those certainties which gave birth to the subject.[61]

Feminist Perspectives on Public Law proposes a more thoroughgoing innovativeness, and sets about introducing feminist theory into the world of public law. In order to do this, we need to address some preliminary questions. First, why have public lawyers to date resisted or denied the relevance of feminist political and social theory? Secondly, why have feminist perspectives on public law been practically non-existent? Unlike other areas of

---

57 *Davy v Spelthorne Borough Council* [1984] AC 262, p 272 (*per* Wilberforce LJ).

58 See Sedley, S, 'The sound of silence: constitutional law without a constitution' (1994) 110 LQR 270.

59 See O'Leary, B, 'What should public lawyers do?' (1992) 12 OJLS 404.

60 Weeks, J, *Invented Moralities: Sexual Values in an Age of Uncertainty*, 1995, Cambridge: Polity, pp ix–x.

61 Loughlin, M, 'The pathways of public law scholarship', in Wilson, G (ed), *Frontiers of Legal Scholarship*, 1995, Chichester: John Wiley, p 186.

the law curriculum – crime,[62] family,[63] health care,[64] employment,[65] legal theory,[66] for example – it is not possible to point to any established tradition of feminist scholarship on 'public law'. Mainstream public law texts do not cite feminism, even amongst their 'alternative' accounts (as sometimes happens in other subject areas). There are several possible answers to these two questions.

Politics, public lawyers and feminism

Some insight may be derived from an exploration of the relationship between feminism and politics. In Phillips' introduction to her collection of work on the subject, she argues that even though 'feminism is politics', it has been much less successful in impacting on political theory or practice than on other disciplines (for example, sociology, cultural studies, social policy or literature):

> Politics as pursued in academic departments is ... surprisingly untouched, for while the literature on gender and politics or feminist political theory has grown from a few seminal articles into a rich diversity of work, 'feminism and politics' is still treated as a discrete object of study, of interest only to those inside it. Sociologists have always included the family among the objects of study. Literary critics have never been able to avoid women writers. Students of politics, by contrast, have taken this as referring to a domain of public power from which women are largely absent. In one of the early discussions of feminism and politics, Joni Lovenduski noted that 'there was never any way that the modern study of politics could fail to be sexist' for 'women usually do not dispose of public power, belong to political elites, or hold influential

62 See, eg, Lacey, N and Wells, C, *Reconstructing Criminal Law*, 1998, London: Butterworths; S, *Ruling Passions: Sexual Violence, Reputation and the Law*, 1997, Buckingham: OU Press; and Smart, C, *Law, Crime and Sexuality*, 1995, London: Sage.

63 See, eg, O'Donovan, K, *Sexual Divisions in Law*, 1985, London: Weidenfeld & Nicolson; O'Donovan, K, *Family Law Matters*, 1993, London: Pluto; Okin, S, *Justice, Gender and the Family*, 1989, London: HarperCollins; and Collier, R, *Masculinity, Law and the Family*, 1995, London: Routledge.

64 See, eg, Sheldon, S, *Beyond Control: Medical Power and Abortion Law*, London: Pluto; Bridgeman, J and Millns, S (eds), *Law and Body Politics: Regulating the Female Body*, 1995, Aldershot: Dartmouth; Smart, C (ed), *Regulating Womanhood: Historical Essays on Marriage, Motherhood and Sexuality*, 1992, London: Routledge; and Sheldon, S and Thomson, M (eds), *Feminist Perspectives on Health Care Law*, 1998, London: Cavendish Publishing.

65 See, eg, O'Donovan, K and Szyszczak, E, *Equality and Sex Discrimination Law*, 1988, Oxford: Blackwells; Lacey, N, 'From individual to group', in Hepple, B and Szyszczak, E (eds), *Discrimination: The Limits of Law*, 1992, London: Mansell, p 99; Morris, A and Nott, S, *Working Women and the Law: Equality and Discrimination in Theory and Practice*, 1991, London: Routledge; and Morris, A and O'Donnell, T (eds), *Feminist Perspectives on Employment Law*, 1999, London: Cavendish Publishing.

66 See, eg, Lacey, N, *Unspeakable Subjects: Feminist Essays in Legal and Social Theory*, 1998, Oxford: Hart; MacKinnon, CA, *Feminism Unmodified*, 1987, Cambridge: Harvard UP; Graycar, R and Morgan, J, *The Hidden Gender of Law*, 1990, Annandale: Federation; Naffine, N, *Law and the Sexes*, 1990, Sydney: Allen & Unwin; and Naffine, N and Owens, R (eds), *Sexing the Subject of Law*, 1997, Sydney: Law Book.

positions in government institutions'.[67] The very definition of the subject matter has made politics peculiarly intransigent to feminist transformations.[68]

Moreover, this definition of the subject matter of politics has led to important feminist 'political' insights developing in other disciplines (such as sociology); for example, explorations of the nature of power, the permeability of the public/private divide and the need for 'bottom-up' analysis. Yet, the strong resistance to interdisciplinarity within politics means that these feminist insights remain ignored.

In the light of the intersection of public law and politics – with its shared emphasis on government institutions – there may be useful comparisons to draw here. Public law has also excluded feminist theory in the construction of its foundational concepts. It rejects interdisciplinarity, and focuses on political elites and established political practices. As Phillips argues, in a climate 'where "the political" still conjures up images of governments and elections and parties',[69] public law, literally and metaphorically, has been viewed as 'a man's world'. This construction also ties in neatly with the 'Founding Fathers' tradition so familiar to classical US political and constitutional thought; the quintessentially male project of politicians and lawyers composing the foundational constitutional text as an exercise in 'nation building'.[70]

Katherine O'Donovan, in providing one of the few feminist critiques of British constitutionalism, highlights some of the effects of the historical absence of a written constitution in the UK. First, there is no foundational document with the potential to generate 'constitutional' values familiar to most liberal democracies. Thus, 'arguments based on equal citizenship, justice for all and equality under the law take on the qualities not of mercy but of mercury, and slip away'.[71] Secondly, the history of exclusion is further solidified by the porous definition of constitutional law itself:

> If the constitution is accepted as existing in an institutional sense, certain consequences follow. Its existence is a matter of tradition and practice. What this means is that the past is always with us. In this context, the past is exclusionary. Women and men of the non-propertied classes were excluded from politics.[72]

---

67 Lovenduski, J, 'Toward the emasculation of political science', in Spender, D (ed), *Men's Studies Modified*, 1981, Oxford: Pergamon, p 89.

68 Phillips, A (ed), *Feminism and Politics*, 1998, Oxford: OUP, pp 1–2.

69 *Ibid*, p 2.

70 See, generally, Yuval-Davis, N, *Gender and Nation*, 1997, London: Sage; Irving, H, 'The republic is a feminist issue' (1996) 52 FR 87; Gilroy, P, *There Ain't No Black in the Union Jack: The Cultural Politics of Race and Nation*, 1987, London: Hutchinson; and Buss, D, 'Women at the borders: rape and nationalism in international law' (1998) 6 FLS 171.

71 O'Donovan, K, 'A new settlement between the sexes? Constitutional law and the citizenship of women', in Bottomley, A (ed), *Feminist Perspectives on the Foundational Subjects of Law*, 1996, London: Cavendish Publishing, p 245.

72 *Ibid*.

This insight can be extended to other aspects of British constitutionalism. When the 'unwritten constitution' can often be reduced to the 'conventions' of political practice – in reality, what actions a patriarchal political and legal elite wish to class as conventional – it is unlikely to be a catalyst for inclusive politics. In view of the under-representation of women in Parliament and amongst the judiciary, there is real significance in the fact that 'the British constitution has always displayed a disjuncture between the theory set out in its textbooks and the reality down in the dirt of political life ...'.[73]

As many legal historians have pointed out, the Oxbridge law schools have played a major role in the 'creation' of a constitutional law tradition. It was Dicey who declared that '[o]ur constitution is a judge made constitution'[74] and 'the lawyers ... played a heroic role'[75] in the exercise. And Heuston proclaimed that: '[t]he doctrine of parliamentary sovereignty is almost entirely the work of Oxford men.'[76] The masculinism of public law therefore operates at multiple levels. Apart from the physical exclusion of women from the world of Oxbridge dons (the environment which produced the classical constitutional law texts), the fundamental doctrines of public law signify masculinist power and understandings (such as the bounded, non-relational concept of sovereignty).

One could also speculate on the effects of the historic absence of a constitutional court in the UK – often the forum for women's groups and other marginalised constituencies to pursue litigation strategies and create a more inclusive public law discourse.[77] An interesting contrast can be made here with the political lobbying and legal campaigns of feminist lawyers at the European level, often proving to be more effective than engagement with domestic institutions.[78] However, it also needs to be emphasised that feminist social policy campaigns in the UK typically take non-legal forms (for example, on health care, education, social services). Even if law provided an appropriate framework, feminist struggles may not take place within a legal system's arenas.

---

73   *Op cit*, fn 9, Morison and Livingstone, p 20.
74   Dicey, AV, *Introduction to the Study of the Law of the Constitution*, 8th edn, 1915, London: Macmillan, p 192.
75   *Op cit*, fn 61, Loughlin, p 166.
76   Heuston, R, *Essays in Constitutional Law*, 1964, London: Stevens, p 1.
77   See, eg, Razack, S, *Canadian Feminism and the Law: The Women's Legal Education and Action Fund and the Pursuit of Equality*, 1991, Toronto: Second Story; and Fudge, J, 'Evaluating rights litigation as a form of transformative politics' (1992) 7 Canadian Journal of Law and Society 153.
78   See Meehan, E, *Citizenship and the European Community*, 1993, London: Sage.

Feminist (dis)engagement with public law

At a number of intersecting levels, therefore – conceptual, educational, and in terms of political practices – public law been constructed in exclusionary and gendered ways. Yet, the question as to why feminist critiques of *public law* are not more common still requires an answer. Phillips ponders a similar question in relation to feminism's relationship with political theory: 'should feminists simply refuse to engage with this dreary universe, or do we have to engage in order to transform?'[79] She argues that it is possible to identify a feminist scholarship on politics of the 'add women and stir' variety (arguably, corresponding with the approach of liberal feminist legal theory). In her view, however, the disillusionment of much 1960s and 1970s feminism with traditional and Marxist conceptions of politics and power has resulted in a subversive rethinking of feminist priorities:

> The problem, if any, was that 'politics' was subjected to such devastating criticism that it threatened to dissolve as a distinct category of analysis ... Representations of masculinity and femininity were seen as forms of control over women just as effectively as the 19th century legislation that had denied them the vote; and the regulation of sexuality – including what many have described as 'compulsory heterosexuality' – was seen as a central mechanism in sustaining sexual inequality. Politics was power, power was everywhere, and politics was no longer much different from anything else.[80]

While this account may, perhaps, downplay the feminist theorising of the state that developed from the feminist materialist tradition,[81] and onwards to feminist poststructuralist writings on the state,[82] Phillips' analysis could explain the absence of direct feminist engagement with public law. The traditional concerns of public law scholarship have not been substantive questions of power (especially in light of the absence of a concept of 'the State' in English law) or issues of gender, class, race or sexuality. When 'the personal is political' and 'politics is everywhere', the focus of feminist legal scholarship may just as easily turn to questions of family, criminal, employment, environmental, European, or health care law; where personal experiences and concerns appear more immediate and relevant. Furthermore, as Morison and Livingstone point out, there is now 'a politicisation along different lines' undermining the significance of established political structures and practices:

> Class movements and traditional political parties are increasingly being superseded by a whole variety of bodies and groups which reflect better the

---

79 *Op cit*, fn 68, Phillips, p 2.

80 *Op cit*, fn 68, Phillips, p 4.

81 See, eg, the 1978 essay by McIntosh, M, 'The State and the oppression of women', in Kuhn, A and Wolpe, A (eds), *Feminism and Materialism*, 1978, London: Routledge, p 254.

82 See, eg, Pringle, R and Watson, S, '"Women's interests" and the poststructuralist State', in *op cit*, fn 68, Phillips, p 203.

kaleidoscope of identities now replacing the hierarchies of traditional politics.[83]

In contrast, when one examines the world of public law textbooks – unwritten constitutions, parliamentary sovereignty, conventions, institutions (Commons, Lords), arcane law making procedures, delegated legislation, procedure based judicial review – it is remarkable how closed it remains. It may also appear less relevant to feminist legal theory in comparison with other subject areas of law. Even the existence of a female monarch, or the tenure of Margaret Thatcher as Prime Minister, did not stimulate a feminist commentary within the traditional public law literature; in contrast to other disciplines which easily recognised the gender implications of women exercising political power.[84]

Whatever the reasons for the previous scarcity of feminist scholarship in the public law field, the intellectual and political landscapes in the 1990s have changed. Reflecting its interdisciplinary origins and maturity as a body of theory, there is now an outburst of feminist scholarship on political values, institutions and practices, which the public lawyer may find harder to ignore. As Phillips suggests:

> [The] double imperative towards critique and recuperation has remained a defining characteristic. Feminists have developed and deepened their critical assessment of the various ways in which politics is conceived. They have increasingly combined this, however, with a calling back to politics, stressing the insights feminism can bring to the theorisation of public power. Some of this recuperates the more self-evidently 'political' preoccupation with women's under-representation in decision making assemblies; some of it focuses on the complex dilemmas that arise in developing legislation for sexual equality; much of it involves a retheorisation of citizenship that takes feminist issues right to the heart of the public domain.[85]

Of course, this is only one account of current feminist engagements with political theory or the terrain of public law. Talk of recuperation and reconstruction remains contested terrain. As Hirschmann and Di Stefano, the editors of *Revisioning the Political* ask: '... is "political theory" something feminists should avoid except from the perspective of tearing it apart?'[86] Their conclusion mirrors the diverse responses from feminists in this volume: some argue for 'rethinking' and some argue for 'restructuring', but 'all result in a call for serious, fundamental change to the face of politics, political theory and political life'.[87]

---

83   *Op cit*, fn 9, Morison and Livingstone, pp 64–65.
84   It should be mentioned here that any feminist critiques of core public law concerns originating from a critical and interdisciplinary standpoint would raise challenges for the 'gatekeepers' of public law knowledge.
85   *Op cit*, fn 68, Phillips, p 5.
86   *Op cit*, fn 3, Hirschmann and Di Stefano, p 3.
87   *Op cit*, fn 3, Hirschmann and Di Stefano, p 19.

FEMINIST PERSPECTIVES ON PUBLIC LAW

The following 10 chapters provide the reader with different feminist perspectives on a variety of public law themes and topics. There is no deep theory behind the order of their presentation. However, three considerations did have some influence. First, as with most edited collections, we expect that many people will read the introductory chapter and then choose their favourite authors or topics according to the titles and their own specific interests; few will read all the chapters in consecutive order.

Secondly, we take the view that the traditional public law textbook approach is very problematic given the nature of governance today. Most texts continue to adopt a 'top-down' descriptive approach, centering public law on the institutions of Crown, Parliament and courts; what one writer has described as 'the living dead of the constitution'.[88] In this collection, we have deliberately set out to avoid the impression that this is the way to understand or 'read' public law.

Thirdly, we recognise that feminism is a rich and diverse field, and we have tried to give a sense of the range of possible feminist perspectives on public law. We reject the idea of a grand feminist narrative on public law or a single method of engagement. Yet, there is much overlap between the different contributions, illustrating central concerns of feminist theory and the potential for dialogue with public law. For example, there are intersecting discussions of the state/power (Murphy, Thomson, Gearey, Cooper); institutions (Whitty, Thomson, McGlynn, Millns, Harvey, Cooper); citizenship (Kingdom, Harvey); rights discourse (Kingdom, Millns); women's participation (Thomson, McGlynn, Gearey); the public/private divide (Whitty, McDonald, Millns, Harvey, Cooper); and gender representations (Whitty, Thomson, McGlynn, Cooper).

We offer a brief roadmap to help readers plot their own routes through this collection. Thérèse Murphy (Chapter 2), writing against much contemporary critical theory, argues for a theorisation of the late modern British state. In Chapter 3, Noel Whitty examines the role and representations of the monarchy in public law textbooks, with a particular focus on the cultural and political aspects of the death of Princess Diana. Michael Thomson (Chapter 4) addresses the issue of women's participation in government, as well as the increasing feminisation of forms of governing, by exploring the phenomenon of New Labour Woman. This issue of female participation is also addressed by Clare McGlynn in her analysis of the gender composition of the judiciary and the impact of women exercising judicial power (Chapter 5). Angus McDonald (Chapter 6) provides an extensive critique of Dicey's

---

88 Kingdom, J, *Government and Politics in Britain*, 1991, Cambridge: Polity, p 253.

influence on the constitutional law textbook tradition and the modernising public law project, arguing for a combined postmodern and feminist engagement with the Diceyan legacy. Adam Gearey (Chapter 7) focuses on the writings of the French feminist, Luce Irigaray, and advances a feminist constitutionalism based on a rethinking of dominant understandings of sovereignty. The current tensions between feminist politics of citizenship and radical democratic politics are explored by Elizabeth Kingdom (Chapter 8), and she proposes a reconceptualisation of rights discourse, drawing on insights from both feminism and radical democracy. Susan Millns (Chapter 9) continues the theme of feminist rights strategies, by examining the adoption of the Human Rights Act 1998 and the jurisprudence of the European Court of Human Rights. Colin Harvey (Chapter 10) presents a detailed account of feminist engagements with Habermas, before providing a case study of asylum law to illustrate the value of feminist perspectives on public law. Finally, Davina Cooper (Chapter 11), combining many of the themes of earlier chapters, explores conceptions of governing power in a series of judicial review cases concerning local government. She also provides an account of connections between feminist theory and judicial review.

In conclusion, *Feminist Perspectives on Public Law* aims to encourage a dialogue between feminism and public law. As outlined above, contemporary public law is fracturing badly. We hope that this collection demonstrates how the critical insights of feminism can be used to critique and revision public law.

CHAPTER 2

COSMOPOLITAN FEMINISM: TOWARDS A CRITICAL REAPPRAISAL OF THE LATE MODERN BRITISH STATE

Thérèse Murphy

INTRODUCTION

In 1989, Catharine MacKinnon published a collection of essays called *Toward a Feminist Theory of the State* in which she argued that the state was male and that gender was an effect of sexualised male dominance.[1] The essays secured MacKinnon's standing as a feminist superstar and, as Wendy Brown notes, also allowed her to make a 'splash in the mainstream'.[2] The book stripped away Anglo-American law's flaunted objectivity, or point-of-viewlessness, exposing its male standpoint and the ways in which it institutionalises men's interests. Together, they documented an unrelenting and pervasive patriarchy in which 'woman' was an effect of sexual subordination, and myriad liberation strategies were jinxed by false consciousness.

MacKinnon herself was undaunted however. She combined her exposé of patriarchy with a call to action, proposing a way to navigate the despair engendered by her account. Basically, her thesis was that although law was flawed, it retained the capacity to recognise and reverse sexual subordination. This, of course, meant that gender equality *was* salvageable and, more importantly, it allowed MacKinnon to use the collection to launch a series of appeals to the US state for gender equality through civil rights law, most famously in the anti-pornography ordinances which she drafted with Andrea Dworkin.[3]

Toward a Feminist Theory of the State had an astonishing impact. It marked the highpoint of feminist grand theory and the manner in which it both shocked and captivated was remarkable. The essays did engender despair, but they also persuaded and energised. There was a sort of magic to their

---

1   MacKinnon, CA, *Toward a Feminist Theory of the State*, 1989, Cambridge, MA: Harvard UP.

2   Brown, W, *States of Injury: Power and Freedom in Late Modernity*, 1995, Princeton, NJ: Princeton UP, p 78.

3   For more detail on these ordinances, see *inter alia*, MacKinnon, CA, *Feminism Unmodified*, 1987, Cambridge, MA: Harvard UP, p 163; Colombo, S, 'The legal battle for the city: anti-pornography municipal ordinances and radical feminism' (1994) 2 FLS 29; Easton, SM, *The Problem of Pornography: Regulation and the Right to Free Speech*, 1994, London: Routledge, p 109.

'paradoxical mix of debilitating pessimism and unfathomable optimism'.[4] Like so many others, I was horrified but smitten: in short, I was a believer.

Ten years on, a lot has changed. Feminist theory and the state are both very different. Moreover, to announce an intention to pursue *a feminist theory of the state* is to risk shame, ridicule or widespread disinterest. Late 1990s' feminist theory has other projects and different priorities, and critique of the state has largely been relegated to feminism's archives. For many feminists, this represents an important step forward. Take Judith Allen, for example. In 1990, Allen argued against feminist theories of the state and in favour of feminist theorising on arenas and processes like policing, bureaucratic culture and masculinity. On her account, the latter represented 'the disaggregrated, diverse and specific (or local) sites that must be of most pressing concern to feminists'.[5] Moreover, she insisted that 'the state' was:

> ... a category of abstraction that is too aggregative, too unitary, and too unspecific to be of much use ... [and] too blunt an instrument to be of much assistance (beyond generalizations) in explanations, analyses or the design of workable strategies.[6]

Allen has a point, but I think she goes too far and, in this essay, I want to argue for theorisation of the state rather than its displacement. I choose this course for two reasons. First, because I have been convinced by the approach towards the state, state power and freedom advocated by US feminist, Wendy Brown. And secondly, because, like Martin Jacques, I think that a 'new Window of the Left' may be opening up in the UK and I would like to see feminism take advantage of this.[7] I suspect, however, that it may be difficult to drum up interest in my proposed feminist theorisation of the state. At present, feminist theorists who are interested in the workings of power are, for the most part, radically disinterested in critiquing *state* power. Moreover, as I shall try to show, many of the feminists who do claim an interest in the workings of the state seem outwitted by its paradoxical and diverse forms, or alternatively disinclined towards critique of the state.[8] Admittedly, feminists are not the only ones in this predicament: as I shall also try to show, a similar malaise infects critical theory more generally, as well as European and public law scholarship.[9]

I am troubled by this state of affairs. I sense a narrowing of democratic possibilities. And I worry about being hemmed in by a combination of

---

4   Jackson, E, 'Catharine MacKinnon and feminist jurisprudence: a critical reappraisal' (1993) 19 JLS 195, p 211.

5   Allen, J, 'Does feminism need a theory of "the state"?', in Watson, S (ed), *Playing the State: Australian Feminist Interventions*, 1990, London: Verso, p 34.

6   *Ibid.*

7   Jacques, M, 'Good to be back' (1998) *Marxism Today*, Nov/Dec, p 3.

8   See below, pp 31–38.

9   See below, pp 24–30 and 31–38.

disinterest, disinclination towards critique of the state and dated analysis. Overall, I am not optimistic about the chances of arriving at a theory of the state that will be adequate to the forms and paradoxes of state power in the late 20th century. The task is daunting, even if one limits it to the British state. Still, I think we should try and I propose to call the attempt 'cosmopolitan feminism'.[10] Cosmopolitan feminism's project will be to articulate and activate a critique of the late 20th century British state.

As will become clear in this essay, I am unsure about whether cosmopolitan feminism will get off the ground. I am also unclear on the shape(s) it might take. However, I do want to try to be clear from the start about what it's not. First, cosmopolitan feminism is not about reifying the state or state power. The cosmopolitan feminist should have no truck with the Orwellian fantasy of earlier state theories. Today, there is little to be gained from resurrecting old Leviathan demons of sovereignty, 'big government' and centralised power, or from protracted debates about the rights and wrongs of being 'in' or 'against' the state, or indeed from a focus on 'conventionally identified institutions'.[11] Thus, the cosmopolitan feminist must live up to her name, always alert to the paradoxical, and sometimes contradictory, nature of late modern state power and its myriad connections and disconnections with other forms of governance. As Wendy Brown explains, late modern state power is complex, and complex power requires complex theory:

> The fact that state power is not unitary or systematic means that a feminist theory of the state will be less a linear argument than the mapping of an intricate grid of overlapping and conflicting strategies, technologies, and discourses of power ... its multiple dimensions make state power difficult to circumscribe and difficult to injure. There is no single thread that, when snapped, unravels the whole of state ... dominance.[12]

Secondly, cosmopolitan feminism is not a socialist *cri de coeur* (although, following Nancy Fraser, I do think that there is a great deal to be gained from working within a framework influenced by concepts such as 'interest', 'exploitation' and 'redistribution').[13] It is now generally accepted that many earlier Marxist and left analyses wrongly eviscerated forms of domination other than class; that their desire to stand apart from liberalism led to a thinning out of respect for democracy; that their emphasis on economic

---

10 I take the idea of 'cosmopolitanism' from David Held. See, *inter alia*, Held, D, *Democracy and the Global Order: From the Modern State to Cosmopolitan Governance*, 1995, Cambridge: Polity.

11 Cooper, D, *Governing Out of Order: Space, Law and the Politics of Belonging*, 1998, London: Rivers Oram, p 9.

12 *Op cit*, fn 2, Brown, pp 177, 179.

13 Fraser, N, *Justice Interruptus: Reflections on the 'Postsocialist' Condition*, 1997, New York: Routledge. See, further, pp 35–37 below.

exploitation denied the harm caused by cultural and political domination; and that their concept of the state was too unified, purposive and functionalist.[14]

Thirdly, cosmopolitan feminism does not turn away from post-theory. I think that feminism has been refreshed by recent injections of postmodernism and poststructuralism; I would argue that their influence has been especially important in developing more sophisticated critiques of power. In addition, post-theory's cultural critique provides a crucial reminder that, however important a feminist theorisation of the state may be, '[n]either domination nor democratic resistance are limited to the venue of the state'.[15]

Against this backdrop, I will use this essay to outline the limitations of much current theorising on the state, as well as the dangers inherent in abandoning state critique. The essay's targets will be British public law scholarship, feminism, and critical theory more generally. As I see it, the disinterest in the state, disinclination towards critique thereof, and dated state analysis that characterise much of this work create the opening for what I have described as cosmopolitan feminism. But, as will become clear, these characteristics also give the cosmopolitan feminist very little to work with. I shall begin with an analysis of the British state, where there is a burgeoning interest in matters to do with the state, but where it also seems that a wonderful opportunity for redesign of the polity – what Bruce Ackerman has called a 'constitutional moment'[16] – may seal around us because of the shortcomings of dominant state narratives in public law. Then, I shall turn to feminism, and to critical theory more generally, in search of more progressive narratives. Unfortunately, this search will throw up more distressing news: feminists and critical theorists have largely abandoned critique of the state. I shall try to explain why this has happened. Finally, echoing Wendy Brown, Colin Sumner and others, I will close the chapter with the following call to action: '[t]he state is still with us and we still need to find the concepts to think it.'[17]

---

14 See, *inter alia*, Phillips, A, 'From inequality to difference: a severe case of displacement' (1998) 224 NLR 143 and Sumner, C, 'Censure, crime, and state', in Maguire, M, Morgan, R and Reiner, R (eds), *Oxford Handbook of Criminology*, 2nd edn, 1998, Oxford: Clarendon, pp 504–05. (I am grateful to my colleague Paul Roberts for bringing Sumner's essay to my attention.)

15 *Op cit*, fn 2, Brown, p x.

16 Ackerman, B, 'The Storrs Lectures: discovering the constitution' (1984) 93 YLJ 1013 (cited in MacCormick, N, 'Democracy, subsidiarity, and citizenship in the "European Commonwealth"' (1997) 16 Law and Philosophy 331, p 333).

17 *Op cit*, fn 14, Sumner, p 505.

A NEW WINDOW OF THE LEFT?
PUBLIC LAW AND THE BRITISH STATE

Contra Allen, I think that to eclipse the state is to relinquish a feminist 'opportunity moment'. In saying this, I am thinking specifically about the UK where, for a variety of reasons, interest in all things statist is running at a recordable high. As I see it, this interest is characterised by varying degrees of optimism, scepticism and crisis, and also by a good deal of fractiousness. Optimism – some might call it utopianism – comes through in the work of scholars like Neil MacCormick and David Held. MacCormick believes that here in Western Europe we may be passing through a 'constitutional moment':

> People talk from time to time about 'constitutional moments', the fleeting junctures of opportunity for radical redesign of a polity, an idea borrowed from Bruce Ackerman's study of the transformations of American constitutional order at great moments of opportunity. Is there such a moment here in Europe in the closing years of the 20th century?[18]

In similar vein, in an essay in *Marxism Today*'s special issue on the 'Blair project', David Held rereads the late 20th century phenomenon of globalisation, arguing that it is multi-faceted rather than monolithic and irrevocably neo-liberal.[19] On Held's account, globalisation is about much more than the rise of neo-liberal deregulation: it is also about an exciting growth in major global and regional institutions, like the United Nations and the European Union; highly innovative forms of governance and law making, including the International Criminal Court; and, more recently, particularly within the EU's post-Maastricht and Amsterdam climate, a burgeoning acceptance of the desirability of intervening in markets.

Here Held is reinforcing his earlier 'cosmopolitan conception of democracy'.[20] Cosmopolitan democracy is about recognising the ongoing diffusion of forms of governance and responding with sophisticated systems of accountability and control. Held's cosmopolitan democrat is very aware of future challenges and opportunities, and little interested in the traditional constitutionalism of sovereign parliaments and 'big government':

> Faced with overlapping communities of fate – with, that is, a world in which the fortunes of individual political communities are increasingly bound together – citizens in the future will need to be not only citizens of their own communities, but also of the regions in which they live, and of the wider global order. They must be able to participate in diverse political communities – from

---

18 *Op cit*, fn 16, MacCormick.
19 Held, D, 'Globalisation: the timid tendency' (1988) *Marxism Today*, Nov/Dec, p 24.
20 *Op cit*, fn 10, Held.

cities and subnational regions, to nation states, regions and wider global networks.[21]

John Morison pursues a similar line when he insists on constitutional renewal as a necessary supplement to New Labour's current constitutional reform project.[22] According to Morison, '[w]hile the proposed reforms are important, and should be implemented, they are not enough by themselves ... [They] miss their target by focusing on a traditional agenda of restraining big government and reviving the role of parliaments through the variable geometry of a newly devolved polity'.[23] Like Held, Morison believes that the nature of the late modern state necessitates new approaches to public power and democracy. Thus, Morison proposes constitutional renewal as the largely unrecognised but vital project for *fin-de-siècle* constitutionalism. This renewal project demands two things: first, the *fin-de-siècle* constitutionalist must tame the 'fugitive power'[24] that operates above, below and through the nation state; and secondly, she must follow through on the insights of radical, communicative and participatory democracy, guiding us towards 'new ways to institutionalise democracy beyond parliaments, committees and codes for conduct there'.[25]

STATE NARRATIVES

These are big ideas. In my view, they are also timely and very welcome. Unfortunately, I suspect that the state narratives currently in use in most legal circles in the UK may prove too linear and far too simple to cope with the challenges presented. Consider the extent of the problem: to start with, one would have to overcome an historical neglect of the concept of the state. Then, one would have to cut through popular assumptions about state helplessness in the face of 'globalizing wall-to-wall capitalism'.[26] It would also be necessary to close down the ongoing circus over sovereignty, especially its star-turns such as the bogey of a 'United States of Europe', the shenanigans of the 'bureaucrats in Brussels', or the vaunting, 'anti-British' ambitions of the Scottish. Moreover, as Morison himself notes, radical state narratives may also be undermined by the pre-modern 'modernisation' of New Labour's constitutional reform project. In short, although state talk is everywhere in the

---

21   *Op cit*, fn 19, Held, p 27.
22   Morison, J, 'The case against constitutional reform?' (1998) 25 JLS 510.
23   *Ibid*, p 525.
24   *Ibid*, pp 526–28.
25   *Ibid*, p 525.
26   *Op cit*, fn 13, Fraser.

UK today, it appears that one can make a sound case for the proposition that it fails to capture 'the state we're in'.[27]

In the following paragraphs, I shall try to give a more detailed account of my suspicions about state narratives in the UK. I want to begin with a couple of personal reflections. First, when it comes to the state, I am unclear on the answers to lots of questions, and sense that I have yet to articulate many others. For example, what is state and what is non-state in today's UK, and when is this a relevant question? Is this particular late modern state everywhere and nowhere, amidst transnationalism and devolution, regulation, partnership and privatisation, susceptibility to global capital and a sometimes distasteful showiness on the world stage in foreign affairs? When did the public/private divide hypostasise into a range of publics,[28] partnerships[29] and 'uncanny half worlds'?[30] What exactly is 'civil society'; and what constitutes the private sphere when there is a growing underclass for whom the state is a 'daily superintendent'?[31] Moreover, if the substance of democracy is unclear, in particular, if 'freedom other than free enterprise'[32] remains elusive, what's the point in a project that seeks to *democratise* the intimate sphere?[33] Finally, what is the promise of subsidiarity? For that matter, what exactly is 'subsidiarity'? And what's all this emphasis on 'citizenship' and 'radical democracy'?

Secondly, I suspect that I make a mess of teaching about the state. For example, I pore over the boundaries of 'state action' in teaching US constitutional law and invoke a traditional civil-libertarian faith in rights based regulation as well as its suspiciousness about 'big government'. Then, in my health care law module, things take a Foucauldian turn and disciplinary power occupies centre stage. Finally, myriad perspectives on the state emerge in my first year course, 'Understanding Law'. Now, one could present these variations as evidence of a teacher's sophisticated unravelling of the late modern state. For instance, Davina Cooper cites the example of a feminist academic at a day's workshop on 'the state and development' who explained that:

---

27 I take this phrase from Hutton, W, *The State We're In*, 1996, London: Cape.

28 *Op cit*, fn 13, Fraser, pp 69–98.

29 See, *inter alia*, Harlow, C and Rawlings, R, *Law and Administration*, 2nd edn, 1997, London: Butterworths, pp 252–94.

30 This was the space to which Mitchell, writing as far back as 1965, consigned the growing number of hybrid institutional forms which defied easy classification as either state or non-state. See Mitchell, JDB, 'The causes and effects of the absence of a system of public law in the United Kingdom' [1965] PL 95, p 113 (quoted in Allison, JWF, 'Theoretical and institutional underpinnings of a separate administrative law', in Taggart, M (ed), *The Province of Administrative Law*, 1997, Oxford: Hart, p 81).

31 *Op cit*, fn 2, Brown, p 196.

32 *Op cit*, fn 2, Brown, p 9.

33 As proposed, *inter alia*, by Giddens, A, *The Transformation of Intimacy*, 1992, Cambridge: Polity; and Weeks, J, *Invented Moralities: Sexual Values in an Age of Uncertainty*, 1995, Cambridge: Polity.

First thing in the morning, with my women and law group, I define the state one way, then differently in the afternoon when I'm teaching law and development. Sometimes I want students to see the state as a contradictory, fluid terrain, sometimes as a coercive, authoritarian apparatus.[34]

Unfortunately, however, I suspect that a different reason explains the varying state forms that emerge in my classes: like so many others, I flop unwittingly between dated accounts of a centralised, sovereign state; fantastical accounts of a state emasculated by globalisation; and the anti-statism of much Foucauldian post-structuralism. Of course, the key question is: why has this been happening?

Carl Stychin has claimed that '[i]n the late 1990s, the nation state sometimes seems to be caught between the local and the global',[35] and it seems to me that, in the UK, observers of the state are trapped in a similar way. To adapt an idea of Neil MacCormick's,[36] observers either tend to look 'forward' by prioritising the local and the supranational and excluding the state, or they look 'back' and persist with a discourse of sovereign states. Very few manage, or even consider, what MacCormick prescribes as essential: a sideways move, or lateral thinking.

Part of the problem is that 'glocalisation'[37] – Zygmunt Bauman's delightful description of the phenomena of globalisation and localisation – has us spooked. And the problems deepen if one takes account of Fukuyama's highly publicised claim that 1989 represented the triumph of neo-liberalism and the 'end of history';[38] or Tony Blair's 1997 promise of an end to ideology;[39] or the (albeit remote) possibility that sovereignty in Western Europe is simply momentarily elusive and 'as certain as anything to fetch up somewhere [either back with fully sovereign states or forward to a European colossus] in due and early course'.[40] On top of all this, of course, there is the mundane but perennial difficulty of knowing how to describe the state in which we live, in particular the fact that 'none of the existing handles quite fit':

... we live in a state with a variety of titles having different functions and nuances – the UK (or 'Yookay', as Raymond Williams relabelled it), Great Britain (imperial robes), Britain (boring lounge suit), England (poetic but troublesome), the British Isles (too geographical), 'This Country' (all-purpose

---

34 Cooper, D, *Power in Struggle: Feminism, Sexuality and the State*, 1995, New York: New York UP, p 60.

35 Stychin, CF, *A Nation by Rights: National Cultures, Sexual Identity Politics and the Discourse of Rights*, 1998, Philadelphia: Temple UP, p 201.

36 MacCormick, N, 'Beyond the sovereign state' (1993) 56 MLR 1, p 17.

37 Zygmunt Bauman, conference address (cited in Yuval-Davis, N, 'Women, citizenship and difference' (1997) 57 FR 4, p 22).

38 Fukuyama, F, *The End of History and the Last Man*, 1992, New York: Free Press.

39 Tony Blair, acceptance speech, general election, 1 May 1997 (cited in Cooper, *op cit*, fn 11, p 173).

40 *Ibid*, MacCormick, p 17.

within the Family), or 'This Small Country of Ours' (defensive Shakespearean).[41]

Thinking about these matters in more detail, it becomes clear that the observer of the modern British state is hampered by the fact that the concept of the state has played little role in the English legal tradition. For example, Harlow and Rawlings note that 'it is a common criticism of public law that it has failed adequately to conceptualise the state', and they go on to agree that 'the term has little legal resonance'.[42] Similarly, Allison argues that the concept of the state has 'played little role in the English common law tradition'.[43] He also cites evidence of a similar historical neglect of the state in English philosophy, political science and history.[44] Moreover, he believes that, of late, the state has become even more indistinct, and notes that a clutch of expert legal commentators now prefer to demarcate the province of public law regardless of the state – whether through an unrelated criterion of public function, regard for context, or a theory of power.[45]

Allison attributes neglect of the state in the English common law tradition to two features: first, the comparative lateness and limited extent of administrative centralisation in England; and, secondly, the theoretical insularity of an English legal profession which was 'preoccupied with remedies, the practice of law, and the law as posited, to the exclusion of political theory with a normative emphasis on the state' and which handed down its preoccupations to 'the early doctrinal writers, such as Hale, Blackstone, Austin and Dicey'.[46] And, paradoxically, as interest in the British state began to emerge in the early part of this century, the task of mapping the state became increasingly difficult. The difficulty, according to Allison, resulted from the increased blurring of the public/private divide, a phenomenon which has since become characteristic of British state administration.

Where tools of state analysis *are* identifiable – for example, sovereignty and the public/private divide – they can seem hopelessly anaemic; fundamentally unable to cope with the tangle of paradoxes presented by the state today. Thus, although 'the state' is beginning to receive lots of attention – for example, devolution has been launched as a flagship political project; we are, finally, 'bringing rights home' in the Human Rights Act 1998; and electoral reform is promised sometime soon – it is unclear whether many of the tools of state analysis currently in use in public law can be of more than

---

41   Nairn, T, *The Enchanted Glass*, 1988, London: Hutchinson Radius, p 93.
42   *Op cit*, fn 29, Harlow and Rawlings, p 7.
43   *Op cit*, fn 30, Allison, p 71.
44   *Op cit*, fn 30, Allison, p 77.
45   *Op cit*, fn 30, Allison, pp 84–88.
46   *Op cit*, fn 30, Allison, p 77.

limited use. As Morison and others have argued, constitutional reform may be central to the New Labour project, but momentous and disorienting developments of a constitutional nature have *already* taken place.[47]

STATE TRANSFORMATIONS

Let's consider a few of these developments. First, consider what Allison has described as 'the indistinctness of the modern state administration'.[48] Allison isolates three developments over the course of this century which he believes have played an important role in accelerating the indistinctness of state administration: first, the series of contractions and expansions in notions of accepted state functions, ranging from the early nightwatchman state with minimal law and order responsibilities, to the welfare state, and more recently, the neo-liberal distaste for the 'nanny state'; secondly, the proliferation of hybrid institutional forms which don't fit a state/non-state classification; and, thirdly, the increasingly close relationship between government and industry, nurtured through governmental bargaining powers. Allison goes on to emphasise that the difficulty of identifying the state and its administration has been compounded by the privatising practices of recent governments. Thus, the 1979–97 Conservative era smeared an already indistinct divide between the public and private sectors by transferring a range of public entities (such as the utility companies) to the private sector, and contractualising public administration through techniques of 'deregulation', 'contracting out', and 'internal markets'. Moreover, its reshaping of government on the model of market ordering has been largely accepted by New Labour: '[s]traightforward privatisation, market-testing, and the purchaser-provider split may have been replaced by newer, New Labour ideas of "contestability", "best value", and partnership but the direction is similar.'[49] And, although it may seem that New Labour's constitutional reform project will render the exercise of public power more distinct and accountable, some commentators have already suggested that the initiative's focus on controlling big government and enhancing representative democracy is outdated:

> Proposals, however well intentioned, about restoring representativeness to the regions, revitalizing Parliament, and ensuring accountability and openness in Westminster and Whitehall are missing the point. Even when such reforms are secured by a new, more emphatic rights approach ... they do not represent anything more than a very modest start on what should be a very much longer journey towards a more truly modern or even postmodern constitutional

---

47 *Op cit*, fn 22, Morison.
48 *Op cit*, fn 30, Allison, p 89.
49 *Op cit*, fn 22, Morison, p 517.

settlement. As we approach the 21st century these reforms seem located in the past.[50]

The second momentous, but largely under-analysed, constitutional development stems from the expanding province of the United Nations (UN) and the European Union (EU), as well as the imminent move to devolution. Together, these open up complex relationships between local, national, European and global systems, creating multiple entry points for law making and legal challenges,[51] as well as a need for new systems of democratic accountability and control. Some commentators – MacCormick, for example – have been keen to press ahead and face up to these opportunities and urgent challenges, but they are in a minority. Thus, MacCormick recently found himself left largely empty handed after trawling the output of some fellow lawyers for ideas on responding to the challenges and opportunities of EU development:

> The community of legal theorists throughout Europe has until very recently, and with but a few honourable exceptions, shown an astonishing lack of interest in the development of European law, in the specific sense of the law of the European Community (EC). Here we have not merely a new legal system, but maybe even a new kind of legal system, unfolding in our faces and all about us. Yet we have largely contrived to ignore it. We have remained, as it were, bewitched with the paradigm of the state and its law. We have greeted this origin of a species with the comfortable complacency of juristic pre-Darwinians ... It seems almost as true that the community of Community lawyers has, with inverse defensiveness, insulated itself from the seductions of theory. Despite the challenge of a claim that here we have law in what is somehow a new form, maybe a new sense of the term 'law', not many scholars seem to have been stirred into deep consideration of the theoretical underpinnings of doctrinal study in EC law.[52]

Of course, as noted above, there is also a danger in getting too caught up in ideas like contractualisation, devolution and globalisation, and thereby eviscerating the role of the state. This danger is particularly acute in relation to globalisation which is frequently, and very misleadingly, presented as leading to 'the end of the state'. Globalisation changes state power; it doesn't destroy it. In fact, as Held has recently pointed out, globalisation has actually stimulated 'a range of government and governance strategies and, in some fundamental respects, *a more activist state*':[53]

---

50 *Op cit*, fn 22, Morison, p 512.

51 Darian-Smith, E, 'Law in place: legal mediations of national identity and state territory in Europe', in Fitzpatrick, P (ed), *Nationalism, Racism and the Rule of Law*, 1995, Aldershot: Darmouth, p 27.

52 MacCormick, N, 'Risking constitutional collision in Europe?' (1998) 18 MLR 517, p 517. See, also, *inter alia*, MacCormick, *op cit*, fn 36.

53 *Op cit*, fn 19, Held, pp 25–26 (emphasis added).

States and public authorities initiated many of the fundamental changes – for example, the deregulation of capital in the 1980s and early 1990s. In other spheres of activity as well, states have become central in initiating new kinds of transnational collaborations, from the emergence of different forms of military alliances to co-operation in the procurement of major new weapons systems. The fact of the matter is that on many fundamental measures of state power – from the capacity to raise taxes and revenue to the ability to hurl concentrated force at enemies – states are, at least throughout most of the OECD world, as powerful if not more powerful than their predecessors.[54]

Moreover, *appearing* to be impaled by global forces, or to be unavoidably caught between the global and the local, can be convenient for the Machiavellian-minded state. As Wendy Brown has argued, a state may be able to play assumed 'impotence' to its own advantage:

> ... like the so called new man, the late modern state also represents itself as pervasively hamstrung, quasi-impotent, unable to come through on many of its commitments, because it is decentralising itself, because 'it is no longer the solution to social problems', because it is 'but one player on a global chessboard', or because it has foregone much of its power in order to become 'kinder, gentler'. The central paradox of the late modern state thus resembles a central paradox of late modern masculinity: its power and privilege operate increasingly through disavowal of potency, repudiation of responsibility, and diffusion of sites and operations of control.[55]

I suspect that there is something of Brown's 'new man' in New Labour. As Stuart Hall notes, the current government has been apt to deal with globalisation 'as if it is a self-regulating, implacable Force of Nature ... like the weather',[56] choosing to adapt us to the strictures of the global economy rather than aiming actively to manage market forces. There is also a whiff of the 'new man' in the government's appropriation of the language of affection and intimacy. Since coming to power in 1997, the Labour Government has set about 'bringing rights *home*', as well as practising 'tough *love*' to 'help individuals to help themselves'. Moreover, it has blurred other boundaries with its evermore complicated range of state/private sector 'partnerships' (as in the educational field).

To sum up: the late 20th century British state is perilous terrain and a quick review of public law suggests that qualified navigators are few and far between. It seems that although there is a great deal of work for the cosmopolitan feminist, she has not been given much to work with. But is the prognosis really this grim? Perhaps feminism and critical theory are more attuned to the forms of modern state power. After all, 10 years ago MacKinnon's theory of the state caught the feminist imagination, and 20 years

---

54 *Op cit*, fn 19, Held.
55 *Op cit*, fn 2, Brown, pp 193–94.
56 Hall, S, 'The great moving nowhere show' (1998) *Marxism Today*, Nov/Dec, p 11.

ago, Marxist state theory generally eclipsed all around it in Left intellectualism. In the next section, I shall consider whether contemporary Anglo-American feminism and critical theory can be said to have a theory of late modern state power.[57] I will start with the arguments of US feminist scholar, Wendy Brown.

'THE STATE WE ARE IN': FEMINISM AND CRITICAL THEORY ON THE LATE MODERN STATE

Brown's project, as outlined in *States of Injury: Power and Freedom in Late Modernity*, is not directly about gender or the state, but rather about 'freedom's contemporary predicament in North America',[58] in particular, the absence of a vital democratic politics of freedom that is alert to the modalities of late modern state power. In *States of Injury*, the late 20th century North American state emerges as a modern Janus – protector and foe, pervasive and intangible, potent and subordinated by privatisation and globalisation, incoherent and dominating – with many different but overlapping political powers. As noted above, it can also be intensely Machiavellian. The question Brown raises is: why are the complexities and contradictions of this type of late modern state power largely unacknowledged in critical theory and progressive political activism?

What, Brown asks, has caused legitimate circumspection about Marxist state theory to lapse into a worryingly pervasive left disinterest in critiquing the state? And, why, simultaneously, has there been a crescendo of appeals to the state for recognition and protection, particularly through rights based juridical adjudication of social injuries such as sexual harassment and hate speech? Brown is worried about the consequences of these developments: what we need, she argues, is to recognise that under such circumstances there is a risk that 'well intentioned contemporary political projects and theoretical postures inadvertently redraw the very configurations and effects of power that they seek to vanquish'.[59]

---

57 I shall limit my analysis to recurring themes in Anglo-American feminism and critical theory. I accept that this generalised approach eclipses pioneering analyses, including Davina Cooper's work on Western governing forms and relations (see, Cooper, D, *Sexing the City*, 1992, London: Rivers Oram; *Power in Struggle: Feminism, Sexuality and the State*, 1995, New York: New York UP; *Governing Out of Order*, 1998, London: Rivers Oram) and Jacqui Alexander's (see, Alexander, J, 'Erotic autonomy as a politics of decolonization', in Alexander, MJ and Mohanty, CT (eds), *Feminist Genealogies, Colonial Legacies, Democratic Futures*, 1997, New York: Routledge, p 63) and Anne McClintock's (see, McClintock, A, *Imperial Leather: Race, Gender, and Sexuality in the Colonial Contest*, 1995, London: Routledge) work on post-colonial states.

58 *Op cit*, fn 2, Brown, p 9.

59 *Op cit*, fn 2, Brown, p ix.

Brown pinpoints particular risks for feminism in abandoning the state as an object of criticism and subject of study.[60] Her starting point is the 'historically unparalleled prominence'[61] of the state in the lives of millions of women in North America (and, I would add, the UK too). She attributes this prominence to two factors. First, the state's near constant presence in many of the issues that interest and divide feminists. Secondly, the centrality of the state in the day to day lives of ever larger numbers of (usually impoverished) woman-supported households. Together, these developments give rise to an expansive, complex and risky dependency. How, Brown asks, ought we to characterise this deepening involvement between women and the state? What is the nature of a dependency that grows out of state protection and regulation? For example, if the state provides and protects, equalises and liberates, does it also dominate, regulate and discipline? To what extent has it become the 'daily superintendent of masculine dominance in late modern life'?[62] And do feminist appeals to the state bolster this 'imperialist public',[63] constructing a 'plastic cage that reproduces and further regulates the injured subjects it would protect'?[64] Moreover, what will happen to millions of women, as late modern states, like the UK, move to impeach dependency and need, championing private economic obligations over erstwhile public ones?[65]

So, why have feminists (and critical theorists more generally) dropped critique of the state from their agendas? In what follows, I propose five reasons for this absence of critique, reviewing each one in turn. At times, I will wander into what may appear to be exclusively North American terrain. However, I would argue that the 'special relationship' between the US and the UK, as manifested, for example, in the Blair/Clinton Third Way, and also in the influence of US authors on British critical writing, makes this apparent detour relevant.

The first factor working against a contemporary feminist theorisation of state is the project's MacKinnonite associations. Late 1990s' feminism has dethroned Catharine MacKinnon. Her work is little cited; very rarely in a favourable way. Over the last decade, her project (and, on occasion, her personal style) has come under heavy fire. The consensus seems to be that she

---

60 Brown's interest in mapping practices of freedom and unfreedom in the late modern state developed out of an earlier attempt at a critical feminist theory of the masculinism inherent in such states. Ultimately, Brown found the latter framework too confining and too open to reification of the state and of gender. For the purposes of this chapter, however, I want to take advantage of these origins.

61 *Op cit*, fn 2, Brown, p 168.

62 *Op cit*, fn 2, Brown, p 196.

63 *Op cit*, fn 33, Weeks, p 13.

64 *Op cit*, fn 2, Brown, p 28.

65 See, *inter alia*, Cooper, D, 'Regard between strangers: diversity, equality and the reconstruction of public space' (1998) 18 CSP 465.

did not add much to our conceptualisations of either 'maleness' or 'the state'.[66]

Secondly, critical thinkers' recent dalliance with post-theory – I'm thinking here specifically of poststructuralism and postmodernism – has created a widespread caution about grand theory, which in turn has caused circumspection about state theory. Basically, state theory is associated with grand theory and, as a result, with bugbears like essentialism. It has fallen out of favour, and local sites (particularly, intimate ones like 'the body' and 'desire') and contingent knowledges have replaced it as the priorities for critical theory. Interest has shifted from 'institutions' to 'discourses' and 'practices', and books like Judith Butler's *Gender Trouble* and *Bodies That Matter* seem to have ousted Marxist tomes in critical theory's bestseller lists. These shifts seem particularly pronounced in feminist scholarship, where the charge of essentialism hit hard. Swathes of feminist theory have turned to 'culture': as Anne Phillips recently explained, '[f]eminists who once sighted politics everywhere are not particularly enthused by the study of politics and are far more readily engaged by work in cultural studies or philosophy or film'.[67]

These shifts can be attributed, in part, to the influence of Michel Foucault's poststructuralism – especially his arguments about the decentered and decentralised character of modern political power. Remember that Foucault argued that:

> We must eschew the model of the Leviathan in the study of power. We must escape from the limited field of juridical sovereignty and state institutions, and instead base our analysis of power on the study of the techniques and tactics of domination.[68]

In the 1970s and 1980s, feminist theories of the state were easy prey for such Foucauldian ideas; in fact, the latter were a welcome corrective to feminism's over-general, rigid and functionalist accounts of state power.[69] As Waylen explains, for much of the 1970s and 1980s 'few feminist analyses went beyond seeing the state as either essentially potentially good or bad for women as a group'.[70] Waylen pinpoints four particular problems with this work.[71] First, it focused on 'the liberal-democratic state in the first world', and gave 'comparatively little attention ... to the gendered analysis of the post-colonial

66 Pringle, R and Watson, S, 'Women's interests and the poststructuralist state', in Barrett, M and Phillips, A (eds), *Destabilizing Theory: Contemporary Feminist Debates*, 1992, Cambridge: Polity, p 57.

67 Phillips, A, *Oxford Readings in Feminism: Feminism and Politics*, 1998, Oxford: OUP, p 2.

68 Foucault, M, *Power/Knowledge: Selected Interviews and Other Writings, 1972–77*, Gordon, C (ed), 1980, New York: Pantheon, p 102.

69 See, *inter alia*, *ibid*, Pringle and Watson.

70 Waylen, G, 'Gender, feminism and the state: an overview', in Randall, V and Waylen, G (eds), *Gender, Politics and the State*, London: Routledge, p 4.

71 *Ibid*.

and Third World state'. Secondly, it swung unhelpfully between 'rather over-general ... overarching macro-theoretical analyses' and 'detailed empirical micro-analyses'. Thirdly, it presented women as 'objects of state policy', characterising the state as 'something "out there" and external to women's lives and women, [as] "done to" by a state over which they have little control'. Finally, where women's engagement with the state was examined, a crude 'them and us' framework was used, such that women were only ever seen as making demands upon the state. In sum then: in 1970s' and 1980s' feminist work, the state was generally presented as a fixed, undifferentiated entity, a force lying 'almost outside society rather than being something which is created in part as a result of the interaction with different groups'.[72]

In the light of these shortcomings, the new emphasis on Foucauldian poststructuralist analyses of power in feminist thinking is, without doubt, a positive development. In addition, it is also worth emphasising that the recent critical vogue for 'culture', noted earlier, is not necessarily an 'anti-politics'; Phillips, for example, cites Michèle Barrett's view that it may help us 'towards a better account of subjective political motivation and open up space for a more explicitly ethical politics'.[73] Still, I remain anxious about the diminution of interest in the state and state power which seems to have crept into feminism alongside the popularisation of poststructuralism and 'the turn to culture'. There are two reasons for this anxiety. First, as Wendy Brown points out, it is arguable that Foucault's insightful and nuanced concept of power has been rendered crude by popularisation, and that what was intended by Foucault as a necessary 'instrument of theoretical ground clearing' has left us blindsided as it:

> ... transmogrifies from methodological strategy to political truth [with the consequence that] two of the most significant contemporary domains of disciplinary power – the bureaucratic state and the organization of the social order by capital – are neither scrutinized by Foucault nor treated as significant sites of power by many of his disciples.[74]

Secondly, despite the valuable insights and general invigoration afforded by the recent feminist emphasis on local sites and contingent knowledges, I worry about a susceptibility to depoliticisation and acontextuality and sometimes find myself doubting the emancipatory capacity of a politics of performativity, visibility and linguistic deconstruction when pitted against dominant economic structures and institutions. I also sense that the 'politics'

---

72 *Op cit*, fn 70, Waylen

73 *Op cit*, fn 67, Phillips, p 2 (citing Barrett, M, 'Words and things: materialism and method in contemporary feminist analysis', in Barrett, M and Phillips, A (eds), *Destabilizing Theory: Contemporary Feminist Debates*, 1992, Cambridge: Polity, p 204).

74 *Op cit*, fn 2, Brown, p 16 notes that Foucault himself sought to dilute over-dichomotous accounts of power in his later work. But, for a feminist account of the bureaucratic state, see Ferguson, K, *The Feminist Case Against Bureaucracy*, 1984, Philadelphia: Temple UP.

of poststructuralism may frighten off many readers: for example, even Anne Phillips recalls:

> … rushing out to buy a new collection of essays published under the title *Feminists Theorize the Political*, a collection packed with fascinating essays, but organised as it turned out, around confirming or contesting the value of poststructuralist theories.[75]

More fundamentally, however, I am concerned about the lack of emphasis in contemporary critical theory on supporting social movements that are struggling for improved life conditions and greater economic justice. I agree with Rosemary Hennessy who argues that many critical theorists need to broaden out from a focus on discourse and gender-play so that consideration is also given to historical practices and contexts and the institutional power of forces like capitalism and imperialism.[76] Hennessy is concerned that critical theory fails to expose the underside of the late modern emphasis on 'lifestyle' and 'individual choice'. She argues that what she describes as 'the aestheticization of daily life' under industrial capitalism promotes 'the pursuit of new tastes and sensations as pleasures in themselves while concealing or backgrounding the labor that has gone into making them possible'.[77] She says that the invisibility of uneven social relations is further compounded by the growth of a professional middle class, and the popularisation of concepts like the 'new man', the 'career woman' and 'lesbian chic' which feed the illusion that patriarchy and exploitation have disappeared. The reality, as Hennessy points out, is that in many industrialised countries, the gap between rich and poor is widening, poverty is becoming increasingly feminised, and gays and lesbians are not all the middle class consumers of popular representations. In addition, she suggests that: 'if gay visibility is a good business prospect, as some companies argue, the question gay critics need to ask is "for whom?". Who profits from these new markets?'[78] In effect, Hennessy is pleading for a new historical materialism; in other words, a critical theory that combines the current postmodern emphasis on discourse and cultural meanings with an understanding of history, context and the impact of class and capitalism.

The third factor working against a contemporary feminist theorisation of the state relates to the protracted and inglorious collapse of Communism. As Fraser suggests, the collapse of Communism seems to have cemented liberal democracy and capitalism, not just as the new world order, but also as the only world order. Thus:

---

75 *Op cit*, fn 67, Phillips, p 2.
76 Hennessy, R, 'Queer visibility in commodity culture', in Nicholson, L and Seidman, S (eds), *Social Postmodernism*, 1995, Cambridge: CUP, p 142.
77 *Ibid*, p 165.
78 *Ibid*, p 173.

... 'liberal democracy' is being touted as the *ne plus ultra* of social systems for countries that are emerging from Soviet-style socialism, Latin American military dictatorships, and southern African regimes of racial domination.[79]

I also agree with Fraser that this has trickled down into left and liberal theory, causing a shift to what she describes as a '"post-socialist" imaginary'[80] wherein an interest in rights and recognition replaces earlier (primarily 1970s') calls for redistribution and attention to economic inequalities. Basically, her argument is that emphasis has shifted from class and economic inequalities to group identity and cultural recognition. In addition, as Phillips explains, celebration of difference, rather than attention to inequality, tends to occupy the epicentre of this '"post-socialist" imaginary', as '[w]e ask ourselves how we can achieve equality while still recognizing difference, rather than how we can eliminate inequality'.[81] The shift is most pronounced in the US, but it is also evident in the UK, as, for example, in the far greater attention that is being paid to constitutional reform by comparison with welfare reform:

> ... this displacement of the economic is precisely what worries so many on the Left in Britain. The radicalism of the new Labour Government is far more evident in its programme for constitutional reform than in any policies for the redistribution of income or wealth; and however much we may welcome this belated attention to questions of democratic accountability, the enlargement of horizons could mean that economic equality drops out of view.[82]

Like Fraser and Phillips, I want to voice some caution about this development; however, I do not want to be misunderstood because, for the most part, I am very keen on what has become known as 'the politics of recognition' or 'politics of difference'. For starters, it is a welcome antidote to the unrelenting class based analysis of earlier left (particularly Marxist) politics. Its emphasis on group identity, and on community, is also an important counter to the increasing focus on the individual. Furthermore, I do not want to deny that there are still large questions that need to be tackled by states in facing up to their own exclusionary cultural legacies, as well as in forging appropriate 'rights of exit' and 'rights of voice'[83] for individuals who are harmed by undemocratic practices within their own communities.

But there are also serious risks attached to the disengagement from analysis of economic inequalities that has tended to accompany the new focus on recognition and rights of difference. In effect, this was why Rosemary Hennessy was trying to caution fellow critical theorists when she expressed concerns about the emphasis on discourse and cultural life in recent critical

---

79 *Op cit*, fn 13, Fraser, p 69. See, also, Marks, S, 'The end of history? Reflections on some international legal theses' (1997) 3 EJIL 449.

80 *Op cit*, fn 13, Fraser, p x.

81 *Op cit*, fn 14, Phillips, p 143.

82 *Op cit*, fn 14, Phillips, pp 146–47.

83 *Op cit*, fn 33, Weeks, pp 152–54.

theory and activism. Therefore, whilst not detracting from the importance of state recognition of group or cultural difference, I do want to emphasise the limitations of many current discourses of difference. The basic problem is that:

> ... these discourses work better for some groups than for others – they work particularly badly ... for that rough category of 'underclass', defined through unemployment or employment insecurity ... discourses of difference 'convey an erroneous impression that they have a capacity to accommodate diversities of all kinds'. All too often, the result is that economic difference is silenced as a significant form.[84]

Of course, in these days of neo-liberalism and globalisation, it can seem as if 'economics' is everywhere, and this may help to explain the general failure to pick up on critical theory's recent elision of economic inequalities. This point also leads me into the fourth possible reason for critical theory's abandonment of state critique.

As pointed out earlier, we tend to assume that globalisation is synonymous with neo-liberalism, and that there are no alternatives to the latter. Thus, there is increasing emphasis on the mobility of capital and of workers; on the unstoppable force of neo-liberalism; and on the importance of economic self-sufficiency and private, as opposed to public, provision for family support, health care and old age. From certain quarters – especially neo-conservative and neo-liberal – there is also virulent criticism of the welfare state, often sneered at as a 'nanny state'. Wendy Brown argues that, in such a climate, critical theorists, who might once have defended critique of the state as a crucial component of democratising projects, may well consider that, today, criticism of the state is 'tantamount to luxury goods in bad times'.[85] A further disincentive to critique is that late 20th century states like the US and the UK are also the sites of acclaimed feminist victories.[86] New forms of legal regulation – sexual harassment, domestic violence, marital rape – have helped individual girls and women to escape violence, abuse and poverty and, as a result, branches of feminism and critical theory have come to believe in, and rely upon, state regulation as a means of escape from oppressive markets or male dominance, regardless of the potentially deleterious consequences for freedom inherent in the accompanying protectionism and surveillance. It is also hard to focus on critique of the state without feeling a sense of guilt about the risks of betraying the growing numbers of women who now depend on the state for day to day living. In sum then, a protective instinct, that locks out critique of the state, seems to have taken hold in the face of attacks on the welfare state and an increasing dependency on state regulation as the solution

---

84 *Op cit*, fn 14, Phillips, p 153, citing Coole, D, 'Is class a difference that makes a difference?' (1996) 77 RP 19.

85 *Op cit*, fn 2, Brown, p 10.

86 *Op cit*, fn 2, Brown, pp 168–71.

to a range of injuries or harms. But, as Brown points out, this protective instinct is very dangerous because:

> ... as capitalism has irreversibly commodified most elements of the private sphere, the domain and character of 'exchange' in the sexual division of labor has been transported from the private and individualised to the public and socialized. The twin consequences are that much of what used to be women's work in the home is now women's work in the economy and that the state and economy, rather than husbands, now sustain many women at minimal levels when they are bearing and caring for children.[87]

Finally, the fifth reason for feminist and critical theory's abandonment of state critique. I am less sure of my ground here but think that it is still worth raising certain concerns. Basically, I want to suggest that radical democracy – or at least some versions of it – may be compounding the abandonment of state theory. In particular, radical democracy's emphasis on citizenship, although meritorious and often inspiring, has paid insufficient attention to the underside of citizenship discourse more generally. This underside concerns the ways in which citizenship can facilitate anti-democratic state interests by functioning as 'a significant marker in the international system of population management'.[88] As Barry Hindess argues, despite the obvious merits of the new citizenship discourse, dominant theorisations of it often underestimate the extent to which it:

> ... provides states with an internationally acceptable rationale for regulating the movements of those who appear (or threaten to appear) on or within their borders as refugees from war and other forms of institutionalised violence, or simply in search of what they believe will be a better life. It helps to keep the poor in their place and, by promoting discrimination against the foreigner, it appears to offer some benefits even to the poorest of citizens who remain at home.[89]

TOWARDS A COSMOPOLITAN FEMINISM

This essay began by proposing feminist theorisation of the *fin-de-siècle* British state as a meritorious and potentially lucrative political and theoretical project. Adapting David Held's ideas, it named the project 'cosmopolitan feminism' and urged its immediate pursuit in the light of a possible new 'Window of the Left'. The essay itself sought to explain why late modern state power requires feminist and critical scrutiny. In addition, it outlined the extent of the task that faces the cosmopolitan feminist. Basically, she has little to draw upon as a

---

87 *Op cit*, fn 2, Brown, p 185.

88 Hindess, B, 'Divide and rule: the international character of modern citizenship' (1998) 1 EJST 57, p 68.

89 *Ibid*.

result of the lack of interest in state theory, the pervasiveness of dated analysis and, in certain circles, a misguided sense of protectionism. This absence makes the task more difficult but no less urgent. Therefore, the key question has to be what, if anything, would constitute a critical stance in this context? That is the project which lies ahead for the cosmopolitan feminist.

CHAPTER 3

ROYALTY AND IDENTITY IN PUBLIC LAW: DIANA AS QUEEN OF HEARTS, ENGLAND'S ROSE AND PEOPLE'S PRINCESS

Noel Whitty

The reign of Queen Elizabeth II is a paradox: a woman presiding over a patriarchal order, organised by primogeniture, the most atavistic aristocratic mechanism to secure masculine power.[1]

The death of Elizabeth II and the subsequent fracture of the hereditary principle were widely seen as the end of the traditional monarchy. The process of public consultation over the succession further diluted the royal mystique. The young King and Queen had done their best, appearing on chat shows, hiring the best script-writers, and keeping their infidelities more or less private ... But in general the nation had grown querulous, either dismayed by the Family's normality, resentful of its cost, or simply tired from bestowing millenia of love.[2]

INTRODUCTION

Within the UK today, the signs of a crisis of political identity (or identities) are everywhere, and the very recent certainties of a robust Britishness now seem quaint.[3] Political parties have set about redefining themselves, the New Labour Government is engaged in 'modernisation', and there is a project to reinvent 'Britain' itself. Should this be classed as an official crisis? Is it just a crisis of political institutions? Or of national identity?

The traditional shell of 'Britishness' is certainly perceived to be threatened by a resurgent Scottish identity. But, the real crisis may be closer to home: 'at the centre and in the elite ... [and] the problems of the English.'[4] As Paxman has argued, '[t]he English are simultaneously rediscovering the past that was buried when "Britain" was created and inventing a new future'.[5] Overshadowing, sometimes fomenting, all of these forces has been the evolving concept of European identity, a political project explicitly aimed at

---

1   Campbell, B, *Diana Princess of Wales*, 1998, London: The Women's Press, p 33.

2   Barnes, J, *England, England*, 1998, London: Jonathan Cape, p 143.

3   Willets, D, 'Who do we think we are?', 1988, London: Centre for Policy Studies (http://www.cps.org.uk/willetts.htm). See, also, Hague, W, 'Identity and the British way', 1999, London: Conservative Party Headquarters.

4   Hewson, R, 'New definitions, new directions', 1997, London: The British Council, *Re-Inventing Britain Conference* (http://www.britcoun.org/studies/stdshewi.htm). See, also, Leonard, M, *Britain, TM: Renewing Our Identity*, 1998, London: Demos.

5   Paxman, J, *The English: A Portrait of a People*, 1998, London: Michael Joseph, p 265.

transcending the limitations of the nation state. The possible fallout from this has been hinted at by Young in his history of the European Union: 'The sacredness of England, whether or not corrupted into Britain, [becomes] a quality setting it, in some minds, for ever apart from Europe.'[6]

The aim of this chapter is to explore the nature of the relationship between one particular political institution and national identities. It takes as its focus an institution that is explicitly *not* included in the New Labour constitutional reform project: the monarchy. My interest is in why an institution that both underpins British public law theory (and, thus, is surely of relevance to any constitutional reform project), and is central to the construction of British political and cultural identities, remains insulated from the reform agenda. Why, in an expansive project of modernisation, has the Blair strategy on the monarchy been perceived as little more than 'grooving with the Heir to the Throne to the strains of Cool Britannia ...'?[7] Furthermore, why has Princess Diana's relationship with the Royal Family been interpreted as providing *new* (as distinct from only making visible for the first time) cultural/political readings of the role of monarchy and women in society. Is the revelation in a Demos opinion poll that 60% of the public agree that '[t]he monarchy's role should be modernised to reflect changes in British life' significant?[8]

Admittedly, some commentators predict that it is only a matter of time before a reformist/republican tide sweeps the traditional monarchy away, as part of the inevitable sentiment of a non-deferential populace in the post-Diana era. Will Hutton is part of this latter group and, like many others, he centres the death of Diana as a defining constitutional moment:

> It is clear that within a generation the monarchy's role will change, and that Britain will look and behave much more like a republic. And the date from which historians will source the change will be Diana's death.[9]

In the first two sections of this chapter, I explore the nature of contemporary monarchy by looking at its representation in the constitutional law textbook. As any first year law student will confirm, flicking through law texts' references to the monarchy is a confusing experience: representations of the monarchy or, more commonly, 'the Crown', rely on a mixture of historical narrative, rituals, personalities and political practices. In contrast to the popular narratives on 'the Royals', the dominant public law representation seems trapped in a time warp from the era of Dicey. While the monarch and the rest of the Royal Family clearly do have political and cultural significance,

---

6   Young, H, *This Blessed Plot: Britain and Europe from Churchill to Blair*, 1998, London: Macmillan, p 1.

7   'Editorial' (1998) *The Independent*, 8 May.

8   Hames, T and Leonard, M, *Modernising the Monarchy*, 1998, London: Demos.

9   Hutton, W, 'Britain is changing' (1998) *The Observer*, 30 August.

public law scholarship maintains its long tradition of deferential and depoliticised commentary.

In the third section, I shall contrast what I term the 'Diana Experience' – and feminist commentaries on it[10] – with the constitutional law tradition. My interest is the political significance of Princess Diana's life and death. Despite Hutton's claim, and in contrast to other legal cultures, such as Australia, there appears to be no popular yearning for a republic. Furthermore, the re-invention of 'Britain' does not seem to entail a rejection of aspects of Britishness that are historically linked to monarchy.[11] I will suggest that the experiences of 'monarchy' are open to different, and contradictory, interpretations. Public reaction to the Diana funeral embodied these contradictions in a most dramatic manner, especially the attempts to reconcile the life and death of a *princess* with either a republican or feminist politics.

My tentative conclusion will be that 'the boundaries of Britishness' are sufficiently fluid to allow people to appropriate the Diana Experience for multiple purposes. Diana can represent a feminist sexual politics, a republican icon, a fairy tale princess, and much more. However, the speed with which Prime Minister Blair stepped forward to quell the 'anti-Palace' currents, indicates that *continuity* of the monarchy above all else is important for the ruling elite, and also that republican predictions may be premature. As Nairn has argued: '[t]he ghost of revolution had materialised, and then de-materialised again.'[12]

ROYALTY AND THE CONSTITUTIONAL LAW TEXTBOOK

Royalty has always had a good press in constitutional law texts. The tone is respectful, if not downright deferential. While students are no longer expected to know the full royal lineage, it is quickly made clear to the reader that constitutional law can only be understood through a royalist lens.[13] Regardless of political reality, key themes about monarchy are copied from

---

10 For one dramatic celebration of Diana, the People's Princess, as a force for feminism and republicanism, see Burchill, J, 'The People's Destroyer' (1997) *The Guardian*, September 2: 'We'll always remember her, coming home for the last time to us, the People's Princess, not the Windsors'. We'll never forget her. And neither will they.'

11 While republicanism has been at the heart of Irish nationalism, contemporary Scottish nationalism has only begun to tentatively embrace it: see Foster, R, *Modern Ireland: 1600–1972*, 1988, London: Penguin, pp 505–11.

12 Nairn, T, 'Breaking up is hard to do' (1998) *Marxism Today*, Nov/Dec, p 43.

13 'Before coming to the study of constitutional and legal history, it is very desirable to have some knowledge of English history in general. The ordinary Englishman is supposed to acquire this at school but for the overseas student, and for anyone who wants to brush up his school learning, Trevelyan's "History of England" may be strongly recommended.' Williams, GL, *Learning the Law*, 1st edn, 1945, London: Stevens, p 41.

text to text: its continuity, stability and the glamour of its pageantry; its lack of political power; and, most emphatically, its guarantee of the national identity.[14] The treatment is generally uncritical, ahistorical and one-dimensional.[15] Even contemporary public law remains caught in the vice of an essentially conservative political mythology about the nature of royalty and national identity. In contrast, other disciplines – such as literature,[16] politics,[17] history,[18] cultural studies,[19] feminism[20] – have increasingly acknowledged the multi-layered meanings of the monarchy.

One possible reason for the deference of public law scholarship may be found in the way that the constitutional law textbook tradition was established.[21] In the absence of a written constitution, 'writers of authority' have taken on an elevated status, influencing successive editions of textbooks. Overwhelmingly, the monarchical dogmatism of Walter Bagehot dominates the textbook. An unbroken narrative is constructed from Bagehot's *The English Constitution* up to the present day:

> The use of the Queen, in a dignified capacity, is incalculable. Without her in England, the present English Government would fail and pass away ... The English Monarchy strengths our government with the strength of religion ... It would be a very serious matter to us to change every four or five years the visible head of our world ... We have come to regard the Crown as the head of our *morality*.[22]

Nearly 130 years later, Bogdanor's *The Monarchy and the Constitution* continues the tradition:

> ... the writings of Bagehot were to attain canonical status. It is known, indeed, that George V, George VI, Elizabeth II, and the Prince of Wales have all studied *The English Constitution*. Since Victoria the changes in the role of the monarchy have been changes in degree and not in kind. There have been no fundamental

---

14 Hitchens, C, *The Monarchy*, 1990, London: Chatto & Windus.

15 'In the 43 years since the Second World War there have been astonishingly few essays in thorough-going criticism.' Wilson, E, *The Myth of British Monarchy*, 1989, London: Journeyman, p 1. See also, Barnett, A (ed), *Power and the Throne: The Monarchy Debate*, 1994, London: Vintage.

16 Townsend, S, *The Queen and I*, 1993, London: Mandarin.

17 Nairn, T, *The Enchanted Glass: Britain and its Monarchy*, 1988, London: Hutchinson Radius.

18 Fraser, F, *The Unruly Queen: The Life of Queen Caroline*, 1997, London: Papermac.

19 Paglia, C, *Vamps and Tramps: New Essays*, 1994, New York: Vintage.

20 Smith, J, *Different for Girls: How Culture Creates Women*, 1997, London: Chatto & Windus.

21 See McDonald, Chapter 6, this volume.

22 Bagehot, W, *The English Constitution*, 1867, London: Henry King & Co, pp 33, 39, 46, 52. It is necessary to emphasise that Bagehot's defence of royalty was primarily motivated by his opposition to universal suffrage. The monarch 'acts as a disguise' because the 'masses of Englishmen are not fit for an elective government' (p 54, original emphasis). Letting 'daylight in upon magic' did not mean what constitutional law students are allowed to think it means.

alterations to the monarchical model as it had evolved by the end of Victoria's reign.[23]

In the era between these dates, constitutional law texts have done little to challenge this mindset, either repeating the political orthodoxy or reducing the monarchy to a few descriptive paragraphs. Consider the following examples. While noting that the Crown had become more associated with 'wealth instead of what used to be called "breeding"', Jennings provides a largely complimentary account: '[t]he State functions more easily if it can be personified.'[24] Hood Phillips, while discussing prerogative powers and the Commonwealth in some detail, provides only a dry history of royal titles.[25] Turpin, as with other writers, includes materials on democracy, constitutionalism and constitutional reform, but never critiques the monarchy itself (while recognising that 'the Queen has still a pivotally symbolic role ...').[26] Wade and Bradley contribute a depoliticised, descriptive account, familiar to generations of law students: the language is such that monarchy is just *assumed* as an inevitable and necessary fact.[27] Even critical public law texts also tend to pay scant attention to the significance of the monarchy. McEldowney, while providing a wide ranging account of public law issues, devotes three pages to the monarchy and references Bagehot as 'useful' reading.[28] In sum, as Mount notes:

> All royal biographers, all newspaper leader-writers and virtually all constitutional writers who have bothered to devote a page or two to the monarchy have followed Bagehot's formula, either tamely repeating it as gospel or rewriting it in their own words.[29]

Not surprisingly, today's first year law students can be taken aback when confronted with the mainstream constitutional law stance. They cannot easily cancel the memories of almost two decades of saturation coverage of 'the Royals' – generally commencing with Prince Charles' search for a Princess, through the televised Royal Wedding, to the marital breakdown, separation, divorce, and finally, funeral. The suspension of disbelief required to enter a public law world that continues to construct an apolitical Royal 'Family',

---

23 Bogdanor, V, *The Monarchy and the Constitution*, 1995, Oxford: Clarendon, pp 40–41.

24 Jennings, I, *The British Constitution*, 5th edn, 1966, Cambridge: CUP, pp 120, 121.

25 Hood Phillips, O and Jackson, P, *O Hood Phillips' Constitutional and Administrative Law*, 7th edn, 1987, London: Sweet & Maxwell, pp 255–61.

26 Turpin, C, *British Government and the Constitution: Text, Cases and Materials*, 1995, London: Butterworths, p 144.

27 Bradley, A, and Ewing, K, *Wade and Bradley: Constitutional and Administrative Law*, 11th edn, 1993, London: Longman, pp 244–74.

28 McEldowney, J, *Public Law*, 1998, London: Sweet & Maxwell, pp 86–88. Harden, I and Lewis, N, *The Noble Lie: The British Constitution and the Rule of Law*, 1986, London: Hutchinson; and Jowell, J and Oliver, D (eds), *The Changing Constitution*, 3rd edn, 1994, Oxford: Clarendon, are silent on the monarchy.

29 Mount, F, *The British Constitution Now*, 1992, London: Heinemann, p 94.

publicly envied and respected as the symbol of the nation, seems impossible. But, apparently, that is what is required. Thus, even though deferential royal commentary is now optional in the UK, orthodox constitutionalism continues to airbrush the reality of the monarch's (and the Royal Family's) life.

Of course, one may ask: does it matter if constitutional lawyers ignore 'the personal difficulties' (as Bogdanor so delicately puts it) and only focus on the official personages and duties; the Queen opening Parliament, the Prince cutting a ribbon? Even if some of the family details are embarrassing and officially concealed or downplayed – the bogus Winsdor name, the pro-Nazism of Edward VIII, the racism, snobbery, alcoholism, affairs and media manipulation[30] – is the *institution* of monarchy not what really matters? I will argue that it is inappropriate to disentangle the two; when dealing with a hereditary monarchy, 'the personal is the political' and vice versa. Family and institution are entwined, impacting on understandings of political authority (through the myriad usages of the 'Crown'), and of British identity. For public lawyers in the 1990s to pretend otherwise is to continue in the fabrication of constitutional myths.

THE CROWN

In this section, I will take a more detailed look at monarchical representations in constitutional law scholarship. What explains the range of these representations, and their sometimes contradictory nature? For example, does historical accident, or underlying authorial purpose, explain the choice of different terms? Constitutional law students may think that it is just a question of language, but there are real *political* consequences to using, and interchanging, the following terms in legal discourse: 'the Crown'; 'the monarch'; 'the Sovereign'; 'Her Majesty's government'; 'Ministers of the Crown'; 'the Queen in Parliament'; 'the Royal Prerogative'; 'Queen's Speech' and so on. What does it mean when public lawyers say in one breath that 'the Crown' equals 'the state' or 'government'; and then in another suggest that one can substitute the words 'the Queen' for 'the Crown'?[31] Or that child prisoners may be detained 'at Her Majesty's *pleasure*'? Even more intriguingly, what is one to make of the claim that the Queen is 'the symbol of national identity'? Thus, while law students are constantly told that the monarchy itself does not have influence, the language of constitutional law continues to

---

30 For examples, see sources as diverse as *op cit*, fn 1, Campbell; *op cit*, fn 15, Wilson; Kelley, K, *The Royals*, 1997, New York: Time Warner; and Hitchens, C, 'The trouble with HRH' (1997) LRB, 5 June, p 24.

31 Le Sueur, A and Sunkin, M, *Public Law*, 1997, London: Longman, pp 45–46, is one of the few textbooks to comment on this terminology.

be saturated with terminology eliding the distinction between Crown and monarchy, with the result that there is a masking of political power.

If we turn to mainstream constitutional law texts, we can identify at least six different, and overlapping, contexts in which the language of Crown/monarch is used. The extent of legitimation of the Crown varies from context to context. The Crown is described in terms of: (a) royal personalities (for example, the Queen); (b) the need for symbolism and ritual; (c) executive, state or prerogative power; (d) regal institutions or actors (such as the Church of England, House of Lords,[32] Privy Council and Lord Chancellor); (e) a description of nationhood; and (f) the construction of British subjecthood.

For this chapter's purposes, I will focus on three contexts: symbolism and rituals; the Crown as nation/state/executive power; and British subjecthood. My aim will be to highlight the ways in which the legitimacy of the Crown is perpetuated – how the preservation of the Crown at the heart of British constitutionalism is made to appear rational and necessary – and how questions of power and identity are constantly submerged. Then, in the next section, I will contrast Princess Diana's funeral with this constitutional tradition in order to problematise public law's assumptions about the role and effects of monarchy in the UK.

Symbolism and rituals

My first example of the uses to which Crown terminology is put concerns the centrality of royal symbolism and public ritual in the constitutional framework of the UK. As Jennings' *The British Constitution*, a historically revered text, explains:

> Certain it is that democratic government is not merely a matter of cold reason and prosaic policies. There must be some display of colour, and there is nothing more vivid than royal purple and imperial scarlet.[33]

Moreover, although Bagehot is cynical about the bringing down of 'the pride of sovereignty to the level of petty life', he also draws attention to the ways in which the symbolism of monarchy might appeal to a female audience, affirming women's apparent disinterest in the real 'business' of politics (as distinct from marriage):

> No feeling could seem more childish than the enthusiasm of the English at the marriage of the Prince of Wales. They treated as a great political event, what, looked at as a matter of pure business, was very small indeed. But no feeling

---

32 It is significant that the current Labour Government's proposals to remove the *hereditary* rights of the 'peers of the realm' scrupulously avoid any questioning of the legitimacy of the monarchy. See *Modernising Parliament: Reforming the House of Lords*, 1999 (http://www.official-documents.co.uk/).

33 *Op cit*, fn 24, Jennings, pp 120–21.

could be more like common human nature as it is, and as it is likely to be. The women – one half the human race at least – care 50 times more for a marriage than a ministry.[34]

What is interesting in these and other accounts is the insistence on royal ritual as a key component of national legitimation. As Bogdanor claims, *only* the monarchy 'can represent the whole nation in an emotionally satisfying way; it alone is in a position to interpret the nation to itself'.[35] This conflation of royalty and national identity ignores the constant inventing and re-inventing of 'tradition' and ceremony by the Royal Family itself. As Hitchens comments, '[t]he thing about the royalist contribution to national ritual ... is the amount of contrivance and greasepaint that it has required and does require'.[36] Warner also highlights that, from the fabricated 'Investiture' of the Prince of Wales in 1911 up to today's television royalty:

> ... the real powers of the monarch have withered away, [as] there has been an increasing growth in public ceremony. Although Queen Victoria was the focus of a popular cult, marked in particular by the tremendous Jubilees towards the end of her reign, her own children married quietly, among relations and friends. But her descendants' weddings are mass solemnities, which, through the medium of television, all the members of the nation and far beyond are invited to attend. The stages of the monarch's reign are marked by fanfares and public pageantry on an international scale.[37]

Even though the monarchical traditions are invented – most notoriously, in the conversion of the House of Saxe-Coburg-Gotha into the House of Winsdor in 1917 – grand ceremonialism is justified as an important sign of stability and continuity in the national order.

The Crown as nation, state and executive power

My second example concerns the range of uses of the concept of 'the Crown' in relation to state authority and executive power. Significantly, most constitutional law texts do not spend much time explaining why there is no concept of the *state* in British public law. In contrast to other democracies, the Crown is the legal entity which takes the place of the state, and to which allegiance is owed. As Jacob attempts to clarify in *The Republican Crown*:

> In Britain [*sic*] the Crown is the sovereign. For other nations, those which have post-Enlightenment constitutions, that sovereignty is the State itself. But there, the State also manages the nation's business. Political theory which seeks to

---

34 *Op cit*, fn 22, Bagehot, p 38.
35 *Op cit*, fn 23, Bogdanor, p 301.
36 *Op cit*, fn 14, Hitchens, p 22.
37 Warner, M, *Monuments and Maidens: The Allegory of the Female Form*, 1985, London: Picador, pp 43–44.

describe Britain as a *state* forgets that the formal structure of our constitution predates the Enlightenment. Our sovereign Crown becomes equated with statehood.[38]

The crucial importance of theorising the late 20th century state, and revealing its gendered nature, is spelt out fully in Murphy's chapter in this volume.[39] My interest here is in highlighting the role of Crown terminology in depoliticising and distorting the concept of the state. I will focus on two important aspects.

First, if, as suggested in constitutional texts, the Crown equals the state – and the state is taken to refer to the political organisation of people and territory – there is immediate confusion. As Nairn points out, in naming the state:

> ... none of the existing handles quite fit: we live in a State with a variety of titles having different functions and nuances – the UK (or 'Yookay', as Raymond Williams relabelled it), Great Britain (imperial roles), Britain (boring lounge suit), England (poetic but troublesome), the British Isles (too geographical), 'This Country' (all-purpose within the Family), or 'This Small Country of Ours' (defensive Shakespearean).[40]

The legally correct title, the one that constitutional lawyers are supposed to use in their lectures to avoid confusing the students, is the United Kingdom of Great Britain and Northern Ireland. And the key word here is 'Kingdom'; not a state or republic but a kingdom, or what some constitutional lawyers quaintly refer to as 'a realm'. So the Crown as state is equated with the United Kingdom, which is taken to represent the 'whole nation'.[41]

This 'whole nation' mentality has further implications for the construction of British identity. As will be discussed below in relation to subjecthood, I do not want to suggest that 'Britishness' cannot, and does not, have multiple and inclusive meanings; in fact, its potential as an umbrella identity is valued by many racial and ethnic groups within the UK. My point is that public law's blurring of the boundaries between 'the Crown' as state, nation and monarchy has consequences for the construction of national identities and limits the debate about the new constitutionalism in the UK.

For example, as New Labour's attacks on the SNP have vividly demonstrated, a political insistence on a unitary British state and dominant British identity as the political and cultural norm for Scotland tends to reinforce an imperial 'English' tradition (and allows nationalists to deploy

---

38 Jacob, J, *The Republican Crown: Lawyers and the Making of the State in 20th Century Britain*, 1996, Aldershot: Dartmouth, p 1 (notes omitted).

39 See Murphy, Chapter 2, this volume.

40 *Op cit*, fn 17, Nairn, p 93. See, also, Colley, L, *Britons: Forging the Nation 1707–1837*, 1992, London: Yale UP; and Crick, B, 'Essay on Britishness' (1993) 2 Scottish Affairs 71.

41 See, eg, Breitenbach, E, Brown, A and Myers, F, 'Understanding women in Scotland' (1998) 58 FR 44.

'anti-English' rhetoric in response). This understanding is not limited to Scotland. One of the key sites of struggle over Australian national identity is the proposal to create a republic: in this debate, British constitutionalism *is* the monarchy and breaking the monarchical link is an essential step towards full nationhood.[42] In the Northern Ireland context, 'the Crown' has been most closely associated with a narrow Unionism, strongly based on devotion to the institution of monarchy; indeed, '[h]ardline Loyalism expresses loyalty not to the Crown in Parliament, but to the monarchy as somehow above Parliament'.[43] Echoes of this Crown terminology sometimes emerge in Northern Ireland cases from the House of Lords:

> There is little authority in *English* law concerning the rights and duties of a member of the armed *forces of the Crown* when acting in aid of the civil power ... In some parts of the *province* there has existed for some years now a state of armed and clandestinely organised insurrection against the *lawful government of Her Majesty* by persons seeking to gain political ends by violent means ...[44]

One would expect some hesitation about this type of constitutional legal discourse in the Northern Ireland context given that the Irish Civil War of 1922 was triggered by the very position of 'the Crown' in Anglo-Irish relations – 'the metaphysical republicanism of the anti-Treaty ultras was matched only by the metaphysical monarchism of the British'.[45]

Secondly, if the Crown equals the state – and state means government institutions and power – there are very problematic consequences attaching to using 'the Crown' as a synonym for government. Historically, the monarch was not amenable to regulation or legal liability, and even though political sovereignty has long since been transferred to Parliament, politicians and judges have been slow to develop a system of public law in response.[46] As Harlow and Rawlings have pointed out, there are obvious dangers in 'allowing a sprawling state apparatus to grow up behind the screen of the personalised image of the monarch like an extension of the royal household':

> The monarchical imagery is absurd, and the legal fiction that power is *not* vested in the Prime Minister, Cabinet and other organisms of the modern state

---

42 See Doyle, T, 'The conservative mythology of monarchy: impacts upon Australian republicanism' (1993) 28 Australian Journal of Political Science 121.

43 Paulin, T, 'Diary' (1998) LRB, 18 June, p 33. See, generally, O'Leary, B, 'The conservative stewardship of Northern Ireland, 1979–97: sound-bottomed contradictions or slow learning?' (1997) XLV Political Studies 663.

44 *Attorney General for Northern Ireland's Ref (No 1 of 1975)* [1977] AC 105, p 136 (*per* Lord Diplock) (emphasis added).

45 Lee, J, *Ireland 1912–1985*, 1989, Cambridge: CUP, pp 51–52. On the complexity of Irish identity, see accounts in Foster, R, *Paddy and Mr Punch: Connections in Irish and English History*, 1993, London: Penguin; and Kiberd, D, *Inventing Ireland: The Literature of the Modern Nation*, 1995, London: Jonathan Cape.

46 See discussions in Sedley, S, 'The sound of silence: constitutional law without a constitution' (1994) 110 LQR 270; *op cit*, fn 38, Jacob; and Allison, J, 'Theoretical and institutional underpinnings of a separate administrative law', in Taggart, M (ed), *The Province of Administrative Law*, 1997, Oxford: Hart, p 71.

but in a royal dignitary incapable, in Blackstone's famous aphorism, not only of *doing* but even of *thinking* wrong, is dangerous. It allows government to benefit from our modern perception of the titular head of state as without political power and confined to dignitary functions.[47]

Thus, allowing Crown terminology to be used as a smokescreen for government diverts attention away from the sites and exercise of power. It mixes the personal and the political with the consequence that the latter is often obscured.

One could also argue that the ease with which government deploys Crown terminology relates not just to the ubiquitiousness of the Crown in the constitutional law tradition, but also to the presence of the Royals in national, public life. Both government and monarchy appear to derive institutional benefit from the inscribing of regality on the national psyche. As Goodrich argues, 'there is an irrefragable significance to the circulation of one symbol, of one icon, of one family'.[48]

The construction of subjects

My third example of Crown terminology concerns the construction of British subjects and flows on from the earlier discussion of 'the Crown' as nation and as state. While a British Nationality Act 1981 now exists, the feudal ideology of monarch/subject still pervades constitutional law.[49] The Oath of Allegiance leaves little room for doubt: 'I, X, swear by Almighty God that, on becoming a British citizen I will be faithful and bear true allegiance to Her Majesty Queen Elizabeth the Second, Her Heirs and Successors according to law.' As Oliver explains:

> At common law, those born 'within the dominions of the crown of England' –
> to adopt the words of Blackstone in his *Commentaries on the Laws of England* –
> were the Monarch's subjects, and as such owed duties of allegiance to the
> Crown. The status of subjecthood was conceived as an essentially personal
> relationship between individuals and their sovereign.[50]

Public law texts, of course, point out that this personal link has now disappeared or receded and that there remains only a symbolic loyalty to a symbolic Crown. In other words, this is a context in which constitutional lawyers appear to explicitly downplay the significance of the monarchy; it

---

47 Harlow, C and Rawlings, R, *Law and Administration*, 1997, London: Butterworths, pp 6–7.

48 Goodrich, P, *Languages of Law: From Logics of Memory to Nomadic Masks*, 1990, London: Weidenfeld and Nicolson, p 219.

49 See Vincenzi, C, *Crown Powers, Subjects and Citizens*, 1998, London: Pinter, pp 280–313.

50 Oliver, D, 'What is happening to relationships between the individual and the state?', in *op cit*, fn 28, Jowell and Oliver, pp 444–45.

seems unduly oppressive to actually insist that everyone *be* a royalist before acquiring British citizenship. Despite this, there remains a gaping hole in public law theory when it comes to conceptualising citizenship. My interest here is in the effects of a monarchical constitution and culture on emerging discourses of citizenship and identity.

If the claim that the monarch symbolises the *nation* is taken at face value, it suggests that British *national* identity necessarily comprises a royalist element. But what aspects of monarchy would be relevant here? Its public representation is of a white, Protestant, aristocratic, patriarchal, heterosexual family unit with a hereditary link to an English feudal past. If the Queen's daily, as distinct from official, activities represent characteristics of 'Britishness', what sort of national life is brought to mind – charity support, attending Ascot, walking Corgis, tweeds and headscarves? Paxman writes of a Britishness that is emblematic of a very particular past:

> The supreme embodiment of the idea of Britain is the country's royal family. The ambition of uniting the kingdom is spelled out in the lumbering list of titles of the heir to the throne: Charles is Prince of Wales, Duke of Cornwall, Duke of Rothesay, Earl of Carrick and Baron of Renfrew, Lord of the Isles and Great Steward of Scotland. The institution of monarchy belongs to the world of red tunics and bearskins, the Union flag and the Gatling gun and Queen Elizabeth and Prince Philip are almost the last representatives of Respectable Society.[51]

Constitutional law never engages with this question of how British identities are constructed. One is just told that the monarchy symbolises Britishness, and British identity itself is never spelt out.[52] As a result, the monarch appears as a depoliticised emblem of a narrow civic identity, the symbolic guarantor of official membership of the UK (such as holding a passport or voting).

The vast literature on identity highlights that Britishness cannot be reduced to this: it is both multi-dimensional and contextual. To take one example: Jacobson, in a study of young British Pakistanis, adopts the concept of different 'boundaries of Britishness' which operate in the popular imagination; thus, instead of a fixed national identity, civic, racial and cultural boundaries exist. While noting the common conflation of 'Britishness' and 'Englishness', her survey identified a *civic* boundary, where citizenship is the main criterion of British nationality; a *racial* boundary where British ancestry or 'blood' defines people as British; and a *cultural* boundary which defines Britishness in terms of values, attitudes and lifestyle.

---

51 *Op cit*, fn 5, Paxman, p 240.

52 Note, eg, the coded silences of *Wade and Bradley: Constitutional and Administrative Law* on immigration: 'During the 1960s, it became necessary for the United Kingdom to impose immigration controls on certain classes of Commonwealth immigrants ... There is wide political interest in immigration. The practice and policies of the immigration authorities are often controversial.' See *op cit*, Bradley and Ewing, fn 27, pp 432, 455.

What is noteworthy here is that the civic boundary – official membership of British society due to legal status – was considered the most incomplete and emotionally unsatisfying expression of national identity. Furthermore, many respondents believed that British identity was widely represented (in explicit and coded ways) as only compatible with whiteness; 'racial' difference conclusively determined the meaning of British ancestry.[53] The cultural boundary was the most complex and had a variety of meanings:

> ... to be attached to the majority language, established religion and cultural heritage of Britain; or to exhibit supposedly 'typical' British moderation, tolerance, reserve and modesty in one's day to day life; or to have knowledge of the famous people of contemporary Britain, and of currently popular modes of speech, dress and food; or to be familiar with the key social and political institutions of modern Britain, and the essentially rationalist, individualist norms which underpin them.[54]

This cultural boundary of Britishness was also the most fluid and, for most respondents, was an inclusive rather than an exclusionary boundary.

This critique has relevance for the discussion of monarchy and identity. Constitutional law texts emphasise the role of the Royal Family in constructing a national identity but they do not consider the messages it transmits about this identity. For example, one could insert the monarch (and Royal Family) into Jacobson's threefold 'boundaries of Britishness'. Depending on the context, the monarchy could represent a civic Britishness; a racially exclusive institution (with its statutory exemptions from the Race Relations Act) and/or a symbolic link to a multi-racial Commonwealth; and a key institution in the cultural reproduction of Britishness. As will become clear in the next section, aspects of royalty do have different political and cultural meanings for different groups. *What* the Royal Family symbolises and *to whom* – and what it has the potential to symbolise or not – remains the contested territory.

The need to theorise British identity in public law is crucially important. A constitutional law tradition which continues to use Crown terminology in a way that perpetuates the status of subject, and draws upon a one-dimensional concept of civic identity, is hopelessly inadequate for engaging in a debate about the meaning of Britishness and a 'United Kingdom' in the late 1990s. While the focus in this chapter is on the monarchy, the re-drawing of the

---

53 See Smith, A, *New Right Discourse on Race and Sexuality*, 1994, Cambridge: CUP, p 8: 'In Powellism, the relation between the white defenders of the true British nation and the anti-British black 'invader' became a nodal point ...' See, also, Herman, D and Cooper, D, 'Anarchic Armadas, Brussels bureaucrats and the valiant maple leaf: sexuality, governance and the construction of British nationhood through the Canada-Spain Fish War' (1997) 17 LS 415.

54 Jacobson, J, 'Perceptions of Britishness' (1997) 3 Nations and Nationalism 181, p 193. See, also, Basit, T, '"I want more freedom, but not too much": British Muslim girls and the dynamism of family values' (1997) 9 Gender and Education 425.

political and constitutional maps in Scotland, Wales and Northern Ireland (and, more broadly, within the European Union), and the new discourses of citizenship, make it an unavoidable project for public lawyers.

THE DIANA EXPERIENCE AND PUBLIC LAW

There is great significance in the fact that Diana, the most internationally visible and discussed member of the Royal Family in the last 20 years, never got anything approaching a commentary in the journals and textbooks that make up the constitutional law world. Even taking account of the monarchical legal tradition described above, there is an extraordinary unreality to reading chapters on 'the Crown' that erase all mention of the royal personality who dominated the British media for a generation. Diana and her actions, and the public perceptions of them, were deemed *politically* irrelevant. Only after her death did Diana appear to have significance for *constitutional law* for the first time; the public reaction to her funeral was recognised as a political (as well as an emotional) act that told us something important about the role of monarchy, citizenship and British identity. Of course, exactly *what* was revealed remains heavily contested.

While traditional public law theory proclaims its concern with democracy and citizenship, it rarely exposes the nature, form and history of oppression, or discusses the role of law in perpetuating or dismantling inequality. Feminist theory, in contrast, aims to collapse any rigid categorisation of social life into the political and cultural or the public and private. Recognising the significance of Diana, first and foremost in gender terms, creates the platform for broader critiques of institutions and power relations between different groups on a variety of grounds such as sexuality, race and class. Feminist perspectives on Diana, therefore, are not just relevant to public law because of what they tell us about the monarchy, but what they tell us about power and social relations generally.

If constitutional law's claim that the monarchy symbolises national identity is altered so that it reads 'Princess Diana symbolised Britishness', what is revealed? The most remarkable fact about all the commentaries is the range of identities that were afforded to Diana: bride, fairy tale princess, mother, charity worker, media icon, victim, survivor, divorcee, single parent, manipulator, feminist, republican, etc. In a 1992 essay, Paglia viewed Diana as possibly 'the most powerful image in world popular culture today, a case study in the modern cult of celebrity and the way it stimulates atavistic religious emotions'.[55] Since her death, the media coverage has continued: 'Even left wing magazines have used her image on their front pages: the *New*

---

55 *Op cit*, fn 19, Paglia, p 164.

Statesman presented a Warhol pastiche; *Red Pepper* gave us Diana as Che Guevara; *Living Marxism* – I kid you not – thought her face worthy of a cover.'[56]

While all this literature is of interest, I want to narrow the focus here to some feminist accounts of Diana's effect on the traditional perceptions of monarchy. Engaging with this critique offers public lawyers a means of interpreting the monarchy in a way that acknowledges its multiple and contradictory meanings, not just in relation to its gendered nature, but in its relationship to republican politics. It should, however, be acknowledged that there is a seductive danger in adopting an ahistorical perspective in this exercise; representing Diana as providing novel readings of royalty while the opportunities may always be there in relation to royal personalities.[57]

Feminist commentaries on Diana disagree on many aspects of her life and also on her political significance. This is illustrated most clearly in critiques of her identification as a feminist and of her relationships with the Royal Family. One notable aspect of her identity was the ability, for a variety of reasons, to transcend the boundaries between monarchy and public; to be both inside and outside 'the Royal Family' or 'the Palace'. McCollum reflects:

> In spite of a longstanding, and at times rabid, dislike of the royal family (I caused scandal in my Ulster Protestant family when I spoke as an anti-royalist on a TV talk show in 1984), I was a big fan of Diana. I did not know her, I never met her, but I admired her and, looking back on her life, I think that feminism has things to learn from it.[58]

McCollum's view is not unanimous within feminism. Thus, while Kelly argues that '[o]ne didn't need much feminist theory to understand that Diana had been used and abused by a powerful man and an extremely powerful family',[59] Cameron points out the contradictions in identifying with Diana, and the ways in which she reinforced monarchical, patriarchal and heterosexist values:

> [It] seems to me that pity would be a more apt feminist response than admiration ... Diana became the 'people's princess' because she, or more exactly her public image, fitted the people's idea of what a princess ought to be: beautiful, glamorous, gentle, sweet and kind. Not to mention vulnerable ... To the extent that she was critical of the role she was forced to play, she was caught up in a basic contradiction: people were prepared to sympathise with her complaints about how hard it was to be a fairy tale princess, only because

---

56 Greenslade, R, 'A Diana effect?' (1998) *The Guardian (Media)*, 17 August, p 2.

57 See, eg, Christopher Hitchens in relation to another 'problem' princess: 'The fascination of Princess Margaret, I suspect, is that she was the forerunner of the public, vulgar Windsor style: now such a drag but then such a sensation', *op cit*, fn 30, p 24; and Lewis, JL, *Mary Queen of Scots: Romance and Nation*, 1998, London: Routledge.

58 McCollum, H, 'Surviving in public' (1997–98) Trouble & Strife, Winter, p 65.

59 Kelly, L, 'Including others' (1997–98) Trouble & Strife, Winter, p 68.

she personified that stereotype so well. She had it both ways. Feminists cannot.[60]

Cameron's perspective is shared by others. Scanlon, for example, considers that women's self-identification with Diana's life was mostly a narrative of private battles around body image and failed relationships, a cult of traditional femininity:

> Even those women journalists who tried to establish what Diana stood for, and acknowledged that the majority of mourners were women, fell into the trap of idealising her, or translating her into a kind of feminist icon, which she most clearly was not ... For many, the way in which her life offered a public record of the private struggles that women have – around eating disorders, self-harm, broken relationships, divorce, family strife, depression – made her death come to symbolise a battle lost, and their own grief was commensurate with this.[61]

One cannot underestimate the power of this representation: as Watson terms it, 'the royal sacrificial victim'.[62] Diana attracted sympathy because of the perception that she had been treated badly by the Palace and Prince Charles (and, only sometimes, by an intrusive media): the (patriarchal) monarchy came to symbolise Diana's misery. But, as Smith pointed out in 1997, Diana herself clung to, even embraced, her 'victim status':

> ... looked at objectively, it is hard to resist two conclusions: that Diana is self-deluding in her assessment of her own situation, and that she has been astonishingly successful in persuading vast numbers of people to collude in that deception ... Her divorce settlement, said to be in the region of £17 million, is not ungenerous compared to the sums that many ex-wives have to live on ... Her chief ground for complaint, in the final analysis, is the old one that she has been denied her rightful role in a fairy tale ... [63]

In the fullest feminist account of Diana to date, however, a different conclusion is offered; for Campbell:

> this woman, who was once such a paradox for modern feminism, came to exemplify its pervasive influence ... It was Diana's treatment as a woman, and her sense that she was sustained by the sympathy and strength of women, that made her dangerous ... The people understood: she had been done down by the bad behaviour of a man who had behaved like a king. The connection between sexism and monarchism was not lost on the people.[64]

It is clear then that Diana is open to different feminist readings. If the role of public lawyers is to identify and *critically* evaluate the values and social and

---

60   Cameron, D, 'A gilded cage' (1997–98) Trouble & Strife, Winter, p 70.
61   Scanlon, J, 'The horrors of heterosexuality' (1997–98) Trouble & Strife, Winter, p 72.
62   Watson, CW, 'Born a lady, became a princess, died a saint' (1997) 13 Anthropology Today 3, p 6.
63   *Op cit*, fn 20, Smith, pp 14–15.
64   *Op cit*, fn 1, Campbell, pp 8, 251.

political implications of the UK's system of government,[65] they should equally be interested in critiquing the monarchy. In order to demonstrate how such perspectives might be integrated into public law scholarship, I want to return briefly to the three contexts discussed above where the language of Crown/monarchy is used. In each context, I will contrast the events surrounding Diana's funeral against the constitutional law tradition in order to problematise its assumptions about the role and effects of monarchy. More generally, I will question the claim that the death of Diana has undermined the centrality of 'the Crown' in British constitutionalism or marks a public yearning for a republic.

Symbolism and rituals

In relation to the traditional symbolism and rituals of monarchy, a contradictory picture emerges when the focus is on the Princess Diana funeral. The Royal Family (especially since the BBC *Panorama* interview)[66] was generally perceived as treating Diana as a traitor (having questioned the right of Charles to be King) and an outsider. Initially, a private funeral was planned by the Palace and only after intervention by the Prime Minister, Tony Blair, did it become a state occasion. The most interesting aspect of this funeral ritual was that, for the first time, the public consciously interpreted – or was represented as interpreting – a royal ceremony differently to the monarchy itself. As Warner points out, the purpose of royal rituals is to demonstrate 'continuity, stability and comfort'; here the mood was troubled, rebellious, demystifying. On this occasion, the explicit and implicit public responses were aimed at making the Queen and the Palace feel uncomfortable: *they* became the outsiders. Thus, the flag-at-half-mast episode, the Queen bowing her head to the coffin, the applause after Earl Spencer's speech and, most vividly, the two sons being brought out to the mourning crowd, had the effect of making a closer connection with dead royalty rather than the living. Certainly, the institution in which national consensus was supposed to be engendered, the Royal Family, was fractured *publicly* – in a way that the marital separations and divorces had never done so.[67]

However, one could easily interpret the public reaction over the funeral of Diana as primarily due to contestation over her status as a *princess*. The repeated insistence that 'the nation' was united in mourning suggested that a

---

65 O'Leary, B, 'What should public lawyers do?' (1992) 12 OJLS 304; *op cit*, fn 47, Harlow and Rawlings, pp 27–28; and see Harvey, Chapter 10, this volume.

66 BBC Television, *Panorama*, 20 November 1995.

67 One could also read the Palace as the aristocratic, *private* institution preventing the people claiming *public* ownership of Diana and her memory. See, generally, Story, A, 'Owning Diana: from people's princess to private property' [1998] 5 Web JCLI; http://webjcli.ncl.ac.uk/.

'closing-in' was supposed to occur; that Diana in her death had to be assimilated back into the folds of the monarchy as was her destiny. As Smith wrote, those who resisted were portrayed as expressing a political message, not an individual or personal sentiment:

> In recent days ... those of us who are not willing to pretend to emotions we don't feel have been getting an ominous message – that we ought to keep quiet. It's a message which is not easy to defy in the face of repeated assertions about the country being 'united in grief'.[68]

On this interpretation, the alleged public desire for royal ceremonialism remains intact. In short, instead of viewing the public reactions to the Diana funeral as a rejection of monarchy and royal rituals, the popular demand to confirm her status as a princess legitimises them.

The Crown as smokescreen for government

It is arguable that the figure who benefited significantly from the events of the Diana funeral was Prime Minister Blair. In the sections above, I have outlined how the Crown has provided a smokescreen for the locus and exercise of government power; in retaining the concept, a 'veil of ignorance' is created as to the distinctions between Crown as monarch and Crown as executive. Focusing on the (usually hidden) relationship between Prime Minister and Buckingham Palace provides an opportunity to assess the benefits to the former in retaining the monarchy in its present form. What explains the motivations behind the Prime Minister's calculated interventions, from the morning of the accident onwards?

> [PM Press Secretary] Campbell's finest moment so far was in the early hours of Diana's death, when he and Blair together, on their mobile phones, composed the 'People's Princess' speech ... Before Blair walked to the church to give his tearjerky performance, Campbell had deputised a local Labour Party member to erect metal barriers and prevent an unseemly media scrum.[69]

Several commentators have argued that the prestige of the Prime Minister was increased through his manipulation of the royal ceremonialism. As the Palace was portrayed as 'out of touch with the people', the influence of the Prime Minister was increased by his adoption of the mantle of head of state:

> In insisting on a large public funeral, in urging the royal family to make a public show of their grief, he loaned them the formidable public relations skills

---

68   Smith, J, 'Comment' (1997) *Independent on Sunday*, 9 September, p 10.
69   Toolis, K, 'The enforcer' (1998) *The Guardian (Weekend)*, 4 April, p 36.

which had won him the election. In the process, he managed the difficult feat of becoming a national rather than a political figure ...[70]

Apart from adopting a 'presidential' posture as Prime Minister, connections were also made between aspects of monarchy and the New Labour project itself:

> The link to Princess Diana is in the domination of emotion over content, and in the individualisation of collective issues. Tony Blair appealed, and continues to appeal, to formless, vague yearnings for an undefined good ... The link between Diana's death and Blair's government may be tenuous, but the feelings were mobilised to create the impression that the 'caring', 'unified' nation in grief was the same nation that voted Tony Blair into power, and that in showing its feelings, the nation somehow endorsed Blair's vision – whatever that really is.[71]

On this crucial occasion, Blair was able to represent himself as on the side of the people; not the Palace. Yet, politically, and behind the scenes, the government worked to ensure that the Royal Family survived intact as an institution.[72] On this reading, prime ministerial omnipotence spreads silently and subtly by rescuing the monarchy from any public discontent. The result is that the 'smokescreen' of the Crown remains intact, hiding the real locus and exercise of political power.[73]

British subjects and identities

Finally, even accepting the media manipulation of some of the public responses, can the funeral of Diana be interpreted as an affirmation of some commonly held national values or identity – in the way that the 1953 Coronation is said to have been? Or did the 'British nation' come together to express the seeds of a republican sentiment? Arguably, Nairn's analysis remains convincing:

> September's funeral-fête showed an England turning away from the British amorial bearings all right, and questing instinctively for a different future. But it may also have displayed a fatal instinct still at work: the one derived from the long historical experience of regality and empire, which is not so easily shed. British popular monarchism established a very powerful fusion of

---

70 Ignatieff, M, 'The meaning of Diana' (1997) *Prospect*, October, p 6.

71 Wilson, E, 'The unbearable lightness of Diana' (1998) 224 NLR 136, p 143.

72 'Blair is not a republican democrat, and saw the attacks on monarchical hauteur as unfair': (1997) *The Observer*, 7 September.

73 Case law helps to further this sleight of hand. Compare 'the Crown ... is in law a corporation sole' with 'the legal concept which seems to me to fit best the contemporary situation is to consider the Crown as a corporation aggregate headed by the Queen': *Town Investments Ltd v Department of the Environment* [1978] AC 359, p 384 (*per* Lord Diplock) and p 400 (*per* Lord Simon) respectively.

nationality and personality, a channelled identity which worked by separation of the charismatic and the political state ... The heart which burst into the streets in September was as yet far from that of a republic. It remains that of a national romanticism.[74]

A tentative conclusion, therefore, may be that Diana's status was derived primarily from her links to royalty. As noted above, much of the outpouring of emotion hinged on whether Diana was to be accorded royal status in death. The suggestion that Diana was not a 'real' or 'royal' princess provoked the public reaction, or 'mini-rebellion', which sought to reconfirm her status. In reconfirming that status – reliving the Royal Wedding, turning out for the funeral procession – the people appeared as *subjects* once again before 'their' Princess.

However, one can also argue that Diana did not serve as a traditional icon of British monarchy. The 'People's Princess' label found general acceptance because, in her support for particular organisations (such as charities for people with AIDS, the homeless and land mine victims), and because of her relationship with Dodi Al-Fayed (a Muslim), she appeared to embrace an non-deferential, inclusive, multi-cultural Britishness.[75] In this sense, Diana was not an icon of whiteness, Christianity, privilege and aristocratic superiority – the traditional characteristics associated with the British Royal Family[76] – but could, instead, be seen as representative of a form of republicanism. As Campbell argues, 'Diana did not create republican sentiment, but she did transform the space in which the public could contemplate their feelings about royalty and republicanism, through the filter of her experience as a woman'.[77]

In a similar vein, Diana represented a paradoxical feminist sexual politics. Her dramatic fracturing of the boundaries between public and private life opened up the monarchy to feminist critiques of its institutional and personal power relations. Despite her desired position to be a princess (and queen) within the patriarchal institution of monarchy, she 'did something that no woman in the Royal Family has done in the 20th century: she called a monarch to account'.[78]

However, there is a danger in over-emphasising the lasting significance of Diana. The Crown retains its central position in legal and political discourses. The monarchy retains its attractions. As a confirmation of the latter in the aftermath of Diana's death, Prince William appears to have been elevated as

---

74 Nairn, T, 'The departed spirit' (1997) LRB, 30 October, p 6.
75 See, generally, Caputi, J, 'The second coming or be-coming of Diana' (1998) unpublished paper.
76 See, generally, McKibbin, R, *Classes and Cultures: England 1918–1951*, 1998, Oxford: OUP.
77 *Op cit*, fn 1, Campbell, pp 250–51.
78 *Op cit*, fn 1, Campbell, p 251. Historically, the monarchy has always been a terrain of sexual politics: see, eg, Thompson, D, *Queen Victoria: Gender and Power*, 1990, London: Virago.

the 'rightful' heir to the throne. In anthropological terms, this could be equivalent to distinguishing between a rebellion against the personal body of the monarch (the unpopular Queen or Prince Charles), rather than the symbolic body of the institution (the House of Winsdor or Royal Family).[79] Thus, when one monarch loses legitimacy, the people may intervene to ensure – not a republic – but a proper succession. The Princess is dead but the Crown lives on.[80]

---

79 *Op cit*, fn 61, Watson, p 6. See, generally, Kantorowicz, E, *The King's Two Bodies: A Study in Medieval Political Theory*, 1957, Princeton: Princeton UP.

80 For a demonstration of how the concept of Crown remains relevant outside a UK context, see Smith, D, 'Bagehot, the Crown and the Canadian Constitution' (1995) 28 Canadian Journal of Political Science 619.

CHAPTER 4

BLAIR'S BABES: GENDER, GOVERNANCE AND POWER[1]

Michael Thomson

Of course women have come a long way, but don't think for a minute that one or two women in Parliament are going to change a damn thing ... [R]emember this Barney, there's more to sex than cold semen running down your leg.[2]

[A] feminist theory of the state requires simultaneously articulating, deconstructing, and relating the multiple strands of power composing both masculinity and the state. The fact that neither state power nor male dominance is unitary or systematic means that a feminist theory of the state will be less a linear argument than the mapping of an intricate grid of overlapping and conflicting strategies, technologies and discourses of power.[3]

INTRODUCTION

Recent decades have seen an increased female presence in the machinery of government and governance.[4] This has been an international phenonenon witnessed in the legislatures of both developed and developing countries. The result of both genuine concern for democratic government and the less noble pressures of party competition, the desire to see more women elected has been largely bipartisan. Many parties have introduced provisions to increase the number of female representatives. This has ranged from the gender quotas of the Norwegian Socialist Left Party in the 1970s to Emily's List and the divisive and contested moves of the Labour Party in the UK in the 1990s.[5]

The inclusion of more women in these positions of authority has arisen from, and maintained, an energetic debate about women's position in, and representation through, state bodies. Whilst domestic and international politics has featured such diverse figures as Margaret Thatcher, Benazir Bhutto and Mary Robinson, the arrival of the media styled 'Blair's Babes' in

---

1   The author would like to thank Kirstie Best, Doris Buss, Davina Cooper, Jenny Morgan, Sally Sheldon and the editors of this volume for their constructive comments on, and patient discussion of, earlier drafts of this paper.

2   Shields, C, *Small Ceremonies*, 1995, London: Fourth Estate, p 78.

3   Brown, W, *States of Inquiry: Power and Freedom in Late Modernity*, 1995, Princeton: Princeton UP, p 177.

4   For a far ranging discussion of women in British politics in this period, see Lovenduski, J and Norris, P (eds), *Women in Politics*, 1996, Oxford: OUP.

5   For a comprehensive discussion of such measures, see Phillips, A, *The Politics of Presence*, 1995, Oxford: Clarendon.

1997 refocused a number of the queries and concerns regarding female participation in, and feminist engagement with, the state. The election of so many women on 1 May 1997 was heralded by many as a step forward for a process of democratic reform which has sought inclusive government and, as a corollary, inclusive democracy. Adding a further dimension to this perception of reform, we have, it has been suggested, seen a feminisation of government:

> Some remark on how government itself has recently become feminised. New Labour certainly presents itself as female, using the language of compassion, forgiveness, apology, understanding and nurturing, qualities conventionally attributed to women. It wants to be loved. The old traditionally male values of constancy, gravitas, restraint, heroism, dignity and honour are seen as belonging to a past world.[6]

Yet is this enough? That is to say, is a greater sexual parity in Parliament and the adoption of a more feminine discourse adequate to make state power both respond to women's specific needs and be sensitive to the gender implications of more general government policy and action? After the honeymoon, after the first welfare reform proposals were made public in December 1997, by the time we were ready to look back and ask what the first year of the new administration had achieved, media coverage of New Labour Woman was a continuous tale of disappointment and betrayal. Implicit in this sense of disappointment was a belief that more women MPs was of itself enough to make a real difference to government.[7] Focusing primarily on the New Labour administration, I want to question this assumption. Yet, I also want to recognise the broader international experience. Whilst being cognisant of this experience, I intend, for reasons that I hope will become apparent, to focus predominantly on the Australian 'femocrats', the women who entered the Australian state bureaucracy in the 1970s.

There are obvious differences between New Labour Woman and the femocrats. Not least are those concerning the point of access into, and the nature of engagement with, state power. Whilst the New Labour Woman is an elected representative, the femocrats were bureaucratic appointments with specifically woman-centred/feminist briefs. The primary danger in playing this parallel out is the conflation of 'woman' and 'feminist'. Whilst, as I have just stated, the femocrats identified themselves as feminists and were explicitly feminist appointments, New Labour Woman is far from this. My focus, however, is expectation. Regardless of the distance just noted there is a proximity regarding the belief held by some, and repeatedly played with by the media, that these women could change the style and substance of

---

6   Weldon, F, 'Big women' (1999) *The Observer*, 10 January.
7   For a discussion of the legitimacy of this expectation see Norris, P, 'Women politicians: transforming Westminster?', in *op cit*, fn 4, Lovenduski and Norris, p 90, pp 90–93.

government. Working with this, I want to move towards illustrating that the same obstacles that exist to meaningful feminist engagement with the state also, to an extent, prevent a greater number of women in government *per se* from destabilising/realigning the gender dynamics of governance. Looking at the femocrats and New Labour Woman and, in so doing, interrogating this more general issue of expectation, I want to build up a picture of state power, as not only complex and contradictory, but also masculine. Whilst recognising the political, historical and cultural differences between New Labour Woman and the femocrats, the issue of expectation and the lessons to be learnt from this earlier period make it a valuable starting point.[8]

At this point it is worth noting my parameters. The focus of this chapter is central government.[9] In focusing only on central government I do not want to suggest that other levels of involvement are unimportant or, equally, unproblematic. Nor do I want to privilege state power at the expense of other sites of power. Having noted these concerns it should also be recognised that some of the observations will be applicable to all levels of state governance. Conversely all analysis must be addressed at a level which recognises specificity, and recognises that such analysis will always be partial and limited.

A TALE OF TWO PARLIAMENTS

The femocrats ... a story of radical reform?

It is the early 1970s and the painful end stages of 23 years of Conservative Government in Australia. Second wave Australian feminism is riding high. There is optimism about political change. The Women's Electoral Lobby (WEL) is founded. It is 'young, dynamic ... politically astute', and 'the

---

8   As Carol Johnson has remarked: 'There are obvious problems in comparing Australian and British experiences, not least Australia's history as a colonial settler economy founded by Britain. However, Australia has also had a long history as a laboratory of social experimentation since the election of the worlds first (short-lived) Labor government in Queensland in the 1890s.' Johnson, C, 'Negotiating the politics of inclusion: women and Labor governments 1983–95' (1996) 53 Feminist Review 102. Failure to realise the value of such a comparison also runs the risk of perpetuating the 'Euro- and US-centrism' which has ignored the political developments and experiences of both Australia and New Zealand (pp 102–03). For a recognition of the historical, political and cultural conditions of possibility and specificity of the emergence of 'femocracy' in Australia, see Watson, S, 'The state of play: an introduction', in *Playing the State: Australian Feminist Interventions*, 1990, London: Verso, p 1; and, in the same collection, Ryan, L, 'Feminism and the federal bureaucracy 1972–83', p 71.

9   See Cooper, Chapter 11, this volume, for a discussion of local government.

political bombshell of 1972'.[10] WEL rates electoral candidates on their attitudes to women's demands. As a result of this extensive campaign, women's issues are made more visible. More sophisticated than the political parties,[11] WEL ensures that women's issues become part of main/malestream political discourse.

Whitlam's Labor Government enters office. It is quick to demonstrate its feminist credentials, it symbolically intervenes in an equal pay case and removes sales tax on contraceptives.[12] Beyond these gestures, it moves to appoint a number of feminists to the staff of several Ministries. In 1972, the Government creates a new political position – an adviser in women's affairs to the Prime Minister. Elizabeth Reid, a philosopher at the Australian National University, is appointed. Simultaneously, offices, sections and councils all emerge to protect women's interests. There is a National Women's Advisory Council, a Women's Affairs Section (later to become the Office of the Status of Women), and policy units are founded in several government departments. The Australian women's movement accesses state machinery as no other women's movement had. Rather than settling for a Ministry or Department of Women's Affairs, feminist concerns are introduced at every level of policy making, implementation, research, development and monitoring. The Office of the Status of Women has access to all Cabinet submissions. The National Women's Advisory Council acts as a conduit between the bureaucracy and women's groups. The economic impact of policies and programmes is audited as each department is now obliged to provide an Annual Women's Budget Statement. The femocrats are born.

What I want to do in this section is to consider this 'feminisation' of government. I want to consider whether this level and form of inclusion is sufficient. In terms of the narrative just told, historical distance allows us to map the changes in the structure of governance whereby women/feminists entered government to an unprecedented degree, yet the broader shift to a political discourse of the free market maintained the inequalities such inclusion promised to address. The election of the femocrats suggested reform. It suggested inclusion and rule by virtue, yet it masked changes in the nature of governance which perpetuated inequalities. These inequalities become recontextualised/obscured within the changing political discourse. Inequality is rewritten as beyond the remit of government. Government's role becomes merely to provide the conditions within which the market can flourish and to mitigate its excesses.

Before I move on to map out this discursive shift and further factors which limited the overall impact of the femocrats, it should be stated that this level of inclusion, the success of the campaign for women to become involved at every

---

10 *Op cit*, Ryan, fn 8, p 72.

11 *Op cit*, Ryan, fn 8.

12 *Op cit*, Ryan, fn 8.

level of state power, did have real gains, even as Whitlam's successors moved to limit the femocrats' power.[13] At a legislative level, the states of South Australia, Victoria and New South Wales, for example, became the first legislative bodies in the world to criminalise marital rape.[14] This was also seen at the level of public service provision with, to provide another example, the New South Wales Child Sexual Assault Programme which, rather than problematising the entire family, targeted the abuse of male power. What needs to be understood, however, is how this potentially radical shift in the gender/sexual composition of government was diffused. The Australian experience is neatly summarised by Anne Goetz:

> As elsewhere, the Australian state's response to the increasingly insistent demands from new social movements for meaningful participation in public decisions was to incorporate movement representatives (among whom femocrats were an important element), but to subordinate these representatives' participatory agendas to managerialist-administrative agendas.[15]

This technology of inclusion and subordination is explained further:

> The characteristic method of incorporation was to elaborate discourses of access and equity in tandem with decentralization, in order to broker needs claims further down the line, hence depoliticizing and rendering them invisible, and with budget cuts to ensure tighter forms of resource rationing. The effect has been to commodify and privatize people's needs in a shift from notions of social citizenship to market citizenship.[16]

This process may be located within a model which recognises a diverse array of technologies deployed by the state to achieve social control. Anna Yeatman, concentrating on Australian public administration personnel, argues that the new legions of technocrats and the shift in discourse from public service to public management marked an expansion in the technologies of control which had been available to the state.[17] Perhaps most helpful from Yeatman's analysis is the recognition of the rise in a new managerialist-economic orthodoxy. This new hegemony replaced a commitment to values and equity whilst, paradoxically, the discourses of inclusion and equity retained a primacy. Yet this analysis is enriched if we start to locate it within an understanding of the nexus between power and masculinity.

---

13 *Op cit*, Ryan, fn 8, p 81.

14 For a brief discussion and bibliography of the marital rape exemption in an international context, see Graycar, R and Morgan, J, *The Hidden Gender of Law*, 1990, Annandale, NSW: Federation, pp 116–18.

15 Goetz, AM, 'No more heroes? Feminism and the state in Australia' (1994) Social Politics 341, p 343.

16 *Ibid*.

17 Yeatman, A, *Bureaucrats, Technocrats, Femocrats: Essays on the Contemporary Australian State*, 1990, Sydney: Allen & Unwin.

Yeatman argues, as have others, that the state is constituted upon a gendered public/private divide. The internal division of labour within its institutions is in line with this more general bifurcation. Within this structure, power and authority are associated with masculinity. It follows from this that the internal logic of the state and its practices is to maintain the current gender/power structure. Whilst it has been stated that the femocrats were involved at every level of government, this needs to be qualified. Replicating general historical employment patterns,[18] the femocrats were only admitted to those sectors associated with what is typically perceived to be women's work – for example, the health, welfare and education departments. Penetration of those departments associated with the masculine 'sphere' could only be achieved if the femocrats were willing to adopt traditionally masculine features, both at the level of personal behaviour, and in embracing the new orthodoxy of financial accountability and public management. The femocrats therefore faced the option of either political marginalisation or participation at the centre of government, but only so long as they jettisoned their transformatory policy ambitions. The result, as Goetz explains, was a sick irony:

> Femocrats became the brokers of the new orthodoxy's residualist welfare strategies that provided safety nets for the losers in the market or the family, without changing the gendered conditions of private dependency or market success.[19]

Whilst reiterating the historical, political and cultural distance between the two experiences, what I want to do now is examine the degree to which parallels exist between the Australian experience and what occured after the 1997 Labour landslide victory. Was the shift towards a greater numerical sexual parity in Parliament accompanied by policy decisions which were sensitive to the need to redress sexual inequality? Or, as in the case of the femocrats, was any progressive agenda diffused?

Blair's Babes

It was 2 May 1997 and the first day of the new Parliament. More than 100 Labour women MPs converged on the steps of Church House. Natasha Walter, writing for *The Observer* seven months later recalled: 'seeing how the sun danced on those bright jackets and their gilt buttons, and how everyone smiled ... How unexpected and grand it looked, all those women, all those dreams.'[20] The tabloids could not believe their luck, here were 'Blair's Babes'.

---

18 See Thomson, M, 'Woman, medicine and abortion in the nineteenth century' (1995) 3 FLS 159.

19 *Op cit*, fn 15, Goetz, p 345.

20 Walter, N, 'Six months hard Labour' (1997) *The Observer*, 30 November.

There was a palpable optimism, a belief
government which could deliver:

> When I first met the five youngest women MPs ba
> their feistiness. They talked impatiently about w
> women, and about changing the systems they found
> their constituencies, about a new style of politics.[21]

Yet, as she concluded, '[t]hat was then'. For many the   wed
'then' provided not just a litany of failed promises or das   , out also a
feeling of betrayal. Women appeared to bear the brunt of   election pledge
to reform the welfare state. This reform became the flagship legislation
programme of the new administration and part of the New Labour 'New
Deal'. On 10 December 1997, the Government confirmed that it was to cut
lone parent benefit premiums, a measure which disproportionately affected
women.[22] Only eight women voted against the cuts, none of these were from
the 'new intake'. Whilst this proved to be the most controversial of the
proposed welfare reforms, there were further proposals. Later that December,
it was suggested that the Government was considering ending free provision
of the contraceptive pill for women not on income support. In January 1998,
maternity benefits became the latest target. Further benefit cuts were
proposed leading to mounting criticism that money was being diverted from
the 'purse' to the 'wallet'. It was also clear that women would gain least from
the proposed 10p rate of income tax and the move to privatise pensions.[23] At
the same time, the Government pursued its intention to spend £26,000 per
head on encouraging the 18–24 year old long term unemployed into
employment. Importantly, three quarters of those receiving such provisions
were men.[24] As Yvonne Roberts noted:

> The remoulding of the country into New Labour's 'New' Britain continues
> apace – and so does the alarm of many women that the highest price exacted in
> this exercise will be demanded from them ... Women will pay dearly – and
> disproportionately to men – unless the Government is persuaded to think
> again.[25]

---

21 *Op cit*, fn 20, Walter.
22 It should be noted, however, that the 'women and children' budget of March 1998
    restored this benefit in another guise.
23 At the same time, it should be recognised that women may have most to gain with the
    introduction of the minimum wage.
24 It is interesting to note Anne Goetz's summary of the Australian experience in this area:
    'the interests of men as a collectivity persistently took priority over women's collective
    interests in policy decisions and implementation. Concern with rising male
    unemployment consistently led to the under-implementation of strategies for gender
    equity in equal opportunities or reskilling programs. The interests of married men
    continued to take priority over those of married women, women with children, and
    working mothers. Eg, though femocrats won the battle against a shift to the family as
    the unit of taxation, in which the second earner is taxed at a higher marginal rate and
    hence discouraged from working, it was at the cost of a continuous increase in the
    Dependent Spouse tax rebate, which benefits married men, and a relentless erosion of
    family allowances, which go directly to women with children.' *Op cit*, fn 15, p 349.
25 Roberts, Y, 'Hard Labour' (1997) *The Guardian*, 4 December.

the failure of the Government to engage with the gender implications of reform proposals, it should come as no surprise that, when it appointed Joan Ruddock Minister for Women, it declined to give her ministerial pay. In a newspaper review of 'those we hated' in 1997, Ruddock was targeted for being the 'invisible minister'.[26] Having reviewed this position, it is interesting to note that, in elevating it to Cabinet status, the job was given to Harriet Harman. In short, the job was given to a Minister who already held a principal portfolio and whose position in the Cabinet was to be short lived. Eighteen months after the election, the brief was divided between two women, again, each had other substantial commitments: Tessa Jowell (Public Health Minister) and Margaret Jay (Leader of the Lords).[27]

In assessing the Government's first year in office, a transitional 'margin of error' has been granted by some critics. The role of government is decidedly different from the role of the Opposition, and the Labour Party had, after all, been Her Majesty's Opposition for 18 years. It is also possible that the criticism of the Government may, in part, be understood by recognising the exceptionally high expectations that had been laid at the new Government's feet. The arguable gender-blindness of the new Government cannot, however, be explained merely in these terms. To understand why women appeared to have shouldered a disproportionate burden in the creation of New Labour's New Britain it is worth returning to the earlier consideration of the Australian femocrats. This story provides an interesting parallel text.

Whilst Blair's project may be seen as heavily intertextual, borrowing – either explicitly or implicitly – from a number of international centre-left experiences, perhaps most notably from the US, the debt to the Australian experience cannot be mistaken:

> There is an echo here of the Australian and New Zealand governments of the past decade, much admired by Blair, which kept some potential critics on-side by championing 'cultural' radicalism – women's and gay rights, environmentalism, the defence of the Aborigines, anti-nuclear policies – as they drove through a convulsive Thatcherite restructuring of their economies.[28]

---

26 (1997) *The Guardian*, 31 December.

27 Neither women are renowned feminists. Indeed, Margaret Jay admits: 'I'm not even sure what feminism is in 1999. I'll probably get into trouble for saying it, but I don't feel part of a sisterhood. Who are they the sisters of, anyway?' (Cited in White, L, 'Labour of Love' (1999) *Vogue* , March, p 307). Similarly, profiled in *The Guardian*, Jay is described as 'not ... a sixties feminist. In truth, her friends say, she was a bit uncertain at first about taking on her other role, as Minister for Women, being unsure what to do with it' (1999) *The Guardian*, 6 February. What she has done, nevertheless, is to launch a government policy document (in November 1998) entitled *Policy Appraisal for Equal Treatment*, designed to facilitate an understanding of 'how policy can have a different impact on different groups in society' and 'to bring this understanding to policy development and work to ensure that the results are fair, lawful and practical, and promote equal opportunities in the widest sense' (available at http://www.cabinet-office.gov.uk/womens-unit/index.htm).

28 Milne, S, 'After the May Day flood' (1997) LRB, 5 June, p 5. This debt has been recognised by Blair. On a visit to Australia in 1995, Blair stated: 'There is a tendency of people on the British Left to look at Europe ... but in many ways the ALP [contd]

Whilst Blair may well have tactically kept potential critics on-side, it needs to be asked whether these critics' agendas have been diffused in the same way. It has been argued, for example, that the failure of New Labour Woman is merely a result of the well tuned machinery of discipline within the Labour Party, the 'culture of fear and obedience that rules'.[29] The dissenter, regardless of sex, risks compromising any career ambition – dissent and you become a 'non-person'.[30]

Whilst the effect of this discipline should not be underestimated, there is also the degree to which discursive shifts in the language of government and governance have undermined any reformatory agendas. There is a clear adoption of the managerialist-economic orthodoxy which diffused the feminist agendas of the femocrats.[31] Whilst it is perhaps contentious to claim that welfare has become purely a cost, as has been argued in the Australian context, the discourses of financial accountability and managing the welfare budget and its claimants does, however, give such an argument increasing credibility.[32] At this point, it is helpful to restate the parameters New Labour set itself. The (perhaps electorally essential) pledge to stick to the preceding Conservative Government's spending targets has shaped the discourse of reform. The provision of welfare services has become less about equity and justice (although these values are still espoused very clearly), and more about financial accountability and management. This shift has been broadcast as 'determined' by externally imposed spending restraints. Reform has therefore

---

[contd] [Australian Labour Party] has far greater similarities than a lot of the European parties and we share many of the same positions.' Quoted in *op cit*, fn 8, Johnson, p 103. Whilst this strategy of inclusion and discipline suggests clear structural similarities, there are further similarities in terms of public expectation: 'The irony of the Australian case is that, unlike the United States, Canada and the United Kingdom, this new economic rationality in public administration – in which equity becomes a cost, not a benefit – was presided over by a Labour government elected on a platform of social equity.' *Op cit*, fn 15, Goetz, p 343. The Labour Government's early proposals on the restructuring of the welfare state carried the same sting of irony particularly for those who fought and gained under the preceding administration. (See Ruth Lister of the Women's Budget Group, quoted in *op cit*, fn 25, Roberts.) This irony is deepened further when we realise that the UK's controversial Child Support Act/Agency was heavily influenced by Australia's Child Support Scheme which was introduced in 1988.

29 *Op cit*, fn 20, Walter.

30 *Op cit*, fn 20, Walter. For an analysis of the loyalty of the New Labour women MPs to the Government as evidenced by their voting behaviour, see Cowley, P, 'Daleks? Labour's rebels are alive and kicking' (1999) Parliamentary Brief, March, p 48.

31 In some areas of welfare management, the fiscal element of the new orthodoxy should not be over stated. Eg, in terms of welfare provision for children, the cost to the public purse has often been a primary concern for government, see Smart, C, '"There is of course the distinction dictated by nature": law and the problem of paternity', in Stanworth, M (ed), *Reproductive Technologies: Gender, Motherhood and Medicine*, 1987, Cambridge: Polity, p 98, particularly p 102.

32 In terms of managing welfare claimants, it is clear that this shift dovetails very neatly with the broader New Labour discourse of 'rights and responsibilities': 'Mr Field [then Welfare Reform Minister] declared that a central aim of the New Labour reform was individual responsibility – to restore the Victorian link between welfare and self-improvement which the 1949 welfare state eroded.' 'Blair's mission to reassure' (1998) *The Guardian*, 16 January.

become about refiguring priorities within the existing budget. It has become about ensuring 'value for money', ensuring that the money goes where it is 'most' needed. After the failure of the New Labour presentation team to smooth out the introduction of the early reform proposals, the machinery was relaunched with renewed vigour. In conjunction with a national welfare reform 'road show', the Social Security Department released a series of files which focused on fraud, inefficiencies and inequities in the current system.[33] Whilst public reaction dictated that the Government provide reassurance that reform would be 'principle' and not 'cut' led, the Prime Minister's speech at Dudley was dominated by the discourse of managing the welfare budget and its claimants:

> We have no choice but to reform the system. Reform will be driven by our principles, not cuts led. It is about delivering a more efficient system ... It will be based on a fairer balance between rights and responsibilities: we will guarantee that people who can, should help to provide for themselves.[34]

As detailed above, this reform driven by the orthodoxy of financial accountability and management has threatened to have very negative effects for women, more specifically, for the poorest women in society. Importantly, these effects are seen as the result of predetermined economic factors, as beyond the control of the current administration.[35] It is also interesting to note that proposed reforms included suggestions that the provision of welfare may become a task of the private sector. Frank Field, giving the 1998 Keith Joseph Memorial Lecture before his resignation as Minister in charge of welfare reform, stated that the Government's aim was to ensure that more people had welfare cover, but that this would not necessarily be provided by the Government. Field talked of partnerships between the public and private sectors.[36] Again, there are clear echoes of the Australian experience, with the commodification and privatisation of individual welfare needs – this shift from social citizenship to market citizenship.[37]

THE *FATHER* OF ALL PARLIAMENTS

In the section above, I outlined how the Blair Government's economic managerial orthodoxy led to policies which were detrimental to women. In

---

33 See 'Blair goes to Dudley: Labour can make a success of welfare if its priorities are clear' (1998) *The Times*, 16 January.

34 Quoted in 'Blair goes back to Beveridge in welfare campaign: Labour affirms its faith in founding principles' (1998) *The Times*, 16 January.

35 It is interesting to note that the 'inevitability' of reform has been exaggerated: 'What's worrying is the way that Labour exaggerates the cost of the system, exaggerates fraud, and exaggerates savings which welfare to work will make.' 'New show, old songs: first get the principles of welfare reform right' (1998) *The Guardian*, 16 January.

36 See 'Pensions safe with us, says Blair' (1998) *The Times*, 16 January.

37 *Op cit*, fn 15, Goetz, p 343.

this section, I want to ask a number of questions and move a step further towards an understanding of state power which will help explain the experiences of both the femocrats and the New Labour Women. In working with these experiences, it is possible to challenge the more general issue of the expectation that accompanies (and promotes) greater gender parity in government. The issue I am seeking to address is where was the challenge to this economic managerial orthodoxy? Where was the expected effect from so many more women in Parliament? Where were the women MPs who wanted to see a better deal for women, a new style of politics? As I have already noted, the well honed disciplinary machinery of New Labour must be implicated in this silence to some extent. Yet, there is also the more structural issue of government as a masculine institution. As Yeatman detailed in her consideration of the Australian administration, the institutions of the state are predicated on, and perpetuate, a more broadly entrenched gendered public/private division. There is a sexual division of labour within which power is associated with the masculine. Whilst the number of women in Blair's first cabinet was unprecedented, like Australia they were primarily only given access to the 'soft' sectors – health, social security and international aid.[38] Not only was there exclusion from the 'hard' sectors, there was a further division in terms of the 'type' of woman admitted to the Cabinet, particularly with higher profile portfolios like health and social security. Whilst it has been claimed that access for the femocrats to the 'hard' sectors was contingent upon 'adopting both the sociological features of masculinity in personal behaviour and the new management style',[39] in the New Labour Government this seems to be the requirement for access to any high profile Cabinet position whether 'hard' or 'soft'. In adopting a masculine standard, the measure of success necessarily becomes detailed in the ability to act within the dominant masculine framework:

> … for many femocrats, success became both a function and expression of their ability to conform to organizational structures and cultures by taking on the sociological characteristics of men in their dress, deportment, managerial styles, and most importantly, in their capacity to minimize the demands of the home.[40]

This pattern of behaviour – most specifically, the adoption of the dominant managerial style – was very clearly witnessed in two of the most controversial

---

38 It is also worth noting that this gendered division of labour is evident at a general parliamentary level. As Virginia Sapiro notes: 'Once women are in office, their committee assignments, initiation of legislation and the topics on which they speak tend to reflect traditional women's concerns … Research … show[s] that perceptions of women among the politically elite are shaped in part by stereotypes, and that sexism plays a role in elite recruitment and promotion.' Sapiro, V, 'When are interests interesting? The problem of political representation of women', in Phillips, A (ed), *Feminism and Politics*, 1998, Oxford: OUP, pp 161, 181.

39 *Op cit*, fn 15, Goetz, p 345.

40 *Op cit*, fn 15, Goetz, p 351.

episodes of the Government's first year. The first, already noted, was the decision to end lone parent benefit premiums. The second was the exclusion of Formula One racing from the ban on tobacco advertising. In each case, the Minister involved – Harriet Harman in the first, Tessa Jowell in the latter – fronted the Government's decision with the dominant New Labour mantra of economic realities and hard decisions. Jowell's involvement in 'Tobaccogate' was seen as clearly contradictory:

> It is ironic that Jowell should have to carry the can for Tony Blair's decision to exempt Formula One from the ban on tobacco advertising when nobody hearing her anti-smoking fervour could doubt that she supports a total ban ... But Blairite discipline required that she take the rap, and discipline is almost as important to Jowell as being a Blairite.[41]

It is the abrogation of values to the orthodoxy of discipline, management and economic accountability which marked both episodes and which characterised the early failure of New Labour Women to match their own expectations and the hopes pinned upon them. Carol Johnson, commenting on the Australian experience, noted that 'the "economic" has functioned as a meta-category which dissolves difference and conflict'.[42] Whilst this was illustrated in the preceding section in relation to New Labour politics, it is clear that difference is also 'dissolved' by the privileging of the masculine.

The examples just cited illustrate the dominance of managerialism and discipline, yet the relationship between masculinity and power has been evident at a number of levels. The early participation of women in the House, for example, was criticised as too courteous. As a result, a woman Labour Whip was appointed with the task of making these Parliamentarians more aggressive and noisy.[43] There is a powerful technology of exclusion: the feminine is marginalised and at the same time the femininity of the women MPs accentuated. Both inside and outside the House, women appear to be women first and Labour MPs second. Clair Ward, one of the new 'intake' reported how colleagues 'look at us as if we are not serious politicians, that we

---

41 'A blot on the perfect Blair Babe – profile: Tessa Jowell' (1997) *The Sunday Times*, 23 November. Shirley Williams in giving an 'end-of-term report' to the new league of 'Blair's Babes' puts a slightly different spin on this episode. Williams, bringing together her own experience, the early experience of Margaret Thatcher and the current Labour Women, claims that women in politics are often used as scapegoats: 'Those who do enter [politics] face a further risk: despite, or perhaps because of their limited influence, women have found themselves made into scapegoats for unpopular policies ... Harriet Harman and Tessa Jowell are today's scapegoats. Indeed, their situation is more painful than mine was. I was held responsible for a policy in which I had not been involved. They are held responsible for policy decisions, such as the reduction in benefits for lone parents, which I suspect they privately oppose.' Williams, S, 'Doing the dirty work' (1997) *The Guardian*, 15 December.

42 *Op cit*, fn 8, Johnson, p 102.

43 McDougall, L, 'House and home' (1998) *The Times*, 17 January.

are just here to decorate the benches and be fashion models'.[44] It is telling to recognise that, whilst women MPs appear to be the focus of greater media attention, it is as women and not as politicians. As Natasha Walter comments:

> ... if these women are getting to be rather well known, it's not always for the reasons they might have hoped. Ruth Kelly is known for having a baby; Yvette Cooper for being engaged to Gordon Brown's advisor, Ed Balls; Claire Ward for being the baby of the Parliament, just 24 when elected; Oona King for having been voted the most beautiful MP ... It's still these women's beauty, youth, their sexiness, that captures the public imagination.[45]

This focus on female MPs as women persists even though female candidates and officeholders have recognised that it is not politically advantageous to emphasise, or even refer to, an interest in women's issues or a home life. Nevertheless, they are forced into a '"woman's role", or at least they are forced to be defined as "women" candidates and politicians rather than, simply as candidates or politicians'.[46]

In noting the privileging of sociologically masculine characteristics, there is value in considering the association Goetz notes between success and the ability to minimise domestic 'ties'.[47] Even with the recent doubling of the number of women MPs, most still do not have any child care responsibilities. Only 22% have children between five and 15.[48] Some of the new Labour MPs have expressed feeling pressure not to start a family. Indeed, research conducted in the House led *The Guardian* to offer the following advice: 'Don't have children: those with pre-school kids or adolescents (10–16) are under most pressure.' Also, '[b]e a man, not a woman. Women tend to be more sensitive and take on more roles in life.'[49] Famously antagonistic to family life, the faltering of early intentions to reform the way business is conducted suggests that the anti-social (or perhaps 'homosocial') aspects of Parliament will remain unchanged.[50]

---

44 *Op cit*, fn 43, McDougall.

45 *Op cit*, fn 20, Walter.

46 *Op cit*, fn 38, Sapiro, p 181.

47 In the Australian context, this point is also made by Watson, *op cit*, fn 8, p 9.

48 *Op cit*, fn 43, McDougall.

49 'Election success turns sour for stressed out MPs' (1998) *The Guardian*, 28 March.

50 This illustrates an interesting point made by Goetz when she states that 'modern masculinity is crisis ridden and contradictory, and modern patriarchy implicates *both* men and women as oppressors and victims, albeit to different degrees, contingent on other factors such as race or class, and with seriously different consequences.' The homosociality of Parliament serves a particular masculinity, harming those, male or female, who value, and want to meaningfully participate in, a family life: *op cit*, fn 15, Goetz, p 346.

At a more basic level, perhaps the most important response to the question of investigating the situation of these women is to look at the place of women in the Government 18 months after the May election. By the time of the 1998 Party Conference, women were conspicuously absent from both the platform and from general party discourse. As Natasha Walter reported from the conference: 'The near invisibility of women at the conference reflects the way women have been sidelined in the Government.'[51] Walter went on to quote a union delegate: 'You just can't say *women* and *feminism* to the Government anymore. Those words don't exist in the New Labour lexicon.'

So far, I have argued that a number of factors may be understood as antagonistic to feminist transformatory political agendas and act as obstacles to greater gender sensitivity from greater sexual parity. Parliamentary procedural life which excludes women, the association between power and masculinity, and the economic managerial orthodoxy which acts to locate equity as a cost, not a benefit, are all implicated in this. In the next section, an understanding of the relationship between masculinity and power will be further developed. Below, it will be argued that this complex relationship moves beyond a privileging of socially masculine characteristics and is played out at a more fundamental level. Questioning the gender of state power emphasises the current limits to women's involvement in participatory politics.

UNDERSTANDING THE STATE

In order to understand the limits to women's engagement with the state, it is essential to understand what we mean by 'the state' in late capitalist culture. The state may be located as a complex, contradictory and morphically dynamic domain. As Wendy Brown has noted:

> The contemporary ... state is both modern and postmodern, highly concrete and an elaborate fiction, powerful and intangible, rigid and protean, potent and without boundaries, decentred and centralizing, without agency, yet capable of tremendous economic, political and ecological effects.[52]

Recognising the state as a 'set of arenas',[53] with its many tensions and contradictions, it becomes problematic, although perhaps inevitable, to talk of 'The State', to talk of 'It', yet:

> [What] we call the state is not a thing, system or subject, but a significantly unbounded terrain of powers and techniques, an ensemble of discourses, rules,

---

51 Walter, N, 'Drowning in a sea of suits' (1998) *The Observer*, 4 October.

52 Brown, W, *States of Injury: Power and Freedom in Late Modernity*, 1995, Princeton: Princeton UP, p 174.

53 Pringle, R and Watson, S, 'Fathers, brothers, mates: the fraternal state in Australia', in *op cit*, fn 8, Watson, p 229.

and practices, cohabiting in limited, tension ridden, often contradictory relation with one another.[54]

This conception of the state raises some important questions. If this domain is so unbounded, contradictory (an 'erratic beast'),[55] and uncertain (a 'contingently articulated, multifaceted phenomena with no fixed form, essence or core'),[56] does this not suggest that it is open to contestation, challenge, negotiation and, ultimately, redefinition? If it lacks agency and intent, how can it be hostile/closed to women and feminist interests? If women MPs are able to overcome the masculine ('men's club') structural obstacles, if they can refigure the position and perception of equity, if a greater sexual parity can break, or at least weaken, the association between masculinity and power, does this not mean that government can represent and respond to women and feminist interests? These claims appear reasonable and form the basis for the positive expectations that were engendered by the increased sexual parity we have witnessed. Yet, underpinning these problems and the failure of a greater number of female political representatives to substantially alter the gender dynamics of politics, is the gender of state power.

Whilst reiterating the state's lack of agency or intent (other than the most partial and temporary) – moving away from an essentialist construction of the state as monolithic – it is nonetheless possible to argue that state power is gendered. There are a number of routes to this end. Rosemary Pringle and Sophie Watson, for instance, argue that 'the discourses that construct the state assume a masculine subject rather than self-consciously defending or creating men's interests'.[57] It is also possible to argue that the state is masculinist, both by locating state power in its historical context and by recognising its current characteristics. In terms of the former, it is difficult to depart from the conclusion that state power is gendered in a way which is antagonistic to women when we recognise that this power has evolved from, amongst other things, male dominance and, more specifically – though not exclusively – male primacy in the public sphere.[58] This conclusion may also be reached if we consider the gendered and sexual foundations of the political structures which existed before the state.[59] Moving on to consider the late modern state's current characteristics, it should be recognised that:

54 *Op cit*, fn 52, Brown, p 174.
55 *Op cit*, fn 53, Pringle and Watson, p 239.
56 Cooper, D, *Power in Struggle: Feminism, Sexuality and the State*, 1995, Buckingham: OU Press, p 61.
57 *Op cit*, fn 53, Pringle and Watson, p 234.
58 *Op cit*, fn 52, Brown, p 174.
59 *Op cit*, fn 52, Brown, pp 187–88.

> ... domination, dependence, discipline, and protection, the terms marking the itinery of women's subordination in vastly different cultures and epochs, are also characteristic effects of state power.[60]

This homology between masculine power and state power is drawn closer when it is recognised that, to a large extent, the law now wields powers previously in the hands of men, powers which set many of the parameters of women's lives. Stated differently, the state has colonised economic, sexual, reproductive and other powers which had, in past ages, been deployed by men.[61]

It is also worth questioning the gender of the notion of 'authority' upon which state power is premised. Kathleen Jones has argued that the focus of feminist work on gender parity in government has left the idea and understanding of public authority unproblematically gender neutral. According to Jones:

> Descriptions of those who act as public authorities – public spokespeople – and of the norms and rules that they articulate, generally have excluded characteristics culturally coded as 'feminine'. In Western political thought, *office, knowledge, judgment* and *will* [the signs or 'marks' of authority] have been connected more immediately to patriarchally gendered masculine rather than to feminine modes of being and action.[62]

Bringing together work by, *inter alia*, Weber and Foucault, Jones details the masculinisation of authority and the corresponding feminisation of the subject. This reading of contemporary state power relies to a large extent on an understanding of the bureaucratisation of modern government. This needs to be explained further. Bureaucratic power has been recognised as the defining characteristic of modern governance. The growth of bureaucratic power has successfully colonised areas previously governed by sovereign or judicial powers.[63] This form of governance is marked by its many normative/disciplinary sites of surveillance and control, of regulation and correction. It may be located as imbricated in the emergence of the pastoral, the 'proliferation of political technologies ... investing the body, health, modes of subsistence, and habitation, living conditions, the whole space of existence'.[64] The bureaucratic networks that mark both the state and the social order allow for the effective management of populations while, paradoxically, the frontiers of the state are 'rolled back'. This management of populations

---

60 *Op cit*, fn 52, Brown, p 173.

61 *Op cit*, fn 52, Brown, p 193.

62 Jones, K, 'What is authority's gender?', in Hirschmann, N and Di Stefano, C (eds), *Revisioning the Political: Feminist Reconstructions of Traditional Concepts in Western Political Theory*, 1996, Boulder, CO: Westview, p 78.

63 Foucault, M, *Discipline and Punish: The Birth of the Prison*, 1991, London: Penguin.

64 Foucault, M, *The History of Sexuality: Volume One*, 1990, London: Penguin, pp 143–44.

through bureaucratic power involves the production of 'disciplined, obedient, rule-abiding subjects'.[65]

Within this paradigm, Jones details the masculinisation of authority from a number of perspectives. Relying explicitly on Foucault, she details the gendered nature of modern state power in its dispersed and disciplinary form:

> ... modern discourses of science, medicine, health, aesthetics, and so forth, contribute to the elaboration of a complex web of authority as control, producing modern subjects as subjugated subjects ... The masculinization of authority follows from the feminization of subjects, subjects whose being disciplined through their bodies represents their 'feminization'.[66]

More specifically, she argues that the modern normalisation of authority as a disciplinary gaze, which involves the subject internalising mechanisms of control, is both gendered and gendering:

> The subject of disciplinary power takes the sovereign into herself making the existence of external controls seem redundant. Since the construction of *to-be-looked-at-ness* is precisely the way that disciplinary power works its effects on all its subjects, it would be accurate to claim that the 'citizen' in the disciplinary state becomes feminized; correspondingly, judgment as the operation of the gaze becomes a masculinized, ocularcentric practice.[67]

It is interesting to note the bureaucratic consequences of some of the New Labour initiatives. Talk of managing the welfare budget and its claimants necessarily involves new bureaucratic structures, seen, for example, with the proposed introduction of means testing for a number of welfare benefits. Of the early New Labour bureaucratic developments, the most poignant, in terms of the current discussion, has been the introduction of interviews for lone parent benefit claimants who are seeking work. Subjecting lone parents to such a literal gaze comes after a sustained period when lone parents have been the focus of a critical and more diffuse public gaze. The establishing of bureaucratic structures, which necessarily involve the gender effects noted above, is itself a masculine process. This bureaucratisation involves the masculinised judgment that Jones argues is inherent in bureaucratic power.

Focusing specifically on the masculinisation of the bureaucrat, and therefore helping to explain why New Labour Women have proved less sensitive to women's interests than many had hoped, Jones further argues that this situation is inevitable given the primacy of 'instrumental rationality' – the use of the most efficient means to achieve established ends.[68] Bureaucratisation, according to Max Weber, 'offers above all the optimum possibility for carrying through the principle of specialising administrative

---

65   *Op cit*, fn 52, Brown, p 193.

66   *Op cit*, fn 62, Jones, pp 82–83.

67   *Op cit*, fn 62, Jones, p 83.

68   *Op cit*, fn 62, Jones, p 80.

functions according to purely objective considerations'.[69] The emphasis on objectivity places rules above persons, including not only the governed but also the officeholder as the privileging of the rules of office depersonalise those in authority:

> Regardless of their sex, bureaucratic leaders are masculinized because they alone are above the merely subjective pull of everyday life; whether they are males or females, their followers are feminized because they are subjected to the soulless commands of rationalized, instrumentalist, and institutionalized manliness.[70]

It has been argued that those who engage with the machinery of the state risk becoming 'more socialised – absorbing bureaucratic culture and processes'.[71] This process of socialisation includes the masculinisation referred to above. It includes both the masculinisation which results from the general culture, and that which results from the bureaucratic process, with judgment as a 'masculinized ocularcentric practice', and the engagement with abstract rationality, procedure and rights – all of which can be allied with socially masculine values.[72]

INCLUSION, INVOLVEMENT, STRATEGY

Part of what this Chapter has done so far is to build up a picture of the obstacles that exist to sustained and meaningful feminist participation in state power. I have detailed the barriers that exist in terms of the fetishisation of the economic, the privileging of values traditionally perceived as masculine, and the masculinist nature of power in the late modern state. Each feature helps us to understand not only why governmental responses to feminist claims are often 'co-optation, diffusion, or symbolic manipulation',[73] but also why government appears largely disinterested in the gender impact of its policies. This process is neatly illustrated in the changes that had taken place in Blair's Cabinet after 18 months. Whilst, on entering office, Blair had created more

---

69 Weber, M, *Economy and Society: An Outline of Interpretive Sociology,* in Roth, G and Wittich, C (eds), 1978, Berkeley: California UP, p 975. Boaventura de Sousa Santos defines bureaucracy as 'a communication form and a decision making strategy based on authoritative impositions through the mobilization of the demonstrative potential of regularized procedures and normative standards.' de Sousa Santos, B, *Toward a New Common Sense: Law, Science and Politics in the Paradigmatic Transition,* 1995, London: Routledge, p 112.

70 *Op cit,* fn 62, Jones, p 81.

71 *Op cit,* fn 56, Cooper, p 118.

72 See Ferguson, K, *The Feminist Case Against Bureaucracy,* 1984, Philadelphia: Temple UP.

73 *Op cit,* fn 38, Sapiro, p 179.

female Cabinet Ministers than any other British Prime Minister,[74] the picture was rather different by the time of the 1998 Labour Party Conference. With the sacking of Harriet Harman and the move of Margaret Beckett from the Department of Trade and Industry (both women having steered through the policies which had most impact for women – the national child care strategy and the minimum wage), there were no longer any women running major domestic departments. Women had been confined to the organisational. Where women remained visible it was as Leader of the Commons, Leader of the Lords, and as Chief Whip.[75] Whilst the importance of these positions cannot be denied, it is significant not only that the occupants were not in control of major domestic departments, but also that they were not in control of significant public expenditure.

Do these obstacles and the manipulation that has been witnessed suggest that engaging in participatory forms of politics is such a limited and counterproductive strategy as to be discarded as an option? Beyond the problems already noted, there are further issues to be aware of before answering this question. It is clear, for instance, that accepting government funding must involve limitations and constraints on feminist objectives and practices.[76] Perhaps more damaging, in becoming a politician, bureaucrat or 'femocrat', you are inevitably drawn into the ethos of the organisation.[77]

Beyond this, given the gendered nature of state power considered in the preceding section, the involvement of women in state bodies clearly becomes an exercise which is problematic. It does not seem unreasonable that suspicion should arise regarding involvement in a power structure which has historically reflected and represented masculinist interests. Under these conditions, it becomes possible to see how women MPs and feminist politics may become involved in reiterating rather than refiguring the conditions and construction of women.[78] As Suzanne Franzway notes: 'The state is not only a site of contest but is itself implicated in that contest and so, necessarily, are state workers.'[79] The position of New Labour women in the welfare reforms

---

74   Margaret Thatcher appointed only one woman to her Cabinet in 10 years, and she only lasted 18 months. When John Major appointed his Cabinet in 1990, after having filled all the Cabinet seats, he realised he had included no women. Gillian Shepard was hastily appointed as Economic Secretary to the Treasury: Ward, L, 'Women on top' (1998) *The Guardian*, 29 July.

75   *Op cit*, fn 51, Walter.

76   Auer, J, 'Encounters with the state, co-option and reform, a case study from women's health', in *op cit*, fn 8, Watson, p 207. Also *op cit*, fn 56, Cooper, ch 6.

77   Eisenstein, H,'Femocrats, official feminism and the uses of power', in *op cit*, fn 8, Watson, pp 87, 100. See, also, Karvonen, L, Djupsund, G and Carlson, T, 'Political language', in Karvonen, L and Selle, P (eds), *Women in Nordic Politics: Closing the Gap*, 1995, Aldershot: Dartmouth.

78   *Op cit*, fn 52, Brown, p 173.

79   Franzway, S, 'With problems of their own: femocrats and the welfare state' (1986) 3 Australian Feminist Studies 49.

which have privileged male public involvement, whilst locating women in the private, supports this contention.

So does this mean that engaging with the formal structures of state power is both futile and politically too problematic? This position seems untenable. It would be an extremely partial account to suggest that the increased number of women in Parliament has had no effect. It is doubtful whether New Labour would have 'reversed' the lone parent benefit cut, or backed down on the proposed means testing for free provision of contraception, without the pressure brought to bear by these women. Whilst New Labour's disciplinary machinery maintains a certain public image, internally, quite a different story is told:

> Let's not be too hard on the women, however. Inside New Labour, the talk is of a Fabian-like success, of how sustained pressure from women MPs and Ministers alike has influenced the big guys. It was that pressure that pushed the Government to its 'women and children' budget.[80]

In terms of the Australian experience, as I have already noted, the femocrats also made real gains. Indeed, such was their success that the Australian New Right may be read as a direct response to the advances made.[81] Whilst these gains are real, that is not to say that they are permanent nor without limitations or conditions, as the emergence of the New Right demonstrates. It is also possible that as advances are made, disciplinary technologies of power may reconfigure. What needs to be recognised is the fragility, contingency and limitation of any gain. As Davina Cooper writes:

> While the state controls particular resources, attempts to gain access to them to further oppositional agendas is important. At the same time, state culture and process will limit and re-form their utility ... The use of state power by oppositional forces will often provoke (intentionally or not) changes to the character and content of its power technologies. Similarly, attempts to undermine state power ... may well lead to transformations in its access.[82]

This does not undermine the utility of engaging with state power from within the structures of government, it merely underscores the need to be strategic, to recognise the limitations, and to foresee the possible costs in terms of 'co-option, de-radicalization, bureaucratism and political diversion'.[83]

---

80 Longrigg, C, 'Babe watch' (1998) *The Guardian*, 27 April.

81 *Op cit*, fn 8, Ryan, p 83.

82 *Op cit*, fn 56, Cooper, p 119.

83 *Op cit*, fn 56, Cooper, p 65.

CONCLUSIONS

It is undeniable that we have seen a shift in the style of government with the electoral success of New Labour. We have, it has been suggested, seen a feminisation of government. This move may be understood at a very mundane level. At a very practical/strategic level the discourse of inclusion may be seen as a way of capturing what was for Blair the electorally decisive female vote. Indeed, the Labour Party has become more 'woman-friendly' in response to its own research and that conducted by the Fabian Society which has highlighted both the dissatisfaction of voters – particularly women – with masculine party images, and the concomitant electoral benefits of having women politicians.[84] Yet this move may also be understood as part of the continual development of more sophisticated forms of governance. In this it can be understood in the same way as Anna Yeatman's identification of the emergence of legions of technocrats and the shift in discourse from service to management.[85] Similarly, it may be read as governance by inclusion and promise, a result of 'the state's desire to maintain its hegemonic position by incorporation and diffusion'.[86] Yet the fulfilment of the promise which keeps potential foes 'on-side' is limited by factors, both said and unsaid, outside governmental control: predetermined spending targets, fiscal policy, convergence criteria and so on.

Yet there remain further limitations which restrict the effect of this 'feminisation' and any possible positive gender effect from the increased female presence in government. The position and role of women in government is determined by a number of factors. These include recruitment procedures and organisational constraints in a political system which is dominated by masculinist values and norms.[87] Further, as Virginia Sapiro argues: 'not the least of the problems is the presence of many female leaders who, to varying degrees, accept and make decisions according to these patriarchal norms.'[88] This was one of the defining characteristics of Margaret Thatcher's premiership, a feature which not only helped to shape the political experience of the 1980s but, as just suggested, continues to influence British political life.

The observation by Sapiro moves us towards a further problem with the expectation of change and the terms within which this is debated. This expectation, as well as the idea of 'Blair's Babes'/New Labour Woman, is ontologically problematic. In many respects, there appears to be an

---

84   *Op cit*, fn 74, Ward.
85   *Op cit*, fn 17, Yeatman.
86   *Op cit*, fn 56, Cooper, p 64.
87   *Op cit*, fn 38, Sapiro, p 183.
88   *Op cit*, fn 38, Sapiro.

essentialising of female participants in state power. There is a construction of the parliamentary woman, in particular, which denies the complexity and diversity of political office and life, and of individuals' relationship to political life. The terms of the debate, more often than not, fail to distinguish between those who entered political life committed to a transformatory agenda and those who are motivated by other forces. This ignores the fact that few women seek or enter political office with the intention of representing women's interests *per se*.[89] Even within the number who are feminists, there are clear differences in their relationship to office. This was evident with the femocrats:

> There is no one pattern of how feminists have negotiated their positions of political and bureaucratic life. Neither is there a distinctive category of 'femocrat'. Some feminists ... joined the bureaucracy as part of a conscious political strategy to achieve reform. Others have been traditional career public servants, while yet others joined the bureaucracy to escape the poorly paid and insecure community sector; some have also joined the bureaucracy because of the closed doors of academia.[90]

Whilst it is important to recognise this diversity and complexity, we should not underestimate the masculinism of state power which is counterproductive to those who do pursue transformatory agendas. This is particularly important as women's relationship to the state expands in late modernity whilst, simultaneously, the state's maleness shifts and becomes more diffuse.[91] There is an irony in the relationship between this shift in the masculinism of state power and the status of contemporary masculinity:

> ... like the so called new man, the late modern state also represents itself as pervasively hamstrung, quasi-impotent, unable to come through on many of its commitments ... The central paradox of the late modern state thus resembles a central paradox of late modern masculinity: its power and privilege operate increasingly through disavowal of potency, repudiation of responsibility, and the diffusion of sites and operations of control.[92]

To be a little parochial, it could be concluded that New Labour has met New Man. This resonates with the charges that were levelled against New Labour by Helen Wilkinson, co-founder of the New Labour-friendly think tank, Demos. Wilkinson, and others, have noted a culture of 'new laddism' surrounding New Labour. Wilkinson cited Blair's 'internal coterie' as predominantly male and argued that 'men remain in charge, with old Labour's macho labourist culture replaced by a subtler, covert and insidious laddishness – all the more alienating for being steeped in predominantly

---

89 *Op cit*, fn 38, Sapiro, p 180. It should be noted that Parliamentarians' attitudes to social issues are more clearly influenced by party allegiance than by gender. See *op cit*, fn 7, Norris, p 103.

90 *Op cit*, fn 8, Watson, p 9.

91 *Op cit*, fn 52, Brown, p 193.

92 *Op cit*, fn 52, Brown, p 194.

middle class values'.[93] This shift may also be considered against a greater male presence at the grass roots level. Against the backdrop of a very visible project of inclusion and feminisation, and after a drive to recruit new members, New Labour members are more likely to be male than old Labour members.[94]

Yet perhaps this analysis, and particularly this point of departure, is too bleak – undeservedly bleak. Within the period analysed above, there were a number of moments which appeared, at some level, to transcend the masculine model of governance I have discussed. Note has to be made, for instance, of Mo Mowlam as Secretary of State for Northern Ireland. She has been central to one of the most significant political achievements of recent times. And, notably, she has been at the heart of perhaps one of the most masculine Ministries. Elements of Mowlam's style have, however, remained distinctly feminine. Whilst this should be noted, it is easy to question its significance. Has Mowlam's 'feminine' style been strategically deployed? Has it been placed to unsettle or disrupt the very masculine governmental politics of Northern Ireland? Would Mowlam's style change if her portfolio were more directly 'economic' – for example, health or social security? Mowlam is clearly a Blairite, and it would be difficult to imagine her not repeating the New Labour mantras which framed a number of the early proposals and which appeared distinctly woman-*un*friendly.

Another element which softens the rather bleak picture detailed above is the idea of progress. Whilst it was noted above that the 1998 reshuffle saw a 'ghettoising' of women into organisational roles, with a quite explicit 'exclusion' from economic portfolios, this account may be seen as partial. Beyond the appointments noted, there was also a significant number of women appointed to the middle ranks. As one new woman MP (not unproblematically) noted:

> These middle ranking appointments are more telling in many ways than the top level jobs. Eventually more women will gain experience and begin to feed through. You can't judge all women on the basis of those few that make it to the top first.[95]

Added to this, the government also appears willing to listen. The 1998 budget did appear heavily influenced by the criticism that followed early welfare reform proposals. As Lynne Jones, one of the Labour Members to vote against the cut in lone parent benefits, noted: '[this is] certainly a hopeful thought to take into any future debates.'[96]

---

93   Wilkinson, H, 'Faced with Labour's lads, I feel like a lover who has been abandoned' (1998) *The Guardian*, 6 August. Also, MacAskill, E, '"New Lads" of Labour attacked' (1998) *The Guardian*, 6 August.

94   White, M, 'Survey gives lie to New Labour "yuppie" image' (1998) *The Guardian*, 4 June.

95   *Op cit*, fn 74, Ward.

96   Personal correspondence.

There is, however, something a little saccharine about finishing here. It feels both over optimistic and perhaps dishonest. Whilst some degree of optimism is not without foundation, the aftertaste is given an edge when this optimism is located within the politics of inclusion which has been discussed. Are these moves about real, sustainable gains, or is this about keeping women 'on-side', about maintaining legitimacy, about 'image'? As at various other moments in history, women's full involvement in government and democracy again appears to be imminent.

CHAPTER 5

JUDGING WOMEN DIFFERENTLY: GENDER, THE JUDICIARY AND REFORM

Clare McGlynn

INTRODUCTION

The judiciary plays a pivotal role in the UK's constitution, comprising, together with the legislature and executive, one of the three branches of government.[1] For this reason, a discussion of the judiciary is customarily included in both public law classes and textbooks. These analyses of the judiciary commonly take the form of an outline of the court structure, the hierarchy of judicial offices and the importance of the independence of the judiciary; such discussions generally forming a preface to a discussion of the law making function of the judiciary and its role in judicial review.[2] Although highlighting the significance of the judiciary's role in the constitution, many analyses tend to treat the judiciary as a given; a predetermined institution, the composition of which is axiomatic. Thus, although the actions of the judiciary are examined by public law scholars and students alike, little consideration is given to possible links between the composition of the judiciary and the fulfilment of its constitutional role.

However, it is precisely because of the importance of the judiciary, not just in the public law field, but in the legal system as a whole, that an examination of the composition of the judiciary, and the potential impact thereof on its role and function, is essential. Accordingly, this chapter aims to interrogate the composition of the judiciary and, in particular, to consider the representation of women. In doing so, the aim is to reveal the extent to which the judicial appointments process is gendered and the impact of this on the legal profession, the nature of judging and the law.[3] In taking a feminist perspective, and centring the discussion on women, it is not suggested that gender is the only factor to be taken into account in assessing the composition

---

1 See Thomson, Chapter 4, this volume, for a discussion of gender and parliamentary government.

2 See, eg, de Smith, S and Brazier, R, *Constitutional and Administrative Law*, 1994, London: Penguin, pp 397–99; Bradley, AW and Ewing, KD, *Constitutional and Administrative Law*, 12th edn, 1997, London: Longman, pp 768–70; Alder, J, *Constitutional and Administrative Law*, 1994, London: Macmillan, pp 278–79.

3 The composition of the judiciary has ramifications beyond the areas identified, but the discussion in this chapter, for reasons of space, shall be confined to these primary themes.

of the judiciary. Indeed, the many analyses of the class and educational background of judges have provided illuminating data and have sparked considerable debate.[4] However, no analysis of gender has been carried out in the UK and the purpose of this chapter is to begin to remedy this omission. Furthermore, in examining the impact of the gender composition of the judiciary, the analysis is intended to reveal the extent to which the judiciary is an institution closed to many groups and individuals, not just women; in other words, feminist analysis is employed in order to reveal the multiple sites of discrimination within the institution of the judiciary.

Accordingly, the chapter begins by examining the gender composition of the judiciary. It proceeds to canvass possible reasons why there are so few women judges and, in particular, considers the closed nature of the judicial appointments process. Having discussed possible reforms to the appointments process which may result in more women being appointed, the chapter turns to consider the potential impact of greater numbers of women judges. This discussion is divided into two main themes. First, the impact on the legal profession will be considered. It will be argued that, in the shorter term, it is in this context that the greatest impact of more women judges will be appreciated. The second theme is the impact of gender on the nature of judging and the content of the law. Both themes consider the profound question raised by many feminist scholars, in particular, Carol Gilligan, as to whether or not women reason in a different 'voice' to men. In this context, the question is whether women judges, by reason of their sex, carry out their functions in a particularly different way to their male colleagues. Although rejecting the essentialism of this theory, it will be argued that a greater number of women judges will make a difference to the nature of judging, but not on the basis of essential characteristics belonging to all women. More women judges will begin to effect change, with consequent effects on the legal profession, the nature of judging and on the content of the law, on the basis that a more diverse judiciary, comprising a broader representation of many presently excluded groups, will bring different experiences and perspectives to their role as judges and that this social experience, not biological destiny, can and will make a difference.

A WOMAN'S PLACE?

No women have ever been appointed to the UK's most senior court, the House of Lords. Indeed, the very name of the supreme court, the House of *Lords*, is suggestive of exclusively male membership. The most senior woman

---

4   See, in particular, Griffith, JAG, *The Politics of the Judiciary*, 1997, London: Fontana.

judge in the UK is in the Court
Court judges. This means that,
whom the law making function
of judges are women.[5] Althoug
only amounts to the appointme
offices (excluding tribunals), w
there has been an improvemer
over recent years, particularly
few women judges. The obviou
is why?

It is oft repeated that the
increase given time for women
former Lord Chancellor, Lc
progress through the profession, it is to be expected that the number of
women within the judiciary will increase.'[8] Such reasoning is, however, far
too simplistic. That history cannot be used as a justification for the very low
numbers of women judges was confirmed by two studies in the early 1990s.
Research commissioned by the Bar Council and the Lord Chancellor's
Department (LCD) in 1992 revealed that women are disadvantaged at the Bar
and in the judiciary in a number of ways which meant that they were not
succeeding as might have been expected.[9] In particular, the report suggested
that discrimination was institutionally present at the Bar and that the judicial
appointments process disadvantaged women. Similarly, a Law Society study
in 1991 found that women had less of a chance of becoming judges than men
and, in the South East, women waited on average two years more than
similarly qualified men for appointment.[10] Underpinning both reports is the
fact that women have been entering and remaining within the legal profession
in large numbers for many years, but are still failing to reach senior positions.
For example, in 1998, 14% of barristers with over 15 year's call were women,
yet only 6% of Queen's Counsel were women.[11] Thus, the argument that
women will in time progress to the most senior levels of the profession,
including the judiciary, is not sustainable. Accordingly, it has been argued
that 'the law is no different from other professions. We cannot count on mere
"mass" to ensure change at higher levels. What we need is concerted action to

---

5   Figures as of 1 June 1998 and quoted from http://www.open.gov.uk/lcd/judicial/
     womjudfr.htm.
6   Hansard Society, *Women at the Top*, 1990, London: Hansard Society, p 45.
7   See http://www.open.gov.uk/lcd/judicial/womjudfr.htm.
8   Quoted in (1995) 145 NLJ 514.
9   TMS Consultants, *Without Prejudice? Sex Equality at the Bar and in the Judiciary*, 1992,
     London: Bar Council and Lord Chancellor's Department.
10   Hughes, S, *The Circuit Bench – A Woman's Place?*, 1991, London: The Law Society.
11   Figures quoted by the Lord Chancellor, speech to 1998 Woman Lawyer Conference,
     reproduced at: http://www.open.gov.uk/lcd/speeches/1998/1998fr.htm.

cial appointments of women'.[12] In the light of this
as focused on the judicial appointments system as
s bar to the elevation of women to the Bench.

APPOINTING JUDGES

are a vast array of different judicial offices, ranging from the most
or judicial offices in the House of Lords and Court of Appeal, to the
extensive number of tribunal appointments. The appointments process for
such a large number of offices will necessarily be complex. However, valid
criticisms can be made of the procedures for appointing judges on the basis
that they are shrouded in mystique, are not fully open or transparent, rely too
heavily on the views of the present judiciary and senior members of the
profession, and are controlled by a government minister, the Lord Chancellor.
Debate regarding why there are so few women judges has tended to focus on
the judicial appointments process, resulting in many reforms of the
procedures since the early 1990s. Debate has, however, moved on and
discussion now centres on the extent of reforms. The first section below will
examine, in broad outline, the judicial appointments process, before going on
to consider proposals for reform.

Although advertisements, job descriptions and interviews have been
introduced for some judicial offices lower down the hierarchy, reforms which
represent a considerable advance on the lack of transparency in respect of the
more senior appointments (High Court and above), the appointments process
remains based on the consultations which take place between the LCD and
senior judges and members of the legal profession.[13] This process of taking
'secret soundings' is the principal focus for criticism in relation to the
appointments process.

A report published by the Bar Council in 1994 included some examples of
the comments made by consultees in the process of taking soundings: 'I am
surprised to see that he is 48, he looks younger'; 'I don't know him personally
but those I have consulted say that he is OK although not very special'; '[ ] QC
says he is not silk material. I do not know him personally'.[14] In view of the
fact that the report supported the consultation process, these samples are
presumably intended to represent the virtue of the system. Although these are
extracts, there appears to be no reference to any selection criteria, rather it
appears that consultees rely on a 'gut' instinct and the views of their

---

12 Kamlesh Bahl, quoted in (1995) 145 NLJ 514.

13 For a detailed discussion of the judicial appointments process, see McGlynn, C, *The
Woman Lawyer – Making the Difference*, 1998, London: Butterworths, ch 7.

14 Hewson, B, 'You've a long way to go, baby ...' (1996) 146 NLJ 565.

acquaintances who do not have to explain and justify their comments. In addition, comments are included from those not on the formal consultee list, and would appear to amount to little more than gossip. Furthermore, it seems clear that judges do not keep contemporaneous records of how they consider barristers to have performed before them, and therefore the consultations rely on remembered perceptions which can quite easily reflect factors which have little to do with the competence of the individual.

Research commissioned by the LCD and Bar Council in 1992 investigated the judicial appointments process and concluded that: 'It is unlikely that the judicial appointment system offers equal access to women or fair access to promotion to women judges … The system depends on patronage, being noticed and being known.'[15] That this is the case is accepted by many judges themselves. Lord Justice Otton remarked at a conference on women lawyers in 1996 that, so long as we have 'male consultors consulting male consultees, women are bound to be at a disadvantage'.[16] A study carried out by the Association of Women Barristers (AWB) sought to test the necessity of 'being known', by hypothesising that the judges consulted tend to recommend, for appointment to the High Court Bench, barristers from their own chambers.[17] The AWB gathered information on all High Court appointments between 1986 and 1996 and on the judges of the High Court, Court of Appeal and House of Lords of the relevant consultation period. Only 58 of 227 sets of chambers were represented by the judicial appointees during the period of the study. Of those 58, seven sets produced no less than 30 judicial appointments. In other words, 29% of all judicial appointees came from 3% of sets of chambers in London, and 2% of chambers in England and Wales.[18] Although the figures involved in this study are small, the results are indicative of the importance of 'being known'. Such a requirement affects women and men alike, but can be particularly onerous for many women who are excluded from the formal and informal networks at the Bar.[19]

In particular, the AWB has argued that membership of the Freemasons by many senior judges, QCs and barristers constitutes an important network from which women are excluded. It is not unreasonable to suppose, argues the AWB, that 'there exists considerable opportunity for informal but important contacts and influence amongst men who practise Freemasonry'.[20] That this is 'damaging to public confidence in the impartiality of the judiciary

---

15 *Op cit*, fn 9, TMS Consultants.

16 Quoted in 'The second Woman Lawyer Conference' (1996) Counsel, May/June, p 8.

17 Hayes, J, 'Appointment by invitation' (1997) 147 NLJ 520, p 521.

18 *Ibid*.

19 See, further, the evidence of the EOC and AWB submitted to the Home Affairs Select Committee on Judicial Appointments Procedures, *Third Report of Session 1995–96, Minutes of Evidence and Appendices*, Vol II.

20 *Ibid*, p 194.

and also to confidence in the impartiality of appointments to QC and the Bench'[21] would appear to be confirmed by the report from Parliament's Home Affairs Committee which recommended that any links between the judiciary and Freemasonry be disclosed.[22]

Women are also scarce, around 6%, among the Benchers of the Inns of Court.[23] The Inns are highly influential bodies, run by Benchers who tend to be either High Court judges or senior QCs. The low number of women Benchers is yet another sign of the lack of informal mechanisms available to women through which it is possible to become 'known' at the Bar. It has therefore been suggested that, 'it is not unreasonable to suppose that [as a Bencher] your chances of judicial appointment, or silk, are improved immeasurably if you lunch with senior judges every day'.[24] Twenty years ago, the Royal Commission on Legal Services recommended that the Inns elect more women as Benchers,[25] but little has changed.

The flaw of the consultations process lies not just with its reliance on patronage and 'being known' but also with the fact that the predominance of men within the list of consultees may affect the outcome. The Equal Opportunities Commission (EOC) has suggested that the use of the selection criteria of 'decisiveness' and 'authority' are subjective and lead to judgments based on individuals' (gendered) preconceptions.[26] In particular, such criteria may be defined in particularly gendered ways.[27] The great danger in an area such as the judiciary, the EOC suggested, is that it has always been largely seen as a masculine area of work, so perceptions of what makes a good judge – and what is 'authority' and 'decisiveness' – are also likely to be masculine.[28] The effect of this, as in many other areas of public life,[29] is that the status quo is replicated as appointers fashion change in their own image.

REFORMING THE JUDICIARY

In view of the serious criticisms of the judicial appointments process, there have been many calls for reform of the process in recent years. The potential

---

21 Home Affairs Committee, *Third Report of Session 1996–97, Freemasonry in the Police and the Judiciary*, para 18.

22 *Ibid.*

23 *Waterlow's Solicitors' and Barristers' Directory*, 1996, London: Waterlow.

24 *Op cit*, fn 14, Hewson, p 565.

25 Royal Commission on Legal Services, 1979, HMSO: London, Cmnd 7648, para 35.29, p 501.

26 *Op cit*, fn 19, Home Affairs Select Committee on Judicial Appointments Procedures.

27 See below, pp 97–98, 105.

28 *Op cit*, fn 19, Home Affairs Select Committee on Judicial Appointments Procedures.

29 *Op cit*, fn 6, Hansard Society.

reforms aimed at refining the present system to make it more open and fair will be examined first, with larger scale proposals being considered thereafter. The first reform must be the introduction of more open selection procedures already adopted for those positions lower down the judicial hierarchy. Accordingly, therefore, advertisements should be placed, selection criteria drafted and job descriptions promulgated. Lay participation in the process, together with the use of meaningful interviews, must be introduced. It may even be that when appointment to the most senior courts, such as the Court of Appeal and House of Lords, is announced, and applications invited, public debate takes place over the various candidates, on their track records, declared opinions and background.[30]

Any selection process must include information on the applicants' performance. The EOC has suggested that a structured monitoring programme should be introduced for those on the lower rungs of the judicial ladder. The aim is for assessment to be more objective and less reliant on the reminiscences of judges.[31] It is encouraging that the Lord Chancellor has announced the introduction of a form of appraisal for newly appointed assistant recorders and deputy district judges, although it remains to be seen what format this will take and whether it will comply with standard equal opportunities requirements.[32]

Even if the present system of consultations is maintained, the least that should be done is for those being consulted to be informed of the available research and literature on the difficulties inherent in making such assessments. Accordingly, the EOC has recommended that, at a minimum, equal opportunities training be given to those engaged in the consultation process so that they may be made more aware of their possible stereotypical attitudes.[33] Similarly, the AWB has criticised the fact that the senior judiciary were not briefed on the findings of the 1992 research commissioned by the LCD and Bar Council which raised so many concerns regarding judicial and QC appointments.[34]

The AWB also recommends that applicants be given clear written reasons why their application for judicial office has been rejected.[35] The Judicial Appointments Division of the LCD does give feedback on applications if requested, but this is not the same as formal written reasons for rejection,

---

30 As suggested by Kennedy, H, *Eve was Framed*, 1992, London: Chatto & Windus, p 268.
31 *Op cit*, fn 19, Home Affairs Select Committee on Judicial Appointments Procedures, p 211.
32 Lord Chancellor, speech to Minority Lawyers' Conference, 29 November 1997, reproduced in full at: http://www.open.gov.uk/lcd/speeches/minlaw.htm.
33 *Op cit*, fn 19, Home Affairs Select Committee on Judicial Appointments Procedures, p 211.
34 *Op cit*, fn 19, Home Affairs Select Committee, p 192.
35 *Op cit*, fn 19, Home Affairs Select Committee, p 191.

matched to the selection criteria and job description, and which can form the basis for challenge. In 1997, the Lord Chancellor announced that he was looking into the possibility of appointing an ombudsperson to investigate complaints from failed applicants.[36] Depending on the powers given to the holder of the office, such as access to confidential documents, ability to publish findings and disciplinary powers, this would be a welcome move.

Many of these reforms, however necessary, would not ultimately exert any significant change on the process of appointing judges. Accordingly, more fundamental change has been on the political agenda for many years. On a number of occasions in Opposition, the Lord Chancellor, Lord Irvine, committed the Labour Party to a 'radical overhaul of the system for appointing judges', including a judicial appointments system with a strong lay element.[37] Lord Irvine said: 'I do not believe that the present system of appointment guarantees that all deserving candidates will be identified and considered.'[38] Lord Irvine has now reneged on his pledge, and has declared that a Judicial Appointments Commission (JAC) is not a priority and that the system of secret soundings works well.

Reform is, however, needed and a JAC would represent a positive step in the right direction. The role, composition, duties and efficacy of a JAC have been debated at great length, and detailed plans have been promulgated by many organisations.[39] All proposals vary in the exact role given to a JAC, from simply recommending appointments to the Lord Chancellor, to making the appointments itself (my preferred option). In addition, there is great variety as to the possible composition of a JAC, with a lay element common in most proposals.[40] Further scope for variation can be found in the methods of selection to be used. The organisation Justice has advocated the use of selection boards, akin to those used for the civil service; the Law Society maintaining that consultation with senior members of the judiciary should remain a feature of any appointments process.[41] Finally, the criteria to be used in making recommendations or selections is open to debate, and the concerns raised over the nature of the criteria for existing judicial appointments must be borne in mind.

Whatever the format of a JAC, the criticisms of the present system are sufficiently incriminating that the advantages of such a commission are

---

36 (1997) *The Lawyer*, 14 October.

37 Lord Irvine, quoted in Dyer, C, 'Women QCs "enjoy reverse bias"' (1996) *The Guardian*, 30 September. See, also, Lord Irvine, 'The legal system and law reform under Labour', in Bean, D (ed), *Law Reform for All*, 1996, London: Blackstone, p 4.

38 Quoted in Gibb, F, 'Labour promises to bear down hard on legal aid costs' (1996) *The Times*, 30 September.

39 Eg, Justice, *The Judiciary in England and Wales*, 1992, London: Justice.

40 House of Commons Home Affairs Committee, *Third Report of Session 1995–96, Judicial Appointments Procedures*, Vol I, paras 133–36.

41 *Ibid*, para 135–36.

considerable. First, by including a lay element in the decision making process, less reliance would be placed on the views of the existing judiciary and legal profession, perhaps reducing the potentially discriminatory habit of appointment in one's own mould, what has been described as 'cloning'.[42] Secondly, the lay element may provide the opportunity for more women to participate in the appointments process. Thirdly, it would ensure that the process was transparent, open to all and accountable to the public. Fourthly, it would reduce the role of the executive by taking judicial appointments away from the total control of the Lord Chancellor or Prime Minister. This would help limit the potential for political interference with the appointment of the judiciary, especially regarding senior appointments. Taken together, these factors may, in time, lead to the appointment of a more diverse judiciary. Ultimately, although reform of the judicial appointments process is required, it must also be recognised that the composition of the judiciary depends on the recruitment policies, as well as the culture and ethos of the legal profession as a whole. Action therefore needs to be taken within the profession to ensure that women lawyers are able to pursue their career choices in an environment free of discrimination. Only then will significant numbers of women reach positions of seniority enabling their elevation to the Bench.

WILL WOMEN JUDGES MAKE A DIFFERENCE?

Having considered the exclusion of women from the judiciary and what reforms may be necessary to begin to effect some change and increase the number of women judges, it is appropriate to consider the impact, if any, of a greater representation of women in the judiciary. This analysis can be broken down into two principal themes. The first relates to the possible impact of increasing numbers of women judges on the legal profession. This discussion focuses in particular on the impact of women judges in role model and mentoring capacities and on perceptions of women in authority. It will be argued that, in this area, the most appreciable differences in the short term might be determined. Drawing on the claims by feminist scholars that women and men reason in a different 'voice', the second theme considers the impact of gender on the nature of judging and the content of the law. It will be argued that a more diverse judiciary, including more women, can begin to effect change as a result of social experience, rather than biologically determined characteristics.

---

42 *Op cit*, fn 30, Kennedy, p 267.

Women changing the legal profession: the impact of women in authority

The composition of the legal profession has changed dramatically in recent years, such that women now comprise equal numbers of entrants to the solicitors' profession and almost equal numbers to the Bar. This is a phenomenon which is replicated throughout the common law jurisdictions and has occasioned much commentary on whether or not this increasing number of women lawyers will alter not just the composition but also the nature of the legal profession to any appreciable extent. The particular focus for this debate has been the work of Carol Gilligan who suggested that men reason from rational, abstract principles or rules, while women are more likely to reason from a care perspective that relies on notions of responsibility, human connection and care.[43] Applying this theory to the legal profession, Carrie Menkel-Meadow has argued that women lawyers may adopt less confrontational, more mediational, approaches to dispute resolution,[44] and that women will be more sensitive to clients' needs and the interests of those who are in relation to each other, for example, clients' families or employees.[45] The application of Gilligan's theory to the large scale entry of women into the legal profession suggests a considerable change in the nature of lawyering.

Gilligan's theory, and its application to the legal profession, has occasioned considerable debate, with many challenging its apparent assignation of certain biologically determined characteristics to women and men. For example, Catharine MacKinnon has argued that for women to 'affirm difference, when difference means dominance, as it does with gender, means to affirm the qualities and characteristics of powerlessness'.[46] In other words, the very characteristics which are said to be feminine are those which are least valued in society. MacKinnon continues that these attributes which Gilligan suggests are female are in fact those which 'male supremacy has attributed to us for its own use'.[47] The difficulty with both Gilligan's theory, and MacKinnon's repost, is that both suggest an essentialism about women. Gilligan adverts to the possibility of being able to attribute characteristics and styles of reasoning to women and men; MacKinnon seeks to persuade us that

---

43   Gilligan, C, *In a Different Voice*, 1982, Harvard: Harvard UP.

44   See, also, Freye, J, 'Women litigators in search of a care-orientated judicial system' (1995) 4 Journal of Gender and the Law 199.

45   Menkel-Meadow, C, 'Portia redux: another look at gender, feminism and legal ethics', in Parker, S and Sampford, C (eds), *Legal Ethics and Legal Practice: Contemporary Issues*, 1995, Oxford: Clarendon, pp 25–56; and Menkel-Meadown, C, 'Portia in a different voice: speculations on a women's lawyering process' (1985) 1 Berkeley Women's Law Journal 39.

46   MacKinnon, CA, *Feminism Unmodified: Discourses on Life and Law*, 1997, London: Harvard UP, pp 38–39.

47   *Ibid*.

none of these characteristics are distinctly female but are imposed by an overweening male supremacy.

The picture is of course more complex.[48] Thus, Sandra Day O'Connor, the first woman to be appointed to the US Supreme Court, has argued that the reliance on Gilliganesque arguments to strengthen the representation of women has considerable drawbacks.[49] O'Connor argues that, just as women are beginning to achieve successes in the legal profession, they are faced with arguments, 'albeit feminist in intention', about how they are so very different from men lawyers and judges.[50] In suggesting that these debates 'recall the old myths we have struggled to put behind us', O'Connor is referring to the jurisprudence of the turn of the century when women were refused access to the courts and to the legal profession on the basis of their different characteristics.[51] In other words, difference has, and will be, used as a means by which to resist the acceptance of women into the legal profession and judiciary.

But difference does need to be recognised. The one relevant difference between women and men lawyers and judges, in the view of O'Connor, is the fact that some women become pregnant, thereby necessitating some time away from the workplace.[52] As a result of this, many women face a glass ceiling, or are sidelined into 'mommy track' jobs. Thus, O'Connor argues, women need to be treated differently to the extent that account must be taken of pregnancy, in terms of leave and pay, but that does not mean that *all* women are different from *all* men in the manner in which they perform their professional obligations. In other words, she is suggesting that, except for the biological capacity to give birth, women and men carry out their professional functions in exactly the same way. Thus, women who do not have children, or who are not acting in any caring capacity, are lawyers the same as men.

However, in seeking to reject any suggestions of difference, O'Connor's argument obscures the impact which larger numbers of women lawyers and judges may yet have on the profession. Greater numbers of women in positions of authority in the law will impact on the ways in which the relationship between women and legal authority is conceived. This chapter has already considered how women are often seen as less authoritative than

---

48 See, further, Carol Smart's discussion of both Gilligan and MacKinnon in *Feminism and the Power of Law*, 1989, London: Routledge, pp 72–89.

49 O'Connor, S, 'Portia's progress' (1991) 66 New York UL Rev 1546.

50 *Ibid*, p 1553.

51 The dominance of the 'separate spheres' theory, that women's skills were in childbearing, rearing and homemaking, while the skills of men were best tested in the public sphere, was the basis for resisting women's attempts to qualify as lawyers. See, further, Sachs, A and Hoff Wilson, J, *Sexism and the Law: A Study of Male Beliefs and Judicial Bias*, 1978, Oxford: Martin Robertson.

52 *Ibid*, O'Connor, a point echoed by Mrs Justice Arden at the 1998 Woman Lawyer Conference, see Gibb, F, 'Sexual bias is still a problem, says a Bar pupil' (1998) *The Times*, 27 April.

men, and therefore less suited to judicial office. One possible reason for this may be found in the traditional conceptualisation of the notion of authority. Kathleen Jones argues that traditionally the concept of authority has been counterposed to the idea of compassion.[53] This dichotomy between authority and compassion is seen as mimicking the differences between men and women: men are authoritative, women compassionate. Thus, Jones argues that 'the dichotomy between compassion and authority contributes to the association of the authoritative with the male voice, [with] the implication ... that the segregation of women and the feminine from authority is internally connected to the concept of authority itself'.[54] Jones therefore argues that transcending this apparent disjuncture between women and authority requires a reconceptualisation of authority. Her suggested reconceptualisation is examined further below, but, for now, it is valuable to reflect on her interpretation of authority.

The very presence of more women judges, and not just a reconceptualisation of authority, will have an impact on understandings of women and authority. The judge is the quintessential authoritative legal figure and women taking on this mantle are able to assume similar authority. The difficulty has been in ensuring that women are seen as sufficiently authoritative to be able to take on that task. Having become judges, and associated with authority thereby, authoritative women become less of an oxymoron, and more conceivable. Thus, in time, the traditional concept of authority itself will come under strain as women are associated more and more with authority.

This will impact on many other aspects of the legal profession. First, for law students and lawyers, the conjunction of masculinity and judicial authority may presently lead to certain assumptions about the appropriate career patterns for women and men in the profession. Thus, an increasing number of women in the judiciary may make appointment thereto a more common aspiration. Furthermore, as Suzanna Sherry has argued, the mere fact that women are judges has an educative function: 'it helps to shatter stereotypes about the role of women in society that are held by male judges and lawyers, as well as by litigants, jurors and witnesses.'[55] It has also been suggested that women advocates appearing before women judges, as opposed to some men judges, find the experience liberating, as they are not seen as 'out of place' and having to justify their presence.[56] Thus, as more women become judges, it may be that the performance of many women advocates improves,

---

53 Jones, K, 'On authority: or, why women are not entitled to speak', in Pennock, JR and Chapman, J (eds), *Authority Revisited*, 1987, London: New York UP, p 152.

54 *Ibid*.

55 Sherry, S, 'The gender of judges' (1986) 4 Law and Inequality 159, p 160.

56 Martin, D, 'Have women judges really made a difference?' (1986) 6 Lawyers Weekly 5.

released from the stereotyping and denigration of many courtrooms, with the consequent effect of them being more successful in their career. Finally, greater numbers of women judges may in turn occasion the appointment of further women judges. As argued above, research commissioned by the LCD and Bar Council suggested that the secrecy of the judicial selection system, the lack of information about criteria, the possible experience of discrimination and patronising treatment from male judges who will determine selection and a professional culture which condones stereotypical and discriminatory remarks, all conspire against women considering themselves for judicial office.[57] A greater number of senior women, particularly women judges, could help, in an informal mentoring capacity, to reduce the dominance of some of these negative impulses. In addition, as women fashion change, in terms of being consulted as part of the appointments process, perhaps they too will fashion change in their own image.

Thus, as argued further below, a greater participation of women in the judiciary may indeed make a difference to our understandings of judging and the legal profession, but this is not likely to come from an essentialist vision of what constitutes uniquely female characteristics, or by rejecting any sense of difference for fear of dominance. The changes to our understandings of judging and the legal profession will come from the fact that because of the way our society has been constructed, many women will bring to their judging very different life experiences and perspectives to the present male dominated judiciary. In particular, the argument is that a more diverse judiciary, meaning not just more women, but also a greater representation of many presently excluded groups, will approach judging in a greater variety of styles, bringing different experiences and perspectives to bear on their roles.

Judgments and gender

In addition to the effects which a greater number of women judges may have on the legal profession as a whole, it is important to consider the role of women judges in relation to their primary activity, that is judging. In other words, will women judges alter the nature of judging, will they judge in ways which are different to men judges and will this have an impact on the content and nature of the law? Such deeply complex questions cannot be answered within the confines of this chapter and the following section will therefore attempt only to sketch some possible responses to these questions.

It has long been argued, most famously by JAG Griffith, that various characteristics such as class, religion, place and type of education, and race

---

57   *Op cit*, fn 9, TMS Consultants, p 24.

have considerable effects on the nature and content of judgments.[58] In particular, Griffith argues that as a result of the background of the judges, there is a 'unifying attitude of mind, a political position, which is primarily concerned to protect and conserve certain values and institutions'.[59] Thus, he argues that the composition of the judiciary does have a particular effect on the content of the law that is produced from the activity of judging. In a similar vein, the organisation Labour Research recently examined the background of the most senior judges, claiming that 'in some areas, the judiciary is more of an elite than 10 years ago', and that this has important consequences for the future of human rights protection.[60] Again, it is being suggested that, because the judiciary is drawn mainly from a particular background, it will determine the outcome of cases in particular ways.

It certainly appears possible that gender may be one aspect of an individual's identity which will affect the performance of his or her judicial functions. Accordingly, numerous studies in the US have been carried out seeking to discover any gender differences in judgments.[61] Despite the dubiety of some of the research methods – how is it decided whether a judgment is given on the basis of gender or some other factor? – it has been suggested that Justice Sandra Day O'Connor of the US Supreme Court dispenses justice with a uniquely feminine jurisprudence which emphasises 'connection, subjectivity, and responsibility', rather than the 'male' concentration on 'autonomy, objectivity and rights'.[62] Similarly, Mona Harrington has argued that, in particular areas of the law, for example, violence against women and sexual harassment, it is 'demonstrably true that women judges ... have brought a markedly different focus to laws applying specifically to women'.[63] However, many others have found 'few, if any, consistent, and statistically demonstrable differences among judges based on gender'.[64]

This debate returns again to questions of what it means to be female, and whether it is possible to say that women reason in a manner which is different to men. Thus, Gilligan's theory of the different reasoning styles of women and men has been employed as reference point for this debate. Her work has informed that of others, such as Robin West, who has sought to construct a

---

58 *Op cit*, fn 4, Griffith.

59 *Op cit*, fn 4, Griffith, p 7.

60 Labour Research, 'Judging from on high' (1997) 86(7) Labour Research 13.

61 See, eg, Aliotta, J, 'Justice O'Connor and the equal protection clause: a feminine voice?' (1995) 78 Judicature 232.

62 Sherry, S, 'Civil virtue and the feminine voice of constitutional adjudication' (1986) 72 Vanderbilt L Rev 543, p 593.

63 Harrington, M, *Women Lawyers – Rewriting the Rules*, 1993, London: Plume-Penguin, p 176.

64 *Ibid*, Aliotta, p 235.

distinctively female jurisprudence based on women's difference from men.[65] West asserts that 'perhaps the central insight of feminist theory of the last decade has been that women are "essentially connected", not "essentially separate" from the rest of human life, both materially, through pregnancy, intercourse [and] breast-feeding'.[66] In other words, men are autonomous beings who experience dissociation with others, who are separate from others, and that this affects their reasoning. So too, as women are connected to others, through various experiences, is their reasoning affected.

The difficulty here, as discussed in relation to the legal profession above, is that of determining what constitutes a female way of judging and what is male. If it is suggested that all women reason in a manner which is different to all men, then it can indeed be seen that a greater number of women in the judiciary would make a considerable difference. However, such a view of women and men belies the reality of the differences between women and in doing so the voices and experiences of some are privileged over others. Angela Harris warns of the dangers of this form of 'gender essentialism' in which, by seeking to distil a 'women's experience' or 'feminism', many different voices of women are ignored.[67] The argument that women have 'different characteristics' to men is too deterministic and assumes that 'women' as a group form an undifferentiated homogenous category according to which all women think the same, have the same experiences and act in the same way. Further, it implies that 'women's' experiences can be described independently of race, class, sexual orientation and other realities of experience. What is essential, Harris argues, is to move away from univocal to mulitvocal theories of women's experiences.[68]

Indeed, it can be seen from West's writing that her examples of connection, for example breast-feeding and sexual intercourse, are not essential to all women, but the experience of some. Similarly, Angela Harris has argued that the experiences of some black women, for example, are 'entirely absent' from West's work.[69] She argues further that seeking to extract an essential female voice from the multiplicity of women's experiences is dangerous, as it privileges certain voices, and also renders the essential voice as different to the (white) male norm, reinforcing that as the reference point, rather than subverting it.[70] Feminists must therefore recognise a 'multiplicity

---

65 See West, R, 'Women's hedonic lives: a phenomenological critique of feminist legal theory' (1987) 3 Wisconsin Women's LJ 81; and 'Jurisprudence and gender' (1988) 55 Chicago UL Rev 1.

66 *Ibid*, West, 1988, p 3.

67 Harris, A, 'Race and essentialism in feminist legal theory' (1990) 42 Stan L Rev 581, p 587. In particular, she focuses her critique on the work of MacKinnon and West.

68 *Ibid*.

69 *Ibid*, p 603.

70 *Ibid*, p 615.

of standpoints, of different versions and visions'.[71] In a similar vein, Regina Graycar has argued that it is important to remember the differences between women such that it may be that 'women judges in Australia have more in common with their white, male counterparts than they have with women who are sole parents living on social security, or rural Aboriginal women, or immigrant women doing piece work'.[72]

Thus, considering sex as the primary referent for decision making is too simplistic. However, it may be that, in the experiences of a person's life and, in particular, the ways in which society constructs particular gender identities, numbers of women judges may make some differences. For example, Regina Graycar has explored how judges resort to what they consider to be 'common sense' when making judgments and that such understandings of what constitutes 'common sense' are often gendered. She gives many examples such as the comment by the Australian Judge Bland: 'it does happen, in the common experience of those who have been in the law as long as I have anyway, that no often subsequently means yes.'[73] Similarly, in the context of a damages claim, a male judge commented that 'the sharing of domestic burdens with the wife is expected of the husband, even where his wife is perfectly healthy'.[74] Judges use their knowledge and understanding of the world, however simplistic and anecdotal, as in the last examples, to construct the common sense approach to factual questions before them. The construction of this common sense approach involves the application of often gendered assumptions about women and men. A more diverse judiciary, including more women, will begin to change the understandings of what constitutes 'common sense', and what perspectives inform the law, by drawing on different perspectives and assumptions.

However, gender should be seen as one factor amongst many which will affect the judgment of judges. A whole manner of perspectives, experiences and views are brought to bear on the processes of reaching decisions. Simone de Beauvoir observed that 'it is impossible to approach any human problem with a mind free from bias'.[75] Inevitably, therefore, every 'decision maker who walks into a courtroom to hear a case is armed not only with the relevant legal texts, but with a set of values, experiences and assumptions that are thoroughly embedded'.[76]

---

71 O'Donovan, K, 'Engendering justice: women's perspectives and the rule of law' (1989) 39 Toronto ULJ 127, p 134.

72 Graycar, R, 'The gender of judgments: an introduction', in Thornton, M (ed), *Public and Private – Feminist Legal Debates*, 1995, Oxford: OUP, pp 265–66.

73 Quoted *ibid*, p 270.

74 *Ibid*.

75 de Beauvoir, S, *The Second Sex*, 1953, Parshley, HM (trans), London: Penguin, p xxxii.

76 Abella, R, 'The concept of an independent judiciary', in Martin, S and Mahoney, K (eds), *Equality and Judicial Neutrality*, 1987, Toronto: Carswell, pp 8–9.

Accordingly, a judiciary which is drawn from a wider range of sexes, backgrounds and ethnicities will bring different experiences to bear on its judgments. Some women, especially as they come through the legal system at present, will often have quite different experiences to their male colleagues, whilst others will have markedly similar approaches to male colleagues.[77] The presence of those who are 'other' 'might alter the institution's character, introducing a different prism and perspective'.[78] In conclusion, therefore, from an outsider perspective, whether it is black, female, gay or lesbian, or some other perspective or identity, a judge may take 'information from the margin to transform how we think about the whole'.[79] As Canadian Supreme Court Judge Justice Bertha Wilson points out, it would be a '[p]yrrhic victory for women and the justice system as a whole if changes in the law come only through the efforts of women lawyers and women judges'.[80] Similarly, US Supreme Court Judge Ruth Bader Ginsburg has argued that a 'system of justice is richer for diversity of background and experience. It is poorer in terms of appreciating what is at stake and the impact of its judgments, if all its members – its lawyers, jurors and judges – are cast from the same mold.'[81]

However, an acknowledgment of the different contexts and perspectives which judges bring to the Bench has resulted in many claims of bias being brought against judges who do not conform to the expected persona of the judge, that is, who are not male and white. As Alison Harvison Young notes, 'it is not coincidental that, at a time when the number of women in the profession and on the Bench has been growing, the concept of bias has begun to show signs of strain ... in its application to judges'.[82] The particular case to which Young draws attention is *RDS v The Queen* in which the judgment of a woman judge of colour, Judge Sparks, was challenged on the grounds that her judgment gave rise to a reasonable apprehension of bias.[83] The case involved a clash of evidence between a police officer who alleged that a black man deliberately ran into him on his bicycle when the officer was trying to arrest another. The arrested man denied the charge. The judge in the case supported

---

77   Although this may not always be the case and may not affect every area of law. Eg, Tobias has noted that the women appointed during the Reagan/Bush presidencies in the US were uniformly 'conservative' in their political outlook. Tobias argues, however, that in certain areas, such as discrimination law, the existence of more women judges will make a difference, despite the conservative tendencies of some: Tobias, C, 'Closing the gender gap on the Federal Courts' (1993) 61 Cincinnati L Rev 1237.

78   Guinier, L, 'Of gentlemen and role models' (1990–91) 6 Berkeley Women's LJ 93, p 99.

79   bell hooks, quoted in Dalton, H, 'The clouded prism' (1987) 22 Harvard Civil-Rights Civil-Liberties L Rev 435, p 444.

80   Wilson, B, 'Will women judges really make a difference?' (1990) 28 Osgoode Hall LJ 507, p 516.

81   Ginsburg, R, 'Remarks for California women lawyers' (1994) 22 Pepperdine L Rev 1.

82   Young, AH, 'Feminism, pluralism and administrative law', in Taggart, M (ed), *The Province of Administrative Law*, 1997, Oxford: Hart, p 344.

83   (1995) 145 NSR (2d) 284.

the testimony of the defendant remarking that the police officer may have overreacted, as officers do, 'particularly when they're dealing with non-white groups'.[84]

The Supreme Court of Canada upheld the judgment of Judge Sparks, L'Heureux-Dube and McLachlin JJ holding that the judge was 'simply engaging in the process of contextualised judging which, in our view, was entirely proper and conducive to a fair and reasonable resolution of the case before her.'[85] Moreover, this mode of 'contextualised judging' is 'not in conflict with the requirement of neutrality which does not require judges to discount their life experiences'. Young states that this case is important as it 'underlines the inescapable fact that Judge Sparks' "baggage" is clearly not the same "baggage" as that carried by predominantly white male judges of the past who have developed the standards of impartiality and objectivity'.[86]

A further example is the case in which a Melbourne solicitor sought judicial review of a planning tribunal decision on the grounds that a tribunal member, five months pregnant at the time of her decision, 'suffered from the well known medical condition "placidity" which detracts significantly from the intellectual competence of all mothers to be'.[87] The challenge was not upheld. This case relied not on the particular experiences, or 'baggage' of the woman judge, but was based solely on her physical condition of pregnancy. Thus, although not strictly a challenge of bias, rather, incapacity, it emphasises the fact that a woman may be challenged not only where she employs her understandings and perspectives to a case, but also on the ground of her biological sex. It also underlines the extent to which the status quo is seen as apolitical. There are no cases in which a challenge has been made to a judge, or other decision maker, on the basis that he was white, male and this had impaired his decision making ability.[88]

Young suggests that we need to move beyond the dichotomy of 'baggage' informing judgment, or the tradition of supposed neutral objectivity. She advocates a more 'discursive' style of judging in which the standpoint of others is taken into account.[89] She suggests that, if the community of judges were more diverse, the comments of Judge Sparks would have not been so deserving of comment. Young concludes by suggesting that the presence of more female judges has not 'revolutionised' the judging or the law, but they are 'expanding the discourse'.[90]

---

84   *R v RDS* Y093–168, 68–69.

85   [1997] 3 SCR 484, para 59.

86   *Op cit*, fn 82, Young, p 346.

87   See Naylor, B, 'Pregnant tribunals' (1989) 14 Legal Service Bulletin 41.

88   *Op cit*, fn 72, Graycar, p 267.

89   *Op cit*, fn 82, Young, p 349.

90   *Ibid*, pp 332, 350. In particular, by adding to the number and variety of dissenting judgments.

In some ways, this suggestion may echo the suggestion of Kathleen Jones that a reconceptualisation of what constitutes authority is needed. It will be recalled that Jones deconstructed the traditional understandings of authority to reveal that it tends to assume a dichotomy between authority and compassion, with the feminine sphere being associated with compassion. In moving beyond this dichotomy, Jones argues for a connection between compassion and authority. Jones quotes William Connolly, who argues that the order which authority imposes 'does not correspond to the world in all its complexities', but that compassion can help 'that which is subordinate to find its own voice'.[91] Jones argues for a concept of compassionate authority which recognises private feelings: compassion has the potential for humanising authority.[92] If women do not speak with authority, Jones argues, 'perhaps their hesitancy reveals the ambiguity, and the choices, behind all rules systems. By reminding us of this ambiguity, the voice and gesture of compassion shocks us into a memory of what has been hidden by the ordered discourse of authority'.[93]

Although not speaking about judging, it is suggested that Jones' conceptualisation of authority and call for compassionate authority has much to lend to a discussion of the role and difference of women judges. If women judges are being seen to bring their gendered 'baggage' to their judgments, perhaps it is because they are bringing compassion, or complexity, or just different life experiences. As Jones notes, their hesitancy, or compassion, may be reminding us of the context and humanity that has been lacking and perhaps it is women who will bring this and begin to bring about a changed perception of what constitutes judging.

CONCLUSIONS

It is undoubtedly the case that progress towards a more diverse and open judiciary is being made. Reforms are being implemented, and more women and lawyers from ethnic minorities are being appointed. This must raise the public's confidence in, and perceived legitimacy of, the legal process. However, in this process, the UK lags far behind other common law jurisdictions. For example, in North America, where more open and publicly accountable appointments procedures have been the norm for many years, women are appointed to the Bench in considerable numbers.[94] Further

---

91 Connolly, W, 'Modern authority and ambiguity', 1984, Amherst: University of Massachusetts, unpublished manuscript, p 21, quoted in *op cit*, fn 82, Young, p 165.

92 *Ibid*, p 165.

93 *Ibid*, pp 165–66.

94 See, eg, Malleson, K, *The Use of Judicial Appointments Commissions: A Review of the US and Canadian Models*, 1997, Research Series No 6/97, London: LCD; and Ginsburg, R and Brill, L, 'Women in the Federal judiciary' (1995) 64 Fordham L Rev 281.

reforms are therefore necessary to ensure that the judiciary is open to a much broader cross-section of the legal profession. It is essential that progress is made towards a more diverse judiciary, and this is particularly so at a time when the judiciary takes on the role of interpreting the European Convention on Human Rights.[95] The inevitable increase in the public's interest in the composition of the judiciary, as it determines human rights disputes, will ensure that it becomes imperative that the judiciary is more representative of society as a whole.

---

95   See Millns, Chapter 9, this volume.

CHAPTER 6

DICEY DISSECTED:
DOMINANT, DORMANT, DISPLACED

Angus McDonald

INTRODUCTION

This chapter attempts a dissection of the body of theory produced by AV Dicey, and the later work of others influenced by or responding to his legacy. It also proposes a new possible appropriation of Dicey to postmodern and feminist ends. There are three stages to the argument. At each stage, the implications for feminist considerations of Dicey are indicated. First, the tradition within which Dicey is dominant is labelled the 'constitutional law' position. Here, the legacy is explored in terms of a specific way of defining constitutional law that seemingly excludes politics. The persistence of this tradition in the undergraduate constitutional law textbook is highlighted, as is the difficulty of specifying a feminist response to Dicey. Secondly, the tradition within which Dicey is dormant is identified as the 'public law' position. This contemporary reaction against Dicey in the name of the modernising public law project in the UK is examined, and the feminist position within the public law paradigm is stated. Thirdly, the possibility of an approach to Dicey in which his influence is neither dominant nor dormant but *displaced* is proposed. This postmodern approach to the constitution is introduced with a comment on the reframing of Dicey's relevance which this allows – and the integration of a feminist perspective which it demands. An encounter between Dicey and feminism is thus made possible.

DICEY'S LEGACY

Dicey's current status is ambiguous. Academia loves an anniversary, and the century since the first publication of Dicey's work, *An Introduction to the Study of the Law of the Constitution*, in 1885,[1] was duly noted. However, the content of the recognition was not always celebratory. It appeared as if many came 'not

---

1   Dicey, AV, *An Introduction to the Study of the Law of the Constitution*, 10th edn, 1967, London: Macmillan (hereafter referred to as *The Law of the Constitution*). Dicey authored eight editions between 1885 and 1915. ECS Wade produced further editions with his own introduction in 1939 and 1959. Dicey's centenary was marked by Jowell, J and Oliver, D (eds), *The Changing Constitution*, 2nd edn, 1989, Oxford: Clarendon.

to praise Dicey but to bury him'. From the perspective of many in the critical camp, Dicey was always the enemy anyway. More than a decade on from the centenary, I wish to remember Dicey once more, as I perceive an unexpected new relevance in his analysis.

If Dicey remains influential, what does his name mark? His reputation is forever associated with three claims, corresponding to the three parts of *The Law of the Constitution*. The claims concern the sovereignty of parliament, the rule of law and the connection between the law and the conventions of the constitution. A presentation of these claims continues to serve as the aperitif to many a course and many a textbook on the constitution. At the heart of Dicey's perspective is this claim: the virtue of the English constitution[2] lies in the assertion that no one is above the law. Dicey means by this, in particular, that no civil servant or government minister is above the law, that officials of the state are subject to the same ordinary law of the land as everyone else. He focuses on the absence of a distinct system of administrative law, by contrast with the French system, as exemplifying the peculiar genius of the English approach.[3]

What has happened to this claim in the intervening century? Undergraduate courses and textbooks are often titled 'Constitutional *and Administrative* Law', and this split more than anything else undermines Dicey. While the constitutional law part of the course or book will utilise Dicey's categories in order to dispel the claim that there is no such thing as a constitution in England, the administrative law part will have to start with a disavowal of the Diceyan stance that there is no such thing as administrative law in England.

Similarly, Dicey's claim that no person is above the law requires two assertions. First, that there is a law of the constitution in England, but that its special character is that it is ordinary law, not law of a special constitutional character. Secondly, that the same ordinary law is pervasive, and there is, therefore, no special system of administrative law. Few now share this second view. I shall focus on the first view, which says that constitutional law in England is ordinary law. This means common law, private law. What Dicey is asserting is the claim that English constitutional law (and the denial of administrative law is part of this overall claim) is not public law. Thus, Dicey stands for the view that *England has no public law*.

---

2   See Whitty, Chapter 3, this volume, for a discussion of English/British identity in public law.

3   The French have, of course, not failed to remark upon the English deception at work here, particularly given recent developments in public law: 'Il n'y a donc pas en Angleterre, tout au moins en principe, un régime juridique propre à l'action administrative. Mais en pratique, l'évolution récente a modifié cette situation en multipliant les textes qui dérogent à la *Common Law* au profit de l'administration.' Rivero, J and Waline, R, *Droit Administratif*, 17th edn, 1998, Paris: Dalloz, p 18.

The tradition that has defined itself against Dicey in the intervening years has marked its disagreement by specifying that its subject matter is not *constitutional* law but *public* law. I wish to investigate the difference between the constitutional law approach and the public law approach. To do this, I must demonstrate what happens to the *public* dimension in Dicey's *non-public* constitutional law. This requires me to read Dicey's *The Law of the Constitution* through the prism of his second major text, *Lectures on the Relation Between Law and Public Opinion in England During the Nineteenth Century*.[4]

DICEY DOMINANT: CONSTITUTIONALISM

The Dicey achievement was to recognise the challenge posed by the absence of a public constitutionality, and to rise to that challenge by theorising the adequacy of a non-public constitutionality. In the absence of a foundational and fundamental constitution, Dicey provided a theory which valorised the non-dimensionality of English constitutionality. Depth, Dicey says, is not necessary. The constitution does not require entrenchment. It does not require extraordinary legislative procedures. It does not require extraordinary courts entrusted with its protection. The constitution can be all on one level – literally, superficial. Dicey's successful attempt to fill the gap in English/UK constitutionality required an appropriate theory – let us call this theory 'constitutionalism'.

Dicey considers the relation of legal science to other disciplines and, indeed, whether there is an object for legal science to read. The title of his key book, read carefully, indicates his stance. He is *introducing* the *study* of the *law* of the *constitution*. Each term counts: each term poses a question. Is there a constitution? Does it have a law, that is, can the law of the constitution be isolated from, say, the politics of it? How can this be studied? How best to introduce such study?

To the familiar question of whether there is a constitution, Dicey observes that the law student will be disappointed if the search is directed to the institutions or the statute book, and will, of necessity, have to turn to the 'writers of authority'.[5] From the lawyers, Dicey finds only a formalism that repeats the orthodox *theory* and neglects the actual *practice* of the constitution; from the historian, only an 'antiquarianism'.[6] From the political theorists, and

---

4   Dicey, AV, *Lectures on the Relation Between Law and Public Opinion in England During the Nineteenth Century*, 1905, London: Macmillan. Coincidentally, it also allows me to mark the passing of another centenary, less celebrated than that of 1985, but just as relevant. It was in Harvard in 1898 that Dicey first delivered this series of lectures on the relation of law and public opinion, developed them at Oxford and published them in book form in 1905.

5   *Op cit*, fn 1, Dicey, p 6.

6   *Op cit*, fn 1, Dicey, p 14.

here Dicey praises Bagehot,[7] he finds a consideration of political understandings, which do not get to the heart of rules of law. He argues that the idea of public opinion is a 'very inadequate solution' to the problem of how political understandings come to be as rigorously obeyed as the commands of law.[8] At this point, Dicey squarely confronts the implication:

> Is it possible that so called 'constitutional law' is in reality a cross between history and custom which does not properly deserve the name of law at all?[9]

It is fore-ordained that this ghost is raised only to be exorcised: Dicey resolves to establish the true field of constitutional law specific to the constitutional lawyer.

He finds his solution in an answer which confronts the need to find a permanent core and banish the ephemeral: in Dicey's argument, this distinction maps onto the distinction between law (permanent) and convention (ephemeral). Therefore, the correct concern of the constitutional lawyer is with the law alone and not the conventional aspect of the constitution. This watertight distinction is precisely the one about which contemporary constitutionalists feel rather more disquiet: even the law element is proving too ephemeral for the lawyer now. It is this factor which is so corrosive of the confidence of the constitutionalist project today.

For Dicey, constitutional conventions clearly fall on the side of politics in any law/politics dichotomy, and are, therefore, of no concern to the constitutional lawyer. Dicey sustains the purity of the legal perspective by drawing a narrow cordon round the purely legal element and simply exiling, as of no interest to the lawyer, any matter tainted by politics. In effect, he makes a common analytical move. He says the subject he is concerned with, constitutional law, is in common but inaccurate usage used to refer to a broader field than its true domain, which, as an expert, he is in a position to clarify. So, we now know to expect of Dicey a positivistic presentation of laws, and this alone. But this he does not deliver. Instead, he delivers what he promises in his preface: what the student needs in order to be introduced to the study of the field. And what is needed at the outset is a *theory*. Dicey expunges conventions, turns his attention to laws alone, and then delivers:

> ... two or three guiding principles which pervade the modern constitution of England[;] ... leading principles [which may] enable [students] to study with benefit ... those legal topics, which, taken together, make up the constitutional law of England.[10]

What Dicey provides, then, are the principles by which constitutionality can achieve a coherence; or, in other words, the doctrine of constitutionalism

---

7   Bagehot, W, *The English Constitution*, 1963, London: Fontana. First published in 1867.
8   *Op cit*, fn 1, Dicey, p 21.
9   *Op cit*, fn 1, Dicey, p 22.
10   *Op cit*, fn 1, Dicey, p v.

which must be present in the mind-set of the constitutional lawyer in order for the existence of constitutional law to be perceived. This distinction between Dicey's exposition of principle, and the too theoretical formalism of which he accused lawyers in relation to the constitution might seem a fine one. But Dicey is confident that whereas, for example, Blackstone's 'habit of applying old and inapplicable terms to new institutions' 'has but one fault; the statements it contains are the direct opposite of the truth',[11] this does not apply to his own fresh formulation of principle.

What Dicey does, therefore, is announce the decline of the old ideas which formerly animated the institutions of constitutional law, those now formalistic ideas of Blackstone's, the venerable principles. But he then proceeds to announce a set of contemporary principles which he claims truly animates the reality of the constitution now, at the time of his writing. While Dicey recognises the redundancy of the old legal perspective, and considers whether the field now belongs to other disciplines, he eventually concludes that a legal perspective animated by new guiding ideas is valid.

DICEY AND PUBLIC OPINION

As highlighted above, Dicey did not only write the book that became the cornerstone of orthodox constitutionalism in the UK. Despite his apparent dismissal of Bagehot's claim of the explanatory value of the notion of public opinion, he also wrote an equally substantial, though now less discussed, text: *Lectures on the Relation Between Law and Public Opinion in England During the Nineteenth Century*.[12] In this section, I will highlight how Dicey's evacuation of the public from his theory of constitutionalism becomes the device for neutralising a public (and, in Dicey's eyes, threatening) democratic politics.

For Dicey, the relationship between law and public opinion starts from the crucial observation of Hume, that:

> As force is always on the side of the governed, the governors have nothing to support them but opinion. It is, therefore, on opinion only that government is founded.[13]

Dicey seeks to apply this insight to 19th century England. Hume's starting point neatly summarises the opinion-politics and power-politics dichotomy found in Dicey's work, and sides with opinion-politics as the true source of stability. In this, he is clear that the ruler could be overthrown at any moment by the superior strength of the masses, and so the crucial question of

---

11 *Op cit*, fn 1, Dicey, pp 7, 8–9.
12 *Op cit*, fn 4, Dicey.
13 *Op cit*, fn 4, p 2.

sustaining the loyalty of the masses is the key question for the rulers.[14] The pessimistic interpretation of this relation is to remind rulers that the power to overthrow them is *always* present as potential and cannot be wished away. The rulers should therefore focus their activities on making sure that the will to use this power, or even better, the knowledge that this power is in their hands, is kept from the people.

Dicey modifies the Humean view in four crucial ways. First, he specifies that public opinion – meaning 'speculative views held by the mass of the people as to the alteration or improvement of their institutions'[15] – is not present in every society. In societies where habit and custom, tradition and instinct, are the dominant forces, there is no public opinion in the Western sense. This gives public opinion a rationalist and Enlightenment shade: it is self-critique, the ability to put into question values, and the exercise of critical judgment. However, Dicey immediately backtracks on the implications of this. Public opinion may fail to be truly public – it may simply be the convictions held by a small, powerful group. He allows that this would still do the work of the idea of public opinion, while failing to be anything more than elite opinion. So, public opinion as an idea implies mass participation, but the absence of the latter does not prevent the function of public opinion being performed in a non-public manner.

Secondly, public opinion may fail to find a site in which it can express itself, and unexpressed public opinion is no public opinion at all. So, it needs an institution, such as a Parliament, in which it can find its voice. These two modifications, while important, are not reservations concerning the concept, but the conditions in which it will flourish. However, the two further qualifications do substantially restrict the notion of public opinion.

Thirdly, Dicey's concept of public opinion is clearly not that of the thinkers of the Scottish Enlightenment. Thomas Reid, who also started from Hume, does perceive public opinion as a judging faculty:

> ... the existence of a common natural base permits the formulation of common judgements which, being such, merit publicity. These judgements form a common opinion latent in all men and women; it is common but at the same time not common because it has been made public, but is public because it has been made common.[16]

This view is a democratic and universal one, an acknowledgment of a human capacity to reason, but one that has a communitarian basis, developed in dialogue with one's peers. Public opinion is the consequence of common

---

14 See the discussion of Bagehot and Plato in McDonald, A, 'The noble lie: critical constitutionalism, criticised', in Hirvonen, A (ed), *Polycentricity – The Multiple Scenes of Law*, 1998, London: Pluto, pp 61–96.

15 *Op cit*, Dicey, p 3.

16 Canel, J, 'The concept of public opinion in the Scottish Enlightenment', in Campbell, T (ed), *Law and Enlightenment in Britain*, 1990, Aberdeen: Aberdeen UP, p 123.

judgment, its medium, but not something arbitrary and contingent. This is not the view of Dicey.

For Dicey, in place of confidence in the judgment of the common mass, there is suspicion, in line with his hostility to collectivism. On the other hand, there is a confidence in the rulers:

> ... public opinion ... is a very complex phenomenon, and often takes the form of a compromise resulting from a conflict between the ideas of the government and the feelings or habits of the governed ... the legislation enacted by Parliament constantly bears traces of the compromise arrived at between enlightenment and prejudice ... The failure of Parliament during the 18th century to introduce reasonable reforms, for instance, was due far less to the prejudices of members of Parliament ... than to the deference ... paid to the dullness or stupidity of Englishmen.[17]

For Dicey, the enlightened law maker is held back by the prejudices and bigotry of the mass, whose revolt against progressive measures is to be feared. Enlightenment, a mass phenomenon for Reid, is a property of the rulers for Dicey. Public opinion has little to do with reasoning and judgment, it is merely a *datum* of which the ruler would be wise to take note. Canel's alternative definition of public opinion fits here:

> After the Enlightenment the triumph of reason gave way to the supremacy of the critical capacity of the individual and public opinion became something arbitrary. Thus, it was considered that all individual opinions are of equal value and can be left to compete against one another in the market place. The one which manages to succeed in the mass media becomes public opinion. Naturally, this concept of public opinion is conditioned by what the state allows to be made public.[18]

This clarifies the rationale of Dicey's stance. His individualism is such that the mass as mass cannot be seen as a source of reasoned judgement. Only when disaggregated into individuals, thus losing the very element of community crucial to Reid's view, can opinion be acknowledged, but this will necessarily be opinion in the market place, as Canel puts it, arbitrary and prejudiced.

Fourthly, Dicey narrows the concept of public opinion in a repetition of the analytical gesture whereby he detached constitutional law from the penumbra which he labelled convention. In relation to public opinion, he purifies the concept to the more strictly delimited notion of legislative public opinion. Opinion concerning the improvement of institutions' is narrowed down to an interest 'only with that kind of public opinion which, since it has told on the course of legislation, may with strict propriety be called law making or legislative public opinion'.[19] This legislative public opinion can be

---

17 *Op cit*, fn 4, Dicey, pp 10–11.

18 *Op cit*, fn 16, Canel, p 123.

19 *Op cit*, fn 4, Dicey, p 17.

found, without the need for wider investigation, 'in the statute book ... or in the volumes of the [court] reports'.[20]

This is a crucial claim and clearly shows how far Dicey is committed to excluding the public from his consideration. 'Public' opinion only registers where legislators or judges acknowledge it. Dicey's anti-democratic attitude is explicit here, and the exclusion, by definition, of any influence derived from a broader notion of public opinion allows him to focus on the influence of individuals instead – Blackstone, Bentham, Shaftesbury and others. Indeed, he argues that 'the advance of democracy' explains nothing in relation to the development of the law precisely because it is not possible to assume that the people are democrats.[21] Dicey, whose view on democracy is best encapsulated in his disdainful reference to it as the extension of 'the influence of mere numbers',[22] finds that ancient privilege need not fear democracy:

> Democracy in England has to a great extent inherited the traditions of the aristocratic government, of which it is the heir.[23]

Against democracy (a French disaster once again), England has a proper respect for heritage.

In a text on feminism and public law, it is important to assess the legacy of Dicey in relation to female participation in the public sphere. If 'no man is above the law' is the key claim, what of woman? Does woman figure at all in Dicey's work on public opinion? The brief answer is 'no'. A few remarks in the lecture on ecclesiastical legislation concerning marriage and divorce and a comment concerning Harriet Martineau[24] do not provide the basis for an analysis of his attitude. The absence of woman in this discourse is of course significant, but, given the absence of the public generally, the lack of substantive references to half the population is not surprising. The male half is only spectrally present, in any case. Dicey achieves this by distinguishing two usages of the word democracy (as with his distinction of political and legal sovereignty): democracy as a condition of society, which he quickly loses interest in; and as a particular kind of constitution. The second usage is then specified as follows:

> [A] constitution under which sovereign power is possessed by the numerical majority of the male citizens; and in this sense, the 'advance of democracy' means the transference of supreme power from either a single person, or from

---

20 *Op cit*, fn 4, Dicey, p 17.
21 *Op cit*, fn 4, Dicey, p 57.
22 *Op cit*, fn 4, Dicey, p 52.
23 *Op cit*, fn 4, Dicey, p 58.
24 See *op cit*, fn 4, Dicey, pp 345–46 and pp 413–16 for examples of the few occasions where 'women's issues' are explicitly addressed by Dicey. Martineau is the only woman to feature amongst Dicey's examination of important opinion formers, a category which includes Charles Dickens and John Stuart Mill. In addition to the remark on divorce, there is a discussion on married women's property rights, pp 369–93.

a privileged and limited class, to the majority of citizens; it means in short, the approach to government by numbers, or, in current, though inaccurate phraseology, by the people.[25]

The significance of the declension must be noted: numerical majority of male citizens; majority of citizens; numbers; and, 'inaccurately', the people. Acknowledgment of the absence of women disappears between definition one and definition two; acknowledgment that these are people disappears between definition two and definition three, and is negatively consolidated by definition four. Consistent with Dicey's attitude that things only become important within the constitutional arena, the numbers referred to mean votes – ballot papers. The question of who cast them is banished.

In conclusion, Dicey's position in relation to law and public opinion can be summarised briefly. Public opinion contains a volatility which makes it a danger to a stable society. It needs to be tamed and taught responsibility. To this end, the transformation of public opinion into legislative public opinion fetters the possibilities of excess by straitjacketing debate into a legal form. In this way, social demands for social change can be renegotiated as the demands of legislative public opinion for changes to laws, thus deferring indefinitely questions concerning social change with greater ambition than a new statute on the books.

The circularity Dicey confesses, whereby public opinion produces law while law produces public opinion,[26] is not seen as a defect, but as a triumph, excluding the possibility of any breach which could interrupt this *repetition of the same*. The risk that the encounter of public opinion and law brings for law, that is, the possibility of unsettling law, is more than compensated for by law's stabilising influence upon public opinion. In other words, constitutionality will institutionalise and re-present public opinion to itself. Dicey's wish to keep politics out of law turns out to be a programme for legalising politics, that is, forcing politics into a legal/constitutional form. This is not the politicisation of law, but the legislation of politics. What Dicey's constitutionalism provides is a device for innoculating us against public democratic politics.

DICEY IN THE CONSTITUTIONAL LAW TEXTBOOK

Dicey's legacy is obvious to any first year law student. Dicey succeeded in defining a legal science, and his view still passes down in an appropriately personalised lineage, along the textbook tradition. In this section, I will demonstrate the continuing influence of Dicey on mainstream constitutional

---

25 *Op cit*, fn 4, Dicey, p 52.
26 *Op cit*, fn 4, Dicey, p 41.

law scholarship, in particular, the ancestry of Bradley and Ewing's *Wade and Bradley: Constitutional and Administrative Law*.[27]

Sugarman has analysed the textbook tradition, and the particular view of legal scholarship which it assumes. In this tradition, the task of scholarship is best fulfilled by establishing the 'coherence and unity' of law, which derives from 'a handful of general principles ..., some common principles or elements which fix the boundaries of the subject'.[28] Exposition and systematisation then become the task of legal scholarship. If giving an exposition of a subject which is coherent, unified and possessed of fixed boundaries is indeed what is required, then it is not surprising that the law textbook tradition is modest in its claims for the need to theorise about its subject matter. The only 'theory' required is one which encourages an ability to bring the subject into focus and to see clearly what its core is.

In the undergraduate textbook, this tends to become a stance of 'objectivity', where, again, only a modest claim to describe is advanced and analysis is deferred or even considered superfluous. The ideal textbook, then, claims to mirror its subject matter, reflecting in its pages an object with an independent autonomous external existence, which would go on as it is with or without the textbook. What is denied is any creative role for the textbook – that it might *constitute* its field of study, that it might, for instance, bring together a variety of areas and demonstrate the hitherto disregarded links between them. All this is sustained by that first act of assuming stable and clearly bounded subject fields.

The context within which legal textbooks are produced is at best indifferent to, and, more commonly, hostile to, 'theory'.[29] Any explicit commitment to a theoretical perspective is viewed with suspicion, as a 'bias' which may skew the perspective of the textbook and diminish its value. From this perspective, there is an assumption that the theory-neutral textbook is possible, preferable and desirable. Such a book would be simply descriptive, a window onto the object of its concerns whose central virtue would be transparency. The image is of a window onto the landscape, or a map of the territory.

If, contrary to this view, the idea that the facts can speak for themselves is rejected in favour of a more mediated view which acknowledges the role of

---

27 Bradley, AW and Ewing, KD, *Wade and Bradley: Constitutional and Administrative Law*, 12th edn, 1997, Harlow: Longman.

28 Sugarman, D, '"A hatred of disorder": legal science, liberalism and imperialism', in Fitzpatrick, P (ed), *Dangerous Supplements*, 1991, London: Pluto, p 34.

29 Lloyd associates this 'hard-headed and pragmatic attitude' with the common law tradition of learning the law in a practical apprenticeship rather than by means of university study: even in the academy, he notes 'the absence of any philosophical tradition informing legal education', resulting in 'scepticism towards theory among judges, legal practitioners ... academic lawyers ... [and] the law student'. See Lloyd, D and Freeman, MDA, *Introduction to Jurisprudence*, 5th edn, 1985, London: Stevens, pp 2–3.

theory in constructing what counts as fact,[30] then we can expect *all* studies of legal phenomena, even the 'descriptive textbook', to have embedded theoretical choices and commitments built in. The theoretical stance of a book will construct not only what count as the facts, but what counts as important, what is central and what is marginal to the topic; in summary, the contours of the field of study itself. In a textbook on constitutional law, it should be possible to detect this process at work.

One of the distinctions at the heart of the enterprise of the descriptive textbook is that between the permanent features of a topic and the ephemeral features. The textbook aims to describe the permanent features of the topic, relegating the ephemeral to marginal comment if acknowledged at all. If this 'works', it can only be on the basis that the topic in question has a degree of stability and permanence. If it is too volatile, then a textbook would be impossible. The textbook must place the permanent features of the topic at the centre of its presentation, but without indicating that this is a choice of focus, which would cast doubt upon its objectivity by suggesting the possibility of another approach to the topic.

Such a reading of a textbook of constitutional law has as its purpose the discovery of how it constructs the topic of 'the constitution' as a permanent and stable object of knowledge, by way of the theoretical choices in which it invests. This is to assert that the textbook tradition is a means by which *a continuity of readings of the constitution is sustained*, and so ana analysis of it may reveal the orthodoxy in constitutional theory. Wherever else this tradition is sustained, the textbook's contribution is the site selected for analysis here. This does not give it any pre-eminent claim, but it is a useful point of departure for a critical reading, given its widespread dissemination and influence. Other critical theories of the constitution all, in one way or another, locate themselves in relation to this orthodoxy.[31]

Any textbook of constitutional law requires a theory of constitutionality to provide a set of concepts which define its subject matter, but is usually self-effacing concerning this theoretical moment, dispensing with such

---

30 This view is in accord with that of Kant, as the opening passages of the *Critique of Pure Reason* state: 'There can be no doubt that all our knowledge begins with experience .... [but] it does not follow that it all arises out of experience. For it may well be that even our empirical knowledge is made up of what we receive through impressions and of what our own faculty of knowledge ... supplies from itself.' See Kant, I, *Critique of Pure Reason*, Smith, NK (trans), 1929, London: Macmillan, pp 41–42. This contribution to knowledge made by 'our own faculty' is what is intended in the discussion by the word 'theory'.

31 Harden, I and Lewis, N, *The Noble Lie*, 1986, London: Hutchinson; Craig, PP, *Public Law and Democracy in the United Kingdom and the United States of America*, 1990, Oxford: Clarendon; Loughlin, M, *Public Law and Political Theory*, 1992, Oxford: Clarendon. The theorists considered all produce commentaries upon the mainstream tradition by way of defining the manner in which their own work departs from the constitutional law orthodoxy. Their work can be classified by contrast as the public law paradigm.

'abstraction' in the opening comments (as in Bradley and Ewing).[32] Thereafter, the textbook usually conceals its theoretical investments behind a facade of objective description of the institutions and practices which constitute its subject matter. It is to these 'theoretical' moments that critical analysis must be addressed.

Above all, the textbook seeks to convey an impression of permanence. It can theorise the constitution, because theory itself is theorised as a neutral tool necessary only as a preliminary move to bring the field of study into focus. In other words, the constitution is theorised as a relatively stable object of study, adapting to new developments, but with a core of continuity. Yet, like all textbooks, new editions are produced. It is worth asking why this might be so. If the situation is as stable as is conveyed in the tradition, why are new editions required at all? To illustrate the extent to which the aspiration to permanence fails, two consecutive editions of *Constitutional and Administrative Law* produced by AW Bradley[33] are here drawn upon: the 10th edition of 1985;[34] and the 11th edition of 1993.[35]

In the preface to the 10th edition, Bradley revealingly reflects on the impermanence of the constitutional law textbook:

> ... it is chastening to reflect on the perishable quality of most books on constitutional law. How attractive it would be to the authors of such books to create an analysis which required the minimum of revision from one decade to the next![36]

The answer to the question why this tedious work of revision is required provides an interesting insight. The first step is that the topic, the constitution, is in a state of development, and so changes in the object necessitate changes in the description of it. But there is more to the issue than this. The perishability to which Bradley refers is compared with an implied claim of immortality for the work of Dicey, in 1985, just passing 100 years old. The enigma of how an analysis becomes a 'classic' and, thereby, immortal is used in contrast to the contemporary descriptive work, which must change to map and reflect empirical change. The classic is a work of constitutional commentary which now attracts its own commentary. Dicey's theoretical stance is now more acknowledged, and its status of descriptive neutrality dropped. Thus, it becomes possible to talk of 'Dicey's theory of the

---

32 *Op cit*, fn 27, Bradley, pp 3–4.

33 The convention that such textbooks continue to bear the names of authors now dead means that this book is still known as *Wade and Bradley*; there are, however, other contributing authors. For convenience, the author is hereafter referred to as 'Bradley'.

34 Bradley, AW with Bates, TStJN and Himsworth, CMG, *Wade and Bradley: Constitutional and Administrative Law*, 10th edn, 1985, London: Longman.

35 Bradley, AW and Ewing, KD with Bates, TStJN, *Wade and Bradley: Constitutional and Administrative Law*, 11th edn, 1993, London: Longman.

36 *Ibid*, fn 34, Bradley, p ix.

constitution', where it would seem incongruous to talk of 'Bradley's theory of the constitution'.

It is in order to maintain the stance of atheoretical transparency that the updating of the textbook must be continued, because to fail to do so would leave yesterday's theoretical investments too evident.[37] In this respect, theory is like fashion: when it is the common sense of the present, it is almost invisible, and simply the context in which we live. It is only with hindsight that we wonder how we could have espoused *that*. Change in theory – in modes of analysis – is as much the imperative that drives updating as change in the object under analysis.

The etymology of *theory*[38] confirms that the process of theorising an object is the search for a point from which one may *gaze upon* the object, see it clearly. Even proponents of the descriptive textbook would accept this job description. The implication is that the securing of a stable point of view is crucial to fixing the meaning of the object. But the anti-theoreticism of the law textbook tradition seeks to occlude this operation, and updating allows a smooth compromise with the evolutions of common sense. This recognition with hindsight of the partiality of past accounts is a process which can be accelerated and brought to bear on contemporary work. It is not necessary to wait for 'classic' status to analyse the theoretical investments of the legal textbook.

In fact, a lineage runs quite directly from Bradley back to Dicey. It was Bradley's former partner ECS Wade who took on the task of editing and introducing Dicey's work after the latter's death. In the 10th edition of Dicey's *The Law of the Constitution* in 1959, Wade's introduction, at nearly 200 pages, occupies almost a third of the book. It is clear that Wade found the framework established by Dicey of continued relevance and usefulness, and it is not too fanciful to see this perspective carried over into the textbook work of Wade with Phillips, then Wade with Bradley, and latterly, that of Bradley and his current collaborators. In this light, *Wade and Bradley: Constitutional and Administrative Law* is the most recent edition of Dicey's work, in the guise of objective science, rather than the opinions of the person. The key question for

---

37   When ECS Wade distinguishes between Dicey's two key works, and calls one 'a textbook ... it has fallen to me on two occasions to edit ... and it has proved possible to ... [adapt] it to contemporary conditions'; while commenting on the other, 'since the book is a work of reflections of an individual, it does not call for editing', he distinguishes quite clearly between a textbook which is impersonal, atheoretical, non-opinionated and objective, and other work where the author's theories, opinions and attitudes are visible. We are to assume that method follows subject: the law of the law, and opinions on opinions. The confidence with which he creates two genres denies the considerable interpenetration of the two styles of writing, an interpenetration which undermines his distinction. Dicey, AV, *Lectures on the Relation Between Law and Public Opinion in England During the Nineteenth Century*, 2nd edn, 1963, London: Macmillan, p 5.

38   'Theory n pl C16: from late Latin, *theoria*, from Greek: a sight, from *theorein* to gaze upon' *Collins English Dictionary*, 2nd edn, 1986, London: Collins, p 1579.

any inquiry into the coherence and continuities of the orthodox tradition will of course concern the degree to which Bradley's theory of the constitution is no longer quite that of Dicey. The most significant difference noticed is *a contemporary loss of confidence*. In Dicey's work, there is a certainty that the concepts developed are adequate to the task of comprehending the constitution. In Bradley, this certainty is notably lacking.

DICEY DORMANT: THE PUBLIC LAW PARADIGM

I have examined Dicey's theory and noted its survival. I have highlighted the silence concerning women in Dicey's writings. I turn now to an alternative understanding of the constitution. In this section, I will argue that the *public law paradigm* stands in clear contrast to Dicey's *constitutional law paradigm* in its recognition of the separation of state and society. Although little cited in the English literature, Hegel's work gives the most precise definition of this split and its consequences, and will be used to analyse contemporary public law critiques of Dicey. However, I will argue in the next section that the public law project paradigm, as an instance of the modernising project, provides feminism with a dilemma, which only a postmodern theory of constitutionality can adequately resolve.

In Hegel's writings, there are two alternative accounts given of a time prior to the separation of state and society. In an early work,[39] a democratic community which could, however counterfactual this might be to the history, have equality of the sexes, is supplanted by an imperial state. This state institutes the public/private divide which will preclude the participation of women in the public realm. This version equates the separation of state and society with the *loss* of ethical community: 'the ethical world corresponded to municipal life and the Greek city ... [; the] universal realisation of the self corresponds to the disappearance of municipal life and the development of the Roman Empire.'[40] With the coming of empire, '[t]he citizen as such disappeared and in his place the private person appeared ... the emperor's will ruled over all; beneath him was an absolute equality. Private law developed and it perfected that equality'.[41]

It should be noted here that, in this version, the private person/citizen dichotomy is not a distinction interior to the imperial period. Citizenship belongs to the ethical community of the city, and private life emerges with the

---

39 Hegel, GWF, 'The difference between Greek imagination and positive Christian religion', in *Early Theological Writings*, Knox, TM (trans), 1971, Philadelphia: Pennsylvania, pp 151–67.

40 Hyppolite, J, *Genesis and Structure of Hegel's Phenomenology of Spirit*, Cherniak, S and Heckman, J (trans), 1974, Evanston: Northwestern UP, p 365.

41 *Ibid*, p 372.

split. To call the public aspect of life after the split 'citizenship' would do damage to the ethical import of the term. This is Hegel's early perspective: an idyll of pagan, ethical life in the city is shattered by the coming of despotic imperial politics which cleaves a gap between society and state, creating the distinction between private life and public life.

In Hegel's second version, taken from *Philosophy of Right*, the same split is re-enacted. But the prior stage now is the primal patriarchal horde rather than the ethical community:

> A nation does not begin by being a state. The transition from a family, a horde, a clan, a multitude to political conditions is the realisation of the idea in the form of that nation. Without this form, a nation, as an ethical substance ... lacks the objectivity of possessing ... a universal ... embodiment in laws. So long as it lacks ... an explicitly established rational constitution, its autonomy is formal only and is not sovereign ... It would be contrary ... to call patriarchal conditions a 'constitution' or a people under patriarchal government a 'state' or its independence 'sovereignty' ... It is the absolute right of the idea to step into existence in clear cut laws and objective institutions, beginning with marriage ... This right is the right of heroes to found states.[42]

In the later Hegel, therefore, the contrast between the ethical life and the legal regime is dropped in favour of an *identification* of the two. It is in a legal state that ethical life is now possible. This legal state begins with the institution of marriage, which distinguishes it from the life of the patriarchal family, which has no constitution, state or sovereignty. A patriarchal family order is thus supplanted by a state founded on the institution of marriage. The institution of marriage will confine women to the domestic realm. But the situation of women before the coming of the state was one of subjection to the patriarchal horde. The possibility of equality for women is occluded totally in either condition; women move from one form of slavery to another.

The long perspective of these Hegelian fragments gives a horizon to my discussion. Two different versions of pre-modernity, the Greek city and the patriarchal horde, are both followed by the separation of the state from society which inaugurates modernity. I will argue that the closure of that gap terminates modernity, allowing the possibility of a postmodern perspective. But, first, it is necessary to demonstrate the relevance of these Hegelian fragments to Dicey's theory.

Hegel's view that the lack of an explicitly established rational constitution denies a nation the title of sovereign would be contested by Dicey. For Dicey, it is this lack which allows the particular national version of sovereignty to emerge in English history. For Dicey there is, precisely, a national sovereignty, even if – *particularly* if – there is no principle of the state and the public realm.

---

42 Hegel, GWF, *Philosophy of Right*, Knox, TM (trans), 1967, Oxford: OUP, p 219.

The starting point here is that there is a simultaneity in the origin of constitutionality, the separation of state and society, the institution of the public/private divide and the absence of women from the world of law. The 'world' which has these attributes is modernity, and it is described by the *public law paradigm*.[43]

By contrast, the English tradition, the *constitutional law paradigm*, analyses the historical evolution of the constitution within a set of assumptions which need not refer to the advent of modernity, the separation of state from society and the public/private divide. Its prime exponent is, of course, Dicey. His theory is undoubtedly a reaction to modernity, particularly, modernity in the guise of the extension of the democratic franchise beyond the propertied class and beyond men, but it is not a modern theory.

Is this a deliberate difference of emphasis between traditional and critical approaches to the constitution? Or are these distinct but overlapping fields? Consideration of the possible relations of the two terms reveals something a little more substantial. We can take *constitutional* (and administrative) law to be a specialised field within the broader field of *public* law. However, Dicey is associated with the claim that the great virtue of the constitutional tradition of England is precisely the claim that constitutional arrangements are governed by the ordinary law of the land. That is to say, perhaps, there is no distinctive public law running alongside private law and no separate hierarchy of courts. In this view, constitutional and administrative law is a branch of *private* law, and the old assertion that we lack a constitution is amended to the claim that we lack a public law of the constitution.

One can argue that the notion of public law only makes sense as a contrast with private law. A constitutional law tradition which does not wish to make such a distinction will view constitutional law as a branch of law in general, a law which is in no way distinct from the rest of private law, and so is a law of rights in persons and in things. Although public law presupposes private law – in order to stand in distinction to the latter – the opposite does not apply. A private law with no public law is conceivable. In effect, this is Dicey's claim. The important corollary of this is that *the state* is not recognised as possessing any special privileges or immunities and is viewed as just another person subject to the law of the land. Again, this is the view with which Dicey is famously associated. The tension in Dicey's thought lies in the question whether this privatised notion of law, this idea of the rule of private law, is compatible with his notion of sovereignty. Dicey appears to intend that sovereignty operate within the rule of law.

---

43 *Op cit,* fn 31, Harden and Lewis; Craig; Loughlin. However, the extent to which this scholarship works with outmoded and exclusionary concepts is significant. See Morison, J, 'The case against constitutional reform?' (1998) 25 JLS 510; and Murphy, Chapter 2, this volume.

PUBLIC LAW, A DILEMMA FOR FEMINISM

If we take the view that a public law perspective is one which explicitly theorises the nature of state power, then we can see why it might seem the obvious perspective for a critical approach which purports to be aware of the realities of politics and society. Such a perspective will theorise the nature of the public/private divide, the absence of a theory of state as opposed to Diceyan conventions of government, and will generally espouse a more transparent and formalised relationship between state and citizen. This will often take the form of demands for a bill of rights and more democratic participation and accountability. Indeed, much of contemporary public law scholarship now reflects these concerns to varying degrees, and all law students will have some familiarity with the 'constitutional reform project.'

It is no surprise that branches of feminism are interested in the public law approach.[44] Feminist perspectives have long focused on the consequences for women of the public/private divide, starting from a critique of the sexist assumption that 'a woman's place is in the home,' and expanding out from this on the theme of securing for women a place in the public world. Note, however, that the focus is on *woman's place*. Within the public law paradigm, what is at stake is a topography. The possible sites and their relations are mapped, then the political demand for admission to places which operate on a principle of gender exclusion is made. The argument takes two forms. Women must be admitted into the public realm, either on the basis of the universalist principle inherent in the notion of citizenship which has hitherto operated only in relation to men; or on the specific assertion of women's participation in public affairs as women, with a framework devised to meet the specific needs and interests of women. It is a matter of showing that the public/private divide has operated against the interests of women, and overcoming this legacy. It is not, however, necessarily a question of dismantling the public/private divide, simply a matter of gaining access to both realms. The private realm, construed as the domestic realm, is also addressed, with the demand that men take their place there also.

How does this relate to Dicey? Clearly, the significance for the constitution of the state/society split and the attendant public/private split is that the Diceyan argument that the constitution is a 'private' historical achievement of a particular community will not work. A universalist claim must be advanced instead. This universalism will be in the familiar form of a declaration of the rights of citizens, or human rights.

---

44 Benhabib, S and Cornell, D (eds), *Feminism as Critique*, 1987, Cambridge: Polity. See Gearey, Chapter 7, Kingdom, Chapter 8 and Harvey, Chapter 10, this volume, for perspectives on the relationship between feminist and public law theories.

However, the argument from Hegel shows that the legal system of the state excludes women. And, as Arendt has argued convincingly, universalist systems of inclusion always work on the basis of an actual exclusion.[45] For Arendt, the other side of citizenship is represented by the person excluded, the pariah; and, in the European tradition, the pariah figure has traditionally been the Jew. Furthermore, as Varikas has demonstrated, the pariah is also a metaphor for the social, political and ethical subjugation of women:

> Arendt stresses the modernity of the pariah, of that figure who initially emerges from a tension specific to the system of universalist legitimation introduced by the French Revolution: the tension between the universalist principle of one general law for all, which founded the nation state and emancipation, and … real discrimination.[46]

It is the excluded woman who makes possible the community of men who participate in public affairs from ancient Athens to revolutionary Paris.

The public law paradigm in the UK, as developed by writers such as Harden and Lewis, Craig, and Loughlin, uses this universalism.[47] It is most evident in the versions which employ a Habermasian template.[48] Arendt's argument shows how feminism can build on this edifice. A critique of the absence of a place for women in universal citizenship, and a development of the location of women in the place of the pariah can be developed into a position arguing that, whilst no man is above the law, no woman is within the law. This means that the feminist critique of the public law model will be in two stages. First, the constitution has to modernise itself into a public polity; then the exclusion of women will be an apparent wrong which can be righted. This clearly reveals the ideology which underpins the public law paradigm. It is a modernist perspective.

The shortcoming of this perspective is also clear: it lies in the ahistorical assumption that the modernist project is a blueprint applicable any where and any time. The relevance of this paradigm stands or falls on the claim that the constitution is best understood as a matter operating within a public law framework. This is not true for English constitutionality, which would first have to become universalist before this mode of analysis could even start to be relevant.[49] In the next section, I want to argue that it is precisely this claim which a postmodern theory of constitutionality can contest. If the possibility

---

45   Arendt, H, *The Jew as a Pariah*, Feldman, RH (ed), 1978, New York: Grove.

46   Varikas, E, 'The burden of our time' (1998) 92 Radical Philosophy, Nov/Dec, pp 17–24.

47   *Op cit*, fn 31, Harden and Lewis; Craig; Loughlin.

48   Habermas, J, *The Structural Transformation of the Public Sphere*, Burger, T (trans), 1989, Cambridge: Polity. See Harvey, Chapter 10, this volume, for a discussion of the influence of Habermas on UK public law theory.

49   *Ibid*, Varikas, p 19, discusses in England 'a very different system of political legitimation which was closer to the notion of … rights *inherited from* ancestors than to the universalist framework', leaving the gap between principle and practice less visible in England than in France.

that the 'public' context of constitutionality has collapsed is conceded, then the public law paradigm is rendered irrelevant.

What, then, is the specific dilemma for feminism? Clearly, a feminist perspective on Dicey founders on the 'non-dimensionality' of Dicey's theory and his particularism. There is no possibility of raising questions concerning society, democracy and women within Dicey's constitutional law paradigm. It might even be argued that this is its whole point. In contrast, feminism can and has defined a position in relation to the public law paradigm which is the new consensus in the UK; a new consensus which now appears to find Dicey wrongheaded. In the face of this consensus, the question of Dicey is rendered irrelevant. It may be, however, that this consensus has inherent weaknesses that feminist critique has exposed. It may be that there is a crisis within the public law paradigm. If so, it becomes significant to realign feminist perspectives not only in relation to the modernising project, but also in relation to the questions raised by postmodern theorising of consitutionality.

DICEY DISPLACED: POSTMODERNISM AND FEMINISM

In this final section, I want to advance what could be called a postmodern position. It turns on the claim that the public law paradigm no longer captures – in fact, never did capture – the crucial features of constitutionality. In particular, it is contended that the spatial focus of public law is deficient: the concepts of the state and the public as terrains for contesting legitimacy are not an adequate theorisation. I want to assert here that the public sphere envisioned by Habermas and his followers has disappeared. It has been colonised by state and media, and has imploded under the pressure.[50] I also want to assert that the nation state has lost its centrality (and that the European dimension should not be forced into a nation state template).[51] If this is all so, then, arguably, women's demand for a public space arrives too late. We thus must think afresh about constitutionality, in another dimension. If the spatial metaphor no longer works, I propose a discussion of the temporalities of constitutions. Let us investigate what emerges from thinking of constitutions as *constructions in time* rather than as *constructions in space*.

We live in a time after the collapse of the spaces of public law. Is a return to the constitutional law paradigm of Dicey therefore in order? I do wish to take from Dicey some elements – in effect postmodern appropriations from

---

50 My argument here is indebted to Negt, O and Kluge, A, *Public Sphere and Experience*, Labanyi, P, Daniel, JO and Oksiloff, A (trans), 1993, Minneapolis: Minnesota UP; Baudrillard, J, *Symbolic Exchange and Death*, Grant, IH (trans), 1993, London: Sage; Baudrillard, J, *Simulacra and Simulation*, Glaser, SF (trans), 1994, Ann Arbor: Michigan UP.

51 Derrida, J, *The Other Heading: Reflections on Today's Europe*, Brault, P-A and Naas, MB (trans), 1992, Bloomington and Indianapolis: Indiana UP.

the premodern – but their import will be displaced. Approaching the question of constitutional temporality, we can see that Dicey's constitutional paradigm is constructed in the past for the present. The ordinary common law of judge made precedent which interprets the constitution ensures this. In contrast, the public law paradigm, with its future oriented constitutional proclamations prescribing how law will be made, is constructed now for the future. Or, after the era of constitution making, the public law paradigm is equally a construct in the past and the continuous present of the constitution. Dicey's theory has a time but no spaces. The public law paradigm has spaces but no time.

Lyotard has commented that '[p]ostmodern would have to be understood according to the paradox of the future (post) anterior (modo)'.[52] The postmodern is that which will have been the case. He also stated that '[t]he artist and the writer, then, are working without rules in order to formulate the rules of what will have been done'.[53] Can this paradoxical tense be relevant to the understanding of constitutions? It piles paradox upon paradox to suggest that the rule maker might work without rules in order to formulate the rules of what will have been done. We can perhaps, however, glimpse a definition of constitutionalising which would not be rule making, and in this way would be closer to the possibility of an ethical practice of justice. In *The Postmodern Condition*, Lyotard argues that:

> Consensus has become an outmoded and suspect value. But justice as a value is neither outmoded nor suspect. We must thus arrive at an idea and practice of justice that is not linked to that of consensus.[54]

He then proceeds to sketch 'the outline of a politics that would respect both the desire for justice and the desire for the unknown'.[55] Here, the consensual, the known, is the rule system of the modern public law paradigm. By contrast, a postmodern constitutionality, attempting to think through this kind of politics, finds in Dicey a resource which is useful precisely because of his lack of reference to the social spaces of the modern paradigm.

Feminism need not fall with modernism. There is a feminism that can work within this postmodern temporality of constitutionalising. There is the time of the constitution and the time of the postmodern. There is also women's time. Kristeva, in her essay 'Women's time', suggests that the loss of the principle of the nation state and trans-European developments have catapulted us into a 'strange temporality ... a kind of future perfect'.[56] She

---

52 Lyotard, J-F, 'Answering the question: what is postmodernism?', Durand, R (trans), in Lyotard, J-F, *The Postmodern Condition: A Report on Knowledge*, Bennington, G and Massumi, B (trans), 1984, Manchester: Manchester UP, p 81.

53 *Ibid.*

54 Lyotard, J-F, Appendix, in *The Postmodern Condition: A Report on Knowledge*, Bennington, G and Massumi, B (trans), 1984, Manchester: Manchester UP, p 66.

55 *Ibid*, p 67.

56 Kristeva, J, 'Women's time', Jardine, A and Blake, H (trans) (1981) 7(1) Signs 13 (also in Moi, T (ed), *The Kristeva Reader*, 1986, Oxford: Basil Blackwell, pp 187, 189).

identifies two temporal dimensions: 'the time of linear history, or cursive time ..., and the time of another history, thus another time, monumental time.'[57] This other history and time, a time of eternity and repetition, is women's time.

Kristeva contrasts the waves of feminism in a way that maps the discussion above:

> ... the women's movement, as the struggle of suffragists and of existential feminists, aspired to gain a place in linear time as the time of project and history ... the movement is deeply rooted in the socio-political life of nations. The political demands of women, the struggles for equal pay for equal work, for taking power in social institutions ... all are part of the *logic of identification*.[58]

But, in a second phase of feminism, she identifies a 'distrust of the entire political dimension', and instead demands 'recognition of an irreducible identity, without equal in the opposite sex and, as such, exploded, plural, fluid, in a certain way non-identical ..., outside the linear time of identities which communicate through projection'.[59] This second phase is aesthetic rather than political (we should remember that the public sphere was once literary before it was political) and its task is:

> ... to counterbalance ... modern communications technology ... to demystify the ... community of language as an universal and unifying tool ... which totalises and equalises ... [and] to bring out .. the multiplicity of every person's possible identifications ... [and] the relativity of his/her ... existence ... this fluidity.[60]

It should be clear that the perspectives of Lyotard and Kristeva are almost identical. Remarkably, both were proposed in 1979, but have not, in 20 years, been posed as a challenge to constitutional thinking in the UK, still dominated by the modern public law paradigm. Kristeva's essay has been discussed recently by Watts,[61] who takes it to task for being post-political, and disabling political activity while valorising cultural activity. I would argue that Watts' analysis is correct, but would disagree with her negative conclusions. A cultural politics of constitutional law – albeit one which does not bow to the imperative of proposing constitutional reform – is conceivable within Kristeva's and Lyotard's perspective, and desirable as an intervention in the contemporary debate over constitutional matters in the UK.

Public opinion, contra Dicey, need not be legislative public opinion. Public opinion can critically, politically, culturally and aesthetically challenge the institutions of law and state. The loss of its space, the public sphere, means that it can manifest only in time. The question is which time; linear and

---

57 *Op cit*, fn 56, Kristeva.
58 *Op cit*, fn 56, Kristeva, pp 193–94.
59 *Op cit*, fn 56, Kristeva, p 194.
60 *Op cit*, fn 56, Kristeva, p 210.
61 Watts, C, 'Time and the working mother' (1998) 91 Radical Philosophy, Sept/Oct, p 6.

historical or monumental and posthistorical? Kristeva's enigmatic suggestion of a monumental time of repetition and eternity captures well the sense of constitutions made in, but beyond, history. If a return to Dicey allows us to rethink constitutions as constructions in time rather than in space, then Kristeva and Lyotard allow us to go beyond the linear time of Dicey's history, and thereby to deal with the twin problematics of women's time and postmodern history. In this exercise, the thread abandoned by Hegel, whereby citizenship in a narrowly public sense is not the embodiment but the opposite of ethical life, is picked up once more.

In conclusion, if my aim is to engineer a collision that becomes visible when Kristeva and Lyotard are put to work questioning the notion of acts of constitution, it remains only to clarify why Dicey is relevant to this task. First, because his 'non-dimensional' theory evacuates space from its considerations and therefore is appropriate to the postmodern situation. Secondly, Dicey is pre-political, a stance recoverable from a post-political perspective. His constitution is inserted in time. It is the linear time of a historical evolution, but this nonetheless allows the contrast Kristeva and Lyotard propose of 'other times'. The discovery of 'what will have been the law' in some way encapsulates the Dicey project. He did not want to write the constitution of England. He wanted to discover it. In other words, Dicey wanted to state what *had been the law*, and in his view *should remain the law*. Of course, his conservatism must be rejected. However, his scepticism concerning modernist constitution building is relevant. The public law paradigm, seeking to determine what *will be the law for all time to come* must also be rejected. Dicey is a resource to be learned from and used, but the perspective which can be developed out of his work relocates his insights to different ends. This is Dicey displaced, raising the possibility of a postmodern and feminist perspective interested in discovering what *could be the law*, what could be *other laws*, and what could be *other than the law*.

CHAPTER 7

TOWARDS A FEMINIST CRITIQUE OF SOVEREIGNTY: GUILD PLURALISM, POLITICAL COMMUNITY AND THE RELEVANCE OF LUCE IRIGARAY TO ENGLISH CONSTITUTIONAL THOUGHT[1]

Adam Gearey

INTRODUCTION

A feminist constitutionalism can be animated by a rethinking of sovereignty informed by a vision of inclusive community. This approach is neither an essentialism[2] nor a separatism: it is, rather, an attempt to develop in public law a thinking already taking hold in other areas of legal scholarship;[3] an elaboration of the work of the French scholar, Luce Irigaray.[4] Although Irigaray has never written exclusively on sovereignty, her work has, at its

---

1   Thanks to Nicky Lacey, Peter Goodrich, Maria Drakopoulou, Sue Millns, Noel Whitty and Mary Grenham.

2   Essentialism is the belief that there is an essential idea of a female essence that is transhistorical and transcultural. See Schor, N, 'This essentialism which is not one: coming to grips with Irigaray', in Schor, N and Weed, E (eds), *The Essential Difference*, 1994, Bloomington and Indianapolis: Indiana UP, p 40. At first, Irigaray was thought of as an essentialist, but there has been a more recent movement to reappraise her work; see Assiter, A, *Enlightened Women*, 1996, London: Routledge, p 30. It is suggested that the essentialism debate does not provide a useful context for Irigaray's later work which is to be examined here, as this work is concerned with the space that exists between men and women. For a questioning of the distinction between equality and difference, see Pateman, C, 'Equality, difference, subordination: the politics of motherhood and women's citizenship', in Bock, G and James, S (eds), *Beyond Equality and Difference*, 1992, London: Routledge.

3   See Goodrich, P, 'Gender and contracts', in Bottomley, A (ed), *Feminist Perspectives on the Foundational Subjects of Law*, 1996, London: Cavendish Publishing, p 17. For a more extensive engagement with Irigaray, see Goodrich, P, *Oedipus Lex*, 1995, Berkeley: California UP; and, also, *Law in the Courts of Love*, 1996, London and New York: Routledge. For developments within American legal studies, see Cornell, D, *Beyond Accommodation*, 1991, London: Routledge. Nicola Lacey has engaged with Irigaray's influence on feminist legal thought in 'Feminist legal theory beyond neutrality', in Freeman, MDA and Halson, R (eds) (1995) 48 CLP 1, pp 1–38.

4   One of the most problematic aspects of Irigaray's work for the anglophone reader is that it comes out of a context of European thought. This is not to suggest that Irigaray is irredeemably difficult, but to argue that Anglo-American feminism tends to make use of Irigaray, or to reject her, from the standpoint of a particular politics or set of philosophical or theoretical assumptions. There are at present, though, valiant efforts to show how Irigaray is central to feminism; on the subject of Anglo American and French feminisms, see Bowlby, R, 'Flight reservations' (1988) 10 Oxford Literary Review 61.

heart, the need to think a shared sociality that is not blind to questions of gender and power, and which roots law in the commonality that exists between women and men. This thinking can be employed as a challenge to the dominant understandings of sovereignty. Irigaray's work also provides a starting point for a feminism which avoids the perennial criticism of oppositional thinking as a 'trashing' that can recover nothing from the ruins. It is possible to show that a rethinking of sovereignty can include an elaboration of institutional forms. To this end, it will be argued that Irigaray's notion of community can be extended by the discourse of guild pluralism which remains present in, but marginal to, contemporary thinking on sovereignty. Instead of conceiving the state as organised on a top-down model of power where authority is seen as pyramidal and enforced by central state agencies, it might be possible to move to a more decentred notion of the state as consisting of a diversity of centres of power. Some feminists may object to this pluralist framework, as it provides no thorough critique of governmental power and no real opposition to market pluralism. At best, it simply relocates power from the centre, and then leaves it unchecked. Moreover, the guild is suspect as it is merely another manifestation of the exclusionary politics of fraternity and brotherhood. It will be maintained that these objections can be taken into account, and a radical re-organisation of state power imagined.

The argument will proceed in four stages. In the first part of this chapter, the dominant theories of sovereignty will be outlined. The second section will argue that, as a feminist analysis of the state developed, scholars looked to Irigaray's writing on rights and that her insights can be extended to a theory of sovereignty. Focus will turn in the third section to Irigaray's theory of love as the foundation of human interrelationship. Irigaray's argument suggests that the presentation of a meaningful constitutional and civil identity for women transforms love into a public dynamic, a political love. This political love will be read into guild pluralist thought, and the possibilities of a political organisation informed by feminism will be developed. In the fourth section, the resonances of guild pluralism with radical social theory will be outlined, thus producing a vision of a social and political arrangement which both articulates the transformative agenda of feminist thought and gives institutional form to a new understanding of sovereignty.

SOVEREIGNTY AND ITS CRITICS: TRADITIONS AND COUNTERTRADITIONS

A feminist engagement with sovereignty is timely. Feminist critique has already addressed the creation of a supposedly objective and universal legal order as inimical to the desires of women, but, as yet, has not substantively engaged with the dominant liberal apologetic of sovereign power. Perhaps the most influential account is that of AV Dicey. It describes Parliament as the sovereign body of the English constitution, able to make or unmake any law.[5] Dicey justified this Leviathan in terms of a positive theory of law which stressed the need for an absolute legal power to found a system of rules allowing social peace and the flourishing of civil society. Parliament's power could be legitimised by the variety of institutional and moral restraints which would effectively prevent it behaving unconstitutionally, even though there could be no legal limitation of parliamentary sovereignty. Ultimately, a tyrannical government would face the sanction of being voted out of office. This aspect of Dicey's account stressed the influence of popular political sovereignty on the constitution. Although Parliament remained legally sovereign, the 'people' retained the power to change government.[6]

While accounts of sovereignty in English law invariably start from this point, one of the subsequent problems is to reconcile Dicey's theory with contemporary reality.

Public law scholarship has tended to relate Dicey's understanding of sovereignty to a particular historical moment and a conception of democratic process which is in need of updating if it is to have any relevance.[7] There are a number of challenges. The impact of European law raises the possibility that sovereignty will become an international rather than a national phenomenon. Running alongside the internationalisation of sovereignty, there is the perceived failure of the legitimisation of government through popular democracy. Dicey's account of political sovereignty has lost a great deal of its authority with the effective domination of Parliament by the executive which has concentrated greater political power in the hands of the Prime Minister and the Cabinet. The ultimate sanction of a general election appears too remote to affect the day to day running of government. Moreover, traditional notions of parliamentary government do not seem sufficient to cope with the challenges of a state that has privatised large areas of its responsibilities and appears reluctant to intervene to any significant extent in a market economy.

A feminist intervention into the theory of sovereignty could build on this perceived 'democratic defect'.[8] Given the existing challenges to national sovereignty from European law, and the developing resistances to European hegemony that stress the local, there is perhaps now the chance to develop a discourse on community that deploys plurality in a direction which can

---

5   Dicey, AV, *An Introduction to the Study of the Law of the Constitution*, 10th edn, 1959, London: MacMillan, pp 92–93.

6   See McDonald, Chapter 6, this volume, for a discussion of Dicey's fear of democratic politics.

7   Craig, PP, *Public Law and Democracy in the United Kingdom and the United States of America*, 1990, Oxford: Clarendon. See, also, Loughlin, M, *Public Law and Political Theory*, 1992, Oxford: Clarendon.

8   Sedley, S, 'Human rights: a 21st century agenda' [1995] PL 399.

imagine forms of social being that articulate both inclusionary visions and new horizons for constitutional thought. As feminism is a broadly progressive movement, any account of sovereignty would have to be based on a theory of social transformation which would develop a version of the 'good life' based on the communal and individual realisation of the potentials of women as well as men. An essential part of this would be a challenge to the hierarchies of power that determine politics as the preserve of a largely male governmental elite and the exclusion of the majority from the political process. A theory of sovereignty would, in other words, not simply describe, but would recommend change and offer visions of possibilities.

What are the resources for this reconstruction? One of the key theoretical problems attached to feminist work is that of the derivation of concepts to inform critique: how is it possible to produce a critical discourse that does not just reproduce the terms of the dominant discourse? If, as feminist critique maintains, the world has always been defined from a male point of view, how is it possible to find an alternative perspective? The approach to be adopted here could be described as genealogical. Genealogy 'looks to the plurality of institutional histories and not only to legitimate forms'.[9] It holds that the objective recovery of history is impossible; historical research is always an invention of the past in the service of the present. Feminist genealogies contend with the construction of dominant discourses; its concern is with what was excluded, fragmentary or suppressed. A genealogy of sovereignty would try to locate the points at which the dominant discourse fails, and attempt to reinscribe the tradition from an alternative perspective. As far as the discourse of sovereignty is concerned, a possibility suggests itself. Sovereignty has always been linked to a notion of community, although this has been defined in a fairly restricted way and linked to ideas of nationhood. It would be possible to borrow from Irigaray's work a rethinking of the basis of community and develop this by linking it to another critical and dissident tradition in the thinking of sovereignty, the notion of guild pluralism.

These resources can be found within the tradition. There has been a forceful critique of a theory of sovereignty which privileges the state as the only form of any social ordering. This critique could be read as a genealogy as it looks not only to dominant interpretations, but to 'splendid failures', and to texts which are 'accidentally preserved.' It builds its argument from a careful rereading of the political tradition, seeking to return to life the 'vague and inchoate, the wan ghosts that seek the substance of institutional form'.[10] The return of this idea is in the service of a contemporary apologetics of popular

---

9   *Op cit*, fn 3, Goodrich, 1995, p 25.
10 Laski, HJ, *The Foundations of Sovereignty and other Essays*, 1921, London: Allen & Unwin, p 7.

sovereignty, the desire that 'community should be master in its own house'.[11] Just as the drive towards the omnicompetence of the state can be traced to medieval political struggles and the writings of the apologists of the power of the prince or the pope, the counter resource can be found in these early texts. The concept of popular sovereignty can be found in Cicero's insistence that the highest law comes from the welfare of the people, in Nicholas of Cusa's recommendation for a parliamentary system, and Marsiglio of Padua's call for sovereignty to express itself as an assembly of the people as a whole. At root, this endeavour returns to the medieval notion of popular sovereignty which resists the coercion of the diversity of community into the form of the state, which can then be controlled by whatever social group holds power.

Although this genealogy is useful, its suppositions and projects need themselves to be genealogised. There is, of course, nothing in it which is inherently feminist; but this is not to suggest that it cannot have profound resonances with feminist work. To build this argument, it is now necessary to turn to the possible critique of sovereignty that emerges from feminist thought.

TOWARDS A FEMINIST ACCOUNT OF SOVEREIGNTY

Sovereignty's absence from the first contemporary feminist analyses of the state is not surprising. It is perhaps difficult to see how this subject has any urgency for a scholarship which first defined itself with studies of pornography, rape and abuse.[12] Any feminist analysis of the state could proceed without becoming distracted by the seemingly abstract preoccupation with a totem of liberal constitutional theory.

Catharine MacKinnon's influential study of law and the state is representative of a tendency of thought which dispensed with any conventional question of sovereignty.[13] MacKinnon presented the liberal state as based on a pretence of gender equality. Law's objectivity, its norms and categories, are male standards which effectively enshrine female sexual

---

11 *Op cit*, fn 10, Laski, p 8.

12 See Allen, J, 'Does feminism need a theory of the state?', in Watson, S (ed), *Playing the State*, 1990, London: Verso, p 21. Allen suggests that the key sites of women's oppression, such as the family and the household, can usefully be approached without being distracted by theories of the state. Feminism 'requires and provides theories of other significant categories and processes' (p 34). Allen's definition of practices anticipates those of Foucauldian feminism, reviewed below. For an approach to social contract theory, see Pateman, C, *The Sexual Contract*, 1988, Cambridge: Polity. Pateman provides an insightful critique of the central writers in this tradition, but does not engage with theories of sovereignty.

13 See, also, Eisenstein, Z, *The Radical Future of Liberal Democracy*, 1986, Boston: Northwestern UP. Eisenstein follows a broadly Marxist line and also dispenses with any category of sovereignty.

oppression and render it invisible, as it does not conform with the male construction of social reality. At the centre of this web of oppression, the state ensures that 'the rule of law – neutral, abstract, elevated, pervasive, both institutionalizes the power of men over women and institutionalizes power in its male form'.[14] MacKinnon's approach thus rejects any liberal legitimisation of the law through either legal or political sovereignty. Analysis had to proceed by a form of consciousness raising which would look to women's own concrete experience to critique male power. This approach has no real use of any analysis of sovereignty; the total system of liberal state law can be entirely condemned.

Difficulties arise when this position is problematised by a feminism that seeks to work within and against the state, and views an analytic like MacKinnon's as impassioned, but ultimately lacking in theoretical depth. Drucilla Cornell's theory of the law and state is an explicit critique of MacKinnon, and an attempt to move the analysis on from the whole scale condemnation of law and legal strategies. At the core of Cornell's project is an affirmation of 'equivalent rights' which would not assimilate women to men's standards, but would effectively enfranchise female realities. It is here that Cornell's work acknowledges a debt to Irigaray. Irigaray's argument is a demand for a legal statement of female identity. This 'right' would make for the 'legal codification' of virginity,[15] a right to motherhood and the enshrining of the obligations of 'mothers-children' in civil law.[16] Also contained in this statement of rights are various strictures that prevent the penalisation of celibacy, and the call for the equal representation of men's and women's interests in all forms of cultural exchange and political and religious representation. These rights would move away from merely attaching criminal sanctions to crimes against women, and would resemble the great enlightenment claims made for the rights of man.

If this approach is accepted, then it seems that feminism is beginning to engage in a different way with a discourse of the legitimacy of the state. To argue that feminism needs to employ both a theory and a practice of rights means that an engagement with the notion of sovereignty is necessary. Although the existing theories that relate sovereignty to rights set out the argumentative territory, they require transformation within a feminist jurisprudence. A brief review can pinpoint both the problems and the possibilities for reinvention. Very schematically, the theories could be divided into three categories. First, classical positivism would link rights to the law determined by the state, and in so doing would return to the command theory

14 MacKinnon, CA, *Towards a Feminist Jurisprudence*, 1989, Cambridge, MA: Harvard UP, p 238.
15 Irigaray, L, *Je, tu, nous*, 1996, London: Routledge, p 86.
16 *Ibid*, p 88.

of law and rights as the creation of government.[17] Secondly, natural law theory would coordinate rights with a transcendent referent, a theory of either God, community or essential humanity. Although there are problems,[18] this theory might, in some ways, be more suitable to feminism, as it immediately opposes the law of the state to a higher 'law'. The neo-Kantian argument, finally, would find values in either a form of natural law or universal human rights which would place limits on the sovereignty of the state.[19] This paper will suggest one possible way forward: an application of Irigaray's thinking of love as immanent to human social relations. Love is not to be associated necessarily with an eroticism, or intimate sexual desire, but taken as a description of community; it is a political love. This may resemble a natural law argument in that it suggests that there are certain characteristics that define human community such as sharing, mutuality, trust and reliance. But this argument needs to be distinguished from developments of natural law to date which have been blind to the definition of sexual difference. It can also be distinguished from natural law arguments as it is inherently transformative, and contains a demand for the refiguring of social and communal relations to take account of both what people share and what makes them different and irreducible to each other. In other words, it requires a reappraisal of the whole question of community as it has been defined in constitutional and political theory.

Recent feminist writing has been very circumspect in its approach to a discourse of community. Notions of sovereignty invariably refer back to questions of nation and belonging, notions which feminism has tried to problematise. In a general sense, feminism has linked community with the exclusion of the other, constructed as different in terms of gender, race or of sexual orientation. Integral to these arguments have been attempts to return to pre-modern or even anti-modern ideas.[20] Feminists have seen these approaches as nostalgic attempts to return to notions of community that are either blind to the problems of gender or include reactionary visions of social solidarity that return women to the domestic sphere. Feminist scholars have also warned against any facile belief in the local and the decentred as necessarily a useful realisation of sexual difference.[21] What must be resisted is 'Rousseau's dream'[22] of a transparent society, organised in such a way as to

---

17 See Lacey, N, 'Feminist perspectives on ethical positivism', in Campbell, T (ed), *Reorienting Legal Positivism*, 1999, Aldershot: Dartmouth.

18 See Davies, M, *Delimiting the Law*, 1996, London: Pluto. Davies is critical of the uses of natural law arguments for feminism.

19 This terminology is drawn from Salecl, R, *The Spoils of Freedom*, 1994, London: Routledge.

20 Frazer, E and Lacey, N, *The Politics of Community: A Feminist Critique of the Liberal-Communitarian Debate*, 1993, London: Harvester Wheatsheaf.

21 Young, IM, *Justice and the Politics of Difference*, 1990, Princeton: Princeton UP.

22 *Ibid*, p 20.

sponsor the face to face and the direct participation in decision making. Such an approach can deny that political relationships are always mediated; it would be naïve to think that a politics could be based entirely on friendship, reciprocity and mutuality when a great many relationships have to take place between strangers. Any viable politics must celebrate the urbanity of modern life, the 'being together of strangers.

However, it is as if the problematisation of community has existed alongside a stubborn need to retain the concept. Writing from a socialist perspective, in particular, has made the rejection of notions of fraternity and brotherhood complex.[23] Although these forms of organisation clearly exclude women, they are essential to any opposition politics. The fear of forced inclusion has also made any simplistic attachment to sisterhood problematic as it duplicates some of the problems of reduction to shared identity. Despite these misgivings, despite the logical appeal of a politics that speaks to self-interest and the resistance to any form of group belonging, the need for community still asserts itself in the affirmation of a 'complex unity that stems from recognising and facing those conflicts that can divide us'.[24] Similar arguments can be observed in the variety of separatist literature on community.[25] The need to live apart as a rejection of the dominant social structures still affirm the possibility of community in the very imagination of an alternative. Given this double bind, or what could be described as the persistence of community, surely the issue becomes the development of a notion of community which does not deny difference, but which still offers some sense of a social universal.

A careful appropriation of the discourse of community which takes these misgivings seriously may be introduced to a feminist jurisprudence. Any notion of community would not have to be reductionist, nor a simple retrieval of reactionary ideas of organic unity.

One final criticism must be addressed. Does the study of sovereignty ignore the possibility that the debate over power has already moved on? Feminist thought which draws on the work of Michel Foucault has certainly produced a relocation of thinking away from the idea of a traditional sovereignty which 'downplays the "power" of the modern sovereign or state'.[26] Power is 'relational', existing in a diversity of social, economic and sexual relationships. The various discourses which create knowledge of the social world effectively organise, define and deploy this power. Writers in the Foucauldian tradition tend to privilege the body and discourse of sexuality as

---

23   Phillips, A, *Democracy and Difference*, 1993, Cambridge: Polity.
24   *Ibid*, p 34.
25   See Munt, S, 'Sisters in exile; the lesbian nation', in Ainley, R (ed), *New Frontiers of Space, Bodies and Gender*, 1998, London: Routledge, pp 3–20.
26   Cooper, D, *Power in Struggle*, 1995, Buckingham: OU Press, p 17.

one of the key areas where power defines people as objects of knowledge to be studied, classified and disciplined. For feminists, patriarchy, or the organisation for power which benefits men rather than women, is one of the principal 'organising frameworks'.[27] Other forms of oppression, such as those based on race and 'normal' sexuality, can be mapped onto the organising grid of patriarchy. Integral to this theory of power is the argument that power cannot simply be escaped or opposed. It is impossible to find the 'outside' of power as it inheres in every form of knowledge. Contestations of power are, however, possible. Every application of power invites subversions and oppositions. Foucauldian feminisms[28] have seen these oppositional moments as the key to feminist thought and practice. Approaches to constitutional discourse would perhaps seek to examine aspects of bureaucracy, policing or the legal construction of the female body which would deal with power at its operational level and hope to discover counter-knowledges and strategic points of resistance. From this perspective, any mode of analysis which returned to sovereignty and a notion of power as existing purely in constitutional arrangements would seem to miss both the sites where power coheres in everyday life and also the sites for its subversions.

The retrieval of a theory of sovereignty will learn from this Foucauldian approach. It will be suggested that Irigaray's retrieval of community deploys a discourse of love which does not seek an outside of power; rather it is a contestation of power. Irigaray's theory of political love takes place within the dominant discourse, both using and distorting traditional concepts. In contesting the meanings supposedly mandated to terms such as community and human nature by political theory, Irigaray creates a counterdiscourse which challenges the traditional exclusion of women from public life at both a theoretical and practical level. A Foucauldian influence continues in the identification of the guild as a legal form, a practice which has always been at the margins of the law. The final influence of Foucauldian feminism is discussed in the fourth part of this chapter, which suggests that a revision of sovereignty must take the form of a decentralised politics; struggles over sovereignty will be presented as taking place at the local level in an account which can sustain the emphasis on the micro-economies of power.

---

27 *Op cit*, fn 26, Cooper, p 11.

28 As Cooper points out, there are many forms of feminism which draw on Foucault's work. It is necessary to acknowledge this diversity which includes Bell, V, *Interrogating Incest: Feminism, Foucault and the Law*, 1993, London: Routledge; Diamond, I and Quinby, L, *Feminism and Foucault: Reflections on Resistance*, 1988, Boston, MA: Northeastern UP; and McNay, L, *Foucault and Feminism*, 1992, Cambridge: Polity.

CONSTITUTING DIFFERENCE, LOVE AND COMMUNITY

To speak of love as the foundation of politics would only be surprising to those who forget the beginnings of the tradition in medieval political theology. In certain senses, this notion of love has always been present in the thinking of community that draws on Christianity.[29] However, it is not the case that Irigaray is simply arguing for a revival of Christian thinking. Although this is a complex aspect of Irigaray's work, and one which undoubtedly has mystical elements, her concern is with a kind of humanism, a thinking of being in the world. At the risk of distorting a complex argument, it could be suggested that some location in Christian thought is important to understand the general dynamics of this position.

The very notion of the rule of law comes out of Christian thought.[30] It could briefly be suggested that the Western political tradition, and hence the tradition of constitutional law, can be traced back to the fusion of classical and Christian culture.[31] Although love had its place in classical, especially Greek philosophy, Christianity is primarily seen as a religion of love. It might seem easy to dismiss this as a scholarship of the obscure, but even a textbook as mainstream as Bradley and Ewing explains that the doctrine of the rule of law has its roots in Christian culture.[32] What limits the law of the state is the belief

---

29 For a somewhat different approach, which nevertheless seizes upon the importance of love in political theory, see Pateman, C, *The Disorder of Women*, 1990, Cambridge: Polity, pp 17–33. Pateman looks at the device of the social contract, and suggests that this is one of the primary justifying fictions of patriarchal politics. It allows a distinction to be made between a state of nature and a civic state. To be a party to the contract, and to enter the politics of the state is to be male and rational. Women are associated with the state of nature and the private realm of the family. In this fiction, women are fitted by nature to the natural ties of love and affection that exist in the intimacy of the family. This sense of love is opposed to a more civil sense of justice in a line of thought that stretches from Rousseau through Locke to Freud. Needless to say, Irigaray's disruption of this thinking is similar to Pateman's. The location in political theology is merely a different starting point. See, also, Jagger, A, *Feminist Politics and Human Nature*, 1988, New Jersey: Rowan and Littlefield.

30 For a development of this point in the theory of sovereignty, see Schmitt, C, *Political Theology: Four Chapters on the Concept of Sovereignty*, Schwab, G (trans), 1985, Cambridge, MA: MIT, p 38: 'The omnipotence of the modern law giver is not only linguistically derived from theology.'

31 See Kelly, DR, *The Human Measure*, 1990, Cambridge, MA: Harvard UP. Kelly shows that Western law can be traced to a conjunction of classical, Judaic and Christian sources. What was unique in the Christian source was the understanding of law as *logos*, a law of God which went beyond the civic. Human law had to be construed as consistent with divine law, as revealed in the Gospels. As much as this is important for the development of law, there is also an antinomianism that is inseparable from the Gospels. See Nygren, A, *Agape and Eros: A Study of the Christian Idea of Love*, 1930, London: SPCM. For a contemporary commentary, see both Millbank, J, *Theology and Social Theory; Beyond Secular Reason*, 1990, Oxford: Blackwells; and Rose, G, *The Broken Middle*, 1992, Oxford: Blackwells.

32 Bradley, AW and Ewing, KD, *Constitutional and Administrative Law*, 12th edn, 1997, Harlow: Longman, p 101.

in the individual worth of each human soul, each human being. One of the earliest systematic treaties on the polis, the city and its constitution, was St Augustine's City of God.[33] Augustine argues that the realisation of love in the human community is central to the realisation of a just polity. This line of thought could be traced through to later philosophers such as Thomas Aquinas. Aquinas' work was immensely influential in medieval political theory in the definition of the law, and this influence is still felt today.[34]

Irigaray can be read as reclaiming this tradition from the perspective of critical thought that acknowledges both its sustaining context in the history of what has been, and sees its work as the reinvention of traditional concepts. There are many aspects of this critique. Irigaray would disassociate love from the masculine deity of Christian religion, whilst not completely rejecting Christianity as an articulation of the mystery that confronts men and women. She would maintain as a kind of foundational myth a notion of love that would allow a certain discourse on community. Love is not just to be associated with the intimate or the subjective. Such an interpretation tends to restrict love to an exclusive association of women as mothers, and defines the order of the civic and the political as one of male objectivity.[35] Separated from the space of individual becoming, love's function in traditional political discourse is to become moulded into a civic or national identity where difference can be subsumed in collectivity.

To rediscover an alternative political love is to reexamine the space between people, between the lover and the beloved: love cannot be identified with an object, such as city or nation, or limited to an essential definition; rather it indicates a space, a difference *between* men and women. Love as difference does not prevent 'commitments' being made between people, commitments that will allow a building of a 'politics of difference', a politics built on a love *to* the other person.[36] This preposition indicates that love is a connective, it signifies an 'indirection' in that the lover does not reduce the

---

33   See Fitzpatrick, P, *The Mythology of Modern Law*, 1992, London: Routledge. Fitzpatrick argues that St Augustine's City of God is central to law's mythological structure. See also Gearey, A, 'Faith, love and a Christianity to come; re-reading St Augustine', in Oliver, P, Douglas Scott, S and Tadros, V (eds), *Faith in Law*, 1999, Oxford: Hart.

34   Aquinas' thought plays a major role in the jurisprudence of John Finnis, the contemporary exponent of natural law theory. It also lies behind the rebirth of Catholic social thought that influenced the founders of the European Union. Key writers include Etienne Gilson, Jacques Maritian and Albert Gortias.

35   For an elaboration of this argument, see Dietz, M, 'Citizenship with a feminist face: the problem with maternal thinking' (1985) 12 Political Theory 19. Dietz suggests that maternal thinking is complicit and reinforces the division between the public and the private that deprives women of a public life. Moreover, the mother-child relationship is inherently undemocratic and bares no relationship to a political relationship. Arguments which use the maternal as a starting point thus tend to lose what should be the real emphasis on issues of community and public power. Political love is not necessarily a thinking of a mother-child relationship.

36   *Op cit*, fn 15, Irigaray, p 112.

beloved to herself, but considers her as an other addressed by a love that presupposes a reciprocity, a space of exchange between two separated people.

Thinking this love means readdressing the definitions of the human nature that have underpinned the social ontologies of political thought.[37] Irigaray does not repeat the mistakes of the philosophers who exclude the female from a thinking of human ontology. For Irigaray, what we find in human nature is sexual difference. Nature is never a single, pure essence; it is already divided. The universal has to be thought on the basis of the two, not the one.[38] In place of 'man' as the single point of reference, there has to be a plural perspective:

> The natural, aside from the diversity of its incarnations or ways of appearing, is at least *two*: male and female. This division is not secondary nor unique to human kind. It cuts across all realms of the living which, without it, would not exist. Without sexual difference, there would be no life on earth. It is the manifestation of and condition for the production and reproduction of life …[39]

This presentation of difference demands a reappraisal of the great themes of the constitutional tradition:

> Man is not, in fact, absolutely free. That is not to say that he is enslaved to a nature and he must overcome it. Nor does it mean he is a slave. He is limited. His natural completion lies in two human beings.[40]

These words weave together the great themes of constitutionalism; the need to achieve man's freedom, his separation from nature and the problematic question of the orientation towards others and the world. As a theory of community, or what holds men and women together by existing between them, it suggests a definition of the human as inherently communicative and, hence, bound to a social commonality. If love is associated with this commonality, then it would cease to be identified purely with domesticity and intimacy, but would become a way of thinking the human community.

THE GUILD

To have any purchase on English constitutional thought, it is necessary to find some way of showing that Irigary's vision of community can have resonances with existing traditions; otherwise the whole project is open to the criticism that it is simply too remote to be of importance. The point of communication

---

37 See Cavarero, A, 'Equality and sexual difference: amnesia in political thought', in *op cit*, fn 1, Bock and James. Cavarero sees the fiction of the state of nature as important to modernist thought as it 'allows the radical elimination of the hierarchical conceptions of the differences amongst men' but makes for a blindness to sexual difference, or a conflation of the political order and 'patriarchalism.

38 *Op cit*, fn 15, Irigaray, p 35.

39 *Op cit*, fn 15, Irigaray, p 37.

40 *Op cit*, fn 15, Irigaray, p 41.

can be found in writings on the guild where community is defined as an associative space, a 'social relationship':

> Society, as a complex of organisations, cannot stand for, or express, all human life within a community, or the whole life of any single human being. Indeed, it is probably true that what is best in men and women escapes almost entirely from the net of society because it is incapable of being organised.[41]

What is essential to human life are our feelings of love and devotion. These have to be expressed in intense personal relationships that find their place in the family. Although the family tends towards society and community as a means of perpetuating itself, it remains inaccessible to organisation. This is a critical moment. There are at least two themes that need to be identified; after the implications of guild organisation have been examined, some important misgivings will be discussed. One can read here an advance on traditional theories of organisation. The end of community is not the state or the nation; nor is it the love of the fatherland or the motherland with its exclusion of the other, but the preservation of the intimate and associative space of love. It is a line of thought which resists a theory of the total state, the reduction of the individual to the whole. Guild organisation presupposes a diversity of centres of economic and political power.[42] Social cohesion depends on the extent to which these groups can co-operate. The theory acknowledges a tension between notions of communal organisation and individual motivation, and seeks to sustain them as an informing tension. Just as Irigaray attempts to associate love with a community of difference, the theory of the guild would attempt to resist the reduction of the individual to the whole or the erasure of specific desires in the name of the greater good of community. It is this idea of social ontology, as divided between the individual and the group, that

---

41 Cole, GDH, *Social Theory*, 1920, London: Methuen, p 55.

42 The key legal problem is thus the recognition of any form of social organisation which claims to found and control itself, and does not acknowledge that its 'being' is granted by the positive law of the state. How is the form of such an association to be understood in law? It is possible to establish a genealogy of this problem. In Roman law, the problem of a plethora of social bodies was resolved by the notion of the *nomen juris* or the fictive person. As the body was purely fictional, it could have no substantive or natural being; it thus derived its very existence from the prince who, as the source of the law, granted legal being. This 'concession theory of corporate life' was massively influential in the both the canonist and continental legal traditions and, through the office of the Lord Chancellor, who was trained as a Roman lawyer, impacted on the common law. The shadow of the concession theory can be demonstrated by reference to the famous *Taff Vale* decision (*Taff Vale Railway Co v Amalgamated Society of Railway Servants* [1901] AC 426). The *Taff Vale* case effectively made unions responsible for the acts of their agents, and hence liable for damages, even though they were not legally constituted as corporations. What lies behind this case, and other union cases, is the idea that unions are composed of a mere collection of individuals and have no legal 'group being'.

underlies the fiction of a sovereignty that can include everyone into a single state and represent every social function.[43]

At the same time, building a theory of social organisation on the family might appear to repeat the tendency of traditional political theory to restrict the female to the family and the home, and to make civic life the preserve of men. To co-ordinate this with feminist thought, as developed by Irigaray, would mean intensifying its positive aspects, whilst resisting the repetition of the conventional identifications of the political tradition.

An essential component of this kind of thinking is a way of articulating the presence of women in public life. It will be suggested that the notion of political love and sovereignty understood as a community of difference can be linked to a form of guild pluralism which, as yet remains marginal to political thinking. Its recovery necessitates a review of how the guild itself has been perceived in legal and political thought.[44] The following discussion of the fragmentary evidence is brief; it is merely a starting point for a possible genealogy which suggests that the guild was not an exclusively male institution; any substantive feminist history of the guild would be a different project.

Medieval guilds were noted for the membership of women.[45] It might be suggested that these bodies allowed women some form of civic identity. They were not organised along feudal lines, but provided a kind of 'artificial family' for their members. This is reflected in the swearing of an oath to guild members rather than a superior figure. The function of the guild was to provide mutual aid, an obligation that was central to the 'ethos' of the guild, and this extended to organising insurance schemes and the care of those who had suffered misfortune. Moreover, guilds had a jurisdiction over their members, the power of law to solve disputes and award penalties.

The legal and political literature on guilds has largely ignored the fragmentary evidence of female membership. It is possible to establish that, in the early middle ages, women were active in guilds and achieved a measure of civic and political power. The cloth and clothing industries were dominated

---

43 For a development of this argument, see Figgis, JN, *Churches in the Modern State*, 1913, London: Longman. The dominant idea of sovereignty can be traced to the influence of Roman law. When the Romans adopted the Aristotelian notion of the state as a people gathered together in one place, they applied the idea to empire, and immediately distorted it. The emperor became the sovereign; the *legitibus solus*. When the Holy Roman Empire replaced the Roman Empire this notion of totality was not rejected.

44 Black, A, *Guilds and Civil Society in European Political Thought from the Twelfth Century to the Present*, 1984, London: Methuen, p 3. The word guild first appeared in Europe around AD 450 and it signified a group held together by a *gilda*, or sacrificial meal held in honour of the dead. This is part of a wider phenomenon. It has often been pointed out that women were linked to the dead in ancient society and to the preparation for burial or cremation. This might suggest a more mythological association of women and guilds.

45 *Ibid*, p 4.

by women, and there were many independent producers. The oldest guild ordinances, dating from Basel in 1226 show that women had equal rights to male guild members and could work, buy and sell under the same conditions. There were exclusively female guilds in Paris and Cologne; and women also had a significant presence in guilds in Frankfurt, Regensburg, Lubech and Quedlinberg.[46] In Frankfurt, by 1370, guilds had gained access to government and held a minority of council seats. This might have meant that women could have voted for government officers, and also, theoretically, have been eligible for government office themselves.[47]

This history indicates that the guild as a form of social organisation was not inherently a preserve of men. Evidence suggests that the guild served as both a locus for the interests of women in employment and as a possible bridge into political life. The prevalence of the guild throughout northern Europe also shows that it was central to the civic fabric of medieval life. How can this approach be made relevant? It could easily be objected that some fragmentary historical evidence and a return to 19th century social thought is an inadequate response to contemporary political and constitutional problems. In the face of such arguments, it is worth returning to the radical agenda of guild thought, where the state is linked to the 'horror of that very economic and industrial oppression which is the distinctive gift of modern capitalism to history'.[48] Although this might provide a starting point, what remains open to question is the construction of an engaged theory of sovereignty which can contend with the particular form of the modern state which increasingly rests not on the absolute state but on the sovereignty of the market.[49] The sovereignty of the market itself has been informed by a market based pluralism, which made use of the strong state to devolve certain aspects of governmental power and responsibility in areas where the market was seen as the primary regulator. Market pluralism was particularly opposed to direct democracy and any notion of progressive social transformation. A picture

---

46   Opitz, C, 'Life in the Middle Ages', in Klapisch-Zuber, C (ed), *A History of Women*, 1992, Cambridge, MA: Belknap, pp 300–03. See, also, Howell, C, 'Citizens and gender: women's political status in northern mediaeval cities', in Erler, M and Kowaleski, M (eds), *Women and Power in the Middle Ages*, 1988, Athens: Georgia UP, p 37. For a consideration of the individual biographies of medieval women and their civic lives, see Barron, CM and Sutton, AF (eds), *Medieval London Widows*, 1994, London: Hambledon. A key source on guilds in England would be Toulmin Smith, J, Toulmin Smith, L and Brenato, L (eds), *English Guilds: The Original Ordinances of More than One Hundred Early English Guilds*, 1870 (reprinted, 1963), os 40, London: Early English Text Society. Research has shown that there is evidence from English guild ordinances that in some cases women had membership as of right, and in others, membership was a privilege. Again, there is evidence of guilds whose membership was exclusively female; but there were also bodies where women had full membership but could not become guild officers. Continental sources return to de Boileau, E, *Livre des Metiers*, de Lespianasse, R and Bonnardot, F (eds), 1879 (reprinted 1980), Geneva: Slatkie Reprints.

47   *Ibid*, Howell, p 47.

48   *Op cit*, fn 43, Figgis, p 57.

49   *Op cit*, fn 7, Craig, p 156.

thus emerges of a state which retains its sovereign powers in many areas of policy making, but has hived off certain functions to powerful economic actors which seem to be beyond any form of public control. Given the hegemony of market pluralism in British politics, and the negative impact it has had on any oppostional discourse or organisation, a contemporary theory of pluralism needs to arm itself against this actuality.

UPDATING THE TRADITION: THE PLURAL STATE AND ANTI-GOVERNMENT

The challenges posed by a strong central state and a largely privatised set of utilities, public services and finance markets can be faced by a rethought relationship between a central power and a decentralisation linked with the guild. This polity can be articulated as a theory of anti-government which has been developed in radical social theory. Anti-government could be defined as a 'scheme to facilitate the self organisation of society outside of government'.[50] It would be wrong to confuse this with an anarchist rejection of the state. It is an attempt to balance the opportunities offered for social transformation by central power with the restraint provided by independent organisations. Linking anti-government to the theory of the guild is essential to the construction of a pluralist polity that is coherent with a progressive feminism.

This schema makes use of the notion of central power. How can this be reconciled with the arguments so far presented? A constitution could be built around devolved guilds operating locally, but with a residual form of overarching public power. The major problem is that of the accountability of any central agency. Central power has to be utilised, but there is the risk that through democratic process a party resistant to change might take control. Keeping this body accountable and ensuring that it can further social change is achievable though an intensification of the traditional division of power into three branches and proliferating the 'overlapping' functions of governmental agencies which ensure no one faction can seize control. Furthermore, harnessing government to social change necessitates the creation of an agency charged with the overall intervention in the control and distribution of both information and expertise as 'the effort to control the sources of technical knowledge and expertise is the natural ambition of unresponsive power'.[51]

It may be relatively straightforward to conceive of a plurality of guilds which organise the economic and political aspects of community and enable

---

50 Unger, RM, *False Necessity; Anti-Necessitarian Social Theory in the Service of Radical Democracy*, 1987, Cambridge: CUP, p 476.

51 *Ibid*, p 450.

self-government and participation and a continued scrutiny of decision making. Councils could be set up for the production and supply of utilities; civic guilds could take responsibility for health care, education and other administrative functions.[52] Problems still remain, however, in the relationship between central and local power. This could express itself in the increased power of the guilds that controlled essential services, and also in the relationship between central power and locality. Both these problems may be resoluable if the idea of decentralisation in anti-government theory could be linked to guild pluralism. There could be a 'conditional right to opt out of the norms established by higher authorities'.[53] Very broadly, this would allow groups who could show that the proposed opt-out was determined by parties of 'relative equality' and that 'the proposed arrangement should not sustain a relationship of subjugation'[54] to reject any directives or recommendations from central authority. Opt-out rights could be incorporated within an operationalisation of a principle of subsidiarity that would devolve power from higher to lower levels of government. Attached to each devolution of power would be a guarantee that it would not serve to preserve or proliferate existing relations of inequality or the sustenance of elite privileges.

A decentralised notion of sovereignty has a vision of a transformed and transforming reinvention of rights at its core. In reinventing any schema of rights, though, account has to be taken of the objections to the form of rights as linked inescapably to the protection of settled property relations. Any claim that rights could be extended and reformed to cover those interests of women not traditionally seen as conducive to juridification would have to take this argument seriously. A possible reply to any argument for the limitation of rights to the form of property would be that this position fails to engage in a sufficiently imaginative way with the transformative dynamic of anti-government. One possible direction is to think in terms of immunity rights, destabilisation rights and solidarity rights. These rights would differ from the presently conceived property rights but would not replace them. They would also contribute to the relocation of power in community and the disruption of monopolies. Immunity rights would be accompanied by destabilisation rights. The former would protect individuals or groups against applications of governmental power and against any form of exclusion from public decision making. Immunity rights would also guarantee an adequate amount of welfare protection. Destabilisation rights would be dedicated to the breaking down of hierarchies of power. Alongside destabilisation rights, solidarity rights would 'give legal form to social relations of reliance and trust'.[55] This last group of rights covers a wide field that includes all aspects of

---

52 Pateman, C, *Participation and Democratic Theory*, 1970, Cambridge: CUP, pp 40–41.
53 *Op cit*, fn 50, Unger, p 486.
54 *Op cit*, fn 50, Unger, p 490.
55 *Op cit*, fn 50, Unger, p 535.

'interdependence' and could be built up from principles already existing in the law of fiduciary relations, the contractual doctrines of reliance and the notion of good faith. This would also give a possible legal form to Irigaray's idea of sexate rights, discussed above.

In any viable counterposition to economic or market sovereignty, there is the need for an increased distribution of resources in touch with a notion of popular empowerment. This could take the form of an appropriation of resources by those excluded from the present commercial and financial sources of power. It would be possible to follow the outlines of one proposal: '[the] key ... the breakup of control over capital into several tiers of capital takers and capital givers.'[56] A capital fund could be established on which individuals and groups could make claims, although capital would be made available to individuals indirectly, after the central fund had allocated it to independent capital trusts. What would be imaginable is a quasi-market overseen by central power; but this would be a long way from market pluralism, as the imperative would be redistribution and circulation of capital rather than its amassing in the hands of a few commercial actors.

It is impossible within the confines of this chapter to develop in greater detail the implications of this radical notion of democracy. The important point is, however, that it returns to a notion of the sovereignty of the community of both mutual reliance and ongoing social transformation. In this associative space, we can express the 'desire to be accepted by one another and to become, through this acceptance, freer to reinvent ourselves'.[57] This passion can be seen as political love or the need to recover the thinking of love as intermediary, the space between or the space of sexual difference through a creative re-reading of the tradition that privileges totality and fixed meaning. Secondly, it means that love cannot be simply identified with an object. Love has to be positioned as a principle of disruption, of difference and non-hierarchy. Moreover, it has to be linked to the visibility of women in public life, the life of the plural state. The discussion of political love is a realisation that sovereignty as the sovereignty of social relationships is, at root, an argument that the state should be imagined as serving the good of people, rather than preserving its own monopolies on power.

REMEMBERING THE FUTURE

This chapter has set up an encounter between the writings of the French feminist Luce Irigaray and English constitutional theory. In this conjunction, it is hoped that there has emerged an alternative vision of sovereignty. What lies

---

56   *Op cit*, fn 50, Unger.
57   Unger, RM, *Passion*, 1984, New York: Free Press, p vii.

behind the reinvention of sovereignty is a notion of human sociability founded in sexual difference. It is an idea of community that has been ignored by conventional constitutional thought. To introduce this kind of thinking to the law is to contend that the law can be a site of transformation. Elaborating this insight has made it necessary to think through a whole tradition which has determined the form of the law, and foreclosed debates about its nature. Irigaray's theory of community must be seen in this oppositional and utopian sense. Her approach is as much performative as descriptive or constative: in describing a community based on love, it initiates a dialogue about its possibility. It must be remembered as well that this is an attempt to redress a balance, to appropriate a constitutional tradition; to give women an objective identity which they have been culturally denied. Utopian dreams? Maybe.

CHAPTER 8

CITIZENSHIP AND DEMOCRACY: FEMINIST POLITICS OF CITIZENSHIP AND RADICAL DEMOCRATIC POLITICS

Elizabeth Kingdom

INTRODUCTION

What is the nature and scope of public law? There are three types of definition: descriptive, analytic and normative. A descriptive definition would comprise an amalgam of the table of contents of standard public law texts and a codification of the topics taught in public law courses. Such a definition will be conservative in the sense that it reproduces prevailing principles, concepts and practices of public law. To overcome that problem, an analytic definition might try to identify the meaning of the term public law, contrasting 'public' and 'private' law and pointing out that 'law' refers to legislation, rules and processes. The difficulties of this type of definition have been clearly documented by Andrew Le Sueur and Maurice Sunkin and they adopt the innovative strategy of supplementing that discussion with vignettes of public law as perceived by a government minister, a citizen and an academic.[1] In including the citizen's perspective, this strategy introduces a normative element, a matter of principle, into the definition of public law, for it emphasises how the constitutional system ought to relate to individual citizens or campaigning groups. The fullest development of this approach is to give a normative definition of public law, a proposal for how public law ought to be studied. Indeed, a standard text of public law opens with the vigorous claim that:

> The starting point for studying constitutional law should ideally be the same starting point as for studying political philosophy, or the role of law and government in society. How is individual freedom to be reconciled with the claims of social justice? Is society founded upon a reciprocal network of rights and duties, or is the individual merely a pawn in the hands of state power?[2]

Quite disarmingly, however, the text proceeds to the observation that '[t]hese fundamental questions are often not pursued explicitly in the study of

---

1 Le Sueur, A and Sunkin, M, *Public Law*, 1997, London: Longman, pp 4–12.
2 Bradley, AW and Ewing, KD, *Constitutional and Administrative Law*, 1997, 12th edn, London: Longman, p 3. See McDonald, Chapter 6, this volume, for an account of the constitutional textbook tradition.

constitutional law'.[3] In fact, the reference at this point to constitutional law facilitates the move away from questions of political philosophy to a technical account of the nature of a constitution, of constitutional law, administrative law, and public international law. By a similar manoeuvre, the opening questions about the relation between the state and society, about the possibility of reconciling individual freedom and social justice, and about rights duties and power – all central topics about the nature of citizenship in political philosophy – are converted into specific questions about the current state of citizenship legislation.

Now, if texts in public law similarly committed to an engagement with the broad questions of political philosophy were to examine political philosophy at greater leisure, they would find a discipline no longer effortlessly dominated by the tenets of liberal democratic theory. It is no longer dominated by the conceptualisation of the state as the impartial guardian of citizens' interests and the provider of political structures enabling citizens to participate in discussions and decision making on matters of national importance. Instead, they would find a discipline where the assumptions of liberal democratic theory have been subjected to a massive critique, primarily by Marxism and by feminism. Marxist theory challenges the political neutrality of the state, identifying law as a key instrument of the state's exploitation of subjects and analysing 'rights' as a bourgeois discourse. Feminist theory, in turn, challenges the gender blindness of Marxism and proceeds to expose state institutions and practices as oppressive of women. Feminism claims that 'rights' are typically understood as men's rights, reflecting men's public life and contemptuous of women's rights, both in the public and in the private sphere. The force of these critiques quite undermines any account of public law which rests on the bland assumptions of liberal democratic theory. Indeed, Paul Craig mounts just such an attack on Dawn Oliver's view of public law.[4] Briefly, while Oliver has charted the expansion of public law to incorporate consideration of basic citizenship rights,[5] Craig shows that she resists the claim that a court might resolve a case by reference to competing political norms and what he terms 'background political arguments' about, for example, primary versus ancillary rights. Craig argues convincingly that Oliver's picture of citizenship is not neutral, that it invokes a somewhat hazy notion of liberal democracy, and that it cannot be separated from political questions about the status of different citizens' economic assets.[6] It is worth noting, too, that Craig's devastating critique of the

---

3   *Op cit*, fn 2, Bradley and Ewing.

4   Craig, P, 'Public law, sovereignty and citizenship', in Blackburn, R (ed), *Rights of Citizenship*, 1993, London: Mansell, pp 308–13.

5   Oliver, D, 'What is happening to relationships between the individual and the state?', in Jowell, J and Oliver, D (eds), *The Changing Constitution*, 1994, Oxford: Clarendon.

6   *Ibid*, Craig, p 313.

vagueness of Oliver's picture of rights and duties incorporates the powerful argument that TH Marshall's analysis of political, social and civil rights can no longer be seen as the unproblematic starting point for public law texts, a point to which I will return in my analysis of feminist politics of citizenship in the section headed 'Feminist politics of citizenship'.[7]

Craig's argument highlights the traditional absence from public law of debates about citizenship and rights in the context of democratic politics. At the same time, in the context of contemporary constitutional reform, Christopher McCrudden and Gerald Chambers have identified 'the emergence of rights' consciousness'[8] and there is evidence that some public lawyers are starting to give more attention to these questions.[9] Further, in this volume, Colin Harvey notes that some public lawyers are committed to the project of identifying shared values in both public and private law, some drawing on the work of Habermas.[10] Even in these more sophisticated texts, however, little attention is given to the voluminous feminist literature on the strengths and weaknesses of liberal democratic politics, on citizenship and women's historic exclusion from it, and on rights.

From a feminist point of view, however, public law's inattention to citizenship and to rights, and in particular to women's rights, is not remedied by the simple inclusion of discussions about the particular claims of women in

---

7   Craig's attack on the parochial nature of prevailing concepts of public law and his insistence that public law be guided by normative principles intimate a further critique of public law which is beyond the scope of this chapter. Briefly, this is the critique of public law in the UK as being too narrowly circumscribed by topics relating only to the UK constitution and to those international legal texts, such as the European Convention on Human Rights, which have a direct impact on UK legislation. It has long been a feminist principle that received divisions of academic disciplines be questioned and that feminists should not be impervious to political developments in other countries. In the case of the study of public law, and of the connected studies of public international law, international law and human rights law, it is salutary for feminists to note the difficulties of marking out clear boundaries. Similarly, feminists may well profit from observing the ways in which features of non-UK constitutions, such as rights discourse, differ from those of the UK constitution. Accordingly, from time to time, I include illustrations which refer to the American constitution, even though it is not possible to make strict comparisons between it and the (as yet) unwritten UK constitution, and I give examples from international law, even though its effect on the UK constitution is, in the absence of constitutional guarantees, uncertain. In this respect, however, one should not underestimate the potential impact on government autonomy of the international treaties, covenants and conventions to which the UK has subscribed. Cf McCrudden, C and Chambers, G, 'Introduction: human rights in British law', in *Individual Rights and the Law in Britain*, 1994, Oxford: Clarendon, p 4.

8   *Ibid*, p 8.

9   Cf *op cit*, fn 4, Blackburn; Feldman, D, *Civil Liberties and Human Rights in England and Wales*, 1993, Oxford: Clarendon; and Hunt, M, *Using Human Rights Law in English Courts*, 1997, Oxford: Hart.

10 Harvey, Chapter 10, this volume, is a relatively rare example of work in the Habermas industry which addresses the pertinence of Habermas for feminist politics. For a useful overview of feminists' ambivalence over Habermas' work, cf Fraser, N, *Unruly Practices: Power, Discourse and Gender in Contemporary Social Theory*, 1989, London: Polity.

these respects. For it is one of the lasting achievements of feminist politics of citizenship that it challenges the capacity of standard concepts in liberal democratic theory to address women's social situation. This chapter contributes to the project of exhibiting the relevance of feminist perspectives to public law with an account of the critique of these standard concepts as developed by feminist politics of citizenship. It also describes the way in which some feminists associated with feminist politics of citizenship are expressing reservations about feminist politics of citizenship, reservations which give rise to the growing literature of radical democratic politics.[11]

Feminist politics of citizenship is a most influential analysis of the obstacles to women's enjoyment of full citizenship status and hence to their full enjoyment of citizenship rights. It offers a variety of explanations for women's exclusion from the full benefits of citizenship and a variety of proposals for their greater inclusion. It would not be an exaggeration to say that this type of feminist politics has been an article of faith for feminists involved in citizenship debates. It is politically disturbing, then, to find that this type of feminist politics being criticised for running counter to democratic politics. Briefly, the criticism is that it is contrary to the spirit of democratic politics that gender claims be given priority over the claims of other political groupings, such as ethnic minorities or even as yet unformed political groupings. This is the position to be found in the texts of radical democratic politics. The project of these texts is to mark the ideological and political mechanisms which serve to exclude from full citizenship not only women but groups which may be structured around many different and changing social identities. In its turn, radical democratic politics is the object of the feminist counterattack that it is inescapably unprincipled in its approach to politics and that it undermines feminist politics.

---

11 The term 'feminist politics of citizenship' is not in standard use, but I introduce it here to capture the main focus of feminist writings on citizenship and on rights in contemporary Western politics. I follow convention in citing Pateman and Walby as its chief exponents, because, as Joni Lovenduski and Vicky Randall have observed, their work has been extremely influential and has advanced feminist understanding of liberal democratic politics. At the same time, Lovenduski and Randall continue, certain central issues, such as the limitations of the concept of patriarchy, remain unresolved: Lovenduski, J and Randall, V, *Contemporary Feminist Politics: Women and Power in Britain*, 1993, Oxford: OUP, pp 8–9. It is to such issues that the literature of radical democratic politics attends. This term is in current use. It is associated with the work of Chantal Mouffe and Anna Yeatman, and I tend to use these authors to illustrate the main features of radical democratic politics. 'Radical democracy' is also a key term in the influential series of public debates, initiated in 1994 in the US, which questioned the unity of 'the Left' and proposed the replacement of socialism as the Left's governing logic with a commitment to 'radical democracy'. Cf Trend, D (ed), *Radical Democratic Politics: Identity, Citizenship and the State*, 1995, Routledge: London. It is arguable that there is some overlap in the scope of feminist politics of citizenship and radical democratic politics, and I discuss this below. For a useful account of the work of key authors in both categories, cf Lister, R, 'Citizenship and difference: towards a differentiated universalism' (1998) 1(1) European Journal of Social Theory 71.

This chapter addresses two linked questions: can feminist politics of citizenship survive the challenge of the radical democratic critique, and can radical democratic politics survive the feminist counterattack?

Below, in the next section, I give a brief account of feminist politics of citizenship. The following section, entitled 'The radical democratic critique,' is a short description of radical democratic politics and of its critique of feminist politics of citizenship. Following that, 'The feminist counterattack' is an account of the feminist counterattack on radical democratic politics. This mainly involves the argument that radical democratic politics is characterised by an absence of principles for the analysis and conduct of feminist politics. Here, I argue that radical democratic politics has a first line of defence which points to a rich resource of political materials for the purposes of engaging in democratic politics, but that this line of defence is superficial and fails to address the persisting force of the charge that radical democratic politics is unprincipled politics. If radical democratic politics is to survive that criticism, I argue that it must address the fundamental question of the nature of principled politics. The section entitled 'Principled politics' begins with an account of this. It is defined as a rationalist conception of politics according to which practical politics and policies can be derived from principles. Using feminist attempts to derive politics from principles, such as oppression and patriarchy, I argue that it is never possible to effect that derivation, and I extend that argument to the impossibility of deriving politics from the type of rights discourse to be found both in traditional democratic theory and in feminist politics of citizenship. I argue that the aspirations of the feminist counterattack in this regard are doomed to failure. The basic assumption of the role of principles which is to be found in the texts of feminist politics of citizenship is accordingly untenable, and it is the strength of radical democratic politics that it recognises the inadequacy of rationalist conceptions of politics for engagement with politics. It is commendable, then, that the texts of radical democratic politics develop a new type of political principle. These political principles are crucial for the development and organisation of democratic politics, but they make no rationalistic assumptions about the derivation of political strategies simply on the strength of invoking democratic principles. The 'Principles of radical democratic politics' section examines some examples of this reconceptualisation of democratic politics. I argue that these approaches also require the reconceptualisation of rights discourse, and, under the heading 'A reconceptualisation of rights', I put forward three suggestions for such a reconceptualisation: rights in general as political heuristics; the concept of citizenship rights as signalling a permanent review of the exclusionary and inclusionary mechanisms of democratic politics; and specific citizenship rights as rebuttable claims. I argue that these proposals are consonant with the project of radical democratic politics and that, whilst they neither prioritise nor dismiss women's rights, they provide a congenial al space for the recognition of the massive backlog of unrealised ... hist claims. Accordingly, whilst the respective projects of radical democratic politics and of feminist politics of citizenship may not be fully reconcilable, they are not implacably opposed.

FEMINIST POLITICS OF CITIZENSHIP

A fundamental tenet of traditional democratic theory is that properly democratic structures provide for the representation of minorities and for their enjoyment of the same protections and rights as all other citizens. The goal of feminist politics of citizenship is to secure those protections and rights for women. The key feature of feminist politics of citizenship is the claim that the political structures and ideologies under which citizenship rights are claimed, whether these are referred to generally as rights or whether they are rights specified by a written constitution, have systematically excluded women from full citizenship status and that, as a result, women have been denied full enjoyment of citizenship rights.

The starting point of feminist politics of citizenship is frequently the observation that the standard texts on citizenship, such as Marshall (on citizenship rights),[12] are marked by an absence of reference to gender. These texts are accordingly criticised for presuming a unitary concept of citizenship which conceals the systematic nature of the exclusion of women from full participation in public affairs.[13] On this view, a key ideological mechanism which serves to exclude women from full citizenship status is the designation of the common concerns of women as private, domestic and non-economic. A most persuasive exponent of this position is Sylvia Walby. To expose the covertly gendered nature of the standard concepts of citizenship, Walby argues for the insertion of an analysis of gender relations into debates on eligibility for welfare benefits, debates upon which citizenship is typically predicated.[14] Similarly, in her analysis of the patriarchal welfare state, Pateman has argued for a patriarchal understanding of citizenship according to which women are faced with an irresoluble dilemma. If, on the one hand, women demand citizenship on a par with men, they are subscribing to a concept of 'citizen' which has been constructed from men's attributes, capacities and activities in the public sphere. Women gain citizenship at the price of becoming lesser men. But if, on the other hand, women demand

---

12   Marshall, T, *Citizenship and Social Class*, 1950, Cambridge: CUP.

13   Pateman, C, 'The patriarchal welfare state', in McDowell, L and Pringle, R (eds), *Defining Women: Social Institutions and Gender Divisions*, 1992, Cambridge: Polity in association with The Open University, pp 227–28. Cf, also, Pateman, C, *The Sexual Contract*, 1988, Stanford: Stanford UP.

14   Walby, S, 'Is citizenship gendered?' (1994) 28 Sociology 379.

recognition of their specific talents, needs and responsibilities in the private sphere, they stay defined as men's dependants and, again, will be allocated an inferior citizen status.[15] Pateman argues forcefully that the social basis for the ideal of the full (male) employment society is crumbling. She urges feminists to exploit the concomitant political challenge to the patriarchal dichotomy – between women and independence-work-citizenship – in order to reach a new understanding of citizenship, one which is not predicated on men's freedom from responsibility from private welfare work.[16]

The brevity of this account of feminist politics of citizenship should not be taken to imply that it has been an insignificant political force. On the contrary, feminist politics of citizenship is an immensely powerful critique of the ideologies and institutions implicated in the construction of citizenship rights. It continues the tradition of first wave feminism and its promotion of the rights of women: it has been the intellectual force behind equal rights campaigns, has had a lasting influence on contemporary politics, and, above all, has upheld the value of women's participation in political life. But it has been subjected to two powerful critiques and, ironically, these are critiques which have frequently been prompted by feminists who have themselves been associated with feminist politics of citizenship, but whose work can also be allied to radical democratic politics. The first critique concerns the problematic nature of rights and the second concerns questions of difference.

The first critique has been to challenge the problematic nature of invoking rights for the purposes of feminist politics. Feminists have argued that rights have been defined and enjoyed on the basis of human attributes which are typically masculine. For example, Catharine MacKinnon has argued that freedom of speech under the American Constitution is effectively the right of men to enjoy pornography, and that the right to equal pay has been eroded by the persistence of the ideology of the traditional male-headed family in which the man's higher pay is justified because he supports his family.[17] But Carol Smart has argued, most feminists would say decisively, that MacKinnon's theory of the state – and law – is essentialist, in the sense that it depends on a division of the population into two categories, men and women, which are defined by reference to the *essential status* of the oppressor and the oppressed. Accordingly, she has warned against over-simple theories of the patriarchal state, on the grounds that they impede feminists' ability to engage with the transformation of social conditions and, in a later work, she pays tribute to the complexity and subtlety of the feminist critiques of rights discourse which

---

15 *Op cit*, fn 13, Pateman, 1992, p 236.

16 *Op cit*, fn 13, Pateman, 1992, p 243.

17 MacKinnon, CA, *Feminism Unmodified: Discourses on Life and Law*, 1987, Harvard: Harvard UP, pp 200, 224. For an invaluable overview of 'the problem of rights' for feminist politics, see Smart, C, *Feminism and the Power of Law*, 1989, London: Routledge, ch 7.

have taken the interrogation of MacKinnon into the sphere of practical feminist politics.[18]

The second critique is usefully introduced through the work of Margaret Thornton. Her compelling work on the masculinity of citizenship falls clearly in the tradition of feminist politics of citizenship. Yet, in her attack on the myth of neutrality in liberal democratic politics, Thornton asks to what extent it is possible for multiple identities to be incorporated within a general concept of the citizen. Thornton asks:

> Can each citizen herself be recognised as a three-dimensional figure, shaped by a multiplicity of factors, including race, class, sexuality, able-bodiedness, and variegated life experiences, rather than a cardboard cutout that can be slotted into a one-dimensional, uniformly grey jigsaw, the pieces of which neatly conjoin to make an inevitably bland picture of 'the citizen' with which few can identify?[19]

With this question, Thornton introduces the concept of difference and clearly intimates its importance for feminists. Thornton herself reverts rapidly to her theme of the masculinity of citizenship, but other feminists have found that raising Thornton's question requires them to address the adequacy of feminist politics of citizenship to new emphases on difference. The problem is this: if, as feminists recognise, there are significant differences not simply between men and women but between women, it follows that feminists can no longer rely on the universal category of 'women' to formulate their politics. They can no longer rely on essentialist categories of gender which conceptualise genders in terms of their permanently defining characteristics. Further, once it is recognised that some groups of women are more advantaged than other groups, including some groups of men, it follows that a democratic politics cannot prioritise the claims of those groups of women simply on the grounds that they are women.[20]

---

18   Smart, C, 'Feminism and law: some problems of analysis and strategy' (1986) 14 International Journal of the Sociology of Law 109. See, also, Kingdom, EF, *What's Wrong with Rights? Problems for Feminist Politics of Law*, 1991, Edinburgh: Edinburgh UP, for a critique of rights which is associated with feminist politics of citizenship but which concludes with an argument for the reconceptualisation of rights which would be more consonant with radical democratic politics.

19   Thornton, M, 'Embodying the citizen', in Thornton, M, *Public and Private: Feminist Legal Debates*, 1996, Oxford: OUP, p 216.

20   I have characterised this matter in terms of the claims of groups. Surprising as it may seem, this is controversial and invokes a debate surrounding the work of Iris Marion Young. Briefly, Young has argued for a conception of justice which acknowledges and affirms group differences: Young, IM, *Justice and the Politics of Difference*, 1990, Oxford: Princeton UP, p 10. But various feminists have been alert to the risks of 'freezing' group identities, such that the claims of as yet unformed groups may be prejudiced. Cf Yuval-Davies, N, *Gender and Nation*, 1997, London: Sage, p 86; and Mouffe, C, 'Feminism, citizenship, and radical democratic politics', in Butler, J and Scott, JW (eds), *Feminists Theorise the Political*, 1992, London: Routledge, p 380. This controversy can be used to illustrate the difficulty of assigning particular authors to the camp of either feminist politics of citizenship or radical democratic politics. I discuss this at the end of this section, where I maintain that they are two separate camps, and I return to the question of how the two camps can be, if not reconciled, then at least seen as not implacably hostile in my conclusion.

The collapse of the concept of universal citizenship, the rejection of essentialist categories of gender, and the celebration of diversity and difference are recurrent themes of writers such as Judith Butler, Nancy Fraser, Seyla Benhabib, Jodi Dean and Iris Marion Young.[21] Their work in reconstructing the concepts of social and political theory is clearly feminist, in the sense that it continues the feminist project of unmasking the alleged neutrality of the state, of citizenship and of rights and of charting the ways in which gender status has persistently worked to disadvantage women. Further, Benhabib remarks of several contributions to her collection on democracy and difference:

> Undoubtedly, the form of difference that is in the forefront of the majority of contributions ... is the oppression of women. Even in those essays ... where it is not the exclusive focus of attention, gender discrimination and the experience of the women's movements are in the background.[22]

Benhabib's remark shows the difficulty of assigning particular authors to the position I describe as feminist politics of citizenship and to that of radical democratic politics, and Nancy Fraser has provided a brilliant account of the complex interrelations between different kind of feminisms and different versions of radical democracy.[23] But she correctly emphasises the mutual suspicion of feminist politics of citizenship and radical democratic politics. This suspicion is clearly illustrated by the link which Fraser makes between radical democratic politics and anti-essentialist and deconstructive politics. The aim of this latter type of politics is to root out universal concepts of gender and to destabilise gender difference and the gender identities that accompany it.[24] Now, this type of politics draws on the literature of postmodernism. At its most general level, postmodernism is the critique of theories which seek to identify – once and for all – the philosophical criteria of truth, certainty and proof for the evaluation of claims to knowledge. In its political form, it is the project of abandoning the tendency of conventional social and political theory to produce essentialist and universalistic theories of society, the state and citizenship. This is the project of radical democratic politics.

---

21 Butler, J, 'Contingent foundations: feminism and the question of "postmodernism"', in *op cit*, fn 20, Butler and Scott; Fraser, *op cit*, fn 10; Benhabib, S, *Situating the Self: Gender, Community and Postmodernism in Contemporary Ethics*, 1992, Cambridge: Polity; Dean, J, 'The reflective solidarity of democratic feminism', in Dean, J (ed), *Feminism and the New Democracy*, 1997, London: Sage; Benhabib, S, 'Toward a deliberative model of democratic legitimacy' and Young, IM, 'Communication and the other: beyond deliberative democracy', in Benhabib, S (ed), *Democracy and Difference: Contesting the Boundaries of the Political*, 1996, Princeton, NJ: Princeton UP; see, also, various chapters in Benhabib, above, and articles in (1989) 99 Ethics, Symposium on Feminism and Political Theory.

22 Benhabib, S, 'Introduction', in *ibid*, Benhabib, p 12.

23 Fraser, N, 'Equality, difference and radical democracy', in *op cit*, fn 11, Trend.

24 *Ibid*, p 204.

This radical democratic critique is extended to challenge the essentialism and universalism of feminist politics of citizenship – its essentialism in conceptualising women as a single and unified group, and its universalism in supposing that all members of that group share the same political demands. Just as Nancy Fraser and Linda J Nicholson point out, feminism and postmodernism have worked largely independently of each other in their respective attempts to generate the conceptual tools of social criticism,[25] so there is a political distance between feminist politics of citizenship and radical democratic politics as conceptualised in this chapter. Agreed, it may turn out that this distance will narrow to the point where feminist politics of citizenship and radical democratic politics will be seen, not as competing views of contemporary politics relating to citizenship and rights, but as complementary developments in progressive and radical politics. Indeed, I argue in this chapter that feminist politics of citizenship is a valuable resource for radical democratic politics. Meanwhile, the mutual suspicion of feminist politics of citizenship and radical democratic politics is undeniable. As indicated above, it is illustrated by the claims that feminism retains forms of universalism and essentialism and that the politics of radical democracy are anemic.[26] It is the first of these claims to which I now turn, with the second claim receiving attention in the section, 'The feminist counterattack'.

THE RADICAL DEMOCRATIC CRITIQUE

One basic premise of conventional democratic theory is that properly democratic political structures provide for the representation of minorities. The theory further stipulates that only those who are not themselves committed to the democratic values of legality and tolerance may be excluded from participation in public life. Feminist politics of citizenship continues the anti-elitist and inclusivist tradition of conventional democratic theory. But, whilst the project of feminist politics of citizenship is to expose the failure of conventional democratic theory to live up to its own norms in the case of women's citizenship rights, the project of radical democratic politics is to mark the ideological and political mechanisms which serve to exclude not only women but groups constructed around many different and changing social identities. This critique is a challenge to the essentialism and universalism found in feminist politics of citizenship which identifies women as a unitary and unified political group.

---

25 Fraser, N and Nicholson, LJ, 'Social criticism without philosophy: an encounter between feminism and postmodernism', in Nicholson, LJ (ed), *Feminism/Postmodernism*, 1990, London: Routledge, pp 19–20.

26 *Ibid*, p 20.

Indeed, it is typical of radical democratic texts to query the legitimacy of gender in citizenship politics and to argue that it is counter to democratic politics to prioritise gender. To represent this position, I cite the work of Chantal Mouffe and Mary Dietz.

Mouffe argues that, within a radical democratic politics, people's participation in the practice of citizenship must be distinguished from their broader social and economic conditions. She does not advocate the disappearance from social life of sexual difference, but she refuses to give it priority in the common enterprise of politics. Rather, she holds that 'in the domain of politics, and as far as citizenship is concerned, sexual difference should not be a pertinent distinction'.[27] Similarly, Dietz has argued:

> A truly democratic defence of citizenship cannot afford to launch its appeal from a position of gender opposition and women's superiority. Such a position would posit as a starting point what a democratic attitude must deny – that one group of citizen's voices is generally better, more deserving of attention, more worthy of emulation, more moral, than another's.[28]

Dietz's critique is directed at 'matriarchalist feminism', effectively, the celebration of the superiority of maternal values. Certainly, it could be argued that only the most extreme form of female supremacism could legitimately be the target of the claim that women are morally superior to men. But the force of Dietz's critique of feminist politics of citizenship as privileging one political group (women) is undeniable. Fraser summarises the dilemma facing feminists in the 1980s:

> ... the need for re-orientation was clear. Only if feminists were willing to abandon an exclusive focus on gender difference could we cease interpreting other difference claims as threats to the unity of women. Only if we were willing to grapple with axes of subordination other than gender could we theorise our relation to the other political struggles surrounding us. Only by abandoning the view of ourselves as a self-contained social movement, finally, could we fully grasp the true situation: that gender struggles were occurring on the broader terrain of civil society, where multiple axes of difference were being contested simultaneously and where multiple social movements were intersecting.[29]

In sum, feminists have been faced with the simple fact that it is neither politically acceptable nor sociologically accurate to identify women as a unitary group – to present women as speaking with one voice. Indeed, feminist politics of citizenship texts are well aware of this.[30] But the strength

---

27 For a pertinent critique of Mouffe, see Cooper, D, 'The citizen's charter and radical democracy: empowerment and exclusion within citizenship discourse' (1993) 2 SLS 149.

28 Dietz, M, 'Context is all: feminism and theories of citizenship', in Mouffe, C (ed), *Dimensions of Radical Democracy: Pluralism, Citizenship, Community*, 1992, London: Verso.

29 *Op cit*, fn 23, Fraser, p 202.

30 Hirchsmann, NJ and Di Stefano, C (eds), *Revisioning the Political: Feminist Reconstructions of Traditional Concepts in Western Political Theory*, 1996, Oxford: Westview.

of a position like Dietz's is in its recognition of the claims of groups other than women and in its attention to the mechanisms of exclusion from citizenship status of many different groups – of multiple voices. For some feminists, as Fraser notes, this recognition of axes of oppression other than gender constituted – and continues to constitute – a threat to the unity of the women's movement. It is not surprising, then, that texts of feminist politics of citizenship have responded with some vigour to the radical democratic critique.

THE FEMINIST COUNTERATTACK

It is, of course, open to feminist politics of citizenship to develop a counterattack on radical democratic politics. At its most general level, the feminist counterattack is the claim that radical democratic politics is unprincipled, in the sense that it provides no principles for the analysis and practice of feminist politics. This position is expressed very forcefully in those texts which criticise the theoretical underpinnings of radical democratic politics, namely, postmodernism's deconstruction of the categories of 'woman', 'gender', 'patriarchy' and 'oppression' and the substitution of a politics of relativism.[31] The feminist counterattack identifies two main effects of this approach – two deficiencies.

The first effect is that radical democratic politics undermines feminism. Caroline Ramazanoglu, for example, argues that the politics of relativism constitutes an attack on feminism as an emancipatory global movement.[32] The implication of this criticism is that radical democratic politics undermines the worldwide experience of women's oppression. Similarly, as Ann Brooks notes, Walby insists that the continued use of the concept of patriarchy is justified because of the widespread evidence of shared oppressions among women.[33] The corollary of this first deficiency of radical democratic politics is that, in demanding recognition of many forms of political protest, it effectively introduces a form of divisiveness between women.

The second effect of the radical democratic critique is that, because it has no means of prioritising political positions, it is anemic, leading to a form of political incompetence and induced political abstentionism. Here are three examples of this type of position. First, Angela McRobbie suggests that, at its least worthwhile, the postmodernism underlying radical democratic politics

---

31 Brooks, A, *Postmodernisms: Feminism, Cultural Theory and Cultural Forms*, 1997, London: Routledge, p 40.

32 Ramazanoglu, C, *Up Against Foucault: Explorations of Some Tensions Between Foucault and Feminism*, 1993, London: Routledge, p 8.

33 *Ibid*, Brooks, p 18.

can amount to little more than an 'overstylised posture adopted by those who can afford to abandon politics'.[34] Secondly, Gregor McLennan challenges the ability of 'ultra-pluralism' to identify which sites of political struggle are central to a particular set of social structures.[35] Thirdly, Brooks argues that the deconstruction of key concepts of feminist analysis renders feminism politically powerless.[36]

Can radical democratic politics make good these two deficiencies? With regard to the first, radical democratic politics can claim that it strengthens feminist politics of citizenship by bringing to prominence the links between feminism and other forms of politics. For example, when Amanda Sebestyen drew up her chart of different forms of feminism in the late 1970s, there was no reference to eco-feminism nor to Black feminism.[37] I would argue that one of the useful effects of the ideas of radical democratic politics is that such an omission would be unthinkable now.[38] Further, it is true that radical democratic politics demands the recognition of many different claims. This could lead to divisiveness as between women, but this effect is not automatic. Certainly, the objective of radical democratic political texts is far from that. Their objective is that the different claims of women and of other political groupings cannot be denied a political voice on any *a priori* basis. Indeed, as will be apparent in the section 'A reconceptualisation of rights', it is incumbent on radical democratic politics to give a hearing to all political agents, even if the outcomes of the political debate in question cannot satisfy all participants.

As to the second deficiency, proponents of radical democratic politics can claim that the demands of radical democratic politics are indeed stringent, in the sense of requiring scrupulous attention to an ever more complex and shifting range of political debates and struggles. Yet there is no reason why that stringency should lead to political abstentionism, nor to political incompetence.[39] On the contrary, it can lead to a strengthening of political competence through the requirement that radical democrats must acquire familiarity with a broad and diffuse range of politics.

To consolidate these two defences, I would argue that only a naïve reading of radical democratic politics makes it vulnerable to the identification of the two deficiencies. This is the naïve reading that radical democrats have no

---

34 McRobbie, A, *Postmodernism and Popular Culture*, 1994, London: Routledge, p 66.

35 McLennan, G, 'Feminism, epistemology and postmodernism' (1995) 29 Sociology 403.

36 *Op cit*, fn 31, Brooks, p 46.

37 Sebestyen, A, 'Tendencies in the movement: then and now', in *Feminist Practice: Notes from the Tenth Year*, 1979, London: In Theory.

38 Barrett, M and Phillips, A, 'Introduction', in *Destabilising Theory: Contemporary Feminist Debates*, 1992, Cambridge: Polity, p 4.

39 The demands of radical democratic politics may lead to individual feelings of helplessness, but that would not mark it out from any other form of politics.

political sources to draw on, or that they wilfully refuse to draw on available resources, in the calculation of democratic politics, as if radical democratic politics starts with a political *tabula rasa*. On the contrary, on their own arguments, radical democrats must use a rich variety of materials: political histories, theoretical innovations and campaign literature. It would be absurd to suppose that these sources would not include materials on feminist politics of citizenship. I shall resume this point in the section 'A reconceptualisation of rights', where I propose that the concept of citizenship rights be viewed as a political heuristic for the open-ended review of the politics of exclusion and inclusion, and where I conceptualise the concept of rights as rebuttable claims.

Meanwhile, it would *seem* to be the case that if radical democratic politics is no longer read in that naïve way, it survives the feminist counterattack. As I shall argue, however, radical democratic politics requires more than this sort of defence if it is not only to make good the two defects attributed to it, but also to address the persisting general criticism, the opening salvo of feminist politics of citizenship, namely, that it is unprincipled politics.

PRINCIPLED POLITICS

Simply to make good the two flaws attributed to it through the simple removal of the naïve reading of radical democratic politics is not, by itself, enough to dispel the feminist counterattack that radical democratic politics is unprincipled politics. This is because the removal of the naïve reading results in no more than the juxtaposition of one set of political resources with another, the mere juxtaposition of the preferred political sources and presumptions of feminist politics of citizenship with the more diffuse political resources of radical democratic politics. The juxtaposition is no more than a redescription of the argument over whether or not radical democratic politics is unprincipled politics. Simply pointing to the more diffuse nature of the political resources of radical democratic politics fails to address the force of the counterattack of feminist politics of citizenship at a more fundamental level. This more fundamental question concerns the role of principles in feminist politics.

There is a time honoured, and indeed, honourable conceptualisation of politics according to which the statement of one or more principles, whether analytic or normative, provides the materials from which practical politics and policies can be derived. This is what I call the rationalist conception of politics, because it stresses the primacy of principles and insists that these principles are the premises which yield political conclusions, as if politics can be logically derived from the statement of political principles. The rationalist conception of politics has been widely assumed both in feminist texts in general and in the specific context of debates about citizenship rights.

To illustrate the rationalist conception of politics, I refer again to Sebestyen's chart. As well as identifying the many forms of feminism prevailing in the 1970s, Sebestyen identified each feminism's answer to a series of questions. These are 'what's wrong?'; 'who benefits/who's the enemy?'; 'how do we fight?'; 'who will fight with us?'; 'how did our oppression originate?'; 'what is our political relation to men?'.[40] So the chart sets out the various feminist doctrines and beliefs and shows how they lead to correspondingly different feminist politics and strategies.

Sebestyen's type of approach was reproduced in many feminist works in the 1970s and 1980s, and it continues to appear in more recent texts. For example, Malcolm Waters distinguishes three main forms of feminism: liberal feminism; socialist feminism; and radical feminism. For each feminism, he identifies the corresponding political strategy: the removal of formal and informal barriers to participation in public structures; the pursuit of general social revolution; and female withdrawal from association with men.[41]

The critique of principled politics

My criticism of rationalist politics is not the overworked claim that rationalist politics is male. Rather, my criticism is that it is not possible to derive politics from principles. Despite the confidence with which feminists have identified the different politics to be derived from liberal feminism, radical feminism, and Marxist feminism, the complexity of political conditions always confounds any such derivation. This can be demonstrated by reference to the examples taken from Sebestyen's chart and to the schema of Waters' analysis.

From the premise of the source of women's oppression identified by traditional Marxists and the identification of women's allies in Sebestyen's first example, it would appear to follow that women's oppression can be ended only, as Waters notes, by general revolution. This is the traditional Marxist view that women should be involved in class struggle, not as women, but as comrades. Yet, as Sebestyen's example shows, the traditional Marxist line has also been open to modification, holding out the possibility that separate forms of organisation can be helpful and may be needed. In other words, the initial premise yields not the one obvious strategy but several, and the implication is that the selection of any strategy would have to be justified in terms of an analysis of the specific political conditions prevailing at the time of any political struggle.

Similarly, although female supremacists and radical feminists have typically been described as adopting a politics of separatism, avoiding political (and sometimes personal) relations with men, both Sebestyen and

40 *Op cit*, fn 37, Sebestyen.
41 Waters, M, *Modern Sociological Theory*, 1994, London: Sage, p 289.

Waters show how even this strategy can become confused. Sebestyen characterises female supremacists, for example, as refusing the support of women who have 'gone over to the other side' and they welcome the involvement of 'male followers'.[42] Similarly, Waters sees radical feminists as facing a choice between separatism and a form of politics which undermines the division of genders into simply that between women and men. Again, it is obvious that the identification of patriarchy as the source of women's oppression fails to mark out allies and strategies. Clearly, these can be determined only after political debate and after an assessment of the effectiveness of one strategy over another.

The impossibility of deriving politics from principles is due to an obvious fact of political life. To put it bluntly, the facts of political life are not such that conflicts are conveniently organised into pure conflicts between homogeneous groups. They are not conveniently organised into conflicts between men and women. They are not even conveniently organised into conflicts between working class men and women on the one hand and bourgeois men and women on the other. Nor are they conveniently organised into conflicts between heterosexual persons and gays and lesbians.[43]

Feminist politics of citizenship is a clear example of the rationalist conception of politics.[44] As noted above, this position identifies the exclusion of one group, women, from enjoyment of rights which have been the prerogative of another group, men. It starts from the premise of the principle of the desirability of full citizenship rights and derives its gender politics from the observation that women do not have full citizenship rights.[45] This is the conventional concept of citizenship which identifies a set of civil, political and

---

42 The reference to female supremacism might appear to be dated, but that form of feminism has resonances with Dietz's critique of matriarchal feminism (see *op cit*, fn 28, Dietz), with persisting – and popular – views of women as morally superior to men in their capacity as carers, and with current debates about whether women should form single sex groups within larger organisations, such as trades unions, as the optimum strategy for empowering women.

43 Kingdom, E, 'Feminism and political priorities', Working Paper No 10, *The Transition to Socialism*, 1982, University of Liverpool: Department of Politics, p 9.

44 In this regard, it shares the fundamental structure of Marshall's account of rights. For, although Marshall has been criticised for his neglect of the exclusion of women from full enjoyment of rights (see Hindess, B, 'Citizenship in the modern West', in Turner, BS (ed), *Citizenship and Social Theory*, 1993, London: Sage, p 33), it is arguable that his formal model can be adapted to accommodate the political objectives of feminist politics of citizenship. This can be done by the simple device of a reference to the relative speed with which citizens come to enjoy the rights he cites.

45 This position has strong *prima facie* political appeal. It underpins the welcome that feminists give to the extension of European Union citizenship rights to a wider range of people, eg, those in part time employment. But feminists are already pointing out that some of these rights are based on models of social and political life which emphasises paid work as the rationale for the receipt of social benefits, to the neglect of unpaid work, such as caring for the sick, which is typically undertaken by women: see Finch, J, 'Women, equal opportunities and welfare in the European Community', in O'Brien, M et al, *Women, Equal Opportunities and Welfare*, 1990, Aston University: Cross-National Research Group.

social rights which are in the process of being extended to an ever wider range of people. Typical examples here are the right to vote, right to equal pay, and the right to freedom of speech.

My critique of the rationalist conception applies with equal force to feminist politics of citizenship. Both standard democratic theory and feminist politics of citizenship begin with a premise of the universal condition of citizenship. To adapt the schema Sebestyen uses, both these theories ask questions such as 'how do citizenship rights come to be possessed?'; 'who actually enjoys these rights?'; 'who does not enjoy these rights?'; and 'should those who currently do not enjoy these rights be accorded them?'.

Standard democratic theory proposes that citizenship rights come to be possessed by virtue of the status of a human being capable of proper participation in public life. It would follow that all such human beings enjoy citizenship rights and that only human beings incapable of participation in political life, such as children, do not enjoy such rights. It would seem to follow that everybody not currently enjoying citizenship rights should be accorded them. Yet democratic theory involves the criterion that citizenship involves the capacity for proper participation in public life, and this test clearly cannot specify in advance which category of persons would or would not qualify. For example, would democratic theory permit the attribution of citizenship rights to terrorists or to convicts?

Again, feminist politics of citizenship acknowledges that citizenship rights are possessed by virtue of the status of citizen, but it points out that most people who have attained that status have been men, whilst many women have been excluded from it. Again, it would seem to follow automatically that citizenship ought to be open to everyone. Yet feminists would surely hesitate to have citizenship rights accorded to convicted paedophiles, to habitual stalkers convicted under the Protection from Harassment Act 1997, or to pro-life groups which mount violent attacks on abortion clinics.

A similar exercise, showing the impossibility of deriving politics from principles can be accomplished with respect to specific rights. Following the identification of a specific right, these questions are asked: 'who enjoys the right?', 'who does not enjoy the right?'; 'should those who do not enjoy that right have it accorded to them?'. Take the right to found a family. Under various international declarations and conventions, everyone enjoys that right. Yet it is clear that, in reality, not all persons do enjoy it. Susan Millns has shown clearly, for example, that persons who are not 'suitable' parents do not enjoy the right to found a family.[46] The implication would appear to be that

---

46 Millns, S, 'Making "social judgements that go beyond the purely medical": the reproductive revolution and access to fertility treatment services', in Bridgeman, J and Millns, S (eds), *Law and Body Politics: Regulating the Female Body*, 1995, Aldershot: Dartmouth, p 79.

everybody *should* enjoy such a right, but, again, democrats and feminists might want to make an exception in the case of convicted paedophiles and child abusers. What about the right to freedom of speech? All citizens of Western democracies enjoy it, with the exception of those who contravene various statutory and common law limits, for example, the Public Order Act 1986. Again, bearing in mind that exception, democrats and feminists have also been much exercised over whether the right to freedom of speech has been used to defend the use of pornography and ought, on that count, to be restricted. Finally, consider the right to freedom of gender and sexual orientation. This right, at its most general level, is enjoyed by all citizens of Western democracies, yet there is widespread evidence of discrimination against persons on grounds of gender preference and there are unjustifiable discrepancies in the age of consent to sexual activity of different kinds. Surely, this right should be accorded to all? Yet, again, the answer is not clear. Should there be no age limits impeding the enjoyment of this right? Should convicted sex offenders and paedophiles be denied full or even partial enjoyment of this right?

The complexity of answers to questions such as 'who should enjoy citizenship rights?' and 'which groups should be accorded specific rights?' make it obvious that there can be no derivation of political strategies from their opening statement of principle – there are always going to be exceptions, deliberations and compromises. On this argument, standard democratic theory and feminist politics of citizenship share all the problems of the rationalist conception of politics.

In contrast, radical democratic politics starts with the recognition that citizenship rights are possessed and denied by virtue of multiple identities and that there can be no definitive answers to questions about the exclusion or inclusion of persons and groups from citizenship and from consequent enjoyment of citizenship rights. An example of the twists and turns of debates about citizenship rights is Le Sueur and Sunkin's case study of the Government Communications Headquarters (GCHQ), what they call 'the government's electronic eavesdropping organisation responsible for collecting signals' intelligence'.[47] They document how, in 1984, workers at GCHQ had their terms of employment changed to refuse them the right to belong to a trade union. As well as government and civil service politics, the European Convention on Human Rights was invoked and the International Labour Organisation persistently criticised the decision. After continued campaigns to reverse the ban, however, GCHQ was privatised in 1995. As Le Sueur and Sunkin remark, this twist in the tale involved contracting out to firms in the private sector, some of whom will have unionised workforces, so that former GCHQ workers would now enjoy the right to join a union, not as a result of

---

47 *Op cit*, fn 1, Le Sueur and Sunkin; *Council of Civil Service Unions v Minister for the Civil Service* [1985] AC 374.

the campaign to do so, but as a result of a quite different political decision.[48] We might also note the way in which rights under the US Constitution can suffer unexpected transformations. Hall has shown how the existence of highly organised and well armed militias, such as the White Alliance and the Illinois Militia, has been used by the pro-gun lobby to defend the constitutional right to bear arms.[49] Radical democratic politics, with its insistence that citizenship rights in general and specific rights come to be possessed or denied in a multiplicity of ways – perhaps through membership of dominant groups, perhaps as a result of specific campaigns – has no problem with the indeterminate nature of answers to questions about the enjoyment of rights. Indeed, it is one of the strengths of radical democratic politics that it recognises the very mixed career of rights.

The mixed career of rights discourse

The above examples show the hopeless project of rationalist politics, the impossibility of deriving, or 'reading off', politics from conventional concepts of citizenship rights. To underline this argument, one should note a feature of the conventional concept of citizenship rights, namely, what might be called the accretionist model of citizenship rights, simply, that rights which once possessed in a democratic society comprise a package which are vouchsafed. But even the most cursory review of rights discourse, especially in public law literature, demonstrates the inadequacy of the accretionist concept of citizenship rights. There is a wide range of 'careers' open to rights. They can be acquired, as under the Acquired Rights Directive 1977.[50] Their enjoyment can be delayed through the imposition of new requirements for citizenship, such as the residency requirements and tests on the Estonian language and Constitution.[51] They can be incorporated or 'brought home' as with the incorporation of the European Convention on Human Rights.[52] They can be lost on the change of status of a nation, as under the transformation of Northern Rhodesia into the Independent Republic of Zambia.[53] They can be restored to groups who enjoyed them centuries ago, as has been the right of Australian Aborigines to reclaim land under the 1993 Native Title Act.[54] They

---

48   *Op cit*, fn 1, Le Sueur and Sunkin, pp 13–21.

49   Hall, A, 'Army of hate has America in its sights' (1998) *Scotland on Sunday*, 19/20 July.

50   Radford, M and Kerr, A, 'Acquiring rights – losing power: a case study in ministerial resistance to the impact of European Community law' (1997) 60 MLR 23.

51   Visek, RC, 'Creating the ethnic electorate through legal restorationism' (1997) 38 Harvard International L Rev 315.

52   Wadham, J, 'Bringing rights home: Labour's plans to incorporate the European Convention on Human Rights into UK law' [1997] PL 75; and cf Millns, Chapter 9, this volume.

53   *Motala and Others v Attorney General* [1992] 1 AC 281.

54   MacKinnon, A, 'Divided continent' (1998) *The Sunday Telegraph*, 11 January.

can be of doubtful value to anybody, as exemplified by the proposal of the Labour Party's Social Exclusion Unit that everybody should have the legal right to run a bank account.[55]

These examples illustrate Barry Hindess' observation that rights discourse is a key organising principle in democratic politics but that, as such, its effects are neither capable of prediction nor automatically progressive.[56] Illustrations include the attraction of opposite rights, as when 'a woman's right to choose' is immediately countered by 'the foetus' right to life' and by 'father's rights',[57] the uncertain outcome of the struggle described above between neo-Nazi militias in the States and defenders of the US Constitution's right to bear arms,[58] and the decision of the Danish Government that neo-Nazis have the right to demonstrate.[59] Indeed, it might be argued that it is precisely because the effects of rights disputes and discourse have been so mixed that recent authors of radical democratic politics texts have sought to identify different organising principles for radical democratic politics, principles which do not have the troubled history of rights discourse.

PRINCIPLES OF RADICAL DEMOCRATIC POLITICS

Radical democratic texts include a number of proposals for political organising principles. Here are four examples. First, in her critique of feminists' pursuit of the unity of community, Iris Marion Young outlines her concrete political vision of inexhaustible heterogeneity and exemplifies this vision with a definition of the unoppressive city as openness to unassimilated otherness. For Young, the city consists in a great diversity of people and groups, with a multitude of subcultures and differentiated activities and functions, whose lives and movements mingle and overlap in public spaces.[60] Young illustrates this vision with the way in which the appreciation of ethnic foods or professional musicians consists in the recognition that these transcend the familiar, everyday life of an individual. To make the point more generally, Young claims that:

> ... a politics of difference lays down institutional and ideological means for recognising and affirming differently identifying groups in two basic senses:

---

55 Farrelly, P, 'Banking for all law proposal angers Big Three' (1998) *The Observer*, 22 March.

56 *Op cit*, fn 44, Hindess, pp 30–32.

57 *Op cit*, fn 17, Kingdom, p 62.

58 *Op cit*, fn 49, Hall, p 19.

59 (1997) *The Guardian*, 20 August.

60 Young, IM, 'The ideal of community and the politics of difference', in *op cit*, fn 25, Nicholson, p 319.

giving political representation to group interests and celebrating the distinctive cultures and characteristics of different groups.[61]

Secondly, Chantal Mouffe puts forward the principle of an 'agonistic pluralism', a pluralism which recognises the ineluctability of political antagonisms.[62] For Mouffe, it is a mistake to search for a neutral concept of citizenship, one which emphasises consensus and unanimity: 'Citizenship is vital for democratic politics, but a modern democratic theory must make room for competing conceptions of our identities as citizens.'[63]

Thirdly, although he does not explicitly situate his work within radical democratic discourse, MJ Detmold offers a powerful critique of concepts of law which fail to recognise ethical and cultural difference in multicultural societies.[64] For Detmold, law is a relation between subjectivities (persons in dispute), whereas power is the imposition of a single sovereign standard on any one or more of the subjectivities perceived to be in the wrong.[65] Justice is rather the recognition of human dignity and it is the function of law to determine if there have been violations of human dignity and, where there have been such violations, wherever possible to return the subjectivities to their original situation. In this way, Detmold is arguing for constitutional equality of subjectivities and for a relational account of the legitimate or illegitimate exclusion of persons from citizenship, for example, in determining if a person is so mentally incapacitated that they are not capable of functioning in human relations.[66]

Fourthly, Anna Yeatman proposes the introduction into decision making processes of the principle of irresolvable difference.[67] On her emancipatory vision of radical democratic politics, there can be no uncontested politics of domination[68] and, in place of the modernist theories of democratic, rationalist consensus, she theorises radical democratic politics in terms of the processes characterised by 'postmodern rhetorics of local, conjunctural, multiple agreements, context bound, and varying by context'.[69]

It is typical of these texts that the principle which they have selected as the basis of their radical democratic politics affords no *a priori* specification of legitimate political claims. That is, the statement of the principle yields no specific political objectives or strategies. For example, Detmold's insistence

---

61 *Op cit*, fn 60, Young.
62 Mouffe, C, *The Return of the Political*, 1993, London: Verso, p 1.
63 *Ibid*, p 1.
64 Detmold, M, 'Provocation to murder: sovereignty and multiculture' (1997) 19 Sydney L Rev 5.
65 *Ibid*, p 11.
66 *Ibid*, p 27.
67 Yeatman, A, *Postmodern Revisionings of the Political*, 1994, New York: Routledge, p 110.
68 *Ibid*, p 32.
69 *Ibid*, p 122.

that the infinite variety of politics be framed by the principle of respect for human dignity affords none but the most tentative assumptions of the lawfulness of relations between subjectivities, and it completely undermines confidence in long cherished legal fictions, such as 'the ordinary person'.[70] Even more strikingly, Yeatman's principle of irresolvable difference effectively incorporates the notion of permanent political debate into its very formulation.

To place these examples in the context of my critique of rationalist politics, it is clear that none of these principles is adopted in the expectation that radical democrats could derive, or read off, practical politics from those principles. To repeat the point, not one of these principles functions in the manner of principles as conventionally understood in rationalist politics, and they are not on that account vulnerable to my criticism of rationalist politics. Rather, each of these organising principles articulates a form of what Yeatman has called 'the democratic politics of difference'[71] which refuses to exclude claims *a priori* and which brings to prominence claims which may have been ignored or suppressed. This politics of difference marks the inadequacy of conventional democratic politics to the analysis of the complex and shifting mechanisms of inclusion and exclusion in the sphere of citizenship rights.

These proposals for organising principles for radical democratic politics are immensely valuable for the way in which they encourage what Nicola Lacey has identified as normative reconstruction in socio-legal theory, including the imagination of different ethical values, relationships and institutions. Part of this project is the reconceptualisation of rights discourse.[72] In taking this position, Lacey recognises that, whatever the strength of feminist critiques of rights discourse, rights discourse is, as it were, part of the political furniture. In this respect, Ann Brooks cites with approval BL Marshall's contention that 'feminism is wedded to the modern by virtue of its rootedness in the space opened up by rights discourse'.[73] Brooks' point is that it is impossible to sever the link between the political origin of feminism and its deployment of rights discourse. It does not follow, of course, that the use of rights discourse is unproblematic.

Indeed, to pursue the metaphor of rights discourse as part of the political furniture and a legacy of modernism, it does not follow that radical democratic politics must engage in the faithful restoration of antiques, buy conventional tables and chairs and set them out in the manner dictated by traditional interior designers. On the contrary, the project of radical

---

70 *Op cit*, fn 64, Detmold, p 16.
71 *Op cit*, fn 67, Yeatman, p 89.
72 Lacey, N, 'Normative reconstruction in socio-legal theory' (1996) 5 SLS 131.
73 Marshall, BL, *Engendered Modernity: Feminism, Social Theory and Social Change*, 1994, Cambridge: Polity, cited in *op cit*, fn 31, Brooks, p 13.

democratic politics demands attention to new conceptualisations of rights discourse. It is to this I turn in my concluding section.

A RECONCEPTUALISATION OF RIGHTS

One major effect of dismantling the rationalist politics of feminist politics of citizenship is that any exceptions to the desired logical derivation of politics from rights claims and any exception to the presumption that rights are politically desirable need no longer be seen as disturbing exceptions to familiar accounts of democracy and of rights. On the contrary, the varied careers of rights can now be seen as normal, par for rights discourse. This is the point to recall the variety of things that can happen to rights as mentioned at the end of the section on 'Principled politics' and also to give some more examples of the mixed and erratic career of citizenship rights as they appear in public law texts. Rights can emerge, as Peter Keller claims for a universal right to ethnic identity in the context of the Council of Europe's Framework Convention for the Protection of National Minorities.[74] In contrast to Marshall's concept of citizenship rights as the product of the emergence of capitalist markets, effectively following the necessary logic of the development of liberal democracy and capitalism, Margaret Somers argues that they are an entirely contingent outcome of the convergence of England's medieval legal revolutions with its regionally varied local legal and political cultures.[75] Dawn Oliver has pointed to the shift under the recent Conservative administration away from citizenship rights, as envisaged by Marshall, to the promotion of the individual as consumer, supporting the notion of citizenship rights as increasingly underpinned by economic status.[76] The time honoured connection between citizenship and the right to vote is challenged,[77] as is the identification of citizenship with any specific range of concrete social and political activities, such as receiving public benefits of any kind.[78]

The above examples are instructive partly because they add to the list of examples of the heterogeneity of citizenship rights discourse. The main reason for reviewing these examples, however, is that, in their different ways, they all constitute a loosening of conventional concepts of citizenship rights. By so

74 Keller, P, 'Rethinking ethical and cultural rights in Europe' (1998) 18 OJLS 29.

75 Somers, M, 'Rights, relationality, and membership: rethinking the making and meaning of citizenship' (1994) 19 Law and Social Theory 63.

76 Oliver, D, 'What is happening to relationships between the individual and the state?', in Jowell, J and Oliver, D (eds), *The Changing Constitution*, 3rd edn, 1994, Oxford: Clarendon, pp 449–50.

77 Lardy, H, 'Citizenship and the right to vote' (1997) 17 OJLS 75.

78 Jelin, E, 'Engendering human rights', in Dore, E (ed), *Gender Politics in Latin America*, 1997, New York: Monthly Review.

doing, they invite a review of the potential of rights discourse both for more sensitive political readings of issues in public law and for engagement with progressive politics. Whilst these texts might not be wholly sympathetic to the project of radical democratic politics, they can be seen as providing the impetus for a review of rights discourse which is consonant with that project. To contribute to that project, I suggest that it is useful to impose on this heterogeneity three different reconceptualisations of rights discourse: rights as political heuristics, rights as signalling a review of exclusionary and inclusionary politics of citizenship, and citizenship rights as rebuttable claims.

The imposition of this threefold reconceptualisation is not a retreat from the project of radical democratic politics, a desperate attempt to find order in the chaos of rights discourse. Rather, it is to be seen as an aide to the intellectually and politically demanding practice of not slipping back into uncritical rights discourse, not defaulting to received concepts of rights. On that understanding, these three reconceptualisations can be read as starting with a general proposal for reconceptualising rights discourse, moving to a more specific proposal for reconceptualising the discourse of citizenship rights, and finishing on a third way of reconceptualising rights discourse, one which engages more directly with the type of legal issues characteristic of public law. In all three of these proposals, it will be apparent that the experience of the women's movements and the literature of feminist politics of citizenship will be a rich political resource. As I emphasised earlier, no engagement with contemporary issues of citizenship and rights can ignore the immense influence of feminist politics of citizenship, whatever the difficulties it faces from the radical democratic critique.[79]

Rights as political heuristics

First, I put forward the proposal that rights be reconceptualised as political heuristics. I have taken the term 'heuristic' from the philosophy of knowledge and action. A heuristic is a principle which is designed to regulate intellectual and practical enquiry. Such a regulatory principle makes no claims to truth or falsity. Rather, it proposes and monitors a line of research. In the course of that research, the heuristic principle may itself come to be modified. This is the proposal that the statement of a right be interpreted as a mechanism for the development of an intellectual and practical agenda.

---

79 Very much in this spirit, the examples which I give in this section are taken from the work of authors who would not necessarily think of themselves as supporters of radical democratic politics. Indeed, they might well identify with feminist politics of citizenship. But their work is, nonetheless, an important resource for the development of the concept of rights as political heuristics, and I invoke their texts to show how rights *can* be conceptualised in this way, regardless of the theoretical leanings of the authors.

In the context of political discourse, the proposal to treat rights as political heuristics is the recommendation that the statement of a right be treated as a mechanism for the development of a political agenda. A political agenda includes, not merely objectives, but also a research programme which investigates, among other things, the implications of expressing a particular campaign in terms of rights and whether alternative political slogans might be more effective. A research programme might well explore the ways in which an extremely abstract right might be 'converted' into workable, concrete objectives. For example, as I have noted elsewhere, the right to bodily integrity could be converted into a series of statements which redefine domestic violence as torture and accordingly bring it under areas of international law not as yet deployed by feminists.[80] Similarly, the assertion of a women's right to reproduce would be viewed as the mechanism for initiating a programme of research into access to new reproductive technology, into the ideologies determining access,[81] and into what lessons can be learned from previous campaigns which employ rights discourse in the context of women's reproductive choices.[82]

The notion of rights as political heuristics can be further exemplified by a consideration of the right to health care. As Margaret Brazier shows, in the party politics surrounding the introduction of John Major's Patients' Charter, the notion of a right to health care was not addressed explicitly; it was a presumption.[83] To view the right to health care as a political heuristic is to recognise that the statement of the right is not to pronounce a self-evident truth that there is such a right, nor that there ought to be. Rather, to see the right to health care as a political heuristic is to initiate a research programme which goes beyond the simple assertion of the citizen's right to health care and which examines both the conditions under which a right to health care might be said to exist and, if it does not, the components of a social policy to bring it into existence. Brazier's discussion of the right to health care would be an invaluable primer. She immediately separates the right to health care into the right to health care on demand (few of those being legally enforceable in the UK) and the right of patients in receipt of health care (several such exist, such as a right to confidentiality). But Brazier then demonstrates the ways in which patients rights within the National Health Service frequently disappear into well entrenched medical paternalism, as exemplified in the decision in *R*

---

80 Kingdom, E, 'Body politics and rights', in *op cit*, fn 46, Bridgeman and Millns, p 16. Sally Sheldon has pointed out to me that this strategy is of questionable value for feminist politics, because it involved the disappearance of a distinctively female experience into the officially gender neutral area of international law. This is a fair point, and I can only reply that it is precisely this sort of calculation that would characterise the analyses necessary to treating rights as political heuristics.

81 *Ibid.*

82 Kingdom, E, 'Transforming rights: feminist political heuristics' (1996) II Res Publica 73, pp 73–74.

83 Brazier, M, 'Rights and health care', in *op cit*, fn 2, Blackburn.

v Ethical Advisory Committee of St Mary's Hospital ex p Harriott.[84] Brazier next breaks down the right to health care into: a right to priority treatment, the interpretation of rights under the 1997 National Health Act as collective rather than individual, the right to emergency treatment, and the right of equality of access. In each case, Brazier picks over how the alleged rights have operated, or been operated, and she concludes that, whilst resort to the courts to define rights is not a trend likely to be reversed, all too often, the victors will be the professionals who seek authorisation for their treatment decisions. This may be a pessimistic view, but Brazier's work can be seen as a vindication of treating rights as political heuristics, for it serves as a corrective to the over-optimistic and glib assertion of the right to health care, recognising the complexity of legal politics in the area of public medicine.

A further illustration of the notion of rights as political heuristics is found in the area of international law. Here, I would invoke my earlier observation[85] that public law may benefit from examining materials which fall outside its immediate scope. In this example, David Berry substantially develops the concept of rights as political heuristics into what he terms the 'expanded integrationist' approach for the determination of political strategies in the context of conflicts between the rights of aboriginal women and the suggested forms of aboriginal self-government in Canada.[86] For Berry, this approach requires two tiers of strategy. The expanded tier is an assessment of the usefulness of existing international law, taking care, for example, that a specific right is contextualised, so as to allow for its different construction in different cultures. A judgment that international law is useful for pursuing a particular right leads into the integrationist tier, at which level a variety of legal techniques and political strategies will be considered.[87] Berry then applies this approach to the complex politics of the practice of clitoridectomy and considers the merits and demerits of several strategies. For example, he considers the politics of viewing the practice as a form of human rights violation, the violation of a woman's right to health. Berry concludes that, while the use of international law could be helpful, because it could permit the selection of reforms most assimilable to a particular culture, the effect of it might be not to stop the practice altogether and only to change the form of the practice, perhaps by substituting safer methods of performing it.[88]

Berry's work is instructive because it shows how rights discourse can be retained for progressive politics, provided that it is used strategically. In this respect it is worth noting that in some other academic contexts authors seem

---

84 [1988] 1 FLR 512.

85 *Op cit*, fn 7, McCrudden and Chambers.

86 Berry, D, 'Conflicts between minority women and traditional structures: international law, rights and culture' (1998) 7 SLS 55.

87 *Ibid*, p 57.

88 *Ibid*, p 59.

to have much less difficulty with the idea of seeing the use of rights discourse as strategic. For example, Ruth Lister argues for a combination of a rights based approach and an approach which emphasises participation for purposes of the theorisation of citizenship.[89] Julia Twigg's work is similarly instructive.[90]

Twigg lists six possible strategic responses to the question of how to integrate informal carers into mainstream service provision, and a rights approach is just one of them. Twigg breaks down the general concept of carers' rights into realisable objectives, such as entitlement to periods of respite, which would effectively constitute 'terms and conditions' of caring.[91] Very much in the spirit of the proposal to treat rights as political heuristics, Twigg outlines a full research programme of the issues which social policy commentators need to assess in order to strengthen the position of carers. Examples include the dominance of rights discourse in their welfare rights tradition of social policy as opposed to rights discourse in relation to service support; the relation between a practical entitlement, such as a respite period, which might have a degree of legitimacy that puts it on a par with the assertion of a moral right; and whether the use of rights discourse in this context works on the assumption that people have common needs.[92]

No doubt, a similar exercise to Twigg's will attend the introduction, if it materialises, of government proposals for the provision of citizenship pensions, that is, state pensions payable to those who have been involved in informal care of friends or relatives for significant periods of time and whose contributions to other pension schemes will have been seriously restricted.[93] Political commentators will monitor closely the operation of any such measure, analysing how such a pension would be paid for, what are the conditions of eligibility, and what its financial value will be. Because informal carers have been on the margins of society for so long, the treatment of carers' rights as political heuristics effectively becomes part of a review of the exclusionary and inclusionary politics of citizenship.

Rights as a review of exclusionary and inclusionary politics of citizenship

Secondly, in the particular context of citizenship debates, rights discourse can usefully be seen as signalling a review of inclusionary and exclusionary

---

89   Lister, R, 'Dilemmas in engendering democracy' (1995) 24 Economy and Society 1.
90   Twigg, J, 'Integrating carers into the service system: six strategic responses' (1993) 13 Ageing and Society 141.
91   *Ibid*, p 160.
92   *Ibid*, pp 161–62.
93   Guthrie, J, 'Bridging the pension gap' (1997) *Financial Times*, 19/20 July.

politics, and here I put forward some illustrations of how that review might proceed.

First, this review might well start with an examination of the mechanisms whereby persons or groups are excluded or included in participation in democratic life. For example, commentators are already assessing, with great attention to detail, how the incorporation of the European Convention on Human Rights proceeds. This will obviously not be a one-off evaluation but a constant review, not least, with respect to the implications of incorporation for women.

Next, the review of inclusionary and exclusionary politics of citizenship could well take account of Dietz's injunction to feminists to take account of struggles both within and beyond their own territory. She recommends bringing to light democratic practices already in existence and using them as inspirations for the struggle for new forms of political life. Dietz's examples include: the Spanish anarchist affinity groups, the Workers' Defence Committee in Poland, and the 'mothers of the disappeared' in Argentina.[94]

Dietz's examples are cited with approval, but it is important to note that the review of inclusionary and exclusionary politics might then proceed to the question of whether exclusions are always undemocratic. For, as Drucilla Cornell has pointed out:

> We cannot escape the comparison of competing normative visions of the good expressed through the appeal to legal principles. Nor do we want all differences to be recognised by the law. To do so carries within it the very real danger of legally freezing well established hierarchies.[95]

To illustrate Cornell's point, we might cite the example of convicted paedophiles mentioned earlier and their problematic status in relation to citizenship rights: to put it crudely, *theirs* is a difference that not many would want formally recognised. Indeed, the need for this caution in the review of inclusionary and exclusionary politics of citizenship is clearly illustrated by all the examples of competing rights claims provided in the critique of rationalist politics above, under the heading 'Principled politics'.

Citizenship rights as rebuttable claims

Thirdly, I put forward the proposal that particular citizenship rights be reconceptualised as rebuttable claims. By a rebuttable claim, I mean a claim which, no matter how powerful its legitimacy may appear to be, has to be viewed with political scepticism. The reconceptualisation of citizenship rights as rebuttable claims has at least two advantages. First, it loosens the

---

94   *Op cit*, fn 28, Dietz, p 79.
95   Cornell, D, *The Philosophy of the Limit*, 1992, London: Routledge, p 104.

presumption that citizenship rights should automatically be granted. For example, where a convicted paedophile might claim the right to protection from harassment from the people into whose community he has moved, that right can be understood as a claim which invites a counterclaim, a rebuttal, perhaps in terms of the safety of the local children, perhaps in terms of the claim that not everybody should have the right to freedom of movement. Secondly, whereas claiming a citizenship right is allied to the discourse of self-evident legitimacy, in the sense that its very statement appears to be without any need for justification, the making of a rebuttable claim forces an investigation of the claim and of its implications, and indeed, whether the particular form of political engagement is best expressed in terms of rights at all.

For example, in the disability movement it is commonplace to argue that the disabled should have full citizenship rights. But R Means and R Smith have shown the risks of adopting this strategy, because, in the context, the disability movement rights discourse has also been the discourse of the New Right. In this discourse, they claim, 'rights are essentially the rights of individuals to pursue their own goals and objectives, and to meet their own needs, free from intrusive intervention from the state'.[96] In the same way, Nira Yuval-Davis has argued that the language of citizenship has become a major resource for New Right politics and that, under the previous Conservative administration, the social rights of the poor, constructed as passive citizens, became at least partially transformed from being entitlements to being the responsibility of charities and voluntary organisations: 'Rights become gifts and active citizenship assumes a top-down notion of citizenship.'[97] In contrast, casting the politics of the disability movement in terms of rebuttable claims alerts campaigners to the political alliances that invoking 'disability rights' may unwittingly invite. At the same time, treating disability rights as rebuttable claims opens up the question of rationing scarce resources and the limitations of the NHS and Community Care Act 1986 in offering not substantive rights but merely procedural justice.[98]

A further strength of the notion of rights as rebuttable claims is that it conveys the toing and froing that can occur, over quite long periods of time, in

---

96 Means, R and Smith, R, *Community Care: Policy and Practice*, 1994, London: Macmillan, p 96.

97 *Op cit*, fn 20, Young, pp 84–85.

98 *Op cit*, fn 20, Young, pp 98–99.

citizenship debates.[99] Here, I would cite the complexities of the apparently simple right to marry. Stephen Whittle gives an account of how, despite the restriction of marriage to heterosexual partners, it was possible for a same-sex marriage to be performed – because one of the spouses, George Scott, was a post-operative male to female transsexual who was registered at birth as male.[100] In that sense, Scott did have the right to marry. But, as Whittle notes, 'the right was removed from heterosexual transsexuals by the judgment of Ormrod J in the now infamous case of *Corbett v Corbett*'.[101] Whittle complains that the UK Government has supported Ormrod J's judgment in all the cases proceeding to the European Court of Human Rights, and he hints that, in the light of competing views of the right to marry held by other contracting parties to the European Convention of Human Rights, there may be a welcome reversal of the weight of opinion given to Ormrod J in *Corbett*.[102]

The continuing battle over the right to marry is also a good illustration of the inconclusive nature of such disputes and of how the conceptualisation of the legitimacy of the parties' claims can shift. In this regard, one might usefully take note of Jodi Dean's argument that rights discourse is not the exclusive ideological property of liberal individualist politics, but can (and, I would add, typically does) feature in the politics of groups and minorities.[103] Indeed, as the voluminous American legal literature on 'suspect rights' and 'discrete and insular minorities'[104] demonstrates, the very construction of groups is itself an issue. Viewing the rights of such groups as rebuttable claims has the advantage, I suggest, of being a shift away from conceptualising legal politics and the politics of citizenship as the implacable stance of one party's rights as against another's. Instead, it captures the frequently long term and inconclusive nature of these forms of politics, with its unpredictable victories, setbacks, muddles and compromises.

---

99 I hesitate to offer this characterisation of rights claims in a textbook on public law whose readers may associate the proposal with the old common law concepts of rebuttal, rejoinder, surrebuttal and surrejoinder. It is not my intention to encourage the reconceptualisation of rights discourse in terms of the archaic language of common law, because it would be absurd to shrink citizenship rights debates to the scale of a small court. But I would not object to the use of this discourse as a historical metaphor, nor to its resonance with the discourse of prebuttal, referral and rebuttal in contemporary constitutional politics in the United States, where President Clinton submitted a Prebuttal to the Referral (the Starr Report, referred to Congress), and followed the Referral with a Rebuttal. (1998) *The Guardian*, 12 and 14 September.

100 Whittle, S, 'An association for as noble a purpose as any' (1996) 146 New Law Review, 15 March, p 336.

101 [1970] 2 All ER 33.

102 *Ibid*, Whittle, p 368. No such change has yet materialised: see *Sheffield and Horsham v The United Kingdom* (1999) 27 EHRR 163.

103 *Op cit*, fn 21, Whittle, p 244.

104 Arriola, E, 'Sexual identity and the constitution: homosexual persons as discrete and insular minorities' (1992) 14 Women's Rights Law Reporter 263.

CONCLUSION

In this chapter, I have exhibited the tension which currently holds between exponents of feminist politics of citizenship and radical democratic texts. In particular, I have shown how, in the last few years, feminists have been forced to review the impact of postmodernism and its political form, radical democratic politics, on feminist politics of citizenship. The role of rights discourse occupies a central place in this literature. My proposals for the reconceptualisation of rights discourse are consonant with those principles characterised above as examples of radical democratic politics. Conceptualising rights as permanently subject to review is part of radical democratic politics' refusal to give automatic priority to any one or more political grouping(s). At the same time, this reconceptualisation of rights invites recognition both of the backlog of feminist politics and of the sophistication and subtlety of feminist critiques of rights discourse. In this way, radical democratic politics does not reject feminist politics of citizenship out of hand. Rather, its critique of any persisting essentialist and universalist assumptions has the progressive effect of opening up the political space, subject to continual redefinition, for feminist politics of citizenship to press the political claims of women and to link them to other groups' claims and struggles.

CHAPTER 9

'BRINGING RIGHTS HOME': FEMINISM AND THE HUMAN RIGHTS ACT 1998

Susan Millns

For men, the family is a realm in which they can expose their 'weaknesses', in which they may embrace without shame the values traditionally associated with women. By relating with women in families, men try to reclaim wholeness. Second, the family is a realm in which men can be bosses. In their families men can express competitive values and other values traditionally considered masculine. Men may be compensated in the family for their failures in the marketplace. *The home is a haven for men.*[1]

The effect of non-incorporation [of the European Convention on Human Rights and Fundamental Freedoms] on the British people is a very practical one. The rights, originally developed with major help from the United Kingdom Government, are no longer actually seen as British rights ... Our aim is a straightforward one. It is to make more directly accessible the rights which the British people already enjoy under the Convention. In other words, to *bring those rights home.*[2]

INTRODUCTION

Since the arrival in power of the New Labour Government in May 1997, a number of cogs which make up the UK's constitutional machinery have been closely scrutinised, found wanting, and have begun to be greased or replaced accordingly.[3] The purpose of this chapter is to address one of the fundamental constitutional modifications which has taken place during the initial period of New Labour Government: the realisation of the project to 'bring rights

---

1   Olsen, F, 'The family and the market: a study of ideology and legal reform' (1983) 96 Harv L Rev 1497, p 1565, emphasis added.

2   Government White Paper on the case for incorporation: *Rights Brought Home: The Human Rights Bill,* October 1997, Cm 3782, paras 1.14, 1.19, emphasis added.

3   Major constitutional developments, in addition to changes in human rights law, have revolved around the projects of devolution for Scotland, Wales and Northern Ireland and reform of the House of Lords. These projects were, of course, in the pipeline before New Labour's accession to power, forming part of their election manifesto commitments.

home'.[4] 'Bringing rights home', to use the rhetoric of New Labour,[5] describes the process of 'domestication' of international human rights law. More specifically, it denotes the incorporation[6] of parts of the European Convention on Human Rights and Fundamental Freedoms (the Convention) into internal UK law,[7] with the effect that individuals can rely on the rights contained within the Convention before the domestic courts, thus avoiding the expense and delay of taking a case before the European Court of Human Rights in Strasbourg.[8] Yet, while speed and cost effectiveness are given as the practical reasons for incorporation, the project has been presented more broadly by New Labour as embodying an ideological commitment on the part of the Government to a better protection of fundamental rights and freedoms:

> For individuals and for those advising them, the road to Strasbourg is long and hard. Even when they get there, the Convention enforcement machinery is

---

4   The debate as to whether or not the UK needs a Bill or Rights and, if it does, whether the most appropriate is an incorporated version of the ECHR has been both heated and longstanding. A sample of the relevant literature includes: Adjei, C, 'Human rights theory and the Bill of Rights debate' (1995) 58 MLR 17; Allan, J, 'Bills of Rights and judicial power – a liberal's quandary' (1996) 16 OJLS 337; Beyleveld, D, 'The concept of a human right and incorporation of the European Convention on Human Rights' [1995] PL 577; Bingham, TH, 'The European Convention on Human Rights: time to incorporate' (1993) 109 LQR 390; Griffith, JAG, 'The political constitution' (1979) 42 MLR 1; Hunt, M, 'The "horizontal effect" of the Human Rights Act' [1998] PL 423; Institute for Public Policy Research, *The Constitution of the United Kingdom*, 1991, London: IPPR; Lord Irvine of Lairg, 'The development of human rights in Britain under an incorporated Convention on Human Rights' [1998] PL 221; Klug, F and Starmer, K, 'Incorporation through the back door?' [1997] PL 223; Laws, J, 'Is the High Court the guardian of fundamental constitutional rights?' [1993] PL 59; Lester, A, 'European human rights and the British Constitution', in Jowell, J and Oliver, D (eds), *The Changing Constitution*, 3rd edn, 1994, Oxford: Clarendon, p 33; Lester, A, 'Fundamental rights: the United Kingdom isolated' [1984] PL 46; Liberty, *A People's Charter: Liberty's Bill of Rights*, 1991, London: Liberty; Wadham, J, 'Bringing rights home: Labour's plans to incorporate the European Convention on Human Rights into UK law' [1997] PL 75; Zander, M, *A Bill of Rights*, 4th edn, 1997, London: Sweet & Maxwell.

5   This phraseology reflects the titles of the Labour Party's Consultation Paper introduced prior to the General Election of May 1997: Straw, J (MP) and Boateng, P (MP), *Bringing Rights Home: Labour's Plans to Incorporate the European Convention on Human Rights into United Kingdom Law*, December 1996, and the Government's White Paper on the case for incorporation: *op cit*, fn 2.

6   The act of incorporation being necessary since the Convention which, although ratified by the UK in 1951, and coming into force in 1953, has never been the subject of domestic implementing legislation.

7   The Human Rights Act 1998 is applicable in Northern Ireland and Scotland, as well as in England and Wales.

8   While it is true that the system for dealing with applications to the Strasbourg institutions changed on 1 November 1998 on the coming into force of Protocol 11, meaning that applications may now be made directly to the European Court of Human Rights and not directed first via the Commission, this procedure will still, inevitably, be lengthier and more costly than a hearing before the domestic courts. For details of the new procedure, see Wadham, J and Mountfield, H, *Blackstone's Guide to the Human Rights Act 1998*, 1999, London: Blackstone, ch 12. The former procedure is outlined in van Dijk, P and van Hoof, GJH, *Theory and Practice of the European Convention on Human Rights*, 2nd edn, 1990, Deventer: Kluwer, chs 2 and 3, with the case for reform discussed in Janis, M, Kay, R and Bradley, A, *European Human Rights Law: Text and Materials*, 1995, Oxford: OUP, ch 4.

subject to long delays. This might be convenient for a government which was half-hearted about the Convention and the right of individuals to apply under it, since it postpones the moment at which changes in domestic law or practice must be made. But it is not in keeping with the importance which this Government attaches to the observance of basic human rights ...[9]

The commitment to give further effect to the rights guaranteed under the Convention[10] has resulted in the adoption of the Human Rights Act 1998,[11] heralded as 'the most significant statement of human rights in domestic law since the 1689 Bill of Rights'.[12] It is this Act and its consequences, set as they undisputedly are to have a 'momentous impact on our legal system',[13] which are under investigation in this chapter. The reason for such scrutiny being that, while excellent work has already been produced on the implications and effects of incorporation,[14] this work has not been explicitly related to the protection of the rights of women and to feminist perspectives on human rights violations.

Yet, feminist scholars have, for a number of years, voiced their scepticism regarding the suitability of (human rights) law to deal with violations of women's rights.[15] In this respect, criticism has operated at two levels. At one

---

9   *Op cit*, fn 2, Government White Paper, para 1.17.

10   In fact not all of the rights contained within the Convention are incorporated, particularly the procedural rights set out in the Convention and Art 13 (the right to an effective remedy) remain unincorporated. The Human Rights Act does, however, incorporate the substantive rights contained in Art 2 (the right to life), Art 3 (prohibition on torture and inhuman and degrading treatment), Art 4 (prohibition on slavery and forced labour), Art 5 (the right to liberty and security of the person), Art 6 (the right to a fair trial), Art 7 (prohibition on retrospective criminal sanctions), Art 8 (the right to respect for private and family life and correspondence), Art 9 (the right to freedom of thought, conscience and religion), Art 10 (the right to freedom of expression), Art 11 (the right to freedom of association and assembly), Art 12 (the right to marry and found a family), Art 14 (prohibition on discrimination in the enjoyment of the rights under the Convention), Art 16 (restricting the political activity of aliens), Art 17 (prohibition of abuse of rights), and Art 18 (limitation on the use of restrictions on rights). The Act also incorporates the rights contained in Protocol 1, Art 1, (the right to peaceful enjoyment of property), Art 2 (the right to education) and Art 3 (the right to free elections). Protocol 6, Art 1, which provides for the abolition of the death penalty is incorporated too and the Government's White Paper sets out, in addition, that Protocol 7 (governing the prohibition on the expulsion of aliens) will be ratified as soon as parliamentary time can be set aside to amend the existing law (*op cit*, fn 2).

11   The Act received the Royal Assent on 9 November 1998. It is anticipated that its provisions will be in force by early 2000, the delay in introduction being due to the carrying out of a programme of judicial education.

12   Straw, J (MP), 'Foreword', in *op cit*, fn 8, Wadham and Mountfield, p ix.

13   *Ibid*, p xi.

14   *Ibid*; Ewing, K, 'The Human Rights Act and parliamentary democracy' (1998) 62 MLR 79; Clements, L and Young, Y (eds), 'Human rights: changing the culture' (1999) 26 JLS (Special Edition).

15   This scepticism is demonstrated in the UK particularly in the work of Carol Smart and Elizabeth Kingdom. See Smart, C, *Feminism and the Power of Law*, 1989, London: Routledge; and Kingdom, E, *What's Wrong with Rights: Problems for Feminist Politics of Law*, 1991, Edinburgh: Edinburgh UP.

level, the adequacy of national and international human rights law in dealing with violations of women's rights has been challenged; it being suggested that the legal interpretation of the concept of 'human' rights has not always been inclusive of 'women's' rights.[16] At a second level, it is the very notion of making claims to *rights* which has proved problematic for feminists, in that the promise of rights in the abstract may appear more attractive than their realisation in practice.[17] These difficulties will be addressed in turn in order to demonstrate the particular feminist objections raised. This initial exploration of feminist scholarship will then be followed by investigation into the provisions of the Human Rights Act 1998 in order to ascertain to what degree it has the capacity to respond to these objections.

FEMINIST PERSPECTIVES ON HUMAN RIGHTS LAW

Are 'women's' rights 'human' rights?

While the rules which go to make up human rights law are couched in gender neutral terms, providing that everyone is entitled to protection of the rights guaranteed therein without discrimination on the grounds of sex, no line is drawn between violations of the rights of women and those of men.[18] This means that the gender-specificity of violations of women's rights is not revealed:

> Human rights principles are based on experience, but not that of women. It is not that women's human rights have not been violated. When women are violated like men who are otherwise like them – when women's arms and legs bleed when severed, when women are shot in pits and gassed in vans, when women's bodies are hidden at the bottom of abandoned mines, when women's skulls are sent from Auschwitz to Strasbourg for experiments – this is not recorded as the history of human rights atrocities to women. They are Argentinian or Honduran or Jewish. When things happen to women that also happen to men, like being beaten and disappeared and tortured to death, the fact that they happened to women is not counted in, or marked as, human suffering ... What happens to women is either too particular to be universal or

---

16 Bunch, C, 'Women's rights as human rights: toward a re-vision of human rights' (1990) 12 HRQ 486; Charlesworth, H, Chinkin, C and Wright, S, 'Feminist approaches to international law' (1991) 85 AJIL 613. With regard, specifically, to the application of the European Convention to women's rights, see Palmer, S, 'Critical perspectives on women's rights: the European Convention on Human Rights and Fundamental Freedoms', in Bottomley, A (ed), *Feminist Perspectives on the Foundational Subjects of Law*, 1996, London: Cavendish Publishing, p 223.

17 *Op cit*, fn 15, Kingdom; and Smart, particularly ch 7 on 'The problem of rights'.

18 Beveridge, F and Mullally, S, 'International human rights and body politics', in Bridgeman, J and Millns, S (eds), *Law and Body Politics: Regulating the Female Body*, 1995, Aldershot: Dartmouth, pp 240, 254. See, further, *op cit*, fn 16, Bunch; Charlesworth, Chinkin and Wright; and Palmer.

too universal to be particular, meaning either too human to be female or too female to be human.[19]

The disjunction between representations of human experience and women's experiences leads to lack of recognition that the injuries suffered by women may be different from those inflicted upon men due to the particularity of women's situation and biological (reproductive) capabilities. So, acts of female rape, for example, have not been recognised as falling within the definition of international human rights violations,[20] just as the inability to recognise the uniqueness of the female capacity to reproduce has led to inadequate protection of the right to bodily integrity and security of the person at international level.[21] Also, while the right to freedom from torture, inhuman and degrading treatment and the right to liberty and security of the person are both recognised by international human rights law,[22] they have not normally been used to cover physical assaults upon women. Catharine MacKinnon argues, therefore, that:

> Women are violated in many ways that men are not, or rarely are; many of these violations are sexual and reproductive ... this abuse occurs in forms and settings and legal postures that overlap every recognised human rights convention but is addressed, effectively and as such, by none. What most often happens to women escapes the human rights net. Abuses of women as women rarely seem to fit what these laws and their enforcing bodies have in mind.[23]

One might object that the adoption of the 1979 UN Convention on the Elimination of All Forms of Discrimination Against Women has sought to address precisely the issue of the lack of specific recognition of women's

---

19 MacKinnon, CA, 'Crimes of war, crimes of peace', in Shute S and Hurley, S (eds), *On Human Rights: The Oxford Amnesty Lectures 1993*, 1993, New York: Basic Books, pp 84–85.

20 *Ibid*. With relation specifically to wartime violence against women in the context of the conflict in the former Yugoslavia, see Buss, DE, 'Women at the borders: rape and nationalism in international law' (1998) 6 FLS 171. More generally, for a study of the use of wartime rape as an instrument of male power, see Brownmiller, S, *Against Our Will: Men, Women and Rape*, 1975, New York: Simon and Schuster. MacKinnon's representation of the inadequacy of international human rights law in dealing with women's rights has not, itself, escaped comment. Suzanne Gibson has argued in response that MacKinnon's characterisation of the sexual violence perpetrated upon women in the former Yugoslavia can be read as a form of 'warnography', and that there is nothing specific about the sexual violation of women as opposed to the physical abuse suffered by men during wartime: 'We must object to the war rape of women on the grounds not that there is anything about rape which requires especial condemnation; not that there is anything about rape which is worse or different, more piquant or more thrilling than what routinely happens to men: but on the grounds that rape is a violation of a basic right of bodily integrity': Gibson, S, 'The discourse of sex/war: thoughts on Catharine MacKinnon's 1993 Oxford Amnesty Lecture' (1993) 1 FLS 179, p 188.

21 *Op cit*, fn 18, Beveridge and Mullally, p 255.

22 Eg, ECHR, Arts 3 and 5.

23 *Ibid*, MacKinnon, p 85.

rights. Yet this text, too, has formed the object of criticism as regards both its substance and its mechanisms for enforcement.[24] With regard to the latter:

> The Convention falls far short of what many feminists would have hoped for ... the only enforcement mechanism envisaged by the Convention is the reporting procedure. Unlike the 1966 Convention on the Elimination of All Forms of Racial Discrimination ... on which the Women's Convention is closely modelled, no provision is made for individual complaints or inter-state complaints. In addition, the number and scope of reservations entered by States Parties has rendered the Convention largely ineffective.[25]

As regards the *substance* of the UN Convention, it is premised upon a commitment to equal treatment to be realised by making available to women those rights which men currently enjoy.[26] Hence, the first Article defines discrimination as:

> Any distinction, exclusion or restriction made on the basis of sex which has the effect or purpose of impairing or nullifying the recognition, enjoyment or exercise by women, irrespective of their marital status, on a basis of equality of men and women, of human rights and fundamental freedoms in the political, economic, social, cultural, civil or any other field.

Fiona Beveridge and Siobhan Mullally are quick to point out that the problem is perceived in terms of distinction between men and women and that consequently the elimination of that distinction is the proposed solution. This is highly unsatisfactory since it 'serves only to reinforce existing norms and values without in any way subverting the inherently gendered nature of the existing rules'.[27] In addition, the UN Convention does not deal specifically with the problem of violence against women, nor does it set out a right to bodily integrity.[28]

Thus, the lack of specific recognition of 'women's' rights as 'human' rights is one aspect of the problem for feminists when scrutinising the desirability of recourse to human rights law at the international and national levels. The second difficulty operates at a more conceptual level, and is with regard to the very usage of the terminology of 'rights'.

---

24 *Op cit*, fn 18, Beveridge and Mullally, p 257.

25 *Op cit*, fn 18, Beveridge and Mullally.

26 *Op cit*, fn 18, Beveridge and Mullally.

27 *Op cit*, fn 18, Beveridge and Mullally.

28 In 1992, however, the Committee on the Elimination of All Forms of Discrimination Against Women did adopt a recommendation on violence against women (CEDAW, General Recommendation No 19, GAOR, 47th Session, 1992, Supp No 38 (A/47/38)), stating that the definition of discrimination contained with the UN Convention included 'gender-based' violence, defined as 'violence that is directed against a woman because she is a woman or that affects women disproportionately'. This was followed by the Vienna Declaration and the Declaration on the Elimination of Violence Against Women (GA Res 48/103, 1993, 20 December) which again identified gender-based violence as a violation of women's rights and, particularly, discrimination against women as a gross and systematic violation of human rights (para 30).

The utility of 'rights' claims

Historically, discrimination against women was sanctioned due to a lack of recognition of women as persons who could possess legal rights.[29] Towards the end of the 19th and beginning of the 20th centuries, however, women were gradually accorded legal personality through judicial and legislative interventions.[30] The formal legal equality granted to women did not, however, put an end to discrimination in many spheres of life and it quickly became apparent that formal legal rights did not (and still do not) necessarily bring with them substantive equality for women.[31] As a result, during the 1980s, wariness began to be expressed that further calls for 'rights' for women might prove to be less than productive.[32] While, on the one hand, rights claims may represent a powerful rhetorical device which, upon identification of the right in question, can result in a degree of empowerment for the rights claimant, on the other hand rights may fail to confer any concrete gains on women and may merely serve as a decoy to distract attention from the substance of the problem. Carol Smart has articulated the difficulty in the following terms:

> We are, therefore, faced with a dilemma. Historically, rights have been almost an intrinsic part of feminist claims. Now rights constitute a political language through which certain interests can be advanced. To couch a claim in terms of rights is a major step towards a recognition of a social wrong ...
>
> It is also the case that to pose an issue in terms of rights is to make the claim 'popular' ... We cannot deny that rights do amount to legal and political power resources. However, the value of such resources seems to be ascertainable more in terms of losses if such rights diminish, than in terms of gains if such rights are sustained.[33]

Smart goes on to give the example of the right to have an abortion, arguing that the provision of abortion rights does not necessarily guarantee that any

---

29 See Bridgeman, J and Millns, S, *Feminist Perspectives on Law: Law's Engagement with the Female Body*, 1998, London: Sweet & Maxwell, ch 1.

30 Sachs, A and Wilson, JH, *Sexism and the Law: A Study of Male Beliefs and Legal Bias in Britain and the United States*, 1978, Oxford: Martin Robertson.

31 For example, in the domain of employment law, attempts to outlaw sex discrimination and to introduce equal pay between men and women have not necessarily resulted in equal treatment for women. See Morris, A and Nott, S, *Working Women and the Law: Equality and Discrimination in Theory and Practice*, 1991, London: Routledge. More generally, see *ibid*, Bridgeman and Millns, ch 2.

32 Eg, Elizabeth Kingdom has cautioned against the adoption by feminists of the slogan 'a woman's right to choose': '[t]he dangers of this strategy call, at the very least, for a reassessment of the use of the slogan ... in so far as, claimed as an absolute right, it constitutes an obstacle to working out means of achieving feminist objectives, means which are politically and legally realisable.' (Kingdom, E, 'Legal recognition of a woman's right to choose', in Brophy, J and Smart, C (eds), *Women in Law: Explorations in Law, Family and Sexuality*, 1985, London: Routledge & Kegan Paul, p 160.)

33 *Op cit*, fn 15, Smart, p 143.

woman who wants an abortion can have one: 'the law may concede a right, but if the state refuses to fund abortions or abortion clinics, it is an empty right.'[34] The point is that the mere existence of a right is not equal to a guarantee that women will be able to enjoy that right. A formal right, without more, may be quite empty if the substantive reality of women's lives is such that they are not in a position to make use of the right.

A second problem identified by feminists with respect to making claims in the form of legal rights is that such claims may merely serve to provoke counterclaims of competing rights. Elizabeth Kingdom has argued that claims for women's rights may, therefore, generate opposing claims on the part of other interest groups – leading to a proliferation of, for example, claims of foetal rights, children's rights and men's rights.[35] Furthermore, popular and political opinion may be more sensitive to the rights of these interest groups than to women's rights. So, for example, were a woman to claim a 'right to reproduce', a man might turn around and assert his right to reproduce also.[36] This might then negatively impact upon the ability of a woman to obtain the termination of an unwanted pregnancy where the putative father did not wish the termination to go ahead.[37] A further example has been seen in the area of child support, where the solidarity of fathers in their opposition to the introduction of the Child Support Act 1991 marked a reassertion of the rights of fathers and demonstrably increased the hostility of fathers (and public opinion) towards mothers.[38]

The scepticism outlined above in respect of rights claims should, however, not be taken to mean that *all* feminists have failed to find merit in making rights claims and that, therefore, the value of human rights law is doubtful *per se*. Feminism is, of course, not a unitary concept; it represents a plurality of

---

34 *Op cit*, fn 15, Smart, pp 143–44. See, also, *op cit*, fn 32, Kingdom.

35 *Op cit*, fn 15, Kingdom. Kingdom has gone on to develop her initial objection to feminist engagement in rights discourse towards a more strategic position according to which she advocates that there are three reasons for feminists to decide to adopt rights discourse: first, where rights discourse is ineluctable (ie, 'the legal-political context in question is so firmly defined in terms of rights discourse that, for any intervention to be successful, it too must be cased in those terms'); secondly, where rights discourse is reasserted (ie, 'where the limitations of rights discourse are judged to be less important than its political effectiveness'); and, thirdly, in order to employ a 'conversion strategy' (ie, 'where feminists can devise ways to convert conventionally conceived "women's rights" into rights which genuinely improve women's position'): see, further, Kingdom, E, 'Body politics and rights', in Bridgeman and Millns, *op cit*, fn 18, p 10.

36 *Op cit*, fn 15, Smart, pp 150–51.

37 Eg, as in the Canadian case of *Tremblay v Daigle* (1989) 59 DLR (4th) 609. Attempts in the UK by putative fathers to prevent women from having terminations have, as yet, proved singularly unsuccessful: see *Paton v Trustees of British Pregnancy Advisory Service* [1978] 2 All ER 987; and *C v S* [1987] 1 All ER 1230, and discussion thereon in Sheldon, S, *Beyond Control: Medical Power and Abortion Law*, London: Pluto, pp 87–90.

38 Knights, E, 'The women's point of view', in Feminist Legal Research Unit (University of Liverpool), *'For Richer or Poorer?' Feminist Perspectives on Women and the Distribution of Wealth*, Working Paper No 2, 1995, Liverpool: University of Liverpool.

positions and perspectives.[39] The range of ideas represented by feminist thought has, not surprisingly, filtered into feminist *legal* scholarship,[40] which has been oriented around, *inter alia*, liberal feminism,[41] socialist/Marxist feminism,[42] radical feminism,[43] cultural feminism,[44] critical race feminism[45] and postmodernism.[46] It is no surprise, therefore, that some feminists have chosen to make recourse to rights arguments in seeking to end discrimination against women. Particularly, in countries which have a strong tradition in the assertion of constitutional rights, feminists have found it appropriate to make use of rights discourse in order to seek out a strategic method of protecting women's interests. In Canada, for example, the Charter of Fundamental Freedoms 1982 has forced Canadian legal scholars to think in terms of rights and to formulate strategies and identify the weaknesses of the rights set out in the Charter.[47] Equally, in the US, feminist campaigners have found it necessary to formulate their discourse around a rights based approach taking account of the constitutional structures (or obstacles) in place. For example, Catharine MacKinnon's campaign to have pornography recognised as the cause of harms against women, which ran into constitutional objections based upon the first amendment guarantee of the right to free speech,[48] led

---

39 On the diversity of feminisms, see Humm, M, *Feminisms: A Reader*, 1992, Hemel Hempstead: Harvester Wheatsheaf; Kemp, S and Squires, J, *Feminisms*, 1997, Oxford: OUP; Tong, R, *Feminist Thought: A Comprehensive Introduction*, 1989, London: Unwin Hyam.

40 See, generally, *op cit*, fn 29, Bridgeman and Millns, chs 1–3; and Lacey, N, *Unspeakable Subjects: Feminist Essays in Legal and Social Theory*, 1998, Oxford: Hart.

41 Atkins, S and Hogget, B, *Women and the Law*, 1984, Oxford: Blackwells; *op cit*, fn 30, Sachs and Wilson.

42 Barrett, M, *Women's Oppression Today: The Marxist/Feminist Encounter*, 1990, London: Verso; MacKinnon, CA, 'Feminism, Marxism, method, and the state: an agenda for theory' (1981–82) 7 Signs 515.

43 MacKinnon, CA, *Feminism Unmodified: Discourses on Life and Law*, 1987, Cambridge, MA: Harvard UP; MacKinnon, CA, *Toward a Feminist Theory of the State*, 1989, Cambridge, MA: Harvard UP.

44 Gilligan, C, *In a Different Voice: Psychological Theory and Women's Development*, 1982, Cambridge MA: Harvard UP; West, R, 'Jurisprudence and gender' (1988) 55 Chicago UL Rev 1.

45 Williams, P, *The Alchemy of Race and Rights*, 1991, Cambridge MA: Harvard UP; Harris, A, 'Race and essentialism in feminist legal theory' (1990) 45 Stan L Rev 581.

46 *Op cit*, fn 15, Smart; Frug, MJ, 'A postmodern feminist legal manifesto (an unfinished draft)' (1992) 105 Harv L Rev 1045; Duncan, S, '"Disrupting the surface of order and innocence": towards a theory of sexuality and the law' (1994) 2 FLS 3; Sandland, R, 'Between "truth" and "difference": poststructuralism, law and the power of feminism' (1995) 3 FLS 4. See, also, McDonald, Chapter 6 and Gearey, Chapter 7, this volume.

47 See Herman, D, 'Beyond the rights debate' (1993) 2 SLS 25; and Herman, D, 'The Good, the Bad, and the Smugly: sexual orientation and perspectives on the charter' (1994) 14 OJLS 589. Prior even to the introduction of the Charter, scepticism with regard to the utilisation of rights discourse was articulated by Canadian feminists: Razack, S, *Canadian Feminism and the Law: The Women's Legal Education and Action Fund and the Pursuit of Equality*, 1991, Toronto: Second Story.

48 *American Booksellers Association Inc v Hudnut* 475 US 1132 (1986).

MacKinnon to advocate a rights based solution, but centred on those rights contained in civil law rather than constitutional law.[49]

Despite, and indeed maybe because of, the feminist scepticism articulated in the UK with regard to rights claims, it is opportune at this juncture to reposition the argument once more at the heart of the discourse on human rights as engaged in by New Labour's project to 'bring rights home'. For the first time, British feminists, like their North American counterparts, have a constitutional 'rights' peg upon which to hang alleged violations of women's/human rights as opposed to the traditional (and less obviously constitutional) common law and legislative pegs hitherto available.[50] Given that the incorporation of the European Convention into domestic law has resulted in a set of rights being built into the UK's constitutional arrangements, the language of rights, and the strategy of making recourse to them, is now very much back on the feminist agenda.

Hence, the remainder of this chapter seeks to address two related matters. First, given the relative limitations of the Convention system in providing equality guarantees (when compared with, for example, European Union law and its more specific commitment to sex equality),[51] what do the Convention and the decisions of the European Commission and Court of Human Rights offer to convince rights sceptical feminists that the interpretation of this body of law is capable of being carried out in a way which is nevertheless protective of women's rights and interests? Secondly, what can feminist legal theory contribute to the development of human rights law in the UK with respect to the application of the new Human Rights Act?

But, before embarking upon these questions and seeking responses to them, it is worthwhile to touch base and take a short detour via 'home' in order to investigate more closely the language being used in the current human rights debate. Whereas above it was the language of 'rights' which was under scrutiny, in the following section it is, instead, more specifically the language and slogans being employed by New Labour in promoting the human rights agenda. While clearly this language has not been employed because of its feminist overtones, and certainly has not been used with the satisfaction of any explicit feminist agenda in mind, it is, nonetheless (rather ironically), not without interest (indeed resonance) to feminist scholarship.

---

49 MacKinnon, CA, 'Francis Biddle's sister: pornography, civil rights, and speech', in *op cit*, fn 43, MacKinnon, 1987, p 163. See, further, Colombo, S, 'The legal battle for the city: anti-pornography municipal ordinances and radical feminism' (1994) 2 FLS 29; Jackson, E, 'The problem with pornography: a critical survey of the current debate' (1995) 3 FLS 49; Lacey, N, 'Theory into practice? pornography and the public/private dichotomy', in Bottomley, A and Conaghan, J (eds), *Feminist Theory and Legal Strategy*, 1993, Oxford: Blackwells, p 93.

50 On the application of human rights law by English courts, see the extensive discussion in Hunt, M, *Using Human Rights Law in English Courts*, 1997, Oxford: Hart.

51 Hervey, TK and O'Keeffe, D (eds), *Sex Equality in the European Union*, 1996, Chichester: John Wiley.

THE LANGUAGE OF LABOUR

As evidenced in the opening citation, drawn from the Government's White Paper on the case for incorporation of the Convention, the slogan 'bringing rights home' describes the process of making directly accessible to British citizens those rights already enjoyed under the Convention. The word 'home' is, therefore, indicative of the UK as a geographical space. In this respect, one reading of the slogan may suggest the desire to promote a nationalist agenda, necessary in order to further the significant contribution made by Britain towards the original drafting of the Convention.[52] A more legalistic interpretation of the rhetoric would highlight that 'home' is indicative of the jurisdiction of the UK courts. It is, furthermore, in tune with the distinction traditionally drawn by international lawyers between states which adopt a 'dualist' as opposed to a 'monist' interpretation of public international law and, therefore, require implementing legislation in order to make the international text directly effective in domestic law.

Yet, are the geographic, nationalistic and legalistic readings of the New Labour human rights initiative the only readings possible? I would suggest not. Those whose ears resonate to the language of feminism may make out the audibility of another message emanating from the slogan. Feminists have long been familiar with the language of the 'home' and the 'domestic' sphere. They have long since learned to distinguish between the 'private' arena of the family and the 'public' arena of the market, demonstrating how women have been excluded from the latter and confined to the former where state intervention is at its most minimal.[53] Is there not, then, an alternative reading of the New Labour slogan to the extent that to talk about bringing rights 'home', to speak of 'domestication', and indeed 'incorporation', evokes a shift in vocabulary toward the use of a language which is more accessible to women and, as such, might promote their deeper engagement with the new human rights discourse?

This suggestion has, at its root, the proposition of cultural feminists that there is a difference in the modalities of expression employed by men and women. Carol Gilligan, for example, has demonstrated that women reason and express themselves 'in a different voice' to men.[54] By using the example of moral decision making, Gilligan argues that women respond to an 'ethic of care', placing greater emphasis on their familial connections and private, domestic relationships than men:

---

52 Detailed in Lester, A, 'Fundamental rights: the United Kingdom isolated' [1984] PL 46.

53 *Op cit*, fn 49, Lacey; O'Donovan, K, *Sexual Divisions in Law*, 1985, London: Weidenfeld and Nicolson; *op cit*, fn 1 Olsen; Olsen, F, 'The myth of state intervention in the family' (1985) 18 Michigan Journal of Law Reform 835.

54 *Op cit*, fn 44, Gilligan.

Given the differences in women's conceptions of self and morality, women bring to the life cycle a different point of view and order human experience in terms of different priorities ... The elusive mystery of women's development lies in its recognition of the continuing importance of attachment in the human life cycle. Woman's place in man's life cycle is to protect this recognition while the developmental litany intones the celebration of separation, autonomy, individuation, and natural rights.[55]

Consequently, it is suggested that women may respond more warmly to the language and the values of home, attachment, domestication and incorporation, while men feel more at ease with the traditional concepts of public law theory founded upon separation (of powers), autonomy and abstract individualism.

Of course, several reservations have to be entered here. First, it should be noted that Gilligan's work has not gone unchallenged by her feminist sisters. She has been rebuked for her appeal to essentialism, and for her failure to recognise that women's values (which privilege caring, attachment and relationships) and women's 'different voice' may be merely one facet of female subordination. Catharine MacKinnon, for example, argues that the different voice attributed to women is simply a product of male dominance:

> *Why* do women become these people, more than men, who represent *these* values? ... The answer is clear: the answer is the subordination of women. That does not mean that I throw out those values. Those are nice values; everyone should have them ... What bothers me is identifying women with [them] ... I am troubled by the possibility of women identifying with what is a positively valued feminine stereotype ... Given existing male dominance, those values amount to a set-up to be shafted.[56]

Gilligan counters that the values articulated by women are, nonetheless, highly positive[57] and, as such, should be more widely assimilated into the legal system.[58] In a climate where UK public law scholars have recognised the increasing importance of 'values' and have identified a common set of values which inspire both public and private law,[59] there may be no better opportunity for feminists to engage in this debate in order to suggest how a

---

55 *Op cit*, fn 44, Gilligan, pp 22–23.

56 Marcus, I and Spiegelman, PG (moderators), DuBois, EC, Dunlap, MC, Gilligan, CJ, MacKinnon, CA and Menkel-Meadow, CJ (conversants), 'Feminist discourse, moral values and the law – a conversation' (1985) 34 Buffalo LR 11, p 74.

57 *Ibid*, p 75.

58 This type of rationale has been followed by other feminists, such as Carrie Menkel-Meadow, who has explored whether mediation as a form of dispute resolution is more fitting to female values of care and connectedness: 'Portia in a different voice: speculating on women's lawyering process' (1987) 1 Berkeley Women's LJ 39.

59 Feldman, D, 'Public law values in the House of Lords' (1990) 106 LQR 246; Oliver, D, 'The underlying values of public and private law', in Taggart, M (ed), *The Province of Administrative Law*, 1997, Oxford, Hart, p 217; Oliver, D, 'Common values in public and private law and the public/private divide' [1997] PL 630.

set of values which is supportive of women's interests may be brought into play. For example, Dawn Oliver's identification in both statute and common law of five core values – those of autonomy, dignity, respect, status and security of the weaker parties[60] – mirrors belatedly much feminist scholarship, and has much to recommend it in terms of both form and substance once combined with feminist analysis.

As far as *form* is concerned, as Oliver explains, 'values' do not constitute 'rights',[61] (which might endear them automatically to rights sceptical feminists) yet they operate to form 'the climate, the "background" against which judges operate'.[62] In this sense, values provide a context for dispute resolution which is both accessible and increasingly identifiable. In their *substance*, the list of five values set out by Oliver is significant in terms of its potential to secure the interests of women. Particularly, notions of dignity, respect and security (of the person) resonate loudly with feminist scholarship and are not far removed from the idea of respect for bodily integrity, already advanced as an appropriate tool for feminist strategy in the context of international law.[63] While some feminists may contest the inclusion within the list of the concept of autonomy, adopting Gilligan's reasoning that this is synonymous with a masculine mode of thought and behaviour,[64] preferring instead the inclusion of a value of care and connection,[65] there are others who might more keenly advocate its inclusion (in a reformulated way) as an

---

60 *Op cit*, fn 59, Oliver, p 218; p 631.

61 *Op cit*, fn 59, Oliver, p 223, although, as Oliver points out, 'rights are expressions of, or means to protect, values'.

62 *Op cit*, fn 59, Oliver, p 224.

63 *Op cit*, fn 18, Beveridge and Mullally, pp 263–65.

64 Autonomy in this context implying also the freedom to participate in the market. The free market construction of autonomy, is nonetheless, challenged by Oliver herself: 'such a narrow view would miss the point I am trying to make, for it does not link with our other key values. It does not, for instance, take account of the issues raised in the law of relationships – marriage, parents and children – where developments over the last century have increased the autonomy of the more vulnerable parties to those relationships, but not to any great degree by reference to market activity': *op cit*, fn 59, Oliver, p 225.

65 Robin West, for example, has chastised American legal thought for being premised upon a 'separation thesis' of what it means to be a human being. She argues, that by embracing this thesis 'all of our modern legal theory ... is essentially and irretrievably masculine'. West counters that women, on the other hand, are 'not essentially, necessarily, inevitably, invariably, always, and forever separate from other human beings: women, distinctively, are quite clearly "connected" to another human life ...'. This connection operates notably on four occasions: during pregnancy, on heterosexual penetration, during menstruation, and when breastfeeding: *op cit*, fn 44, West, pp 2–3.

appropriate mechanism to protect women from intrusion upon their person.[66] This might be particularly so where foetal health and rights are pitted against those of women.[67]

It may be, therefore, that the language of New Labour, in conjunction with the developing public law project to uncover a set of underlying values, has the potential to enhance the promotion of women's interests by, on the one hand, resonating with a female mode of thought and behaviour, and, on the other, representing a step away from the traditional rights based approach of public law scholarship. There is, however, a further reservation which may be raised with regard to a feminist reading of New Labour's human rights message. It may be objected that one should avoid confusing the text of the message with substantive change. 'Bringing rights home' does not necessarily entail bringing rights *into the home*, or more generally into the private sphere, the location in which abuse against women has been traditionally invisible and gone unacknowledged.[68] It is well established that, in principle, international law agreements do not create obligations for private parties,[69] but only for states, and the Human Rights Act itself is confined in its application to violations or rights carried out by public authorities.[70] Caution should, therefore, operate against making presumptions that the Human Rights Act will necessarily be capable of redressing the harms suffered by women in the private sphere. While feminists have long recognised that 'the personal is political', this recognition has not necessarily filtered through to the legal interpretation of women's rights (as will be seen below). In which case, a feminist interpretation of the new human rights agenda as responsive

---

66   Eg, Nedelsky has argued that, while feminism must retain the basic value of autonomy because of its centrality to feminist concerns, it should reject the attachment of autonomy to liberal individualism and seek out its subjective element, that is 'the actual experience of autonomy', instead: Nedelsky, J, 'Reconceiving autonomy: sources, thoughts and possibilities', in Hutchinson, AC and Green, LJM (eds), *Law and the Community: The End of Individualism?*, 1989, Toronto: Carswell, p 240; see, also, Nedelsky, J, 'Law, boundaries, and the bounded self' (1990) 30 Representations 162; Stychin, CF, 'Body talk: rethinking autonomy, commodification and the embodied legal self', in Sheldon, S and Thomson, M (eds), *Feminist Perspectives on Health Care Law*, 1998, London: Cavendish Publishing, p 211; and Bridgeman, J, 'Skeletal frames and labouring women: the impact of the female body upon medical treatment decision-making' (conference paper), *Gender, Sexuality and Law: Reflections; New Directions*, International Conference, Keele University, 19–21 June 1998.

67   As, eg, where a woman has refused her consent to a caesarean operation against medical advice. See Wells, C, 'On the outside looking in: perspectives on enforced caesareans', in *ibid*, Sheldon and Thomson, p 237.

68   This is particularly so with regard to sexual and physical 'domestic' violence. For a discussion of examples of the injustices caused by this exclusion, see Fox, M, 'Legal responses to battered women who kill', in *op cit*, fn 18, Bridgeman and Millns, p 171.

69   This is not to say that the application of international human rights law to private parties has gone unexplored: Clapham, C, *Human Rights in the Private Sphere*, 1993, Oxford: OUP.

70   HRA 1998, s 6. See *op cit*, fn 8, Wadham and Mountfield, ch 5. Nevertheless, see, also, *op cit*, fn 4, Hunt.

to women's concerns risks remaining at the level of a reinterpretation of language rather than demonstrating gains in terms of legal substance. To this end, the final section of this chapter will examine the extent to which the personal has come across as (a)political with regard to recent applications of the European Convention by the Strasbourg authorities. These applications and the way they fit with the new scheme of relationships operating between the UK Parliament and courts following incorporation will be considered and the prospects for an enhanced interpretation of Convention rights from a feminist perspective examined.

THE PERSONAL AS POLITICAL: CONVENTION RIGHTS AND WOMEN'S INTERESTS

The (temporary) resolution of the Bill of Rights debate in the UK, involving, as it does, the adoption of the Human Rights Act 1998, has necessitated the formulation of a new relationship between Parliament and the courts. The formula adopted, on the one hand leaves parliamentary sovereignty intact, while on the other it permits some courts (the High Court and above) to issue a 'declaration of incompatibility',[71] signalling the fact that in the court's view there has been a legislative violation of the Convention. The declaration does not render the Act of Parliament ineffective, but it acts as a signal to Parliament and to the public at large that, in the court's view, a violation of a fundamental right has occurred.[72] While it is likely that the courts will strive to interpret statutory provisions in conformity with the Convention rights in order to minimise the need to have recourse to the 'declaration of incompatibility',[73] the Act also imposes an obligation on domestic courts and tribunals to interpret legislation, wherever possible, in a way which is

---

71 HRA 1998, s 4(2).

72 HRA 1998, s 10 outlines a 'fast track' procedure for the amendment of legislation in order to bring it into line with the protection of the right allegedly violated. The appropriate government minister will be able to amend the legislation by an Order requiring the approval of both Houses of Parliament before taking effect. However, the minister is not obliged to make an Order, nor is Parliament obliged to approve it: 'It is a power to remove an incompatibility, in response to a clear finding from the United Kingdom court or from the Strasbourg Court. Even when there is a clear finding of incompatibility, the Government may decide not to use the power because the subject needs full consideration by Parliament in the normal way. Or Parliament may make it clear that it wishes to consider the matter more fully by declining assent to the remedial order. In this way also, the Bill respects the central sovereignty of Parliament.' Lord Irvine of Lairg LC, 'Address to the Third Clifford Chance Conference on the Impact of a Bill of Rights on English Law', 28 November 1997: www://open.gov.uk/lcd/speeches/humn-rts.htm.

73 *Op cit*, fn 8, Wadham and Mountfield, p 47.

consistent with the Convention rights[74] and demands that they take account of the decisions of the Strasbourg institutions in doing so.[75]

While, therefore, it was noted above that only public authorities are obliged to comply with the terms of the Human Rights Act, the obligation upon the courts to interpret legislation in conformity with the rights set out in the Convention has the effect that the Convention will be potentially relevant in cases between private parties.[76] For feminists, this is an exciting prospect, given the often private and domestic nature of harms perpetrated against women.[77]

The interpretative power of the courts, however, is harnessed by the Act to interpreting domestic law in line with the decisions of the Strasbourg institutions. It must, therefore, be asked whether this case law carries with it the prospect of a positive construction, with regard to the protection of women's rights. Given that the Convention does not contain an explicit clause protecting sex equality,[78] it is necessary to investigate the case law governing the substantive rights contained within the Convention. To this end, two areas of particular concern to women's lives – sexual violence and abortion – will be analysed in the remainder of this chapter in an attempt to uncover to what extent the Strasbourg institutions have been able or willing to contexualise issues of women's rights in terms of female experience, despite the abstract

---

74 HRA 1998, s 3(1) states that: '[s]o far as it is possible to do so, primary legislation and subordinate legislation must be read and given effect in a way which is compatible with the Convention rights.'

75 HRA 1998, s 2(1) states that: '[a] court or tribunal determining a question which has arisen in connection with a Convention right must take into account any–
(a) judgment, decision, declaration or advisory opinion of the European Court of Human Rights,
(b) opinion of the Commission given in a report adopted under Article 31 of the Convention,
(c) decision of the Commission in connection with Article 26 or 27(2) of the Convention, or
(d) decision of the Committee of Ministers taken under Article 46 of the Convention,
whenever made or given, so far as, in the opinion of the court or tribunal, it is relevant to the proceedings in which that question has arisen.'

76 See op cit, fn 4, Hunt, for discussion of the potential application of the Convention rights to disputes raising issues of private law rights.

77 It might be envisaged that the potential of the Convention to reach into the private sphere of women's lives may involve rather more an increased application of the criminal law as opposed to the common law. However, the potential relevance to claims of injury based upon tort law should not be denied given that feminist scholarship has identified strategies for addressing harms to women on the basis of actions in private law: Howe, A, 'The problem of privatized injuries: feminist strategies for litigation', in Fineman, MA and Thomadsen, NS (eds), At the Boundaries of Law: Feminism and Legal Theory, 1991, New York: Routledge; Conaghan, J, 'Gendered harms and the law of tort: remedying (sexual) harassment' (1996) 16 OJLS 407; Conaghan, J, 'Tort litigation in the context of intra-familial abuse' (1998) 61 MLR 132.

78 ECHR, Art 14 prohibits discrimination on the grounds of, inter alia, sex, but is not free standing and can, thus, only be used in conjunction with the alleged violation of one of the substantive rights or freedoms contained within the Convention.

and individual way in which the Convention rights are framed. The reason for choosing these examples is not to suggest that they are the *only* issues which offer a point of contact between women's experiences and the rights guaranteed under the Convention.[79] Rather, the reason for the choice is that, should the Strasbourg (and national) authorities prove unable to recognise the gender dimension of these issues – which are so obviously of concern to women – then there is little prospect of recognition of the gendered nature of other harms which have a less obvious (but, nonetheless, equally important) impact upon women's lives.

Sexual violence

It has already been highlighted above that the lack of a specific right to bodily integrity in international human rights texts has been found problematic by international lawyers[80] and the introduction of such a right proposed as a solution.[81] No exception to the rule, the European Convention contains no specific right which operates to protect the integrity of the human body and which might, therefore, be called into play in cases of sexual assault against women. Nevertheless, this is not to say that issues of sexual violence have not been raised before the Commission and Court. Cases which have found their way to the Strasbourg institutions have raised important questions concerning the nature of violations of the female body perpetrated by private individuals, but where the state also has had a role to play in being responsible for, or responding to, the harm caused.

A number of Articles of the Convention have proved pertinent in this respect, most notably Art 8 which, in its first paragraph, guarantees the right to respect for private and family life, home and correspondence.[82] This Article has been interpreted to mean that it is incumbent upon the State to take positive measures to ensure that the right to respect for private and family life is not violated by private parties.[83] Hence, in *X and Y v The Netherlands*,[84] a case involving a 16 year old woman with learning difficulties who was sexually assaulted by the son in law of the directress of the private institution

---

79 Other points of contact might include, eg, the protection of the rights of female prisoners and those of female prostitutes as they encounter the criminal justice system; equal access to welfare benefits; equal pay; protection against sexual harassment; the rights of single mothers; and recognition of discrimination on the basis of lesbian identity.

80 *Op cit*, fn 18, Beveridge and Mullally.

81 *Op cit*, fn 18, Beveridge and Mullally, pp 263–65.

82 ECHR, Art 3, which prohibits, *inter alia*, 'inhuman and degrading treatment', has proved of less utility due to the extreme gravity of treatment which must be demonstrated in order to bring a successful claim under this heading. See *op cit*, fn 8, Janis, Kay and Bradley, ch 5.

83 *Marckx v Belgium* (1979) 2 EHRR 330.

84 *X and Y v The Netherlands* (1986) 8 EHRR 235.

in which she lived, and against whom no prosecution was brought, the European Court of Human Rights found that:

> Although the object of Article 8 is essentially that of protecting the individual against arbitrary interference by the public authorities, it does not merely compel the state to abstain from such interference; in addition to this primarily negative undertaking, there may be positive obligations inherent in an effective respect for private or family life. These obligations may involve the adoption of measures designed to secure respect for private life even in the sphere of the relations of individuals between themselves.[85]

The Court went on to observe that, nevertheless, the choice of means to secure compliance with Art 8 in the sphere of relations between individuals was, in principle, a matter to be decided by the particular state concerned, and fell within the 'margin of appreciation' to be left to each Contracting Party.[86] While the Dutch Government argued that a criminal sanction would be unsuitable in this particular case because 'to go too far in this direction might lead to unacceptable paternalism and occasion an inadmissible interference by the state with the individual's right to respect for his or her sexual life'[87] and suggested that a civil remedy would be more appropriate in the circumstances, the Court was not persuaded. It found, instead, that the protection offered by the civil law was insufficient:

> This is a case where fundamental values and essential aspects of private life are at stake. Effective deterrence is indispensable in this area and it can be achieved only by criminal law provisions.[88]

Finding that the state of criminal regulation in the Netherlands was insufficient to offer adequate protection to Ms Y, the Court held unanimously that a violation of Art 8 had occurred.

This solution is indeed welcome to the extent that it sets out clearly that the state cannot draw the boundaries of public and private sphere activity always as narrowly as it might desire. It cannot hide behind a front of private relations in order to abdicate responsibility, even with regard to the activity of individuals, nor is it permitted to exceed an acceptable 'margin of appreciation' in its tolerance of private sphere sexual or 'domestic' abuse. Furthermore, the recognition by the Court of the fact that it was Y's sexual being which was in danger of violation, as opposed to the sexual freedom of her abuser, demonstrates a commitment on the part of the Court to balance rights and freedoms in the light of the particular circumstances and experiences of the victim of sexual assault.

---

85 *X and Y v The Netherlands* (1986) 8 EHRR 235, para 23.

86 *Ibid*, para 24. Hence, other instances of childhood sexual abuse may remain unaddressed because of national rules on limitation periods. See, eg, *Stubbings and Others v UK* (1997) 23 EHRR 213 and discussion thereon in *op cit*, fn 77, Conaghan, pp 140–44. See, also, Wright, J, 'Local authorities, the duty of care and the European Convention on Human Rights' (1998) 18 OJLS 1.

87 (1986) 8 EHRR 235, para 25.

88 *Ibid*, para 27.

This approach has set the scene for a more recent intervention by the Court in the context of sexual violence perpetrated by the act of rape within marriage.[89] This intervention, involving two actions brought against the UK, is particularly significant in that it marks an alignment of Convention rights with UK law, and might, therefore, be taken as an indication of the approach which UK courts could be expected to adopt when tackling similar issues of sexual violence in future. Again, welcome in its contextualisation of the nature of the abuse, the Court tendered a decision which once more went some way towards recognising the particularity of the violation at stake.

The cases of *SW v UK* and *CR v UK*[90] arose in response to the landmark decision of the House of Lords in *R v R*,[91] in which it was decided that the marital rape exemption, which had for so long held strong, was anachronistic and should be ended.[92] Following convictions for the attempted rape of his wife (in the case of CR), and for the actual rape of his wife (in the case of SW), the applicants applied to the European Commission of Human Rights claiming that the convictions amounted to a violation of Art 7 of the Convention which sets out the principle of non-retroactivity of the criminal law. Both the Commission and the Court found unanimously that no violation had occurred, it being recognised that the judiciary was perfectly entitled to amend the criminal law in order to secure its adaptation to changing social circumstances:

> There will always be a need for elucidation of doubtful points and for adaptation to changing circumstances ... Article 7 of the Convention cannot be read as outlawing the gradual clarification of the rules of criminal liability through judicial interpretation from case to case, provided that the resultant development is consistent with the essence of the offence and could reasonably be foreseen ...

> The essentially debasing character of rape is so manifest that the result of the decisions of the Court of Appeal and the House of Lords – that the applicant could be convicted of attempted rape, irrespective of his relationship with the victim – cannot be said to be at variance with the object and purpose of Article 7 of the Convention.[93]

The Court did not, however, stop at this point and it is here that the effect of the decision as far as its further reinterpretation in the domestic courts is

---

89 *SW v UK* and *CR v UK* (1995) 21 EHRR 363. See Palmer, S, 'Rape in marriage and the European Convention on Human Rights: *CR v UK, SW v UK*' (1997) 5 FLS 91.

90 *Ibid*. Although representing two separate actions, the cases, given their similarity, were joined in the interests of the proper administration of justice with a single Chamber being constituted to hear both.

91 *R v R* [1991] 4 All ER 481.

92 For a range of views on the background and implications of this decision, see Barton, J, 'The story of marital rape' (1992) 108 LQR 260; Lees, S, *Ruling Passions: Sexual Violence, Reputation and the Law*, 1997, Buckingham: OU Press, ch 6; O'Donovan, K, *Family Law Matters*, 1993, London: Pluto, pp 1–9.

93 *SW v UK* and *CR v UK* (1995) 21 EHRR 363, paras 36/34 and 44/42.

significant, marking out the approach to be adopted upon rights being brought home. The Court went on to make a broader point regarding the nature of sexual violence and its relationship with the overall purpose of the Convention:

> What is more, the abandonment of the unacceptable idea of a husband being immune against prosecution for rape of his wife was in conformity not only with a civilised concept of marriage but also, and above all, with the fundamental objectives of the Convention, the very essence of which is respect for human dignity and human freedom.[94]

Of course, the Court does not need to be congratulated upon its appreciation of the anachronism of the marital rape exemption, indeed, it might have even been appropriate that some comment be made to express surprise that the exemption had been tenable for so long. What is of significance, however, is the recognition by the Court that sexual violence perpetrated against a wife is unacceptable because of its inconsistency with the fundamental tenets of the Convention. Thus we can gain from this an understanding of what lies at the essence of the Convention, at least for the Strasbourg authorities, that is, 'respect for human dignity and human freedom'. It will quickly be apparent that the fundamental values articulated here by the Court are not dissimilar to those key values set out by Oliver as the foundations for UK public and private law, and which, it was argued above, do offer some hope for a more feminist articulation of fundamental constitutional values. Particularly, the clarity of the appeal for the need to respect human dignity has much to recommend it to feminist analysis. It may not have escaped the attention of the European Court that this concept has become the rising star of constitutional jurisprudence elsewhere in Europe and, as such, has been interpreted as a value that has the capacity to protect the integrity of the physical human body.[95] An interpretation back home of the need to protect women against sexual assault in order that their human dignity be respected would go some way towards addressing the absence in the Convention of a specific right to bodily integrity. Indeed, it may be a more welcome prospect than the explicit articulation of a new right, given that the concept of human dignity is capable of a broader application than a narrow right to bodily

---

94   *SW v UK* and *CR v UK* (1995) 21 EHRR 363, para 44/42.

95   In France, eg, the constitutional value of the protection of human dignity was 'discovered' by the Constitutional Council in 1994 from an inspired reading of the Preamble to the Constitution of 1946 during its control of the conformity to the Constitution of new legislation on bioethics: Decision No 94-343-344 DC of 27 July 1994. The concept has since been interpreted by the Constitutional Council to include the right to decent housing: Decision No 94-359 DC of 19 January 1995. It has also been developed by the Conseil d'Etat (the highest administrative court) in order to justify the ban on dwarf-throwing competitions in the name of safeguarding the dignity of the dwarf participant: CE, ass, 27 October 1995, *Commune de Morsang-sur-Orge* and *Ville d'Aix-en-Provence*; see Millns, S, 'Dwarf-throwing and human dignity: a French perspective' (1996) 18 JSWFL 375.

integrity (ensuring respect of both mental and physical integrity) and, furthermore, would act as a constant value against which *all* judicial decisions should be measured.[96]

Abortion

A second issue which has caused much concern to feminists engaged in rights discourse has been that of reproduction and, more specifically, abortion politics. It is pertinent, therefore, to survey the position of the Strasbourg authorities on this matter in order to ascertain the scope for a post-Human Rights Act interpretation of the compatibility with Convention rights of domestic legislation, particularly s 1(1) of the Abortion Act 1967 (as amended by s 37 of the Human Fertilisation and Embryology Act 1990) which details the circumstances in which an abortion is lawful in Britain.[97] As will be seen below, however, abortion politics is not simply confined to the question of when a termination may be legitimately performed (and how the rights of the foetus should be balanced against those of the pregnant woman), but may also interconnect with wider questions, particularly those of the fundamental freedoms of expression and information. Hence, in terms of its applicability, the Convention in itself neither permits nor prohibits abortion, nor does it explicitly protect a woman's right to choose or a foetus' right to life. This is not to say that the rights guaranteed by the Convention are without relevance in

---

96 As has begun to happen in France: see Millns, *ibid*; Edelman, B, 'La dignité de la personne humaine, un concept nouveau' (1997) *Dalloz*, chron, p 185; Mattieu, B, 'La dignité de la personne humaine: quel droit? Quel titulaire?' (1996) *Dalloz*, chron, 282; Saint-James, V, 'Réflexions sur la dignité de l'être humain en tant que concept juridique du droit français' (1997) *Dalloz*, chron, p 61. In the UK, dignity has in fact already been identified as an aspect of privacy by David Feldman ('Secrecy, dignity, or autonomy? Views of privacy as a civil liberty' (1994) 47 CLP 41). In addition, however, it is important to note that the concept has importance beyond the realm of privacy, being particularly applicable in other contexts and to other fundamental rights, such as the right to equality.

97 The provisions of the Abortion Act 1967 do not extend to Northern Ireland where legal terminations are still subject to the guidelines set out in *R v Bourne* [1939] 1 KB 687. In the rest of the UK, the amended s 1(1) applies, to the effect that a termination is lawful where it is performed: 'by a registered medical practitioner if two registered medical practitioners are of the opinion, formed in good faith–

(a) that the pregnancy has not exceeded its 24th week and that the continuance of the pregnancy would involve risk, greater than if the pregnancy were terminated, or of injury to the physical or mental health of the pregnant woman or any existing children of her family; or

(b) that the termination is necessary to prevent grave permanent injury to the physical or mental health of the pregnant woman; or

(c) that the continuance of the pregnancy would involve risk to the life of the pregnant woman, greater than if the pregnancy were terminated; or

(d) that there is a substantial risk that if the child were born it would suffer from such physical or mental abnormalities as to be seriously handicapped.'

See, further, *op cit*, fn 37, Sheldon, ch 6.

the context of abortion. It might be argued, rather, that Art 2, which provides that '[e]veryone's right to life shall be protected by law', should be interpreted to include the foetus within its ambit. Equally, it might be pleaded that Art 12, which governs the right of men and women of marriageable age to marry and found a family, supports the criminalisation of abortion. On the other hand, Art 8 might be invoked to support a woman's right to choose to terminate a pregnancy in the context of her right to respect for private and family life. In addition, Art 10, which protects freedom of expression, may become relevant with regard to the dissemination of information about abortion.

Given the absence of an explicit statement with regard to the legitimacy of terminations within the text of the Convention itself, and given the controversy to which debate on abortion invariably gives rise,[98] the act of interpretation of the rights guaranteed under the Convention is bound to be challenging at both European and at domestic level. Sally Sheldon has convincingly argued, however, that before the UK courts, abortion has been increasingly transformed from a political to a medical issue, regarding which, the courts have habitually shown deference to medical opinion.[99] In a not dissimilar fashion, and yet without recourse to a specific medical discourse, it is notable that the European Commission and Court of Human Rights have also been successful in effacing the politics of abortion from the cases before them, keeping them instead decontextualised and tightly nailed to discussion of the abstract Convention rights at stake.

Abortion and rights

In the case of *Bruggemann and Scheuten v Federal Republic of Germany*,[100] the Commission considered a restriction of the law on abortion which had been implemented in Germany following a liberalisation of the law which was challenged on the basis that it constituted a violation of Art 8. The Commission concluded that there was no violation of the right to respect for private life because abortion did not relate solely to private life and therefore not every aspect of the legal regulation of terminations constituted an interference with a woman's privacy. In making this assessment, the Commission failed to consider whether a foetus was a 'life' within the context of Art 2 and also whether it was a person within the terms of Art 8(2) which permits a justifiable interference with the right guaranteed under Art 8(1)

---

98 A clear presentation of the arguments put forward by anti-choice and pro-choice advocates is to be found in Morgan, D and Lee, RG, *Blackstone's Guide to the Human Fertilisation and Embryology Act 1990*, 1991, London: Blackstone, pp 38–40.

99 *Op cit*, fn 37, Sheldon, ch 5.

100 *Bruggemann and Scheuten v Federal Republic of Germany* (1981) 3 EHRR 244.

where this is necessary to protect the rights of others. In *Paton v UK*,[101] where a husband had sought to prevent his wife from having a termination, the Commission found that the right to life and health of the mother limited any right a foetus might have. There was, consequently, no attempt to deny that the foetus had a right to life, but nor was any attempt made to draw the boundaries of when life might be said to begin. But, not insignificantly with respect to safeguarding women's choice, the Commission rejected the husband's claim to a right to be consulted about a termination, a claim also founded upon Art 8.

The Commission in both *Bruggemann* and *Paton* has, therefore, been placed in the position of having to arbitrate in a dispute where conflicting rights (woman/foetus, woman/putative father) are at issue. The overall result is compromise and a lack of clarity. The failure to tackle the abortion question head-on may, thus, create difficulties in interpretation for British courts, should they be called upon to interpret the domestic legislative provisions on abortion in conjunction with the Strasbourg case law. The possibility of judicial intervention is not remote, with constitutional lawyers already pointing out that the legitimacy of UK legislation permitting abortion is ripe for challenge given the nature of the rights under the Convention.[102] Yet, between the medicalisation of home judicial interpretation of abortion law, and the ambivalent nature of the Commission's interpretation of the Convention rights applicable, the depoliticisation of judicial interpretation of abortion looks unlikely to alter. This means that the furtherance of a politics of abortion grounded in women's reproductive choice is unlikely to be realised in the near future.

Abortion and information

Furthermore, beyond the conceptualisation of abortion as a conflict between rights of foetus, mother and putative father, a further instance of the depoliticisation of abortion politics by the Strasbourg organs has arisen in the context of the Art 10 guarantee of freedom of expression discussed by the Court in two cases: *Open Door Counselling, Dublin Well Woman Centre Ltd and Others v Ireland*[103] and *Bowman v UK*.[104] Both cases demonstrate a desire to draw the line of freedom as broadly, and the inference of politics as narrowly,

---

101 *Paton v UK* (1981) 3 EHRR 408.

102 Ewing, K and Gearty, C, 'Terminating abortion rights?' (1992) 142 NLJ 1696.

103 *Open Door Counselling, Dublin Well Woman Centre Ltd and Others v Ireland* (1993) 15 EHRR 244. See *ibid*. For discussion of the historical background on the law on abortion in Ireland, see Whitty, N, 'Law and the regulation of reproduction in Ireland: 1922–92' (1993) 43 Toronto ULJ 851.

104 *Bowman v UK* (1998) 26 EHRR 1. See Millns, S and Sheldon, S, 'Delivering democracy to abortion politics: *Bowman v UK* (1999) 7 FLS (forthcoming).

as possible; a strategy which is not without implications for a feminist politics of abortion law.

In the former case, a petition was brought by two counselling organisations challenging an injunction granted in the Irish courts which restrained the organisations and their agents from helping pregnant women to travel from Ireland in order to obtain abortions abroad.[105] The petitioners argued that the injunction breached their rights under Art 10 and Art 8 and was discriminatory on the ground of sex under Art 14. The European Court found, by a 15:8 majority, that there was a breach of Art 10 because of the breadth of the injunction. While the Irish Government had argued that freedom of expression was not breached because the aim of Irish law was to protect the right to life of the unborn (under Art 2 of the Convention), the Court reiterated that, although there was no such thing as a common standard of European morality and Ireland had some discretion in the matter, this discretion was, nevertheless, subject to the scrutiny of the Court. Given that it was not an offence to seek an abortion outside Ireland, the prohibition upon information was an improper restriction upon freedom. While, on the one hand, many feminists who advocate the right to choose would welcome this decision as furthering choice, it is not wholly unproblematic in that it persists in a reading of the text of the Convention which largely precludes a feminist interpretation by denying the relevance of the female body and sexual politics to the precise legal point under discussion. In short, the issue is still characterised as one of information, not women's reproductive choice (or, indeed, lack of it).

A similar point has been made in the context of European Union law following the case of *SPUC (Ireland) v Grogan*,[106] in which the Society for the Protection of the Unborn Child sought to prevent the dissemination, in Ireland, of information in student handbooks about abortion clinics in Britain. A preliminary reference to the European Court of Justice to ascertain whether this amounted to a breach of EU law on freedom to provide services found that, while abortion did constitute a service, the link between the information provided by the students and the service provided by British clinics was insufficiently strong to amount to an interference in the provision of the service by the discontinuance of the information. The decision demonstrates the supremacy attached to the legal text (in this case, to the market values inherent in the Treaty of Rome), at the expense of consideration of the issue

---

105 For examples of the many ways in which access to information about abortion is restricted throughout the world, see Coliver, S (ed), *The Right to Know: Human Rights and Access to Reproductive Health Information*, 1995, Pennsylvania: Pennsylvania Press; and discussion thereon in Whitty, N, 'The mind, the body and reproductive health information' (1996) 18 HRQ 224.

106 *SPUC (Ireland) v Grogan* [1991] ECR I-4733. See Flynn, L, 'The body politic(s) of EC law', in *op cit*, fn 51, Hervey and O'Keeffe, p 301.

within the specific context of abortion politics, highlighted by the exclusion of the information/service providers from the internal market.

The dangers inherent in this market based approach have been noted by Derek Morgan and Robert G Lee in their analysis of the interplay of services and rights in the context of the freedom to receive medical (fertility treatment) services under EU law and the decision of the Court of Appeal in *R v Human Fertilisation and Embryology Authority ex p Blood*.[107] Morgan and Lee effectively highlight the troublesome nature of the requirement to justify rules aimed at protecting social and moral values in order to satisfy an economic imperative:

> *Blood* begins to explore the fundamentals of a common social policy in the European Union which has everything to do with economics, even the economics of reproductive life, which is beginning to emerge strongly as the binding parameter for a Union which *can find no other guiding principle*.[108]

The inability to find alternative guiding principles beyond the market (in the case of EU law) and beyond the *negative* freedom from censorship in the dissemination of information (in the case of the Convention) is not conducive to a contextualisation of matters of reproductive health, nor to a practical consideration of the limits of the rights granted. Hence, no attempt is made to analyse the extent to which the counselling information which was provided in Ireland to pregnant women was effective in facilitating the choice of these women to undergo a termination or not, that is, in establishing whether the women actually understood the information given. Furthermore, the articulation of freedom of expression and information, without the imposition of more *positive* obligations upon the state (such as, for example, an obligation to finance counselling services) simply highlights the emptiness of the right concerned for those women who do not have the economic or social means to seek out and obtain access to counselling and termination services.[109]

The use of freedom of expression to defend access to information about abortion is, therefore, not unproblematic for a feminist employment of rights strategies because of the non-contextual manner in which the issue is discussed. Furthermore, free speech may be used in ways which are profoundly antithetical to the interests of women's groups campaigning for abortion. In the US, for example, s 507 of the Telecommunications Act 1996 contains a provision which criminalises the distribution or receipt of any information on the Internet relating to where and how to obtain an abortion.

---

107 *R v Human Fertilisation and Embryology Authority, ex p Blood* [1997] 2 All ER 687; Morgan, D and Lee, RG, 'In the name of the father? *Ex parte Blood*: dealing with novelty and anomaly' (1997) 60 MLR 840. See, also, Hervey, T, 'Buy baby: the European Union and regulation of human reproduction' (1998) 18 OJLS 207.

108 *Ibid*, Morgan and Lee, p 855.

109 See *op cit*, fn 105, Whitty, p 235, where the author argues that '[a] reproductive health approach not only requires a critique of the information that is provided to women in order to expose the dominant ideologies and biases which underpin it, it also requires the existence of supportive environments where this process can occur and informed choices can ultimately be reached'.

This provision is claimed not to violate the first amendment guarantee of free speech (defined as *political* speech) as, according to Supreme Court jurisprudence, the advertisement of a service is defined as *commercial* speech and can, as such, be regulated by the Government.[110] In this respect, feminists may have rather more to lose than to gain in terms of the implications of employing free speech and freedom of expression claims in order to secure the dissemination of abortion information.

A further instance of the inability to address the relevance of abortion politics by judicial authorities has been demonstrated in the recent decision of the European Court in *Bowman v UK*,[111] in which Mrs Bowman, a leading UK anti-choice activist, petitioned the Strasbourg institutions after being prosecuted for distributing one and a half million leaflets in election constituencies throughout Britain which set out the various candidates' views on abortion and embryology. The prosecution, which was formed on the basis of a contravention of s 75(1) of the Representation of the People Act 1983 (prohibiting any expenditure in excess of £5 being incurred by any person[112] with a view to promoting or procuring the election of a candidate), was ultimately not upheld on a technicality,[113] yet it was found by the Court that a violation of Art 10 had occurred.

The importance of this decision for feminist abortion politics, however, lies not so much in its finding of a violation of Mrs Bowman's freedom of expression, but rather in the context of the ongoing anti-choice campaign to reposition abortion at the heart of electoral politics. First, the leaflet produced by Mrs Bowman concerning the views of the electoral candidates was represented as a means of providing the electorate with 'factually accurate' information and thus promoting democracy and electoral choice. This factual accuracy was never contested by the Court despite the highly emotive nature of the language employed in the leaflet.[114] Secondly, the leaflet contained an

---

110 See Wells, C, 'Abortion counselling as vice activity: the free speech implications of *Rust v Sullivan* and *Planned Parenthood v Casey*' (1995) 95 Columbia LR 1724.

111 *Bowman v UK* (1998) 26 EHRR 1.

112 Other than candidates, their election agents and persons authorised in writing by the latter.

113 Bowman had been summonsed after the one year time limit for prosecution had passed.

114 One candidate, Alison Mahon (Labour) is described as follows: 'Mrs Mahon is a leading pro-abortionist. As an MP she voted to allow abortion up to birth for handicapped babies. She voted for the compulsory enrolment on a published register of doctors with a conscientious objection to abortion despite warning that it could be used as a blacklist. She also voted to allow human embryos to be used as guinea-pigs in programmes including the testing of drugs and other experiments.' The choice of 'facts' and utilisation of language here is, however, highly selective. Could Mrs Mahon not equally have been described as a leading 'pro-choice' MP? Did she not, rather, vote to extend the provision of abortion services until term where two doctors believe that termination is necessary because of serious risk of grave foetal disability and vote to allow human embryos to be used in approved and regulated scientific programmes including investigation into infertility and other diseases? See further, *op cit*, fn 104, Millns and Sheldon.

image of a free-floating foetus at 10 weeks gestation. As has been argued by Petchesky, this type of representation has the power to abstract and then present as truth an image which is partial and inaccurate in that it eclipses all visibility of the body of the pregnant woman and denies her role in the gestation process.[115] The foetus is represented as an autonomous individual, abstracted from all context, despite the clear inaccuracy of the image. Thus, the leaflet distributed by Bowman was carefully loaded in a way which seems antithetical to an accurate and *informed* debate on abortion politics. Indeed, it runs quite counter to Bowman's suggestion that her actions were intended as a means of facilitating democratic choice. On the contrary, the Court's decision, in inscribing once more within Art 10 a *negative* right to freedom of expression (that is, prohibiting the censorship of what individuals may say) does nothing to address the absence of positive obligations on the part of the state to enhance the opportunities for speech traditionally denied to those who lack the power and resources necessary in order to secure a platform from which to be heard.

This approach is markedly in contrast with that of the Court in relation to the positive obligations incumbent upon the state in the context of sexual violence. In this respect, the inconsistency as regards interpretation may be a source of confusion for domestic courts when using the Strasbourg case law to inform domestic decision making in cases raising issues of body politics. Equally, the lack of politicisation in the context of abortion politics may be contrasted with the contextualisation of questions of female sexual abuse and, again, may generate problems with respect to interpretation and consistency of approach.

CONCLUSION

Despite the lack of consciousness of an overtly feminist perspective in the decision making of the Commission and the Court, and despite the lack of regard to the politicisation of their actions, particularly in the area of reproductive choice, the case for a more feminist reinterpretation of domestic legal provisions in the light of the rights under the Convention is certainly not lost. At a broad level, Stephanie Palmer has noted how the very novelty of this situation has created a space in which feminist perspectives may act to destabilise contemporary discourses:

> ... the introduction of the European Convention into domestic law may provide an opportunity to unsettle existing discourses. A space may be created which would allow women's perspectives and experiences to enter into the

---

115 Petchesky, R, 'Foetal images: the power of visual culture in the politics of reproduction', in Stanworth, M (ed), *Reproductive Technologies: Gender, Motherhood and Medicine*, 1987, London: Polity, p 62.

law. There could be openings to ask previously unasked questions and to reframe debates. The introduction of a formal declaration of rights will not solve political and social conflicts within society but it can heighten awareness of the conflicts. It has the potential to mobilise movements, to influence political debate, and, perhaps, to bring about social change.[116]

At a more specific level, the commencement of the project of articulation of constitutional values, which would include dignity, respect and security of the person, is most welcome from a feminist perspective. Enhanced by the European Court's reading of the fundamental objectives of the Convention as encompassing both the respect of human dignity and human freedom, the space created for a domestic reinterpretation of human rights discourse in the UK offers judicial authorities the occasion to prove that home is indeed where the heart is as regards the recognition and protection of women's rights and interests.

What should be stressed, however, is that feminist recourse to rights strategies is inherently a risky business, which carries with it the prospect of both gains and losses. Rights strategies *can* be effectively pursued by feminists and, in this sense, we should not be afraid to seek them out, remaining alert to the dangers and pitfalls associated with doing so. It may be, for example, that we need to expose further the fact that rights strategies can prove counterproductive to women's interests if they fail to address the often disempowering nature of rights litigation for the individual litigants. Thus, the elite group of white, middle class women lawyers involved in cases such as *Open Door Counselling* may have had little in common with the women counsellors (and the women uncertain as to whether to terminate a pregnancy) whose interests they represented before the courts. In this respect, it is important to reduce the extent to which litigants (despite an eventual successful outcome) feel distanced from the process unfolding before them as their lives and experiences are filtered through the legal system and their claims are translated into the 'appropriate' legal rights and remedies, losing in that translation all contextualisation.[117]

It is obvious, too, that feminists cannot afford to pass up the opportunity created by the introduction of the Human Rights Act to engage in rights litigation in areas of concern to feminist politics. In a climate where women litigants such as Diane Blood and Phyllis Bowman have proved extremely effective in their use of rights discourse (sometimes achieving results which feminists may find difficult to support), to abandon the terrain of rights to the opponents of feminism would be irresponsible. What appears necessary,

116 *Op cit*, fn 16, Palmer, p 242.

117 It is precisely this translation/reduction of female experience into existing legal categories which is criticised by Carol Smart as disempowering for women, and which leads her to suggest that it is 'important to challenge the power of law and to insist on the legitimacy of feminist knowledge and feminism's ability to redefine the wrongs of women which law too often confines to insignificance': *op cit*, fn 15, Smart, p 165.

instead, is to seek to maximise the potential of the Human Rights Act by broadening our strategic usage of rights claims. While this chapter has been confined to two areas of immediate and evident concern to women's lives – sexual violence and abortion – the Human Rights Act offers the scope to move beyond this and to address the impact of the Convention upon areas where rights litigation has hitherto largely failed to bite. Thus, for example, female prisoners, recipients of welfare benefits, victims of sexual harassment, single mothers and individuals concerned about the politics of sexual identity may all find within the Convention rights a new source of legal arms with which to further the recognition of hitherto hidden gender based harms and inequality. It is in this respect that the gender blindness of human rights law can begin to be challenged more effectively on both international and home territory.

CHAPTER 10

ENGENDERING ASYLUM LAW: FEMINISM, PROCESS AND PRACTICE

CJ Harvey

INTRODUCTION

There is extensive soul-searching going on in the public law community. While some of this can be attributed to the present restructuring of the constitution, and to the revolution in public administration in modern times, the issue seems to run deeper. Values are back in vogue among public lawyers, with some, for example, arguing for the judiciary and public law scholars to be more explicit about the democratic values which guide them.[1] In an ambitious project, Dawn Oliver has sought to unearth common values in both public and private law.[2] The search appears to be on in public law for a new paradigm to orient practice in an increasingly complex legal world. Both internal and external pressures are causing a rethink of basic aspects of the subject. This is a particularly appropriate time for public lawyers to address the challenges presented by feminist theory.

Feminist theorists have been at the forefront of attempts to unmask law's pretensions and its questionable claim to embody reason, neutrality and universality. Insights from feminist theory now offer the means to interrogate all aspects of modern public law and policy. It is interesting to watch public

---

1   See Harlow, C and Rawlings, R, *Law and Administration*, 1997, 2nd edn, London: Butterworths, pp 27–28: 'Like Craig, we are concerned with the search for values, accepting law's educative and symbolic roles. Our response to the question "What should public lawyers do?" would be that they have a responsibility critically to evaluate the institutions, processes and systems of administration, exposing to public gaze the values on which both are premised.' See, also, Oliver, D, 'The underlying values of public and private law', in Taggart, M (ed), *The Province of Administrative Law*, 1997, Oxford: Hart, p 217; Oliver, D, 'Common values in public and private law and the public/private divide' [1997] PL 630. Cf Cotterrell, R, 'Judicial review and legal theory', in Richardson, G and Genn, H (eds), *Administrative Law and Government Action*, 1994, Oxford: Clarendon, p 13, p 32: 'We have noted that the appeal to community values, whether in courts, in the writings of legal philosophers, or in the consciousness of political leaders and opinion makers is likely to be an appeal to those values that the person making such an appeal ascribes to the community.' Also Feldman, D, 'Public law values in the House of Lords' (1990) 106 LQR 246; and Loughlin, M, 'The pathways of public law scholarship', in Wilson, GP (ed), *Frontiers of Legal Scholarship*, 1995, Chicester: John Wiley, pp 184–85; Harlow, C, 'Changing the mindset: the place of theory in english administrative law' (1994) 14 OJLS 419.

2   *Ibid*, Oliver, in Taggart. The five key values she identifies are autonomy, dignity, respect, status and security.

lawyers now problematising issues which have been central to feminist theory for some time. Whatever the precise reason for the new interest in the blurring of the public/private, it is important that more use is made of those fields of inquiry where the divide has traditionally been questioned.

It is the suggestion in this chapter that new forms of 'functionalist' thought share a common purpose with strands of feminist theory.[3] The link will be deliberately made in order to demonstrate how a procedural conception of public law can accommodate new insights which challenge core aspects of current law and practice. The project is essentially about reforming current law and practice in the light of 'new voices' entering the discourse. By gesturing at antagonisms and tensions which presently exist, we should be able to offer a rational reconstruction which is inclusive and at least actively grapples with the task of understanding the totality of the human experience in legal contexts. Underpinning this search for common values and defensible background theories of public law, which are relevant to today's world, is a desire for coherence in the face of increased societal complexity. As the 'fact of pluralism' gains acceptance, there is concern about discontinuity and fragmentation. Some, for example, have wondered what is now distinctive about public law and suggested ways the subject might move forward.[4] This ambition to construct unity in the midst of diversity and pluralism lies at the heart of a number of modern trends in legal and political theory. Is it still possible to recognise the situated nature of our lives and work while retaining a link to rational decision making and even (the deeply unfashionable) concept of universalism? An alternative question might be: why be concerned about the turn to particularity and difference. Many schools of thought, including important strands of feminist legal theory, now advance a politics of difference and welcome the move from grand theory to the local and particular. It is a mistake to view these debates as removed from the day to day life of public law. These themes from social and political theory can be unearthed in many of the current disputes in the subject and have important implications for any modern discussion of equality and social justice.

Feminist theory goes to the core of these debates. By revealing the distortion and oppression perpetuated and masked by rationalism and universalism, feminism invites powerful suspicion of past theories of law and democracy. In this chapter, an attempt is made to take this perspective seriously and examine some of the implications. To illustrate the value of the feminist perspective on public law, the chapter includes a case study from the frequently neglected area of asylum law. Feminist theorists have presented some of the most influential criticisms of refugee and asylum law in the past

---

3   Young, AH, 'Feminism, pluralism and administrative law', in *op cit*, fn 1, McTaggart, p 331.

4   Loughlin, M, *Public Law and Political Theory*, 1992, Oxford: Clarendon.

decade. This critique has been used to confront the legal regime with political strategies which have yielded some success in practice. It is the claim of this chapter, contrary to some feminist theorists, that this strongly suggests that engagement with law can lead to politically progressive results. This is not the same as saying that legal regulation will solve all the problems of modernity but that properly conceived it can contribute to *facilitating* consensual governance. It is important that feminist scholars do not join the ranks of those neo-conservatives who either erase normativity and projects of reconstruction in the face of societal complexity or retire to the realms of the esoteric.

FEMINISM AND CRITICAL PUBLIC LAW SCHOLARSHIP

The feminist perspective on public law joins a growing band of critical work in the field. Much of this work displays a commitment to inclusive democratic governance. It is suggested here that feminist theorists can make a valuable contribution to what has been termed the functionalist approach to the subject. There has always been a strong attachment to theories of participatory democracy among certain schools of public law thought.[5] Ultimately traceable to the influence of sociological positivism, philosophical pragmatism in the US and utilitarianism in the UK, the functionalist school places emphasis on the important facilitative role of government. In this model, law and the constitutional state fulfil a vital part in societal integration and emerge for the purpose of securing regulation in the public interest. Reacting against the preference for a minimalist state evident in the work of Dicey, Hayek and, more recently, Nozick, functionalists welcomed the emergent administrative state and the opportunities it offered for securing social justice. The canvas upon which functionalists operate has tended to be much broader than normativists. Studies have focused in detail on public administration and the policy making process in an attempt to move beyond court centred obsessions in public law.[6] Given the use made in this work of a variety of 'new perspectives', its advocates are natural allies of feminist theorists in the attempt to 'open up' public law.

The importance of interdisciplinary work is now recognised in critical debates in public law and several attempts have been made to draw upon

---

5   See *eg* Morison, J and Livingstone, S, *Reshaping Public Power: Northern Ireland and the British Constitutional Crisis*, 1995, London: Sweet & Maxwell; Harden, I and Lewis, N, *The Noble Lie: The British Constitution and the Rule of Law*, 1986, London: Hutchinson; Prosser, T, 'Towards a critical theory of public law' (1982) 9 JLS 1.

6   Eg, Black, J, *Rules and Regulators*, 1997, Oxford: Clarendon; Baldwin, R, *Rules and Government*, 1997, Oxford: Clarendon; Galligan, DJ, *Due Process and Fair Procedures: A Study of Administrative Procedures*, 1997, Oxford: Clarendon; Galligan, DJ (ed), *A Reader on Administrative Law*, 1996, Oxford: OUP.

social theory to see what light can be shed on the subject.[7] Recent critical literature in public law has, for example, made use of the critical theory of, among others, Habermas.[8] Given the extent to which this social theorist holds to universalist claims, it is perhaps surprising that his work has been so well received by some feminist theorists. On reflection, however, it is understandable: perhaps the attraction lies in discourse theory's commitment to real world radical democracy and critique in the face of the corrosive neo-conservative strands in some postmodern and poststructuralist work. It is widely acknowledged that the discourse theory developed, with its radical democratic implications, is useful in analysing the pathologies of modernity and in indicating constructive ways forward.

RESPONDING TO COMPLEXITY WITH PROCEDURALISM?

At a time when the 'fact of pluralism' has become an almost universal given, it is unsurprising that some theorists seek comfort from procedural models.[9] There is, however, little that is particularly novel about this turn to process in law.[10] The attempt to unearth the core of reason in legal and democratic practices is a well established tendency. Habermasian proceduralism is yet another effort to chart this path. Versions of the model he advances are proving influential among some public law theorists. There remain, however, a number of substantial problems from a feminist perspective. Some understanding of Habermasian theory is necessary before examining the use made by feminist theorists of dialogical models and the criticisms advanced.

It is beyond the bounds of this chapter to map in detail the intricacies of Habermas' work. Although reductionist, certain key themes can be extracted. Central to his project, and a point often neglected by those who criticise the minimalist nature of the theory, is the commitment to radical democracy. In our postmetaphysical world, it is no longer the job of theorists to prescribe totalising theories to be imposed by elites coercively on individuals and groups. This explains why proceduralism is so important in his theory of law and democracy.[11] At the core of this work is a turning away from subject

---

7   Eg, Leyland, P and Woods, T (eds), *Administrative Law Facing the Future: Old Constraints and New Horizons*, 1997, London: Blackstone, pp 374ff.

8   Eg, Birkinshaw, P, *Freedom of Information: The Law, the Practice and the Ideal*, 1996, 2nd edn, London: Butterworths, pp 15–18; Lewis, N, *Choice and the Legal Order: Rising Above Politics*, 1996; London: Butterworths, pp 17–21.

9   See Chambers, S, *Reasonable Democracy: Jürgen Habermas and the Politics of Discourse*, 1996, London: Cornell UP, pp 17–29.

10   Duxbury, N, *Patterns of American Jurisprudence*, 1995, Oxford: Clarendon, pp 205–99.

11   See, generally, Habermas, J, *Between Facts and Norms: Contributions to a Discourse Theory of Law and Democracy*, 1996, Cambridge: Polity. For comment on the work, see Salter, M, 'Habermas's new contribution to legal scholarship' (1997) 24 JLS 285; Rosenfeld, M, 'Law as discourse: bridging the gap between democracy and rights' (1996) 108 Harv L

centred reason to a dialogical model of rationality.[12] This is founded on the belief that the philosophy of consciousness has led consistently to a dead end and, in modern times, has resulted in a turn to destructive forms of nihilism and neo-conservatism.[13] The communicative model painstakingly developed is based on the deceptively simple proposition that, in all attempts to reach understanding in dialogue with others, there are certain embedded presuppositions which have a normative content. Most controversially, these presuppositions are claimed to have universal underpinnings which transcend context and location and which potentially offer a basis for continuing critique. In this model, reason cannot be simply reduced to its instrumental forms and the importance of communicative rationality must be acknowledged.

The attraction of this work for public lawyers lies in its utility as a way of understanding and criticising modern trends in law and policy development. Most intriguing is the attempt made to draw together two strands of legal thought which have tended to be viewed as opposed. In the discourse theory of law and democracy, human rights and popular sovereignty are internally connected. This is particularly relevant in the public law sphere where funtionalism and normativism have often been thought of as two quite distinct mindsets.

FEMINISM AND THE COMMUNICATIVE CONCEPTION OF RATIONALITY

As indicated above, the communicative model has potential in the public law sphere which the case study below will seek to draw out. Before embarking on this, the feminist critique of this body of work needs to be examined. Can the theory withstand these criticisms or must it necessarily be reconstructed in order to be of use to feminist scholarship?

---

11 [contd] Rev 1163; McCormick, JP, 'Habermas' discourse theory of law: bridging the gap between Anglo-American and Continental legal traditions?' (1997) 60 MLR 734; Harvey, C, 'The procedural paradigm of law and democracy' [1997] PL 692; Dyzenhaus, D, 'The legitimacy of legality' (1997) XLVI Toronto ULJ 129. See, also, 'Habermas on law and democracy: critical exchanges' (1996) 17 Cardozo L Rev (Symposium Issue), pp 767–1643; Deflem, M (ed), *Habermas, Modernity and Law*, 1996, London: Sage; Alexy, R, 'Basic rights and democracy in Jürgen Habermas's procedural paradigm of law' (1994) 7 Ratio Juris 227. On related themes, see Bohman, J, *Public Deliberation: Pluralism, Complexity and Democracy*, 1996, Cambridge, MA: MIT.

12 Habermas, J, *The Theory of Communicative Action Volume 1: Reason and the Rationalisation of Society*, 1984, Cambridge: Polity; *The Theory of Communicative Action Volume 2: Lifeworld and System: A Critique of Functionalist Reason*, 1987, Cambridge: Polity. For an interesting study, see Cooke, M, *Language and Reason: A Study of Habermas's Pragmatics*, 1994, London: MIT.

13 Habermas, J, *The Philosophical Discourse of Modernity*, 1987, Cambridge: Polity.

The discourse theory of law and democracy has its problems and prospects.[14] The priority given to the right over the good is not novel in political theory. Taking his lead from Kant, Rawls is possibly the best known modern defender of a procedural model. In modern times, suspicion has been cast on this approach. Proceduralism is always open to the criticism that it simply fails to acknowledge its own substantive commitments. Critics point to the abstraction[15] of the theory and the image of the self which it perpetuates.[16] Proceduralism, it is claimed, cannot avoid reliance upon a substantive concept of the good life and holds out a form of disengagement that has proved attractive but which is ultimately untenable. It is not difficult to see why this has proved unpalatable to some feminist theorists. Replacing the Rawlsian original position with the presuppositions of communicative action to ground a dialogical model simply does not convince those opposed to versions of neo-Kantian universalism. Despite the fact that Habermas clings to much that feminist theory has traditionally found unacceptable, his work has attracted reserved support from a number of critics. The univeralism, formalism and abstraction of this body of work is, however, dubious from the perspective of an oppositional tradition that has witnessed all these things operate in the service of domination and oppression in the past.[17] Specifically, the following criticisms might be made:

(1) it is naive to think that, given the different interpretations of needs and wants that consensus is ever going to be a possibility;

(2) communicative equality as envisioned by this theory is simply too idealistic;

(3) the totalising and system building urges evident in this work are in some sense intrinsically 'male'.

Here, we will examine these criticisms further with reference to some feminist theorists who have been attracted by this work. The first obvious problem is that, until very recently, Habermas has neglected feminist theory.[18] He has, however, recognised the clear emancipatory potential of the feminist

---

14 For interesting criticism, see Rosenfeld, M, *Just Interpretations: Law Between Ethics and Politics*, 1998, Berkeley and Los Angeles: California UP, pp 114–49.

15 Cf Rawls, J, *Political Liberalism*, 1993, New York: Columbia UP, pp 44–46.

16 Sandel, M, 'The procedural republic and the unencumbered self' (1986) 12 Political Theory 81. Cf Taylor, C, *Philosophy and the Human Sciences: Philosophical Papers 2*, 1985, Cambridge: CUP, pp 187–210. Cf Rorty, R, *Contingency, Irony and Solidarity*, 1989, Cambridge: CUP, pp 65–69.

17 See, generally, on these issues and problems with the traditional republican conception of participation, Young, IM, 'Polity and group difference: a critique of the ideal of universal citizenship' (1989) 99 Ethics 250; Young, IM, *Justice and the Politics of Difference*, 1990, Princeton, NJ: Princeton UP, pp 96–121.

18 Cf Fraser, E and Lacey, N, *The Politics of Community: A Feminist Critique of the Liberal-Communitarian Debate*, 1993, London: Harvester Wheatsheaf, p 145.

movement.[19] His concept of the public sphere has proved popular but has not gone uncriticised.[20] The conception of the bourgeois public sphere is said to be idealistic.[21] The republican public sphere, as it emerged in France, was constructed around a male conception of speech and behaviour to the exclusion of women. Other public spheres existed which he fails to account for. Thus, critics like Fraser explore conflicting historical evidence which suggests that the public sphere held up by Habermas was, in practice, an ideological legitimation of class rule.[22] The notion that we should claim this model as a normative ideal with which to measure modern democracy is thus problematised. Rather than reject this approach, however, Fraser builds on the blind spots exposed to argue for a more complex notion of the public sphere which recognises the plurality of competing publics.

The theme of colonisation of the lifeworld is problematic if we consider the family, for example. The term 'colonisation' can perpetuate a view of the institution which is misleading. Some would argue that it is not a matter of an 'alien' force entering this sphere, but it is the institution itself which is questionable.[23] This is a general difficulty with Habermas' conception of the system/lifeworld distinction. It freezes elements which are much more fluid in reality and may restrict new thinking which uncovers the complexity of this relationship. Connected to this, the argument that symbolic reproduction is central to the constitution of the lifeworld, while material reproduction belongs to the realm of the system, has been criticised. Fraser has argued that material reproduction is at the heart of the family and it is women's unacknowledged role which is masked by such a divide. On conceptions of citizenship, Habermas' approach is also suspect from a feminist perspective. The concept depends on capacities which are said to be connected to 'masculinity'. Pateman, for example, has noted how women's consent is reinterpreted and that the whole notion of citizenship is gendered.[24] Her critique of social contractarianism is particularly good.[25] But, while a useful critique of contract theory, it misses the mark when applied to the communicative model.

---

19 White, S, *The Recent Work of Jürgen Habermas: Reason, Justice and Modernity*, 1988, Cambridge: CUP, pp 123–27.

20 Fraser, N, *Justice Interruptus: Critical Reflections on the 'Postsocialist Condition'*, 1997, London: Routledge, pp 69–98.

21 *Ibid*, p 73.

22 *Ibid*, p 76.

23 Fraser, N, 'What's critical about critical theory?', in Meehan, J (ed), *Feminists Read Habermas: Gendering the Subject of Discourse*, 1995, London: Routledge, p 29.

24 Cf Lister, R, *Citizenship: Feminist Perspectives*, 1997, London: Macmillan, p 196, even though citizenship is a concept which was formed on the basis of exclusion it is still useful.

25 Patemen, C, *The Sexual Contract*, 1988, Cambridge: Polity. Cf *op cit*, fn 9, Chambers, p 23, stating that proceduralism is not the same as contract theory.

In general terms, proceduralism is, today, the object of sustained criticism from a variety of perspectives. Feminism combines with the new 'contextualism' of Sandel, Taylor, Walzer, MacIntyre, and postmodernism to challenge any attempt to reinvent neo-Kantianism for the modern age. We are all situated selves in a way that has been neglected by theories which draw their inspiration from Kantianism. This Hegelian critique is not new and has been, I believe, answered fairly convincingly by Habermas.[26] For feminism, the emphasis on the concrete other is central.[27] Abstract, disengaged formalism has too often masked partial and distorted perspectives. While 'masculine theorists' focus on autonomy and independence from others, some feminists have emphasised connectedness and intimacy. The construction of freedom in terms of the rational ego is straightforwardly problematic from a feminist perspective, but it is precisely this 'deformed' conception of freedom, detached from solidarity and emancipation, which critical theorists have habitually attacked.[28] In other words, critical theorists have consistently challenged 'disengaged' reason.

Some of the implications of this debate are perhaps best explored on the terrain of moral theory. Universalism has always been an important aspect of the Habermasian project. The fear which motivates this impulse in his work is well understood. He finds it unacceptable that a theory should be dependent on the life of one particular political community. Even those who are sympathetic have wavered on the strength of his attachment to universalism. Some suspect that this arises from the specifically German context within which Habermas writes. In contrast, it is interesting to note how Rawls has retreated from this position in recent times.[29] In addition to the clear Kantian orientation, Habermas has also relied on a Kohlbergian paradigm in understanding postconventional morality. In the light of debates which have followed the publication of Gilligan's *In a Different Voice*,[30] this reliance is open to question. The ethics of care confronts the abstract formalism of Kantianism with the concrete other and actions which are not necessarily grounded in reciprocal obligations.[31] Habermas' response has been that care is not built into the communicative presuppositions of discourse, but that the principle of solidarity is. All participants recognise the other as an equal

---

26 See Habermas, J, *Moral Consciousness and Communicative Action*, 1990, Cambridge: Polity, pp 195–215.

27 Cf Lacey, N, *Unspeakable Subjects: Feminist Essays in Legal and Social Theory*, 1998, Oxford: Hart, pp 125–64.

28 See McNay, L, *Foucault and Feminism: Power, Gender and the Self*, 1992, Cambridge: Polity, p 102.

29 Rawls, J, 'The idea of an overlapping consensus' (1987) 7 OJLS 1; Rawls, J, 'Justice as fairness: political not metaphysical' (1985) 14 Philosophy and Public Affairs 223.

30 Gilligan, C, *In a Different Voice*, 1982, Cambridge, MA: Harvard UP.

31 See *ibid*, Habermas, pp 175–81.

person and thus there is an embedded concern with the fate of all others.[32] Benhabib's difficulty with Habermas and Kohlberg is that they have a very narrow conception of the moral domain.[33] The moral relates to issues of justice and is concerned only with providing impartiality in the modern context.[34] The justification of moral norms is, in addition, separate from their concrete application. Justice and the good life are distinct, the former can be universalised, the latter can not. For Benhabib, as with Gilligan, the obligations and relations of care are central to a modern understanding of morality. The challenge for discourse ethics is, therefore, to expand the notion of the moral domain to include the concrete other and the ethics of care. However, this is not a case of either/or. If the moral domain is suitably expanded, then universalism which is attached to justification is still possible. The model of discourse ethics could thus be reshaped in the light of such criticisms.

The argument advanced here is that, despite the flaws in this version of proceduralism, it does provide a useful model for examining public law. The proceduralist understanding disavows a grounding in substantive values for a reason which departs radically from traditional versions of formalism and universalism. Modern universalism in critical theory is profoundly interactionist in orientation. This model is content to unearth the rationality in our democratic practices and encounters with others and thus leaves everything to participants. The utility of this model for feminist perspectives on public law is that it recognises the dilemma of difference while holding on to the tools of reconstructive critique. To point to continuing inequality in practice as a reason for rejecting this thesis misses the point. All that Habermas is attempting to do is unearth the rationality in our everyday encounters and attempts to reach agreement. This provides a means for distorted communication (based on manipulation, coercion, economic inequality) to be diagnosed and addressed. By exploring the area of asylum law below, this chapter tries to show how a version of this model can help us to understand what is happening when social movements seek active political engagement with areas of public law and policy.

It is no longer plausible for elites (no matter which progressive movements they happen to adhere to) to construct a unified theory of the good life to be imposed on citizens of modern democracies. Modernity must construct its normativity out of itself, it can rely on no other transcendental source. It is through the interaction between citizens within legally institutionalised

---

32 See Honneth, A, 'The other of justice: Habermas and the ethical challenge of postmodernism', in White, S (ed), *The Recent Work of Jürgen Habermas: Reason, Justice and Modernity*, 1988, Cambridge: CUP, pp 289, 316ff.

33 See Benhabib, S, *Situating the Self: Gender, Community and Postmodernism in Contemporary Ethics*, 1992, Cambridge: Polity.

34 See, generally, *op cit*, fn 26, Habermas.

spheres of communication and connected channels of discussion and debate that this happens. The model values difference while recognising the intersubjective and social (in the sense that we are socialised through language) nature of our lives and thought. Rather than retreat into atomised conceptions of difference, the conversational model takes seriously the challenges faced in modern pluralist societies and the need for understanding, agreement and consensus in the regulation of social life. It allows us to diagnose distorted communication and thus offers a firm grounding for critique. It also takes the immanent normativity of modernity, as this is reflected in the relationship between the rule of law and democracy, seriously. There are clear links between this work and modern forms of republicanism. The difficulty with traditional republican theory is that it tended to neglect the importance of difference and plurality by seeing them purely as privatised and egotistical. By constructing difference as special pleading, groups could be marginalised because of their alleged failure to contribute to the common good. The result was a desire for unity and promotion of homogenous cultural contexts which perpetuated exclusion from the public sphere of deliberation.[35] The communicative model addresses these weaknesses by acknowledging the nature of difference, while trying to keep open the channels of communication which make democratic dialogue possible and consensual regulation at least a theoretical possibility.

This is important for any radical project at a time when romantic rejections of modernity are widespread. Often, such projects of negation take for granted their own reliance on that which they wish to abandon.[36] Revealing contradiction and exposing indeterminacy is an understandable reaction to law's pretensions, but we should remember that there is no necessary link between this activity and progressive politics. Carl Schmitt would have been just as welcoming of this insight with its emphasis on the ubiquity of power politics and cynical instrumentalism.[37] It is in the reconstructive project forged as a result of the exposure of legal participants to the voices of marginalised others that the potential for meaningful reform opens up.[38] It is suggested, in this chapter, that the communicative model offers a useful tool

---

35 See *op cit*, fn 17, Young.

36 Cf Scheuerman, W, *Between the Norm and the Exception: The Frankfurt School and the Rule of Law*, 1994, London: MIT, pp 245–48, arguing that CLS rejection of the determinacy of law should not automatically be seen as progressive. He notes how a similar position was used by right wing authoritarians in mid-century Germany to launch an attack on democracy.

37 See, eg, Schmitt, C, *The Crisis of Parliamentary Democracy*, 1988, London: MIT. Cf Dyzenhaus, D, *Legality and Legitimacy: Carl Schmitt, Hans Kelsen and Hermann Heller in Weimar*, 1997, Oxford: Clarendon, pp 38–101; Neumann, F, *The Democratic and the Authoritarian State: Essays in Political and Legal Theory*, 1957, New York: The Free Press.

38 Cf *op cit*, fn 27, Lacey, p 11; Cotterrell, R, 'Must legal ideas be interpreted sociologically?' (1998) 25 JLS 171, pp 187–88. See, also, Nelken, D, 'Blinding insights? The limits of a reflexive sociology of law' (1998) 25 JLS 407.

for feminists concerned to challenge the dominance of institutional and cultural forms of oppression.

Law functions in both material and symbolic ways. The material aspect of the law is connected to its coercive and instrumental character. Regulation in the area of immigration and asylum straightforwardly excludes, on its face, and functions in order to sanction, for example, the deportation of individuals from the UK. This is the brute face of the law. Law does, however, also function symbolically to reproduce dominant images of regulated populations.[39] The images which law produces both shape and reflect distorted and partial perspectives which can be challenged by drawing upon work that exposes this and tries to reshape doctrine and the practice of law accordingly.

That the slogan 'the personal is the political' may be unpalatable to some should not lead to a rejection of the core of truth which it contains. A worthwhile contribution of feminist theory is to have decisively undermined the traditional conception of the public/private divide.[40] The story is now very familiar, but worth retelling, if only in outline form. In general terms, classical liberal political theory was committed to the division of the public and private spheres.[41] The private was that sphere which was not subject to legal regulation: in other words, a space where society and its norms would not intrude. These theories were linked to individualism and had their corollary in a conception of autonomy which was reliant on negative liberty or 'freedom from' rather than 'freedom to'.[42] Classical liberalism thus tended towards an anti-perfectionist view of the state.[43] Its purpose was not to make individuals good, but simply to create the framework whereby individuals could pursue their freely chosen ends. As with a number of classic theories of liberalism, the model of human nature adopted was that of the abstracted, or disengaged,[44] subject defined in universalist language (although, abstracted

---

39 Cf O'Donovan, K, *Sexual Divisions in Law*, 1985, London: Weidenfeld and Nicolson, pp 19–20; Cotterrell, R, *Law's Community: Legal Theory in Sociological Perspective*, 1995, Oxford: Clarendon, pp 221–48.

40 See *op cit*, fn 27, Lacey, esp pp 71–97; *op cit*, fn 17, Young; Young, IM, 'Impartiality and the civic public: some implications of feminist critiques of moral and political theory', in Benhabib, S and Cornell, D (eds), *Feminism as Critique: Essays on the Politics of Gender in Late Capitalist Societies*, 1987, Cambridge: Polity, p 74.

41 Cf *ibid*, Lacey, p 72, noting that the public/private divide is evident in Marxist literature. She is also critical of the way the terms are used in analysis. By reifying conceptions of the public and private, the blurred nature of the divide is neglected and this can perpetuate explorations which fail to focus on concrete social practices.

42 See Berlin, I, *Four Essays on Liberty*, 1969, Oxford, NY: OUP, p 171; Mill, JS, *On Liberty*, 1974, London: Penguin, p 63. Cf Raz, J, *The Morality of Freedom*, 1986, Oxford: Clarendon, p 425.

43 See Barry, B, *Political Argument*, 1964, London: Routledge and Kegan Paul, p 66.

44 For an examination of the background to the rise of 'disengaged reason' and the distortions which it has wrought, see Taylor, C, *The Sources of the Self: The Making of Modern Identity*, 1989, Cambridge: CUP, pp 143–58; *op cit*, fn 16, Taylor, ch 1.

from context, this 'individual' was often driven by highly specific and all too human instrumentalist goals). The emergence of the social sciences in the 19th century lead to scepticism about the idealism implicit in much political philosophy. Confronted with empirical knowledge of everyday oppression and exploitation normative, political theory seemed naive. A split (which continues to this day) between a normative political philosophy (always open to criticism for being abstracted from reality) and social science (always open to the accusation that it submerges or fails to acknowledge its normative commitments) began to open up. For those concerned with tackling the root causes of disadvantage and inequality, normative political philosophy was (and continues to appear) much too cosy and, on occasion, seemed to slide in the direction of apology.[45] The difficulty, which is still with us, and which all those concerned with human rights protection inherit, including feminist theorists, is how to give due recognition to two things: first, the situated nature of our lives and thought; and, secondly, the structural factors which drive the tension between legal and factual equality, as revealed by the social sciences. Is this possible while, at the same time, holding onto the universalism, and normativity, of, for example, human rights law discourse? The politics of difference, while vital in recognising the pluralism of modern societies, is an insufficient response to this dilemma.

Having placed this discussion in context, it is necessary to extract core elements of feminist theory which are of relevance here. The straightforward starting point is that feminist theory can not be reduced to any one particular insight, it is a diverse body of scholarship.[46] For the purposes of this article, it is enough to trace some of the core themes: deconstruction of the public/private divide; distrust/rejection of universalist moral, political and social theory; suspicion of normative political philosophy and the disengaged image of the self; emphasis on context and the situated nature of our practical reasoning; explorations of the structural factors which contribute to the gap between legal and factual equality. As has been argued in this chapter, these themes are part of the ongoing conversation of modernity. It was not long before the insights of feminist theory began to impact upon refugee law scholarship.[47] One of the first gaps exposed was the absence of specific

---

45 See Dewey, J, *Reconstruction in Philosophy*, 1957, Boston: Beacon, pp 191–92. See, also, Dewey, J, *Liberalism and Social Action*, 1935, New York, GP Putnam.

46 For an interesting discussion of what this might mean for political practice, see *op cit*, fn 17, Young, pp 218–20.

47 See UNHCR Executive Committee (UNHCR EXCOM), Conclusion No 39 (1985), para (k) which: 'recognised that states, in the exercise of their sovereignty, are free to adopt the interpretation that women asylum seekers who face harsh or inhuman treatment due to their having transgressed the social mores of the society in which they live may be considered as a "particular social group" within the meaning of Article 1A(2) of the 1951 United Nations Refugee Convention.' Greatbatch, J, 'The gender difference: feminist critiques of refugee discourse' (1989) 1 International Journal of Refugee Law 518; Johnsson, AB, 'The international protection of women refugees' (1989) 1 International Journal of Refugee Law 221.

reference to gender as an enumerated ground of persecution. It is worth noting that the guidelines which have been adopted, and that are discussed below, do not alter the basic position that gender is not included as a ground of persecution in refugee law. In addition, the systematic neglect of the experiences of women is highlighted.[48] This is now combined with recognition of the problems fostered by a distorted view of the refugee experience. The structural factors which dictate who migrates and to where have also been explored. This has fed into a general theme in critical refugee law scholarship, one aspect of which is the questioning of refugee law's traditional focus on asylum. The fact is that the majority of the world's refugees are women and yet the majority of asylum seekers in, for example, Europe are men. Another result of this criticism is that the internally displaced now receive much more international attention than was the case in the past.[49] It is evident from this very brief discussion that feminist theory has much to contribute to critical explorations of refugee law.

GENDER AND ASYLUM LAW

This section of the chapter uses the communicative model to examine the gender critique of asylum law and the results that this is having in practice. As Fraser has argued, a critical social theory should operate with its eye firmly fixed on the work of those oppositional social movements with which it has 'a partisan, though not uncritical, identification'.[50] In refugee and asylum law in recent years the main dissenting voices have focused on the blindness of the law to the specific experiences of women refugees.[51] One of the major critical trends in this area of late is the contribution made by feminist theorists and activists to ongoing debates about the future of refugee and asylum law. There has been an acceptance that the law is not the purely neutral edifice it is often claimed to be. This merges with growing concern, from a variety of perspectives, that both its substance and its practice may disguise partial perspectives on the totality of the human experience. A number of writers have begun to expose its one sided nature and the ways in which its substance and its practical application neglect the specific experiences of women

---

48 *Op cit*, fn 47, Greatbatch.

49 See Report of the Representative of the Secretary General on Internally Displaced Persons, UN Doc E/CN.4/1998/53.

50 *Op cit*, fn 23, Fraser, p 21.

51 See, generally, Indra, D, *Engendering Forced Migration: Theory and Practice*, 1998, New York: Berghahn; Crawley, H, *Women as Asylum Seekers: A Legal Handbook*, 1997, London: ILPA and Refugee Action; Bhabha, J and Shutter, S, *Women's Movement. Women Under Immigration, Nationality and Refugee Law*, 1994, Stoke-on-Trent: Trentham; Spijkerboer, T, 'Woman and refugus status: beyond the public/private divide' (1995) 7 International Journal of Refugee Law 756.

refugees.[52] This work seeks to demonstrate that the promise of universalism held out by the words of refugee law is not fulfilled in practice. It is the aim of this section to explore aspects of this critique and demonstrate the specific ways it is having a practical impact on law and policy.

Refugee law is dominated by the 1951 Convention relating to the Status of Refugees and its 1967 Protocol.[53] The Convention contains a well known definition of the refugee[54] and some important protections, most notably, Art 33(1) (*non-refoulement*). Although this is not an unlimited obligation, as, for example, Art 3 of the European Convention on Human Rights is (Art 33(2) contains a specific exception),[55] it is the cornerstone of this particular regime of protection. It specifically prohibits a state from returning a refugee. The principle has gained such widespread international recognition, that it is now regarded by some as a norm of customary international law, even though its precise scope outside the 1951 Convention is uncertain.[56]

Trends elsewhere in international law are having a substantial impact on the protection of refugee and asylum seekers. General human rights law has emerged as a valuable mechanism for supplementing the more obvious deficiencies in refugee law.[57] The European Convention system is proving useful,[58] but other instruments could be mentioned.[59] In the context of developments elsewhere in human rights law, refugee law is now showing its age. The definition of refugee is limited to civil and political rights, a fact which neglects the interdependent nature of all human rights and other recent

---

52 Eg, Tuitt, P, *False Images: The Law's Construction of the Refugee*, 1996, London: Pluto, pp 33–35.

53 189 UNTS 150; 606 UNTS 267.

54 Convention Relating to the Status of Refugees 1951, Art 1A(2).

55 'The benefit of the present provision may not, however, be claimed by a refugee whom there are reasonable grounds for regarding as a danger to the security of the country in which he is, or who, having been convicted by a final judgement of a particularly serious crime, constitutes a danger to the community of that country.'

56 Goodwin-Gill, G, *The Refugee in International Law*, 1996, 2nd edn, Oxford: Clarendon, pp 117–71.

57 See, eg, *Chahal v UK* (1996) 23 EHRR 413. For comment, see Harvey, C, 'Expulsion, national security and the European Convention' (1997) 22 EL Rev 626.

58 See Mole, N, *Problems Raised by Certain Aspects of the Present Situation of Refugees from the Standpoint of the European Convention on Human Rights*, 1997, Council of Europe, Human Rights Files, No 9.

59 Eg, UN Convention Against Torture and Other Cruel, Inhuman or Degrading Treatment or Punishment, GA Res 39/4; *A v Australia* (1997) UNHRC Comm No 560/1993; see (1997) 3 International Journal of Refugee Law 506; UN Convention on the Rights of the Child 1989, Art 22. For a revealing examination of the broader human rights issues raised by expulsion, see Matas, T and Aiken, S, 'International human rights law and legal remedies in expulsion: progress and some remaining problems with special reference to Canada' (1997) 15 Netherlands Quarterly of Human Rights 429. See, also, Clark, T, 'Human rights and expulsion: giving content to the concept of expulsion' (1989) 1 International Journal of Refugee Law 155.

trends in the law.[60] The delegation of the application of refugee law to states may have had the short term advantage of securing consent to the original treaty but, in practice, it has meant substantial inconsistency and the devaluation of principles of refugee protection. The loose commitment of states to refugee protection allows the regime to be swept along by the stronger tides of state interest. Without an international supervisory mechanism to offer principled interpretation of the law, the Convention has suffered from restrictive interpretation by national decision makers. This problem has been recognised and some states have now accepted the need to attach the meaning of the definition to other developments in human rights law,[61] or to co-operative regional arrangements.[62] Progressive developments in human rights law suggest that refugee law may eventually be rendered paradoxically peripheral to the real needs of the majority of the forcibly displaced. At present, and certainly within the UK context, refugee law remains central, primarily because official recognition of the status gives rise to legal entitlements which are unavailable to those who do not receive it.[63] In the UK, as in many other states, refugee status is a privileged status, granted only to a minority of forced migrants. An issue for the future will be clarifying, in precise terms, the rights of all those forced migrants in the UK and elsewhere in Europe who are granted some 'lesser' humanitarian status.

It is time to focus on the argument developed here. The thesis defended is that feminist legal theory may be employed in this area of public law to show how reconstructive critique can help to bring about legal and policy reforms. This should be of interest to those who wish to see how theoretically informed critique of the law might be transformed into constructive practical proposals for concrete change. It is suggested that this essentially reformist agenda is an appropriate way forward. To be critical in this modest sense is to test the law on its own ground. By highlighting the distortions in the perspectives of those

---

60 Cf OAU Convention 1969, 1000 UNTS 46, Art I(2); Cartagena Declaration on Refugees 1984, OAS/SerL/V/II66, Doc 10, rev 1, pp 190–93.

61 See Hathaway, JC, *The Law of Refugee Status*, 1991, Toronto: Butterworths, pp 104–05.

62 See EU Joint Position on the Harmonised Application of the Definition of the Term 'Refugee', in Art 1 of the Geneva Convention of 28 July 1951 Relating to the Status of Refugees, 4 March 1996.

63 A recognised refugee is granted leave to remain. The Home Office's current position is to grant 12 months' stay and then a further three years upon renewal. Refugees are eligible for indefinite leave to remain after four years. A recognised refugee has a right to family reunion. Compare this with someone who is granted the discretionary humanitarian status of exceptional leave to remain (ELR). Anyone who is granted ELR receives leave to enter or remain but the position is less secure than the recognised refugee. Continuing leave to remain is dependent on the conditions prevailing in his or her country of origin. Those granted ELR have to wait seven years before eligibility for indefinite leave to remain arises, they have no right to family reunion, see Macdonald, IA and Blake, NJ, *Macdonald's Immigration Law and Practice*, 1995, 4th edn, London: Butterworths, pp 418–20.

tasked with law and policy making and application, law may be reinterpreted and designed to fit the new picture that emerges of the experience of the refugee.

REFORMING REFUGEE LAW AND POLICY: CHALLENGING DISTORTED PESPECTIVES

At the centre of the current gender critique of refugee law lie concepts of equal treatment and equal access to determination systems within states which connect interestingly with the procedural understanding defended above. It is suggested here that the challenge in refugee law at present is to reconstruct law and practice on the basis of this norm of substantive equality.

One leading writer in immigration law has recently advocated the deployment of a cultural jurisprudence as suited to the demands of the area:[64]

Cultural jurisprudence aims to explore ways in which the development of the law can be informed by an understanding of culture so that values of justice can be enhanced and expanded to apply to all populations that come within the jurisdiction of the law.[65]

Although broadly defined, it is welcome recognition of an existing problem and provides a framework for future research. The emphasis placed on a heightened measure of cultural sensitivity on the part of all those tasked with law application is particularly relevant to the concerns of this chapter.[66] While the focus of Juss' work is the fostering of pluralist democratic values in racially and ethnically diverse societies, the gender dimension should also be recognised. 'Race', ethnicity *and* gender must be central concerns of any 'new' cultural jurisprudence. The issue addressed in this section is how the insights revealed by the critique described previously can be translated into meaningful institutional change in the light of this 'new' cultural jurisprudence.[67]

When considering the landscape of refugee law today, one of the more significant developments is the adoption of gender guidelines by a number of states. Efforts to mainstream a gender perspective in law and policy development, while neglected in the past, are now beginning to emerge as key

---

64 Juss, S, *Discretion and Deviation in the Administration of Immigration Control*, 1997, London: Sweet & Maxwell, pp 10–39.

65 *Ibid*, p 5.

66 *Ibid*, pp 18–19: 'Cultural jurisprudence is vital where the actors operate in a relatively unconstrained legal field, laying emphasis on the exercise of wide discretionary power, which requires cultural training and sensitivity.'

67 For some interesting thoughts on how this might be addressed in the interviewing process in asylum cases, see Hinshelwood, G, 'Interviewing female asylum-seekers' (1997) International Journal of Refugee Law (Special Issue) 159.

issues in European and public law.[68] Within the European Union, a number of new strategies are being employed in order to achieve the aim of equal opportunity for men and women. It appears that the feminist critique which underlies such new thinking is beginning to have an impact on asylum law. In recognition of past failure to address adequately the experiences of women within the asylum determination process, some states have decided to adopt measures which will encourage a less distorted approach to refugee determination in the future. The United Nations High Commissioner for Refugees (UNHCR) played a significant role in this process. In 1991, it issued Guidelines on the Protection of Refugee Women[69] and the Executive Committee of the UNHCR has adopted several Conclusions on the problems encountered by refugee women.[70] Following this, Canada, the US, and Australia adopted gender guidelines which seek to embed a gender perspective within the determination process.[71] In order to explore the nature

---

68 See European Commission, Incorporating Equal Opportunities for Men and Women into all Community Policies and Activities, COM/96/97/Final; European Commission, Progress Report on Equal Opportunities, COM/98/122/Final. These outline new structures that have been put in place and ones that are recommended in order to mainstream equal opportunities, this includes: awareness raising; training; preparation of guidelines; tools for gender impact assessments; and gender proofing. See, also, Council Resolution, Integrating Gender in Development Co-operation, 20 December 1995; Council Conclusion, Gender Issues in Development Co-operation, 18 May 1998.

69 EC/SCP/67, 22 July 1991. See, also, UNHCR, Interviewing Applicants for Refugee Status: Training Module, 1995, ch 4 ('Interviewing women refugee applicants'); UNHCR, Guidelines on Preventing and Responding to Sexual Violence Against Refugees, 1995. See, also, UN Fourth World Conference for Women, Beijing Platform for Action, UN Doc A/CONF.177/20/1995.149(i).

70 UNHCR EXCOM Conclusion 73, Refugee Protection and Sexual Violence; UNHCR EXCOM Conclusion 64, Refugee Women and International Protection; Conclusion 60, Refugee Women; Conclusion 54, Refugee Women; UNHCR EXCOM Conclusion 39, Refugee Women and International Protection.

71 Australian Department of Immigration and Multi-Cultural Affairs, Guidelines on Gender Issues For Decision-Makers, July 1996; US Immigration and Naturalization Service, Considerations for Asylum Officers Adjudicating Asylum Claims From Women, 26 May 1995; Canadian Immigration and Refugee Board, Guidelines on Women Refugee Claimants Fearing Gender-Related Persecution, 9 March 1993 (updated November 1996). See Anker, D, 'Rape in the community as a basis for asylum: the treatment of women refugees' claims to protection in Canada and the United States: Part I' (1997) 12 Bender's Immigration Bulletin 476, p 478: 'The Canadians did more than issue the guidelines. The IRB took active steps to implement and monitor them … the IRB has conducted ongoing educational programs designed to educate immigration officials on fundamental human rights principles and gender issues in asylum. As a result of this monitoring, when critical issues have been identified the IRB has been able to respond with specific training'. As she notes, there have, however, been resource problems. For a useful analysis of the gender guidelines in context, see Macklin, A, 'Refugee women and the imperative of categories' (1995) 17 HRQ 213. See, also, Oosterveld, VL, 'The Canadian guidelines on gender-related persecution: an evaluation' (1996) 8 International Journal of Refugee Law 569; Wallace, R, 'Making the Refugee Convention gender sensitive: the Canadian Guidelines' (1996) 45 ICLQ 702.

and scope of these guidelines, the Canadian Immigration and Refugee Board (IRB) Guidelines will serve as an illustrative example for the purpose of this chapter.[72]

First, a brief outline of the Canadian asylum determination system.[73] Few would disagree with the proposition that Canada has shown the way in designing a respected asylum determination system. The authorities have taken the time, and made the effort, to invest in an administrative and adjudicative system structured to secure fair decision making. In contrast to the UK, the Canadian system has gained a marked level of legitimacy among those who participate in it. A number of factors combine to foster this, including a more engrained 'human rights culture'. This is not to exaggerate the strengths of the system, it is subject to continuing criticism within Canada. However, it does offer a useful model for comparison at a time when most states in the European context are engaged in a 'race to the bottom' in the area of asylum law. It is evident that a human rights paradigm has emerged in the Canadian asylum context which is proving influential in other states.

The Immigration and Refugee Board (IRB) was created in 1989 and it is Canada's largest tribunal. It is an independent administrative tribunal with quasi-judicial functions. It consists of three divisions, one of which, the Convention Refugee Determination Division (CRDD), assesses asylum claims. It sits usually in two person panels with assistance from a Refugee Hearings Officer (RHO). Initially, a claim is assessed by a Senior Immigration Officer in order to determine whether the claim is eligible to be heard by the CRDD. If eligible, the claim may be advanced to the CRDD for determination. The RHO is responsible for conducting background research into the claim. The process is specifically designed to be inquisitorial. Members of the CRDD are required to write reasons, even for positive applications in gender-related cases, though in law reasons are required only for negative decisions.[74] There is no appeal from a decision of the CRDD, but it may be judicially reviewed if the leave of

---

72 Note that other Guildlines have now been adopted by the Chairperson: Guidelines on Detention, March 1998; Guidelines on Civilian Non-Combatants Fleeing Civil War Situations, March 1996; Guidelines on Child Refugee Claimants: Procedural and Evidential Issues, August 1996.

73 This outline draws on the information provided on the IRB website (http://www.irb.gc.ca) and Justice, ILPA, ARC, *Providing Protection: Asylum Determination in Canada Supplementary Report 2*, 1997.

74 See Bernier, C (Special Advisor to the Chairperson, IRB, and Senior Advisor on Gender Equality, Department of Justice, Canada), 'The IRB Guidelines on Women Refugee Claimants Fearing Gender-Related Persecution' (1997) International Journal of Refugee Law (Special Issue) 167, pp 167–68: 'We do ... require that the Members write reasons even for positive decisions on gender-related claims (by law only negative decisions must always be given in writing), and we expect Members to justify any departure from the Guidelines.' She cites the following from the decision of the Federal Court of Canada in *Narvaez v Minister of Citizenship and Immigration*, FC-TD, 9 February 1995, p 6: 'While the Guidelines are not law, they are authorized by sub-s 65(3) of the [Immigration Act] and intended to be followed unless circumstances are such that a different analysis is appropriate.'

a Federal Court judge is obtained. The Federal Court has held that in relevant cases it is an error of law to ignore the guidelines.[75] The Immigration Department is not a party to the proceedings, unless the issue of exclusion arises. The CRDD does not have the power to grant asylum, this is the responsibility of the Immigration Department. If a positive decision is made, the applicant is granted refugee status and may then apply for permanent residence status. Refugee recognition rates are markedly higher than in the UK. On average, 60% of asylum applicants are granted refugee status, compared to a figure somewhere between 3-5% in the UK.[76]

The Chairperson of the IRB has the power to issue guidelines.[77] Gender guidelines were adopted by the Chairperson in March 1993 and updated in November 1996. Although they are not legally binding (this fact has attracted criticism),[78] they are generally regarded as having had a progressive impact on the determination system.[79] As to content, they promulgate a step by step analysis of the refugee definition, highlighting precisely when and where a gendered perspective should inform the decision making process. The General Proposition is worth citing:

> Although gender is not specifically enumerated as one of the grounds for establishing Convention refugee status *the definition of Convention refugee may properly be interpreted* as providing protection for women who demonstrate a well founded fear of gender-related persecution by reason of any one, or a combination of, the enumerated grounds [emphasis added].

Although a woman's claim must go through the same process as a man, she is permitted, if a request is made in writing, to have women CRDD members present, a woman RHO and a woman interpreter. On procedural matters, emphasis is placed on sensitivity to the specific experiences of women, with appropriate training provided to officials. In addition, on substantive issues of refugee law, the guidelines promote a gendered perspective on all important aspects of the interpretation of the law.

---

75 *Mohamed v Canada (Secretary of State)* (1994) 73 FTP 159.

76 *Op cit*, fn 73, IRB website and Justice, p 1.

77 Immigration Act, s 65(3).

78 *Op cit*, fn 71, Oosterveld, pp 580–83.

79 See *op cit*, fn 71, Anker, p 482, she does, however, note some problems: 'not all the decisions reviewed have demonstrated the same sensitivity to women. Moreover, there is reason for concern in the termination of the working groups and termination of the internal reports on gender reasons ... But the Canadians are clearly "ahead of the rest" and their example has had a remarkable effect outside Canadian borders.' *Op cit*, fn 73, Justice, pp 14–15: 'The guidelines issued by the Chairperson are extremely important in informing good decision making ... The guidelines are important not only because they state (and arguably expand) the definition of refugee; but also because they provide the decision maker with a series of necessary steps and relevant questions, as the building blocks in satisfying themselves as to whether the definitional criteria have been met. This assists a rigorous and consistent approach to decision making, which applicants and their representatives can expect to rely on (the guidelines are publically available).' *Op cit*, fn 71, Macklin, p 275.

The promulgation of guidelines in Canada is evidence that women's NGOs have been successful in lobbying the administration there in a way that groups in the UK have not. Further to this, the success of the guidelines cannot be attributed solely to their formal enactment. A further factor is the willingness of the relevant authorities to try to ensure that they become meaningful in the culture of decision making, through the use of working groups and training programs. As to matters of adjudication, the position has also been advanced by the willingness to connect interpretations of refugee law to other developments in the international law of human rights.[80] A human rights paradigm has emerged which helps to keep refugee law relevant. The Canadian example illustrates the use that may be made of guidelines. Formal adoption appears to be only a first step in the effort to promote an institutional culture which is conducive to the effective interpretation and application of refugee law.[81] It is evident that the legal construction of the refugee within states is dependent on the community of interpreters of refugee law in important ways. While the law's image of the refugee has undoubted rhetorical and symbolic power, it is within the administrative and adjudicative systems of individual states that the 'refugee' emerges.[82] The culture of decision making, and therefore the institutional networks within which the community of interpreters of refugee law operate, is central: institutional and cultural contexts are key factors in the construction of the refugee. One of the arguments advanced by critics of the UK system is that there is a pervasive culture of disbelief or suspicion. Rather than continue to lament the clearly narrow definition of refugee law, what this suggests is that more attention needs to be paid to the 'social construction of protection' in its institutional setting. The point is to examine the institutional factors which define protection *as well as* the principles of protection. A project of reform must keep in view both institutional design and the norms of human rights and refugee law. However, getting institutional design right is not in itself enough. Creating systems which allow women's voices to be heard is not the end of the story. The regulation of asylum needs to be constructed in a way that facilitates understanding and communication also.[83] This is a clear implication of the Canadian example and flows directly from a commitment

---

80 Eg, *Canada (Attorney General) v Ward* (1993) 2 SCR 689, 103 DLR 4th.

81 See *op cit*, fn 74, Bernier, pp 168–69: 'Essentially, our Guidelines seek to remove the blinkers that too often cause us to approach refugee claims by women according to the more familiar situation of men refugees. This was acheived moreover, within the terms of the 1951 Convention.'

82 This helps to shift attention away from an exclusive concern with the legal rule and toward empirical work on, eg, the culture of public administration. The point is *not* to discourage a focus on rules but to encourage a more comprehensive approach to analysis.

83 In a different context, see Black, J, 'Regulation as facilitation: negotiating the genetic revolution' (1998) 61 MLR 621.

to proceduralisation. In other words, legal regulation is not about aggregating the contribution of all those who act within this institutional context but, rather, translating the different 'languages' of participants into a form that makes fair decision making more likely. There are valuable lessons here for those who advance a gender critique of the UK's arrangements.

RETHINKING REFUGEE LAW: OVERCOMING PARTIALITY IN THE UK ASYLUM CONTEXT?

In the UK, this area is governed primarily by the provisions of the Asylum and Immigration (Appeals) Act 1993 (IIAA), as amended by the Asylum and Immigration Act 1996, as well as the main immigration statutes and rules including, most importantly, the Immigration Act 1971. In the UK, a claim to asylum is defined as:

> ... a claim made by a person (whether before or after the coming into force of this section) that it would be contrary to the United Kingdom's obligations under the Convention for him to be removed from, or required to leave, the United Kingdom; and 'the Convention' means the Convention relating to the Status of Refugees done at Geneva on 28th July 1951 and the Protocol to that Convention.[84]

As to the precise status of the Convention in UK law:

> Nothing in the immigration rules (within the meaning of the 1971 Act) shall lay down any practice which would be contrary to the Convention.[85]

For all practical purposes, the Convention has been incorporated into domestic law. It is beyond the remit of this chapter to go into details of the precise procedures (which are at the time of writing under review).

All aspects of asylum law and practice present specific problems for women refugees. It must be emphasised that the problems of women refugees begin long before they arrive in the UK. A substantial number of the women involved have fled from countries where they have been raped, tortured and abused.[86] Human rights concerns do not commence with the asylum process.

The story of the development of asylum law is now familiar.[87] After years when it received minimal coverage, it now features frequently in public law

---

84   AIAA 1993, s 1.
85   AIAA 1993, s 2.
86   Luping, D, 'Women's rights' (1998) *Liberty*, Autumn, p 4.
87   See, generally, Nicolson, F and Twomey, P (eds), *Current Issues in UK Asylum Law*, 1998, Aldershot: Ashgate.

debates. The increase in the number of asylum applications[88] caused problems for the UK's inadequate administrative arrangements. The result was legislative and other action aimed at curbing abuse of the procedures and, although not defined as official policy, reducing overall numbers.[89] A variety of defensive regulatory strategies were adopted to achieve this, including the use of concepts which have gained widespread recognition in Europe. As Amnesty International has stated, there is a general reluctance to improve asylum systems in Europe because they are now viewed by states as 'pull factors' for general immigration.[90] In procedural terms, in the UK, an attempt was made to speed up the entire administrative process.[91] Working on the disputed premise that the majority of asylum seekers came to the UK solely for economic reasons, the Government also embarked, *inter alia*, upon a policy of welfare restrictionism.[92] Overall, a formidable array of legal and policy tools were used in order to construct this regulatory strategy. Possibly the most pressing problem at present is the backlog in applications.[93] As indicated a review of the process is underway but, as some have noted, New Labour have thus far failed to improve substantially on the record of the

88 In 1997, there were approximately 32,500 applications for asylum made in the UK (HC Deb 305 col 143, 27 January 1998. In 1997, appproximately 3,985 were granted asylum, 3,115 ELR with 28,945 refusals. As to appeals, 21,090 were determined by the adjudicators of the IAA with 1,135 allowed, 18,255 dismissed and 1,660 withdrawn. The IAT received approximately 1,570 appeals with 55 being allowed, 305 dismissed and 445 remitted to adjudicators (HC Deb 305 col 283, 28 January 1998).

89 Home Office, 'Minister affirms plans to stamp out abuse of asylum system', Press Release, 19 September 1997. The Home Office announced the establishment of an inter-Departmental task force to look at the issue of abuse. See Home Office, *Annual Report 1998–99*, para 17.1: 'The main elements of policy are to ... ensure that asylum decisions are both swift and fair and fully meet the United Kingdom's obligations towards refugees under international law.'

90 Amnesty International, *Europe: The Need for Minimum Standards in Asylum Procedures*, June 1994.

91 See, generally, Harvey, C, 'Restructuring asylum: recent trends in UK law and policy' (1997) 9 International Journal of Refugee Law 60; Harvey, C, 'The right to seek asylum in the UK and "safe countries" [1996] PL 196; Harvey, C, 'Taking human rights seriously in the asylum context? A perspective on the development of law and policy', in *op cit*, fn 87, Nicolson and Twomey, pp 201–23.

92 Eg, Asylum and Immigration Act 1996, ss 9–11, Sched 1; Housing Act 1996, ss 161, 183, 185–87, Sched 19, Pt VIII; Housing Accommodation and Homelessness (Persons subject to Immigration Control) Order 1996 SI 1996/1982; Homelessness Regulations 1996 SI 1996/2754; Housing Accommodation and Homelessness (Persons subject to Immigration Control) (Amendment) Order 1998 SI 1998/139; Allocation of Housing and Homelessness (Amendment) Regulations 1997 SI 1997/631; Homelessness (Persons subject to Immigration Control) Amendment Order 1997 SI 1997/628; Social Security (Persons From Abroad) Miscellaneous Amendments Regulations 1996 SI 1996/30; Feria, M, 'Commentaries on the Social Security Persons from Abroad (Miscellaneous Amendments) Regulations 1996' (1996) 10 Immigration and Nationality Law and Practice 91. There were well founded concerns expressed that s 8 of the 1996 Act would have negative implications for racial equality: see Commission for Racial Equality, *The Asylum and Immigration Act 1996: Implications for Racial Equality*, October1996. See Immigration (Restrictions on Employment) Order 1996 SI 1996/3225

93 Note KPMG Peat Marwick, *Review of Asylum Appeals Procedure*, 1994, London: Home Office/Lord Chancellor's Department.

Conservative Government.[94] It is difficult to identify in a precise way at this stage the possible gender impact of the proposals contained in the White Paper,[95] but a number of issues can be identified which are of relevance. In terms of effective legal regulation, the deployment of an integrated approach to the immigration control system[96] may make sense. However, asylum and immigration should operate according to quite different systemic logics. While consequential reasoning is often appropriate in the immigration context, it is not in relation to asylum. States are obliged not to return prescribed categories of protection seekers regardless of the behaviour of the individual or the implications of this for broader immigration control imperatives. As stated, the backlog in decision making causes huge problems for refugees and there is an urgent need to address it in an effective way. The commitment to achieving this through speeding up procedures may impact disproportionately on women asylum seekers in the absence of reform of the system. Women asylum seekers encounter particular problems which are, as yet, not satisfactorily addressed in the current system. The emphasis on speed may compromise any attempts to mainstream a gender perspective in the asylum process in the future. A safety net scheme for asylum seekers which does not comprise of cash payments and is based on a 'no choice' philosophy is also problematic. These are just some of the areas of concern. There are, no doubt, other difficulties which will arise for women refugees as the Labour Government carries forward a regulatory strategy which does not depart in its essentials from that pursued by the previous administration.

The general failings of the UK asylum system have been exposed, and there are now numerous calls for reform.[97] Although, in other states, institutional recognition has been given to the specific experiences of women within the asylum determination process, this is yet to impact seriously on the UK.[98] The adoption of guidelines in other states, detailed above, has sparked

---

94 Stevens, D, 'The Asylum and Immigration Act 1996: erosion of the right to seek asylum' (1998) 61 MLR 207.

95 *Fairer, Faster, Firmer – A Modern Approach to Immigration and Asylum,* Cm 4018. See, also, Home Office/Lord Chancellor's Department, *Review of Appeals: A Consultation Paper,* July 1998, London: Home Office/Lord Chancellor's Department.

96 *Ibid*, White Paper, para 8.6.

97 Eg, Justice, ILPA, ARC, *Providing Protection: Towards Fair and Effective Asylum Procedures,* 1997; Amnesty International, *Slamming the Door: The Demolition of the Right to Seek Asylum in the UK,* April 1996; Amnesty International, *Cell Culture: The Detention and Imprisonment of Asylum-Seekers in the UK,* December 1996.

98 See Storey, H, 'Country Reports: UK' (1997) International Journal of Refugee Law (Special Issue) 71. Acknowledging that sensitivity is shown to all applicants and that UK policy 'is generally compatible with that set out in the United States guidelines ... We have not yet identified a need to issue *separate* guidance on dealing with applications from female asylum seekers in the United Kingdom'. Cf Shah, P, 'Quarterly legal update' (1997) 11 Immigration and Nationality Law and Practice 95, pp 95–101: 'The Canadian Guidelines could provide a useful model for implementation in the UK where government have already declared that it has no specific policies to deal with women's claims.'

calls for the UK to take a similar approach.[99] In July 1998, the Refugee Women's Legal Group (RWLG) published *Gender Guidelines for the Determination of Asylum Claims in the UK*. The RWLG was established in 1996 with the specific aim of building a gendered perspective into refugee law. In June 1997, the RWLG published *Women as Asylum Seekers: A Legal Handbook*.[100] It will be interesting to see whether the Labour Government will be prepared to follow other states and adopt such guidelines. It is suggested in this chapter that the adoption of guidelines, combined with a commitment to their practical application and enforcement, would play a part in attempts to mainstream a gender perspective in the asylum process.

While formal adoption of gender guidelines in the UK would be a welcome development, it is important to note that much can be achieved, within the existing legal framework, to promote an understanding of refugee law which is no longer mired in a partial perspective. There are issues surrounding equal access to refugee status determination procedures which should be of concern regardless of whether a state has adopted specific guidelines.[101] The flaws contained in refugee law are well understood, but there is still scope for doctrine to be revitalised.[102] As the Canadian Guidelines state, refugee law *properly interpreted* includes the protection of women and can recognise their specific experiences. The argument is that a gender perspective should be mainstreamed in the application of current law and practice. A somewhat different argument is that gender might be included specifically in the 1951 Convention definition. While this might seem like an obvious strategy from a liberal feminist perspective, there are difficulties. In the current international climate, states are unlikely to accept

---

99 *Op cit*, fn 73, Justice, Recommendation 5: 'Guidelines and policies for dealing with particular countries or groups of applicants should be published by the Asylum Division for the use of first instance decision makers, after consultation with UNHCR and refugee advocacy groups. The guidelines should refer to the criteria under the 1951 Convention and wider forms of extra-Convention protection. They should help decision makers apply those criteria in a structured way and should pay particular regard to sensitive issues such as gender, religious and cultural difference, sexual preference and other developing areas.'

100 RWLG, *Women as Asylum Seekers: A Legal Handbook*, 1997, London: ILPA and Refugee Action.

101 EXCOM, Conclusion 73, Refugee Women and International Protection, para c; EXCOM, Conclusion 82, *Safeguarding Asylum*, para d(i), drawing attention to the importance of 'access, consistent with the 1951 Convention and the 1967 Protocol, of asylum-seekers to fair and effective procedures for determining status and protection needs'.

102 Fitzpatrick, J, 'Revitalising the 1951 Convention' (1996) 9 Harvard Human Rights Journal 228. Cf *op cit*, fn 71, Macklin, pp 259–60, responding to arguments about adding gender to the 1951 Convention, she states: 'The trouble with framing any persecution of women as "persecution because of gender" is that it can reinforce women's marginalisation by implying that only men have political opinions, only men are activated by religion, only men have racial presence, etc. In other words, it may create and sustain the stereotype that men "own" the categories of oppression that are not explicitly "gendrified". On the other hand, the trouble with *not* acknowledging gender as a discrete basis of persecution is that it masks the specificity of women's oppression.'

any widening of the 1951 Convention definition. In fact, recent events indicate that states are more likely to narrow the definition. In this context, there is much merit in the tactic of mainstreaming a gender perspective in the law as it exists at present. In many senses, this also presents the more radical challenge for advocacy groups.

EXPOSING PARTIAL PERSPECTIVES

To further illustrate the usefulness of the model deployed in this chapter for a feminist perspective on public law, two recent asylum cases will be examined. The focus above on guidelines highlighted the importance of building a gender perspective into the administration of asylum. Here, the role of other institutional actors – the courts – is examined. This is not to 'romanticise' their role, as Sterett has noted, this is too often the approach of legal theory.[103] Although, as noted above, the courts have recently been active in challenging government in this area, it is important to place this in the context of an open political struggle over the terms of policy with a diverse range of institutional actors involved. The aim is to suggest how, during the process of adjudication, at whatever level of the judicial hierarchy, legal doctrine might be approached anew after exposure to new voices entering the discourse and the critique explored above. Linked to the critical perspective defended elsewhere in this chapter, the argument is based on the premise that doctrinal work in law is a rational reconstruction of 'raw law' which is unavoidably shaped by the paradigm within which the jurist undertaking the task functions.[104] New insights derived from feminist criticism of current law and practice can contribute to more inclusive, rational reconstructions in future. The practical obstacles to this, however, continue to be substantial.

Both these cases concern women asylum seekers and the interpretation of one of the most controversial aspects of refugee law, the 'particular social group' category. They help to illustrate how women's applications for asylum have been reconstructed in asylum law. The focus here is on the law's image of the woman refugee, but one must not lose sight of the structural factors which impact specifically on women asylum seekers. Procedural and evidential difficulties are also part of the everyday experience of the woman refugee.[105] The paradigmatic understanding, which appears to infect all

---

103 Sterett, S, *Creating Constitutionalism? The Politics of Legal Expertise and Administrative Law in England and Wales*, 1997, Ann Arbor: Michigan UP, p 158.

104 Cf MacCormick, N, 'The ideal and the actual of law and society', in Tasioulas, J, *Law, Values and Social Practices*, 1997, Aldershot: Dartmouth, pp 15, 23: 'At least from the time of Gaius, and probably earlier, there have been legal scholars at work, capturing raw law and systematising it, but at the same time transforming it.'

105 The policy of welfare restriction ostensibly designed to 'deter economic migrants' is also a major structural problem for women seeking asylum.

aspects of asylum law and practice, is that of the politically active (in the public sphere) male persecuted by the state. The claims of women may never reach the determination process because of a focus on male relatives during the interview stage. Women may be reluctant to volunteer information in the presence of other family members. The reality is that a woman who flees a state where she has suffered persecution may find that, on entering the UK, she encounters similar mindsets in her attempt to secure 'refugee' status. The vulnerablility of the woman refugee is acute. The feminist perspective on refugee law thus extends to all aspects of its interpretation and application. This includes: procedural issues, such as interviews and credibility assessments; the meaning of 'persecution' and the test of 'serious harm'; as well as establishing the grounds of persecution. There have, for example, been recent advances in recognising female genital mutilation (FGM) and other forms of violence against women as persecution within the terms of the 1951 Convention.[106] It is accepted that experiences specific to women do amount to persecution for asylum purposes.[107] This is part of a general movement in international human rights law to recognise, as the phrase goes, women's rights as human rights.

For a woman to claim asylum successfully, the following legal obstacles must be overcome. She must be outside her state of origin; be unable or unwilling to seek the protection of the state; possess a well founded fear of being persecuted; be able to bring this within the stated grounds of persecution: race, religion, nationality, membership of a particular social group and political opinion. Only after all these hurdles have been successfully negotiated can she claim to be a 1951 Convention refugee. There is no autonomous internationally agreed definition of all these terms. The UNHCR's Handbook[108] is useful, but it is not legally binding and some of its

---

106 'Matter of Kasinga BIA Interim Decision (13 June 1996)' (1997) International Journal of Refugee Law (Special Issue) 213. See Helton, AC and Nicoll, A, 'Female genital mutilation as ground for asylum in the US: the recent case of In Re Fauziya Kasinga and prospects for more gender sensitive approaches' (1997) 28 Columbia Human Rights L Rev 375: 'The vast majority of the world's refugees are women ... yet the majority of those claiming and receiving asylum in the United States are male. This reality suggests that asylum law, both inherently and in its implementation, currently may operate in a discriminatory manner and may fail to offer women the same level of protection it offers male asylum seekers.' See, generally, UNHCR Division of International Protection, 'Gender-related persecution: an analysis of recent trends' (1997) International Journal of Refugee Law (Special Issue) 79.

107 See Castel, JR, 'Rape, sexual assault and the meaning of persecution' (1992) 4 International Journal of Refugee Law 39; Patel, KP, 'Recognizing the rape of bosnian women as gender-based persecution' (1994) 60 Brooklyn L Rev 929, p 935: 'While some US courts have acknowledged that rape is a form of persecution, these same courts, at times, have refused to grant asylum to victims of rape because they were not persuaded that the claimant was raped on account of one of the five enumerated grounds.' In the context of the European Convention on Human Rights, see Aydin v Turkey (1997) 25 EHRR 251. See, also, Report of the Expert Group Meeting on Gender-Based Persecution, Toronto, Canada, 9–12 November 1997, EGM/GBP/1997/40–42.

108 UNHCR, Handbook on Procedures and Criteria for Determining Refugee Status under the 1951 Convention and the 1967 Protocol Relating to the Status of Refugees (reedited Geneva, January 1992).

passages are not precise enough for practical application.[109] The interpretation and application of the phrase is delegated to the authorities in individual states. Inconsistency in approach is thus a recognised problem. In order to try to respond to this, the courts in the UK have acknowledged the importance of looking at various materials, such as: jurisprudence from other common law jurisdictions; the UNHCR's Handbook; the views of academic writers; and (worryingly) non-legally binding instruments which have emerged from the EU process of co-operation.[110]

As stated above, both cases under examination were argued under the 'particular social group' ground. Where there is doubt, this has tended to be the ground under which the claims of refugee women have been brought.[111] It is not the aim of this section to examine the ongoing and well established debate surrounding the precise interpretation of this phrase. A point that may usefully be made here, however, concerning this debate, is that (despite the fact that it is odd to think of women in terms of a 'social group') gender should be regarded as an 'innate or unalterable characteristic' for the purpose of examining the applicability of the 'particular social group' category.[112] Rather than engage in argument about this ambiguous aspect of the present law (which, at the time of writing, is to be considered by the House of Lords), what is suggested here is that we return to basics and re-examine the law with 'fresh eyes' and see whether some of the more established categories of refugee law prove more fitting. The thesis defended here is that the 'political opinion' ground may be a more appropriate basis on which to ground claims by women who confront institutional discrimination or male social/cultural

---

109 Eg, *op cit*, fn 108, UNCHR, para 77: 'A "particular social group" normally comprises persons of similar background, habits or social status.'

110 *Adan v Secretary of State for the Home Department* [1998] 2 WLR 702 (HL), *per* Lord Lloyd, p 709; *T v Secretary of State for the Home Department* [1996] AC 742; [1996] 2 WLR 766; [1996] 2 All ER 865 (HL), *per* Lord Lloyd, p 779; *R v Secretary of State for the Home Department ex p Robinson* (1997) *The Times*, 1 August.

111 See *op cit*, fn 71, Canadian IRB, Section III, where the category is given extensive treatment.

112 See *op cit*, fn 61, Hathaway, p 161: 'This formulation includes within the notion of social group: (1) groups defined by an innate, unalterable characteristic; (2) groups defined by their past temporary or voluntary status, since their history or experience is not within their current power to change; and (3) existing groups defined by volition, so long as the purpose of the association is so fundamental to their human dignity that they ought not to be required to abandon it.' See *Canada (Attorney General) v Ward* (1993) 2 SCR 689, 103 DLR 4th. See UNHCR Division of International Protection, 'Gender-related persecution: an analysis of recent trends' (1997) International Journal of Refugee Law (Special Issue) 38: '[A]s a developing area of law it is increasingly recognized that gender-related persecution is a distinct form of persecution which may properly fall within the Convention definition of refugee.' EXCOM, Conclusion 39, Refugee Women and International Protection, para k: 'Recognized that states, in the exercise of their sovereignty, are free to adopt the interpretation that women asylum-seekers who face harsh or inhuman treatment due to their having transgressed the social mores of the society in which they live may be considered as a "particular social group" within the meaning of Article 1A(2) of the 1951 United Nations Refugee Convention.'

dominance.[113] To place the claims of refugee woman in the 'social group' category may be appropriate in many cases, but it is problematic. The contention here is that it perpetuates a way of constructing the woman refugee which is fundamentally flawed.

The first case is *R v Immigration Appeal Tribunal ex p Shah; Islam and Others v Secretary of State for the Home Department*.[114] This involved two Pakistani women who had been falsely accused by their husbands of adultery. If returned, they claimed, they would be abused by their husbands and subjected to punishment under Sharia law, with the possibility of death by stoning. The claims of the two women were on the whole argued under the 'particular social group' category. This has proved to be one of the most elusive phrases in refugee law and there has been much commentary on it. This can be roughly divided between those who see it as a 'catch-all' and those who argue that the drafters intended a more restrictive conception. The liberal interpretation has the merit of humanitarianism and suggests that the important focus should be on the persecution expected upon return and not on the reasons for this. The difficulty here is why the drafters of the Convention included a list if it was meant to have so little impact in practice. The issue of the applicability of the *ejusdem generis* principle is a somewhat distinct but related theme. It has been argued that, given the prominence of civil and political rights in the other grounds of persecution, 'particular social group' should be intrepreted in the same way. While one can acknowledge the logic of the argument, it seems too restrictive to adopt such an approach. In the case under discussion, Waite LJ stressed the importance of trying to harmonise the UK approach with that adopted in other jurisdictions. He opted for the following construction of the category after an examination of the 'international' jurisprudence, 'members of the group must share something which unites them, and which sets them apart from the rest of society and is recognised as such by society generally'. Their claims were rejected as the court felt that they were not members of a 'particular social group'.

It is disappointing that the court decided not to consider the women in this case as members of a 'particular social group'. This reflects a particularly restrictive approach by a judiciary straightforwardly concerned about the implication of their judgment for immigration control. The indeterminancy of the legal rules on this occasion was conveniently resolved by opting for a

---

113 Cf *op cit*, fn 71, Canadian Guidelines, Section II: 'A woman who opposes institutionalised discrimination against women, or expresses views of independence from male social/cultural dominance in her society, may be found to fear persecution by reason of her actual political opinion or a political opinion imputed to her (ie, she is perceived by the agent of persecution to be expressing politically antagonistic views).'

114 [1998] 1 WLR 74 (CA). At the time of writing, a ruling from the House of Lords was expected, this does not impact on the analysis here, which focuses on how the facts were categorised.

restrictive approach. This is not, however, the central reason for including the case in this analysis. The aim here is to deconstruct the law's image of the woman refugee in this context. The law can only deal here with the claims in a way which is highly revealing of a number of distortions. The law seems blind to the women's stories and instead tries to assimilate them to a passive legal category which denies the nature of their lives and actions. In this process, difference is not taken seriously in an attempt to assimilate the lived experience of women refugees to legal categories which promote distortion. The critique developed as a result of listening to the voices of women refugees leads to a reconstructive project which may be used by representatives and decision makers, but is, in the first instance, more likely to form part of the stragegy of relevant social movements.

To see what is meant in practice by this argument, one must look again at the facts and how the claims of these women are reconstructed in the legal context. The facts in the case were not in dispute, the sole issue was the precise interpretation of 'particular social group'. Let us examine the facts again. Shahanna Sadiq Islam married in 1976 and, from an early stage of the marriage, she suffered abuse from her husband. This abuse was to worsen progressively. The increased intensity of the abuse was triggered by an incident which occurred at the school where she worked. She had tried to prevent two politically opposed groups from fighting. She had not intervened for a political reason but one of the groups regarded her actions as such. For this she suffered harassment from supporters of one of the factions involved, who also made allegations to her husband that she had been unfaithful. The domestic violence against her intensified and she was hospitalised as a result. The situation was made worse by Sharia law which held out the possibility of punishment for sexual immorality. After a brief stay with her brother, who was threatened by unknown armed men, she came to England and applied for asylum.

A number of 'social groups' can be imagined into which this claim might be located but, to further the thesis defended in this chapter, we will consider the other grounds. Can, for example, a political opinion not be imputed here? This point was considered by Waite LJ, but only in relation to her public activities at the school, in other words, the public display of 'peace keeping' was not enough to impute onto her a political opinion. If we return to the previous discussion of the public/private divide, could this case not, however, be recast along somewhat different lines. For a start, simply focusing on public displays of political opinion excludes resistance within the private sphere against private acts of harm committed by a spouse or partner. Should such localised resistance to private displays of power, in the general societal context which existed here, not be regarded today as the expression of a political opinion? If feminism, as a political ideology which has gained widespread legitimacy, has cast the personal as the political, is it not at least plausible to argue such claims under this category? In modern times, it seems unduly narrow to limit the definition of the political to traditional forms of political action in the public sphere. Could one not impute to a woman who resists and seeks refuge from domestic violence a political opinion, *feminism*? It seems to be the case that 'political opinion' is being artificially restricted. At one level, this can be seen as law fulfilling the political role of deterring immigration. The reality of this position is masked and legitimised by the terms of legal discourse here. However, if we examine this more closely, we can also see the gendered nature of the image created. The legal construction of the political in this context is a distorted and partial one. It reflects a gendered conception of the political and neglects the many and varied types of localised struggle and resistance which circumvent traditional notions.

At a slightly different level, the US Guidelines explicitly recognise that an applicant who can show the requisite fear of persecution because of her beliefs about the role and status of women in society may be eligible under political opinion.[115] To counter claims that this would cause overwhelming evidential problems, or lead to an overburdening of the system, a number of responses might be made. First, the refugee determination procedure already struggles with ever-present evidential difficulties. If, in principle, someone is a 1951 Convention refugee (which, it must be emphasised, precedes in principle formal recognition), the problem of obtaining evidence is not reasonable justification for exclusion. Secondly, the person involved must still bring her claim within the other aspects of the 1951 Convention before she can successfully claim to be a refugee.[116] The argument advanced here is limited to rethinking the established grounds in an inclusive way. It is not supportive of a wholesale lowering of existing standards which would undermine the credibility of the refugee protection regime. The logic of the argument is simple: by highlighting the present partial and distorted interpretation of

---

115 See *Fatin v INS* (1993) 12 F 3d 1233, 1242 (3rd cir): 'In this case, if the petitioner's political opinion is defined simply as "feminism" she would presumably satisfy the first element, for we have *little doubt that feminism qualifies as a political opinion within the meaning of the relevant statutes.*' See Report of Expert Group on Gender-Based Persecution, Toronto, Canada, 9–12 November 1997, EGM/GBP/1997/44: 'the meeting agreed that feminism constitutes political opinion for the purposes of defining who is a refugee ... It noted that behaviour by a woman that does not conform to cultural or social norms with respect to gender roles may be construed as political opinion with respect to gender roles or the political opinion, feminism ... [p]ersecution as a result of expressed or imputed feminism, or failure to conform to conventional gender roles, or because of activities during armed conflict or imputed opinion as a result of the opinion of family members should all be regarded as persecution on the grounds of political opinion for the purposes of the Refugee Convention.' See *op cit*, fn 71, Canadian Guidelines, Section II, on political opinion.

116 'Domestic violence is not a random crime; it is a gender-specific violation of the rights of women. It often implicates the most fundamental of human rights: the right to life, and to freedom from torture and cruel, inhuman and degrading treatment ... There is a clear basis for granting asylum protection in cases of domestic violence.' Anker, D, Gilbert, L and Kelly, N, 'Women whose governments are unable or unwilling to provide reasonable protection from domestic violence may qualify as refugees under United States asylum law' (1997) 11 Georgetown Immigration LJ 709, p 744. See, also, Thomas, D and Beasley, M, 'Domestic violence as a human rights issue' (1993) 15 HRQ 36.

'political opinion' we can begin to engage constructively with those excluded by the practical construction of protection.

The same reasoning can be applied to Syeda Khatoon Shah's claim. She again suffered years of domestic violence, finally fleeing to England in 1992. Her claim was argued solely on the 'social group' ground and, again, it is suggested that the political opinion argument should at least have been considered as a possible grounding for the claim. It is not suggested here that these claims would necessarily have succeeded under the 'political opinion' ground – as presently interpreted by the courts, they would not – or that they are the best possible examples of claims which might come within the 'political opinion' ground. The intention is to encourage a re-think of interpretative strategies in other cases by gesturing toward other ways of thinking about the activities of women asylum seekers. Sincethis was written, the House of Lords has overturned the judgment of the Court of Appeal.[117] In this landmark ruling, the majority adopted an impressively liberal interpretation of 'social group'.[118] However, this does not affect the substantive argument advanced here.

Another example will help to illustrate the argument further. *Ouanes v Secretary of State for the Home Department*[119] involved a claim to asylum by an Algerian woman who had been employed by the Department of Health as a midwife. During the course of her employment, she was required to give contraceptive advice. The difficulty was that fundamentalists in Algeria opposed this aspect of government policy, leading the respondent to flee because of a fear of persecution. The Immigration Appeal Tribunal held that Algerian midwives employed by the government in this context did constitute a 'particular social group'. The Secretary of State successfully challenged this interpretation of the law. As with *Shah/Islam* the aim is not to explore whether the woman involved did below to a 'particular social group' (there are grounds for favouring the IAT's interpretation in this instance).

As to the facts, in October 1994, she was told that: 'she must wear the veil and cover her arms and legs or "her day would come".'[120] In November, a man threatened her in the health centre where she worked, again, insisting that she wear the veil. In another incident, she asked a patient to remove her veil, the patient refused and threatened to report her to the fundamentalists. Since her arrival in the UK, her nephew had been killed and there was documented evidence of a midwife being kidnapped and beheaded. There had been other incidents which confirmed this general picture of events. On these facts, her case was brought within a 'particular social group' and the argument about its precise meaning ended up in the Court of Appeal. Rather

---

117 *Islam v Secretary of State for the Home Department; R v IAT ex p Shah* (1999) not yet reported (HL). See http://www.parliament.uk/.
118 See Harvey, C, 'Mainstreaming gender in the refugee protection process' (1999) 149 NLJ 534.
119 [1998] 1 WLR 218 (CA).
120 *Ibid*.

than dwell on this, I want to explore the facts again and apply the same analysis as that discussed above. Given the experiences of the individual involved in this case, is it really necessary to place this claim exclusively within the monolithic 'social group' category? As in the examination of *Shah/Islam*, the suggestion here is that this effectively connives in a construction of 'female passivity' which is highly inappropriate, given the part played by women in such situations. Here is an example of a woman, working in a health centre, suffering repeated threats and intimidation for the work she is doing and the life choices she has made, that is, giving contraceptive advice to other women in Algeria as well as her refusal to wear the veil. To rely solely on the 'social group' category in this context is to undermine the active role of women in societies such as Algeria who are struggling against the violence and intimidation of fundamentalist groups. Such activity is 'political' and surely should be viewed as such in any modern interpretation of refugee law.

These cases highlight how a gendered perspective on asylum law provides fascinating insights into one problem with this area of law. There are, of course, many other aspects of asylum law which could be subjected to a similar critique but which go beyond the bounds of this chapter. It is at this point that a turn can be made from the deconstruction of the law's image of the refugee to reconstruction. This is where the communicative model sketched earlier provides a useful bridge between theory and practice. It also offers a grounding for critique at a time when a number of schools of thought have sought to pour scorn on the notion. To gesture at the continuing existence of oppression in practice, in no way undermines a model which merely seeks to unearth the fragments of reason in our social practices. The hard work of achieving practical change remains to be done by those social movements committed to a transformative politics that can distinguish and justify itself through dialogue. The difficulty with those who claim that it is all about strategic manipulation, power and the acceptance of the reality of brute conflict in social and political life is that they can provide no basis beyond an often crude (existentialist inspired) decisionism for their actions. In rejecting this form of decisionism, this chapter has attempted to show that deconstruction must be followed by reconstruction and that this is best explained by those like Benhabib, Fraser and Habermas, who advance (in different ways) versions of communicative models. In testing the model, asylum law was used to indicate how the feminist perspective on public law has contributed, through the action of social movements, to gradual change.

CONCLUSION

The thesis defended in this chapter is one borne from a recognition of the sins of omission in refugee law. It is part of a process of acceptance of the unavoidably partial nature of our perspectives. As a community of inquirers engaged, in all good faith, in an attempt to reconstruct the law, we are striving towards impartiality by recognising our present limitations. Conversations in social democracies must always be open to those movements which highlight distortion in past practice and ongoing oppression. This inclusive process, which recognises the importance of a multiplicity of public spheres, is vital for the continuing legitimacy of law. In pragmatist terms, we never know whether we have arrived at the finally correct model and to reach such a point would be a dangerous closure of the continuing conversation of social democracy. The key to an enlightened and ethical asylum policy is, thus, to accept our own limitations, and the partial nature of our perspectives, and then be prepared to work forward towards impartiality in dialogue with others. The project of modernity, as it is made manifest in legal discourses, advances incrementally as we work through the tension between the situated nature of our lives and work and the constant need to engage in rational discourses with universalist underpinnings. When we approach the interpretative task of reconstructing legal meaning, it is important to do so with as comprehensive an understanding of the totality of the human experience as it is possible to have. One way this can be achieved is by creating procedures for encouraging the voices of the silenced 'others' to be heard. Once this has occurred, however, these voices must be listened to, and there must be a willingness to rethink traditional structures of legal argumentation. This chapter has tried to take the challenge of the feminist perspective on public law seriously. Exploring feminist critiques of, for example, the public/private divide, the intention is, at the symbolic level, to defend a reconstruction of refugee law in the light of the new voices which are entering the discourse. On the material level, the aim is the straightforwardly instrumental one of promoting practical legal and policy reforms of adjudication and administration which will nurture a culture where fair decision making becomes possible. Working in good faith with this conversational model involves the adoption of a pragmatic disposition on the part of participants and one that is open to revision of entrenched interpretations. Such a critical model is one way in which we can try to give a voice to those who have suffered, and continue to suffer, in silence. One practical way to achieve this aim, it has been suggested, is to return to what seem like well established interpretative positions with 'new eyes'. What we find is that interpretations have solidified around partial and distorted perspectives on the totality of the human experience. It is suggested that the communicative model defended in this chapter offers the most convincing way forward for feminist scholars who do not wish to abandon the project of modernity. By adopting this model, it is possible to diagnose modern pathologies and work toward constructive ways forward. Ultimately, this is based on the insight that to make the moral claim that the current hegemonic language game is grounded in distortion and oppression is to put forward an argument which has a truth content and universalist underpinnings. Resignation might be superficially appealing, but is ultimately not the way to address the complex problems faced by modernity.

CHAPTER 11

PUNISHING COUNCILS: POLITICAL POWER, SOLIDARITY AND THE PURSUIT OF FREEDOM[1]

Davina Cooper

... it is not, in general, the business of local authorities to punish people who have committed no legal wrong.[2]

INTRODUCTION

This chapter is about local government abusing its power in pursuit of political ideology at the expense of companies, voluntary organisations, and individuals. Demanding compliance, this is also a story of punishment: meted out by local government to innocent actors and bystanders caught in the political crossfire.

But who are the storytellers, and what is their investment in this narrative? To address this question, we must shift the scale of inquiry – from the micro-politics of the local to the practices of the courts, including, and in particular, their self-identified role as upholders of private freedoms against state power.

The plausibility of judicial commitments to 'freedom' is clearly debatable. However, one context where the courts have presented their actions as such concerns local government policy. Here, particularly in connection with left wing councils, the courts have jumped to restrain municipal activity – protecting civil society from *ultra vires* policies and practices. Yet, to define council policies as *ultra vires* is already to internalise a judicial gaze. For the contours of local government's mandate and remit depend largely on judicial activity.

Court attempts to restrict municipal action have been apparent in a range of areas. However, one which has generated particularly rigorous judicial activity, and forms the subject of this chapter, concerns the withdrawal by local government of funds, land and contracts from bodies whose actions they oppose. Such council practice escalated in the 1980s as urban councils came under the control of left wing Labour groups.[3] Determined to use the council as a political tool, despite the growing constraints placed upon them,

---

1   Thanks to Didi Herman, Sue Millns and Noel Whitty for their excellent comments and suggestions.

2   *Per* Staughton LJ, in *R v Greenwich LBC ex p Lovelace* [1991] 3 All ER 511, p 526.

3   Boddy, M and Fudge, C (eds), *Local Socialism?*, 1984, London: Macmillan; Gyford, J, *The Politics of Local Socialism*, 1985, London: Allen & Unwin; Cooper, D, *Sexing the City: Lesbian and Gay Politics within the Activist State*, 1994, London: Rivers Oram.

leaderships looked to their 'private', as well as 'public', powers to make their mark – and make it publicly. In part, this strategy reflected a wider vision of local government's purpose – to include international and industrial solidarity as well as housing provision, education and refuse collection. However, it was also a consequence of Conservative central government's neo-liberal agenda which reoriented local government away from direct service provision to contractually procuring services from others.

The withdrawal of contracts, funds and licences thus needs to be placed within the wider political context of the 1980s and early 1990s, with the development of compulsory competitive tendering, privatisation, and central-local conflict. We can then see what I shall call 'transactional'[4] withdrawal as simultaneously performing two functions: first, using the remaining forms of power available to local government to pursue a socialist or social welfarist politics and, secondly, subverting, through 'misuse', the neo-liberal logic apparent within the government's emphasis on contractual relations.

Wheeler,[5] *Shell*,[6] *Times Newspapers*,[7] and *Fewings*[8] are perhaps the best known cases in this area. They concern, respectively, the refusal to let a local club use a council run rugby stadium after several club members chose to play in apartheid South Africa; a boycott of Shell products on the grounds that Shell subsidiaries traded in South Africa; the cancellation of *Times* owned newspapers from municipal libraries in solidarity with staff engaged in a serious industrial dispute; and the withdrawal of permission from the Quantock Staghounds to hunt deer across council owned land in Somerset's Quantock Hills. Given that these four cases raise important administrative law issues, it is surprising how little critical attention they have received as a group. For the most part,[9] such analysis as does exist either takes the form of a short casenote or is incorporated within a broader discussion of administrative law doctrine and theory,[10] tensions around constitutional

---

4   By 'transactional', I refer to a range of exchange relationships, including licences and procurement. Not all involve financial forms of consideration; in the case of grant giving, for instance, the transaction involves an agreement to abide by certain conditions in exchange for funds.

5   *Wheeler v Leicester City Council* [1985] 2 All ER 1106.

6   *R v Lewisham LBC ex p Shell UK Ltd* [1988] 1 All ER 938.

7   *R v Ealing LBC ex p Times Newspapers Ltd* (1986) 85 LGR 316.

8   *R v Somerset County Council ex p Fewings* [1995] 3 All ER 20.

9   A different approach is taken by Dawn Oliver, who considers these cases from the perspective of regulating state power and ownership. This approach is closer to my own, although the direction our analysis takes diverges radically. See Oliver, D, 'State property and individual rights' (1988) 25 Coexistence 103; see, also, Nardell, G, 'The Quantock Hounds and the Trojan Horse' [1995] PL 27; Loughlin, M, *Legality and Locality*, Oxford: Clarendon, 1996, pp 172–75, 177–82.

10   Jowell, J and Lester, A, 'Beyond *Wednesbury*: substantive principles of administrative law' [1987] PL 368; Allan, T, 'Pragmatism and theory in public law' (1988) 104 LQR 422; Richardson, G and Genn, H, *Administrative Law and Government Action: The Courts and Alternative Mechanisms of Review*, 1994, Oxford: Clarendon.

freedoms, such as freedom of expression,[11] or the status of moral/political governance objectives.[12]

This work is important, and my own analysis draws from it. At the same time, this chapter aims to address somewhat different issues. Analysing the cluster of late 20th century cases involving transactional withdrawal, I am concerned with why council actions in this area provoked so much judicial hostility. To address this question, I draw on a range of theoretical perspectives. These include communitarian and liberal theory as well as Foucauldian and feminist analysis.

Since this book concerns the application of feminist principles to public law, let me say something about their application in this area. Developing feminist theory in the context of transactional withdrawal cases is certainly far from straightforward. To begin with, there is almost no British writing on judicial review from a feminist perspective.[13] This general absence may be due to the fact that feminist analysis tends to focus on relations, discourses or ethics involving women. Since gender is not an explicit central focus of much administrative law, it is not immediately apparent what a feminist analysis would contribute. However, further reflection suggests that feminist theory may prove relevant and illuminating. In relation to general public law principles, as other chapters in this volume demonstrate, feminist theory offers an analysis of the embodied (and abstracted) citizen, as well as critiquing historically gendered concepts such as the public domain, the state, rationality, the rule of law and political authority.[14] In addition, so far as the specific case law discussed in this chapter is concerned, feminist theory provides useful analytical insights into the meaning of power and community, as well as a normative framework that generates questions about state/civil society relations,[15] and the nature of domination and freedom. Feminist theory has also developed analysis of the way in which gender meanings extend beyond men and women, to wider cultural values. This last is an important point for it allows us to explore the resonances and connections

---

11   Allan, T, 'Rugby, recreation grounds and race-relations: punishment for silence' (1985) 48 MLR 448; Allan, T, 'Racial harmony, public policy and freedom of speech' (1986) 49 MLR 121; Barendt, E, 'Libel and freedom of speech in English law' [1993] PL 449.

12   Logie, J, 'Party policy and the law' (1988) 138 NLJ 307; Carter, S, and Kinloch, I, 'Local authorities and moral judgments' (1994) 144 NLJ 1474; Welstead, M, 'A hunting we will go' (1994) The Conveyancer 416; Cram, I, 'Public authorities, political protest and judicial review' 1995 24 SLT 213.

13   For an interesting Canadian discussion of administrative law from a feminist perspective, see Young, A, 'Feminism, pluralism and administrative law', in Taggart, M (ed), *The Province of Administrative Law*, 1997, Oxford: Hart.

14   See, eg, Hirschmann, N and Di Stefano, C (eds), *Revisioning the Political: Feminist Reconstructions of Traditional Concepts in Western Political Theory*, 1996, Boulder, CO; Westview.

15   Clearly, feminist work is not the only literature to critique state/civil society relations; nevertheless, it does provide useful insights, see, for instance, Pringle, R and Watson, S, 'Women's interests and the post-structuralist state', in Barrett, M and Phillips, A (eds), *Destabilising Theory: Contemporary Feminist Debates*, 1992, Cambridge: Polity.

between the way men and women – the masculine and feminine – are understood and the discourses that constitute other social phenomena.

Feminist theory also has something to say about punishment,[16] and it is the portrayal of councils as punishing, through the withdrawal of contracts, resources, and licences, which lies at the heart of my analysis. I therefore begin by exploring the rhetorical value and implications of this term, drawing on feminist theorist Judith Butler's work on drag as well as Foucauldian notions of discipline. The second section of the chapter goes on to explore more broadly why the courts proved so hostile towards local government action in the cases discussed; I focus here on freedom, commercial state practice, and community. Finally, I bring the different strands together by applying the metaphor of the 'monstrous feminine'[17] to the courts' portrayal of local government. My argument is that the applicability of this metaphor lies in the courts' depiction of local government as both inadequate and excessive – importing inappropriate familial norms of conduct into the public domain.

THE PUNISHING COUNCIL

The concept of the 'punishing council' highlights the two aspects of my discussion: the way in which councils, according to the courts, abuse, coerce and exact revenge from local residents, organisations and companies and, at the same time, the punishment the courts mete out to councils in return. In this section, I focus on the first aspect, I return to the second below.

The notion of local government as punishing pervades the cases. Yet, in what way can the withdrawal of contracts and licences, largely for political reasons, be seen as punishment? This is not punishment as the courts might punish through fines or imprisonment, nor does it involve physical violence. What it does entail is the placing of significant pressure on individuals and corporations. According to Dawn Oliver, this is enough:

> ... the state has at its disposal many resources on which individuals and private organisations depend and which can be deployed so as to influence those individuals and organisations and to manipulate their behaviour. It is in consequence unnecessary for physical coercion to be invoked by the state in the pursuit of many of its policies.[18]

---

16 For a critique of feminist strategies that prioritise punishment for injuries undergone, see Snider, L, 'Feminism, punishment and the potential of empowerment' (1994) 9 Canadian Journal of Law and Society 75.

17 See Braidotti, R, *Nomadic Subjects*, 1994, New York: Columbia UP, ch 3; Thomson, M, 'Legislating for the monstrous: access to reproductive services and the monstrous feminine' (1997) 6 SLS 401.

18 *Op cit*, fn 9, Oliver.

Cases of transactional withdrawal fall into three categories. The first – the cluster of cases with which Dawn Oliver is principally concerned – involve the (threat of) withdrawal of council resources and contracts to pressure private individuals, organisations and corporations to act in specific ways, for instance, to oppose apartheid, government training schemes or to resolve industrial disputes. Judicial discomfort at the extent of this pressure is made particularly explicit in *Shell*.[19] Lewisham Council there decided to boycott all Shell products (providing reasonable alternatives existed), and to encourage other authorities to take similar action, to persuade Shell subsidiaries to withdraw commercially from South Africa.[20] A council press release stated: '[m]illions of pounds of pension fund investment, contracts for fuel oil for schools, council buildings and vehicles and many other Shell products are being targeted.'[21]

The second set of policy decisions involve councils banning activities on ideological, political or ethical grounds. In the early 1990s, rural authorities prohibited hunting across their land on grounds of animal cruelty,[22] while urban councils, in the 1980s, attempted to forbid fascist organisations from using council premises for meetings.[23] Here, unlike the first category, there is nothing the organisation can do to make the council change its mind. Local government is not wielding its power as a political stick, but rather using its authority to remove undesirable activities and groupings from its vicinity.

The third group of cases I mention for completeness, although I will not discuss them further. They concern punitive action taken, not for political reasons, but rather because the appellant has breached council rules, behaved rudely, caused a nuisance or otherwise disregarded council policy. Cases in this category include the withdrawal of market traders' licences from council administered markets, ejecting travellers from council controlled land, and removing council representatives from school governing bodies.[24] In this cluster of cases, unlike the other two, the courts recognise the councils' right to penalise through the withdrawal of permission. Thus, decisions emphasise the need for local government to behave, in such cases, in a quasi-judicial manner. The courts focus on the procedure for attributing 'culpability' as well as the

---

19 *R v Lewisham London Borough Council ex p Shell UK Ltd* [1988] 1 All ER 938. See, also, *Martin v City of Edinburgh District Council* (1998) Scots Law Times, 20 May, p 329.

20 Through the organisation initiated by Lewisham – Joint Action Against Apartheid.

21 *R v Lewisham London Borough Council ex p Shell UK Ltd* [1988] 1 All ER 938, pp 942–43, Neill LJ.

22 *R v Somerset County Council ex p Fewings* [1995] 3 All ER 20.

23 See *Verrall v Great Yarmouth Borough Council* [1981] 1 QB 202; *Webster v Southwark London Borough Council* [1983] 1 QB 698.

24 See, for instance, *Brunyate and Another v ILEA* [1989] 2 All ER 417; cf *R v Greenwich London Borough Council ex p Lovelace* [1991] 3 All ER 511; see, also, *R v Hendon Justices and Others ex p DPP* [1993] 1 All ER 411.

choice of penalty.[25] Where applicants succeed, it is often because the council has not lived up to judicially laid down standards of fairness and natural justice.[26]

While in this third category judging and punishing are not seen as antithetical to municipal activity, my focus is on the first two groups of cases, where the exaction of penalty is deemed fundamentally unacceptable. Lord Roskill declared in *Wheeler*, 'persuasion, however powerful, must not be allowed to cross that line where it moves into the field of illegitimate pressure coupled with the threat of sanctions'.[27] In *Shell*, Neill LJ makes a similar point, 'a council cannot use its statutory powers in order to punish a body or person who has done nothing contrary to English law'. The courts thus portray local government in these cases as having erroneously appropriated a judicial function. In other words, these are not cases where councils have failed to act as proper judges (as in category three) but where, according to the courts, they should not be acting as judges at all.

In treating councils as having misappropriated a judicial role in their bestowal of punishment, the courts draw on a very wide definition of punishment. Any local government policy might constitute punishment if it involves the withdrawal[28] or reallocation of contracts, committee appointments, licences or grants on grounds – moral, ideological or regulatory – that are inconsistent with the courts' understanding of the governing legislative instrument.[29] Clearly, such a judicial framework is open to critique on normative grounds. My aim, however, in this chapter, is rather to consider why the courts adopted this perspective and the implications of their doing so. Certainly, questions of personal motive are difficult, if not impossible, to uncover, and this chapter largely leaves them to one side. What I wish to focus on instead are, first, the rhetorical power of the label 'punishing'; and, secondly, the relationship between transactional withdrawal and neo-liberal/communitarian judicial ideologies.

---

25 See, for instance, *R v Brent London Borough Council ex p Assegai* (1997) *The Independent*, 12 June.

26 See, for instance, *R v Barnsley Council ex p Hook* [1976] 1 WLR 1052, p 1060, *per* Scarman LJ.

27 [1985] 2 All ER 1106, p 1111.

28 This may also generate benefits for those becoming the new recipients of contracts, funding or access to land thanks to its withdrawal from others. This is often ignored.

29 Though see, also, *R v Secretary of State for the Environment ex p Greenwich London Borough Council* (1990) 22 HLR 543, p 551. Here, the Minister was held not to be 'punishing' Greenwich and other councils in the formula drawn up for housing revenue subsidies pursuant to the Local Government and Housing Act 1989. The court held the Minister was entitled to declare some forms of lawful expenditure would attract support, while others did not.

RHETORICAL VALUE

The phrase 'punishing councils' offers a powerful means of attacking, and thus circumscribing, a wide range of council decisions. It suggests that councils have both lost sight of, and exceeded, their proper function in their drive to bend others to their will; and implies that in victimising those who refuse to comply, local government has wrongly and defectively appropriated the courts' role. The defectiveness of local government's action is apparent on several counts. First, it is politically, rather than legally, motivated; it therefore lacks detachment and objectivity. Secondly, the scale of punishment is disproportionate to the harm caused.[30] Thirdly – and this is, for the courts and many commentators, fundamental – it involves punishing *lawful* behaviour.[31]

This account of judicial concern focuses on the *way* local government punishes, rather than the very fact that it does so. Yet, the existence and form of municipal punishment cannot be adequately separated within judicial discourse. Their intertwined nature is perhaps more clearly apparent if we draw on the metaphor of the 'drag judge' to illuminate the court's approach. 'Drag' suggests a reinvention of the self through appropriating the norms of the 'Other' (usually, the forbidden Other). While traditionally dismissed as a mere theatrical performance or parody, critical theorists have legitimised drag by identifying its political significance in the destabilisation of the original.[32] In other words, drag's ability to resituate itself as that which it copies interrogates the authenticity of the latter – suggesting it too is a copy. Adopting this analysis, we might suggest that the reason for the courts' hostility towards local government in these cases lies in the threat municipal punitive action poses to the courts' own coherence and integrity. If local government can 'pass' as juridical, then what special status do the courts retain? Are they too simply passing – actively performing the fictional judge?

The problem with this line of argument is that it assumes what needs proving: the destabilising quality of drag which largely lies in the inability to distinguish copies from self-identified originals. An alternative interpretation – which rejects the notion that drag successfully passes – is to see drag as entrenching the 'original' by revealing its distance from, and focusing

---

30 For a discussion of attempts to apply proportionality principles to British law, see Boyron, S, 'Proportionality in English administrative law: a faulty translation?' (1992) 12 OJLS 237.

31 See, for instance, *op cit*, fn 10, Jowell and Lester, pp 376–77: a central principle of legal certainty is that there should be no punishment without breach of the law.

32 See, generally, for discussion in this area, Butler, J, *Gender Trouble*, 1990, New York: Routledge, pp 137–38. Cf Butler, J, *Bodies that Matter*, 1993, London: Routledge, pp 125–37; Champagne, J, 'Stabat Madonna', in Frank, L and Smith, P (eds), *Madonnarama: Essays on Sex and Popular Culture*, 1993, Pittsburgh, PA: Cleis; Flannigan-Saint-Aubin, A, '"Black gay male" discourse: reading race and sexuality between the lines', in Fout, J and Tantillo, MS (eds), *American Sexual Politics: Sex, Gender and Race since the Civil War*, 1993, Chicago, IL: Chicago UP.

attention on, the failed imitative character of copies. In this way, the courts' repeated construction of local government as punitive can be seen as a strategy for fortifying the courts' own authenticity – accentuating the foundational character of judicial identity through (mis)reading the performance of local government as hyperbole or excess.[33] In other words, only the courts can judge properly; attempts by local government will inevitably fall out of bounds because to judge is not *at the essence of what local government is*.

This explanation for the courts' rhetorical emphasis is grounded on an assumed articulation between punishment and law – that punishment, outside the private domain, is something only law enforcers properly can do. However, if punishment and law are uncoupled, we can understand the courts' rhetorical strategy as generating two other discursive effects. In the first, punishment functions as a shorthand for discipline; in other words, as an extra-legal technique for producing submissive, normalised subjects.[34] Disciplinary analysis has spawned a considerable literature, including that of feminists, on the ways in which women's bodies are constituted as childlike, manageable and restricted.[35] There are echoes of this analysis in the transactional withdrawal cases. In *Wheeler*,[36] *Liverpool*[37] and *Shell*,[38] the courts identified council action as similarly driven by the desire to discipline resistant bodies – to compel their submission: to deter future rugby players from visiting apartheid South Africa; to pressure Shell to amend their international economic policy; and to persuade Liverpool's voluntary sector to withdraw from government training schemes.[39]

---

33 Cf *op cit*, fn 32, Butler, p 22.

34 Foucauldian work has spawned extensive debate about the relationship between law and discipline, see Hunt, A, 'Foucault's expulsion of law: towards a retrieval' (1992) 17 Law and Social Inquiry 1; Hunt, A and Wickham, G, *Foucault and Law: Towards a Sociology of Law as Governance*, 1994, London: Pluto. For analysis of Foucault's use of discipline, see Dews, P, *Logics of Disintegration: Post-Structuralist Thought and the Claims of Critical Theory*, 1987, London: Verso, p 161; Fraser, N, *Unruly Practices: Power, Discourse and Gender in Contemporary Theory*, 1989, Cambridge: Polity, p 22; Simons, J, *Foucault and the Political*, 1995, pp 31–32. While the courts implicitly identify municipal punishment as 'not law' thanks to its extra-legal status, the councils do draw upon a range of juridical forms, including contract, ownership, and statutory powers/procedures.

35 See, for instance, Bartky, S, 'Foucault, feminism and the modernization of patriarchal power', in Diamond, I and Quinby, L (eds), *Feminism and Foucault: Reflections on Resistance*, 1988, Boston, MA: Northeastern UP.

36 [1985] 2 All ER 1106.

37 (1988) 154 LGR 118. This case concerned a decision taken by Liverpool Council to withdraw grant aid from organisations that participated in the Conservative government's Employment Training Scheme.

38 [1988] 1 All ER 938.

39 Cf *R v Somerset County Council ex p Fewings* [1995] 3 All ER 20 and the National Front municipal hall rentals, *Verrall v Great Yarmouth Borough Council* [1981] 1 QB 202; *Webster v Southwark London Borough Council* [1983] 1 QB 698, where the attempt to engineer submission is not articulated to the continuation of the organisation's activity in an acceptable manner, but rather to its general termination or removal.

Yet, there is also a paradox or tension in treating transactional withdrawal as a disciplinary strategy. In the main, Foucauldian work on discipline has placed considerable emphasis on surveillance. 'Observation allows one to exercise normalising judgment, punishing all deviations from the norm.'[40] Bodies are trained to behave appropriately through a technology of hierarchical watching where those subjected never know when the gaze is present. Here we have, to some degree, the reverse, since the removal of grants, contracts and licences involves the *withdrawal* of local government's gaze or recognition.

Does this make municipal action counterdisciplinary? Yes and no. Surveillance is, arguably, only one amongst a range of disciplinary techniques; in addition, withdrawal in the cases discussed here was undoubtedly preceded by extensive examination and surveillance. Nevertheless, the judicial articulation of punishment to withdrawal does suggest an alternative interpretation. According to this, local government is bent, not on submission or normalisation, but on expulsion/forgetting.

Do discipline and forgetting provide conflicting interpretations of the same decisions or is reconciliation possible? The latter may be achievable if we see discipline/forgetting as relating to the different categories of cases outlined above. While the courts depict councils in the first category as intent on disciplining the stubbornly perverse to engineer their rehabilitation/ normalisation within the community (for example, *Shell*[41] and *Wheeler*);[42] in the second category, local government is depicted as condemning the irrevocably sinful to exclusion and neglect (for example, *Fewings*).[43]

FREEDOM

I am concerned with a fundamental freedom which this country has prided itself on maintaining, and for which much blood has been spilt ...[44]

In my judgment, if the decision of the council in the present case is lawful, there is a dangerous risk to those fundamental freedoms of the individual ... Basic constitutional rights in this country ... are based not on any express provisions ... but on freedom of an individual to do what he [sic] will save to the extent that he is prevented from so doing by the law.[45]

---

40 Simons, J, *Foucault and the Political*, 1995, London: Routledge, p 31.
41 [1988] 1 All ER 938.
42 [1985] 2 All ER 1106.
43 [1995] 3 All ER 20.
44 *Per* Watkins J, in *Verrall v Great Yarmouth BC* [1981] 1 QB 202, p 205.
45 *Per* Browne-Wilkinson LJ, in *Wheeler v Leicester City Council* [1985] 2 All ER 151, pp 157–58.

The courts' emphasis on punishment in the cases discussed here is clearly intended to send signals that councils have overstepped their mark. But why have the courts proven so hostile to transactional withdrawal? Progressive local government activism, during the 1980s, did not only take a punitive form. It also involved attempts to expand the positive freedoms of vulnerable or disadvantaged groups. While these latter initiatives encountered extensive criticism and derision from the media, Parliament and local opposition groups, they less frequently formed the basis for judicial review.[46] Opponents saw the bestowal of resources on disadvantaged groups, such as minority ethnic communities and lesbians/gays, as a form of special treatment that undermined equality, but, generally, they restricted their opposition to conventional political arenas. In contrast, policies that challenged negative freedoms – freedom *from* state interference – frequently ended up in the courts. Freedom became that which the council was withdrawing. For the courts and their applicants, freedom had no relationship to the beneficiaries of council action – anti-fascists, minority ethnic communities, trade union members, or even deer.

This refusal to recognise 'positive' freedoms highlights the distance between the courts' approach and that of feminist theorists. While feminist conceptions of freedom vary, one important strand focuses on connection rather than separation; in other words, the expression of freedom both entails and is grounded upon the support of others. This approach centres the socio-economic and political backing necessary for many people to achieve greater choice.[47] At the same time, the courts did *feminise* the applicants before them. Fascists, hunters, oil companies and newspaper owners were represented as vulnerable and unprotected when confronted with local state power. While some, such as voluntary groups, were deemed to be inherently powerless, the courts identified the impotence of others as emanating from their pejorative status. In *Verrall*, for instance, the court portrayed the National Front as the victims of left authoritarianism, unable to hold their annual conference because no local authority would rent them a hall.[48]

---

46 There are some exceptions, for instance, race equality policies in relation to education. Resource reallocation policies were also challenged, on grounds, *inter alia*, of a breach of fiduciary duty. I discuss this further in *Governing Out of Order: Space, Law and the Politics of Belonging*, 1988, London: Rivers Oram, ch 4.

47 See Hirschmann, N, 'Revisioning freedom: relationship, context, and the politics of empowerment', in Hirschmann, N and Di Stefano, C (eds), *Revisioning the Political*, 1996, Boulder, CO: Westview; Lacey, N, *Unspeakable Subjects*, 1998, Oxford: Hart, pp 77–78.

48 See, also, Denning MR, in *R v Barnsley Metropolitan Borough Council ex p Hook* [1976] 1 WLR 1052.

Local government and contractual freedom

Yet, if the courts were so concerned with protecting freedom that they would restrict municipal action in order to do so, how could they ignore the freedom of local government, in particular, the freedom to contract?

Conventionally, British courts have affirmed local government's contractual freedom and shown reluctance to interfere by means of judicial review. Sue Arrowsmith argues that the courts tended to treat contractual disputes involving public bodies as private law matters unless there was a sufficient public law element.[49] While there are exceptions, this tended to mean treating local government as a 'normal' partner within a 'private' contractual relationship in which both sides were deemed 'free, rational and equal'.[50] However, in the cases discussed here, the courts did not see local government as acting normally. From their perspective, the contracts could not be treated as operating between two equal, legal persons because one party – the council – was not only exploiting its superior power, but was also acting for reasons beyond those of a 'private' legal person. Motivations such as animal cruelty, apartheid and fascism took council decisions outside of the common law's regulatory framework.

Yet, the irony here is that while the courts treated local government's reference to political considerations as precipitating judicial review – a legal form that relates to bodies as *public* bodies – the *public* status of local government was not sufficient to justify or validate the decision. In fact, it achieved the reverse, since the courts left private bodies with more leeway to take action on 'political' grounds. This 'organising out' of politics in relation to local government problematises the feminist claim that liberal discursive practices, such as those of the courts, locate politics within the public sphere. While this is broadly true, in the sense that liberalism tends not to see the private domain as political, not all public institutions are permitted to act politically.[51] Cases such as *Fewings*[52] stress the limits placed on local government *qua* a public body. While a private body is presumed to possess

---

49   Arrowsmith, S, 'Judicial review and the contractual powers of public authorities' (1990) 106 LQR 277. See, also, Fredman, S and Morris, G, 'The costs of exclusivity: public and private re-examined' [1994] PL 69; Cranston, R, 'Reviewing judicial review', in *op cit*, fn 10, Richardson and Genn. See *R v Basildon District Council ex p Brown* (1981) 79 LGR 655; cf Dunn LJ, p 672 with Lord Denning, p 663; *R v Wear Valley District Council ex p Binks* [1985] 2 All ER 699; *R v National Coal Board ex p National Union of Mineworkers* [1986] ICR 791, pp 794–95.

50   See, generally, Naffine, N, *Law and the Sexes*, 1990, Sydney: Allen & Unwin, p 53.

51   There are instances where the courts have recognised positively local government's political character. Indeed, in *Derbyshire County Council v Times Newspapers Ltd* [1993] 1 All ER 1011, p 1017, the court identified the council's democratic, elected, governmental character as the reason for denying Derbyshire the right to sue for defamation.

52   See, in particular, the High Court decision: [1995] 1 All ER 513.

the residual freedom to do that which is not forbidden,[53] a public body, whose powers derive from statute, cannot.[54] Local government freedom, according to judicial *dicta*, is, in a sense, a positive rather than negative freedom. It is a 'freedom to' derived from its legally inscribed role and functions rather than a 'freedom from'. Yet, this 'freedom to' does not include the pursuit of an ethical agenda where negative freedoms are at stake, save with explicit statutory permission.[55]

In saying councils cannot exercise the freedom of private actors, we nevertheless encounter a paradox. The constraints placed on local government are based on a framework that both constitutes and steers local government towards acting as a private body.[56] In the main, what the courts mean by this is that local government should resemble a commercial organisation, governed according to norms and discourses of managerialism, efficiency, financial accountability, and customer service.[57] To this extent, court decisions constitute normative local government as masculine, grounded in the values of the private, commercial domain. At the same time, as I have suggested, local government is not expected to behave as an autonomous, independent body. Repeatedly, judgments stress its subordinate and limited authority, suggesting a far more inconsistent gendering than portrayal as a private commercial body might imply.

We are thus confronted with two interlinked contradictions: first, the courts expect local government to act as a private, commercial body while withholding the negative freedom commercial bodies possess; secondly, the courts measure local government against a masculine ideal, while largely forcing it to conform to a feminised paradigm of powerlessness. These

---

53 Powerful private bodies are increasingly becoming subject to quasi-public law restrictions: see *R v Panel on Take-overs and Mergers ex p Datafin plc* [1987] 1 All ER 564; cf *R v Jockey Club ex p Aga Khan* [1993] 2 All ER 853, especially *per* Hoffmann LJ, p 875. For discussion generally, see Woolf, H, 'Public law – private law: why the divide? A personal view' [1986] PL 220, pp 224–25; Oliver, D, 'Is the *ultra vires* rule the basis of judicial review?' [1987] PL 543; Borrie, G, 'The regulation of public and private power' [1989] PL 552, p 558; Pannick, D, 'Who is subject to judicial review and in respect of what?' [1992] PL 1.

54 See *R v Basildon District Council ex p Brown* (1981) 79 LGR 655, p 663. The limits on local government contrast with central government's residual freedom (analogous to that of a 'natural' person) to undertake acts for which it neither has statutory permission nor prerogative powers where no countervailing legal rights exist: see Harris, B, 'The "third" source of authority' (1992) 109 LQR 626. Harris, however, suggests that, where government is not acting as a 'natural' person, for instance, using contract to regulate activities in pursuit of government policy, specific statutory approval should be required. For critique of Harris' assumptions, see *op cit*, fn 9, Nardell, p 28. See, also, Daintith, T, 'Regulation by contract: the new prerogative' (1979) 32 CLP 41.

55 See, for instance, *per* Laws J, in *R v Somerset County Council ex p Fewings* [1995] 1 All ER 513, p 530.

56 See Dignan, J, 'Policy-making, local authorities and the courts: the "GLC Fares" case' (1983) 99 LQR 605, p 614, for discussion of *Gesellschaft* law.

57 See Clarke, J and Newman, J, *The Managerial State*, 1997, London: Sage; I also develop this analysis in more detail in *op cit*, fn 46, Cooper, ch 4.

contradictions are apparent in a range of municipal contexts, they proved, however, especially pronounced in the transactional withdrawal cases. What is particular about these cases is the way in which they force the courts to confront neo-liberal norms in tackling the relationship between local government and commercial activity. When, if ever, are contracts unfair? To what extent can economic actors use their economic strength to achieve results? Fundamentally, if local government is to function as a neo-liberal state, on what basis can restraints on its commercial activity be imposed?

SEPARATING SPHERES OF ACTION

These questions confront the divide between public and private activity – a division that has proven a central theme of much feminist analysis over the last 10 years.[58] Feminist work on the public/private has proven useful in understanding political hostility towards municipal policies which appear over-interventionist. For instance, opposition to lesbian and gay equality was partly framed in terms of people's 'right' to hold bigoted opinions without state intervention as well as the 'right' not to confront 'deviant' sexualities in the public domain.[59] However, while the defence of private opinion emerges in several of the cases discussed here, the emphasis on a single public/private divide does not explain opposition to transactional withdrawal more generally. In particular, it fails to explain why the cancellation of relations – the denial of the Other's 'face' – appeared to the courts to be so problematic.[60] It also does not explain the nature of boundaries, norms and interactions between multiple – as opposed to binary – social spheres.

To some extent then, I want to suggest, we can see judicial hostility to local government as tying up with the defence of social pluralism. Within a modernist, liberal imaginary which sees the world as divided into multiple, discrete fields and systems,[61] a just distribution of resources requires different allocative modes within different spheres. The distribution of resources within a family, for instance, is, and should be, based on entirely different principles to the distribution of welfare benefits by the state or the distribution of jobs

---

58 There is a vast feminist literature on the public/private divide, see O'Donovan, K, *Sexual Divisions in Law*, 1985, London: Weidenfeld and Nicolson; Lacey, N, 'Theory into practice? Pornography and the public/private dichotomy' (1993) 20 JLS 93; Thornton, M (ed), *Public and Private: Feminist Legal Debates*, 1995, Melbourne: OUP.

59 See Cooper, D, *Sexing the City: Lesbian and Gay Politics within the Activist State*, 1994, London: Rivers Oram, p 157.

60 Unless one argues that the courts adopted a pro-feminist perspective that opposed local government's refusal to recognise – and give public status to – certain 'private' actors. In other words, privacy – an absence of state recognition – becomes something imposed rather than chosen.

61 See, for instance, Walzer, M, 'Liberalism and the art of separation' (1984) 12 Political Theory 315.

within an economy. Local government's mistake in the cases discussed here was to cross these boundaries so that commercial decisions – lettings, procurement, licences, etc – became made on non-commercial grounds.[62] Considerations that might be valid in relation to twinning activities or 'political' action had gone and exceeded their narrow legitimate domain. How narrow this domain proved to be is evident in *Times Newspapers*, where Watkins LJ declared that even library selection and procurement – well within the realm of legitimate municipal action – would not be lawful when 'taken on purely political grounds'.[63]

The *Times Newspapers* case not only demonstrates politics out of control, it also involves a sullying of commerce. According to the court, industrial disputes should be settled according to good economic sense, not through external pressure. As Watkins LJ declared, 'the ban imposed ... was inspired by political views which moved the borough councils to interfere in an industrial dispute'.[64] As well as being unfair, such interference also precipitates, in the court's eyes, a distorted market outcome since resolution is contingent on an extraneous influence.

But should social spheres be treated as normatively discrete? Aside from romanticising the market as a mode of distributing resources (in those cases which focus on commercial parties' freedoms), a further problem lies in the assumption that fields have – empirically or ideally – an inner, single[65] rationality and purity that should remain undistorted.[66] In *Times Newspapers*, industrial relations and library selection were treated as having their own appropriate mode of operation. However, library decisions are innately ideological, in terms of what gets purchased or rejected.[67] In the case of newspaper markets and industrial relations, politics, including central government intervention, has always been evident. If there is, then, no clear division between different allocative spheres or systems – and if the courts know this – why do they act as if there is? One answer may be strategic. Fortifying domains as economic arenas, in the way that the courts have done, can be seen as rendering hegemonic an economic logic. The feminist writer, Nancy Fraser, argues this has two interconnected effects. First, it functions to

---

62   See, for instance, *R v Derbyshire County Council ex p Times Supplements Ltd and Others* (1990) 140 NLJ 1421.

63   *R v Ealing London Borough Council ex p Times Newspapers Ltd* (1986) 85 LGR 316, p 326.

64   *Ibid*, p 329.

65   See Gutmann, A, 'Justice across spheres', in Miller, D and Walzer, M (eds), *Pluralism, Justice and Equality*, 1995, Oxford: OUP, p 103.

66   See Rustin, M, 'Equality in post-modern times', in *ibid*, Miller and Walzer, p 31; *op cit*, fn 53, Oliver, p 566, where she argues that the market should be respected.

67   This rarely receives attention unless councils choose to remove previously accepted works from libraries, such as children's writer, Enid Blyton, on grounds of perpetuating racist/sexist stereotypes.

exclude certain matters from public debate; secondly, it disadvantages economically subordinate groupings.[68]

The judicial economising of municipal politics is a twofold strategy. It stops local government from crossing boundaries – making economic decisions on political grounds. In addition, and more significantly, it stops councils from demanding that other bodies – sports clubs, voluntary organisations, corporations – behave likewise. In *Shell*,[69] the demands placed by Lewisham Council upon the applicants are judicially spelled out in some detail. Not only did Lewisham ask Shell to ensure its subsidiaries withdrew from South Africa, but Shell was also required to publicly condemn apartheid. Through such a series of linkages, the courts imply, the virus of politics and ideology spreads through commercial decision making.[70]

Yet, there is a problem in explaining judicial behaviour in the maintenance of separate spheres. It does not marry with the courts' defence of private action on grounds of freedom of expression. In other words, the courts have not argued that firms should be allowed to do business where they wish for reasons of profit, but that actors within civil society, including corporations, should not be stopped from expressing – and pursuing – their own lawful opinions.[71] What the courts have constructed here is not an antagonism between public sector contracting and private commercial freedom, but a conflict between local government, straining against its bounded freedom to contract, and negative, corporate freedom of expression.[72] In the words of

---

68   Fraser, N, *Justice Interruptus*, 1997, New York: Routledge, p 88.

69   [1988] 1 All ER 938.

70   A form of contagion analogous to the sexualised or racialised Other exceeding their own domain; on this point, see, generally, Stoler, A, 'Sexual affronts and racial frontiers: national identity, "mixed bloods" and the cultural genealogies of Europeans in colonial Southeast Asia' (1992) 34 Comparative Studies in Society and History; Herman, D, *The Antigay Agenda: Orthodox Vision and the Christian Right*, 1997, Chicago, IL: Chicago UP, ch 2.

71   See *Verrall v Great Yarmouth Borough Council* [1981] 1 QB 202; *Webster v Southwark London Borough Council* [1983] 1 QB 698. However, in the apartheid cases, the courts only pursue this argument part way. In *Wheeler* [1985] 2 All ER 151, *per* Ackner LJ, p 153, *per* Browne-Wilkinson LJ, p 156, the Court of Appeal stressed the *reasonableness* of the Rugby Club's response. Sir George Waller also referred to the (legitimate) body of opinion which saw sporting links as a means of reducing segregation (p 160). Similarly, in *Shell* [1988] 1 All ER 938, the court drew attention to the fact that Shell did not defend apartheid, but simply questioned whether disinvestment was the best possible approach. In these two cases, then, the courts emphasised the different ways of opposing apartheid; local councils could not oblige individuals or organisations to choose their route.

72   To what extent do these cases concern freedom of expression? In *Wheeler* [1985] 2 All ER 151, p 160, Sir George Waller claimed the restriction was not on expression but on rugby players sporting in South Africa. However, the sanctions were not due to the English Rugby Football Union touring South Africa but because the Leicester Football Club failed to condemn the tour and discourage attendance (see Lord Roskill, in *Wheeler*, [1985] 2 All ER 1107, p 1110). Freedom of expression presumably includes the right not to express particular opinions. Other cases, involving National Front meetings, hunting and government training schemes, concern freedom of assembly and association, for both the applicant and council.

Browne-Wilkinson LJ in his dissenting judgment in *Wheeler*, it involved negotiating between 'the right of a democratically elected body to conduct its affairs in accordance with its own views and, on the other, the right to freedom of speech and conscience enjoyed by each individual in a democratic society'.[73]

If companies and sports clubs can legitimately express and act upon *political* beliefs, why, then, do the courts want to stop local government from acting similarly? I have already suggested that one important factor is local government's deployment of its commercial powers; however, linked to this is judicial hostility towards what appears to be municipal attempts to convert the private sector and civil society into ideological amplification for local government's own views. Lord Templeman makes this point in *Wheeler*, when he states, 'the laws of this country are not like the laws of Nazi Germany. A private individual or a private organisation cannot be obliged to display zeal in the pursuit of an object sought by a public authority and cannot be obliged to publish views dictated by a public authority'.[74]

Judicial fear of an expansionist municipal project is also given voice in *Liverpool City Council*.[75] Lloyd J there offered two illustrations of the repercussions facing groups who decided to participate in the Government's Employment Training Scheme (ETS) against the declared wishes of Liverpool Council. One concerned a training centre largely aimed at Liverpool's black communities. Having decided to participate in the ETS, the group was informed: 'the Sub-Committee instructs the Director of Education to withdraw all funding and to cease all co-operation from the start date of the Scheme.' The centre withdrew from participating. Lloyd J declared: 'We do not know the reason for this. But if it was wholly or in part due to the threat of withdrawal of funding, the coercion of the Council had proved effective.' The other project was a mobile library service for elderly people. 'When the association decided to participate in Employment Training, the Council demanded the return of some thousand books it had lent to the association.'[76]

In these cases, local government functions within the judicial imagination as a monstrous lifeform whose tentacles penetrate and feed upon civil society. In the above case, for instance, Lloyd J declared: 'The fact that the council has made alternative arrangements for providing a mobile library service is beside the point.' Yet, in a sense it is the point. For the council are replacing a voluntary organisation which refuses to comply with an administrative council structure that has no choice but obedience.[77] This point goes back to

---

73   [1985] 2 All ER 151, p 156; see, also, *op cit*, fn 10, Jowell and Lester, p 373.

74   *Wheeler v Leicester City Council* [1985] 2 All ER 1106, pp 1112–13.

75   (1988) 154 LGR 118.

76   *Ibid, per* Lloyd J.

77   See, also, *Brunyate and Another v ILEA* [1989] 2 All ER 417, esp p 421, where Lord Bridge of Harwich declared that allowing authorities to remove non-compliant governors on grounds of their non-compliance usurped the governors' independent function.

my earlier discussion of discipline. Within the first category of cases, in which councils seek to engineer compliance through contractual pressure rather than terminating relations, local government intensifies its disciplinary gaze to achieve submission.[78] However, where subservience proves impossible to generate, the courts suggest, opposition and independent voices are eliminated; local government then expands to fill the space civil society has vacated.

I explore this issue further in my final section in relation to the 'monstrous feminine'. Before doing so, however, I wish to consider a different question: what role has community played within the judicial critique of transactional withdrawal? Has it mitigated the courts' emphasis on negative freedom by introducing other values, such as connection, collective responsibility and social concern, or does it reinforce a judicial bias towards the liberal individual?

COMMUNITY

While the courts do not use the term community in these cases in any extensive way, conceptually, it underlies many of their judgments. It is also evoked more directly in other guises: as public, population, residents, local people, voters/electorate. To delve more deeply into the courts' portrayal of community, I want to draw also upon what might seem at first glance to be an opposing analysis. Feminist writing has explored community in ways that range from identifying it as the place where subjectivity is constructed to celebrating counter-cultural collectivities pursuing prefigurative, post-patriarchal norms, such as the separatist communities of Greenham Common Women's Peace Camp.[79] The three perspectives upon which I wish to focus here are: first, the equation of community with subordinated constituencies, such as women, gay men, and minority ethnic communities; secondly, radical democratic scholarship which positively identifies community as the place of public dialogue constituted according to shared norms of equality and freedom;[80] and thirdly, community as a hierarchical network of relations defined and organised by its exclusions.[81]

---

78 For use of a civil action to achieve similar effects, see *per* Lord Keith, in *Derbyshire County Council v Times Newspapers Ltd* [1993] 1 All ER 1011, pp 1017–18.

79 There is a vast feminist literature on community, see, eg, Young, I, 'The ideal of community and the politics of difference', in Nicholson, L (ed), *Feminism/Postmodernism*, 1990, London: Routledge; Frazer, E and Lacey, N, *The Politics of Community*, 1993, Hemel Hempstead: Harvester Wheatsheaf.

80 A key proponent of this approach is Chantal Mouffe: see Mouffe, C (ed), *Dimensions of Radical Democracy*, London: Verso, 1992; Mouffe, C, 'Feminism, citizenship and radical democratic politics', in Butler, J and Scott, J (eds), *Feminists Theorise the Political*, 1992, London: Routledge.

81 *Ibid*, Young.

These last two feminist approaches bear interesting similarities to Roger Cotterrell's work.[82] In recent writing, Cotterrell has explored community: first, as a 'freely chosen association between individuals and between social groups on the basis of values held in common'; and, secondly, as 'imperium'[83] – 'a vertical relationship of domination between a political authority ... and each subordinate person'.[84] Cotterrell uses these terms to think about the place of judicial review within wider social and political processes.[85] However, his framework is useful here in thinking about how the courts imagine the relationship between local government and its constituents.

Of Cotterrell's two models, associative community is the least prevalent within the judgments discussed in this chapter. Where it does exist, however, it takes one of two forms. The first – echoing more Habermasian feminist writing[86] – equates community with the discursive public sphere – a place of conversation and political debate. Within this approach, freedom of association and expression are valued for their contribution to the construction and maintenance of a thriving dialogic realm. This is particularly apparent in *Derbyshire*, where the court criticises the council for attempting to use civil litigation as a way of suppressing local opposition.[87]

The second version of associative community focuses on groups of people with shared interests, values or experiences, for instance Black/Asian communities in Lewisham and Leicester. Yet, while these collective interests are given some legitimacy, they run into conflict with the courts' other concern: individual freedom. How this tension is juridically balanced depends on the way the courts interpret the governing statutory framework. For instance, in *Shell*, the court held that Lewisham could decide lawfully to boycott a company trading in South Africa if it was done to pursue good race relations under the Race Relations Act 1976.[88] However, economic exclusion

---

82 Cotterrell, R, 'Judicial review and legal theory', in *op cit*, fn 10, Richardson and Genn.

83 For discussion of 'imperium' in a different context, see, also, *op cit*, fn 54, Daintith.

84 *Ibid*, Cotterrell, p 20; see, also, Cotterrell, R, 'A legal concept of community' (1997) 12 Canadian Journal of Law and Society 75.

85 See *ibid*, fn 82, Cotterrell, pp 24–34.

86 For a feminist approach to the discursive public sphere, see Fraser, N, *Justice Interruptus*, 1997, New York: Routledge, chs 3 and 4.

87 *Per* Lord Keith, in *Derbyshire County Council v Times Newspapers Ltd* [1993] 1 All ER 1011, p 1017: 'It is of the highest public importance that a democratically elected governmental body ... should be open to uninhibited public criticisms. The threat of a civil action for defamation must inevitably have an inhibiting effect on freedom of speech.'

88 *R v Lewisham London Borough Council ex p Shell* [1988] 1 All ER 938.

could not be undertaken in order to put economic pressure on the firm. In the case of *Shell*,[89] this additional motivation vitiated the decision as a whole.[90]

These two judicial models of community share common ground with the first two feminist frameworks outlined above. However, they also differ in key ways. First, while community *qua* public sphere reveals similarities with feminist radical democracy analysis, its depiction of key values diverges from a feminist emphasis on equality, deconstruction and social transformation. Instead, the courts, adopting a more conservative 'republican' position, identify the public sphere as the place of shared common sense knowledges, norms and values. While this may involve critique, it tends to be a critique of change rather than a critique of foundational liberal truths and norms. Yet, this republican approach is also not consistent. In other instances, the courts identify the public sphere as a normatively thin place in which different interests negotiate each other. Here, community is little more than a set of procedures and places that contain, facilitate and manage antagonism.

The second, substantial difference between feminist and judicial discourse relates to the balance between community interests and individual freedoms. While many radical pluralist feminists now place more value than previously on individual freedoms, there is a marked difference in determining what constitutes an unacceptable brake on such freedoms. For the court in *Shell*,[91] economic harm to commercial interests falls within this category. In contrast, feminist notions of harm might place more weight on the damage Shell caused by trading in South Africa than on the injury meted out to them. This is not to suggest that feminists agree on what constitutes harm. However, while there is disagreement on the seriousness, in particular, of linguistic or textual forms,[92] feminists have tended to equate harm with dominance, violence, poverty and marginalisation, rather than with challenges to traditional property/economic interests.

Cotterrell's second, imperium paradigm focuses on the relationship between state and constituency. Here, community refers to constituencies whose interests are jeopardised by local government action. In both the *Times Newspapers*[93] and *Fewings*[94] cases, the courts depict community as the victim of local government's inappropriate exercise of imperium. In the case of *Times Newspapers*,[95] the court declared that Ealing Council's decision to introduce a

---

89 *R v Lewisham London Borough Council ex p Shell* [1988] 1 All ER 938.

90 The difference between these two rationales – the one legal, the other not – seems slight. It suggests the courts construct as meaningful a distinction between a boycott for local symbolic reasons which is acceptable, and one which aims materially to impact upon a company and nation's economy which is not.

91 *R v Lewisham London Borough Council ex p Shell* [1988] 1 All ER 938.

92 Compare, for instance, MacKinnon, CA, *Only Words*, 1993, Cambridge, MA: Harvard UP with Butler, J, *Excitable Speech*, 1997, New York: Routledge.

93 (1986) 85 LGR 316.

94 *R v Somerset County Council ex p Fewings* [1995] 3 All ER 20.

95 (1986) 85 LGR 316.

boycott revealed how little attention they paid to local people. According to Watkins LJ, the council had 'readily and easily available a weapon which they proceeded wilfully to use regardless of the library requirements of the public which should have been, but was not then, their concern'.[96] Laws J expressed a similar view over Somerset's hunting ban. 'I consider it highly unlikely that ... Parliament intended to confer powers upon local authorities which would enable them, piecemeal, to impose upon local communities their individual perceptions of the ethics of the matter.'[97]

The portrayal of local government dominating subordinated communities ironically parallels feminist theories of the patriarchal state.[98] However, within the latter, the state is seen to condense – or function as an instrument of – male power and interests against women as a class. In contrast, within these cases, it is hard to identify any coherence in judicial depictions of local government's agenda. Councils seem simply intent on achieving control or power over their local community, a community that is, in many of the cases, similarly unmarked. Yet, as feminist work has demonstrated, this kind of unmarking or abstraction does not render the community an inclusive one. While the courts may believe they are concerned with common shared interests, the abstracted person they have in mind, as the *Times Newspapers*[99] case suggests, is someone with interests met through conventional library purchases (who is not offended by sexist or racist writing).

Thus, within judicial discourse, community is not only at odds with local government, but also at odds with politics/ideology. It is the political that diverts local government from its proper focus – that stops it from seeing. In this second, imperium model, political debate and controversy do not further, or function as an expression of, the public interest, but detract from it. For the public are identified as inherently apolitical, with no interest in the politics of library book selection, or in using local government more generally as an arena for the contestation, development or expression of shared norms.

To sum up this discussion of community, it seems that, to some degree, community did operate to mitigate the judicial attack on local government. This was particularly apparent in the South Africa related cases where the courts did recognise councils' need to pursue good race relations in the interests of local, multicultural populations. However, with this exception,

---

96 (1986) 85 LGR 316, p 332.

97 [1995] 1 All ER 513, p 530.

98 Kuhn, A and Wolpe, AM (eds), *Feminism and Materialism*, 1978, London: Routledge and Kegan Paul; Showstack Sassoon, A (ed), *Women and the State*, 1987, London: Hutchinson; Franzway, S *et al*, *Staking a Claim: Feminism, Bureaucracy and the State*, 1989, Cambridge: Polity; Watson, S, *Playing the State: Australian Feminist Interventions*, 1990, London: Verso; Brown, W, 'Finding the man in the state' (1992) 18 Feminist Studies 7; Cooper, D, *Power in Struggle: Feminism, Sexuality and the State*, 1995, Buckingham: OU Press; Jones, K, 'What is authority's gender?', in Hirschmann and Di Stefano, *op cit*, fn 47.

99 (1986) 85 LGR 316.

judicial talk about community largely functioned to deepen the attack on local government. Transactional withdrawal cases, for the most part, depict councils as undermining community:[100] restricting public dialogue and debate; disregarding the values and interests of local people; and, perhaps most heinously, granting to 'fake' constituencies the authority to determine local norms against 'real' community interests.[101]

MONSTROUS COUNCILS

We have seen how the courts' attack on local government focused on three issues: local government's misappropriation of the entitlement to punish; its attack on traditional freedoms in pursuit of partisan, political norms; and the domination of local communities and thwarting of civil society. In response to these offences, the courts saw themselves as having no alternative but to punish in return. The sanctions they imposed included, but also exceeded, formal remedies; for the well publicised character of many of the cases meant judicial review proffered a public spectacle of local government's subordination and humiliation. Unable to exceed narrowly defined statutory powers, local government was re-presented as a minor creature of statute. In particular, the use of specific performance and certiorari orders compelled local government to comply with pre-existing commitments and to undo 'irregular' changes. Through their actions, the courts infantalised, and thereby crushed, local state attempts to redetermine the nature, terms and parties to its relationships: local government would have to share its 'toys' and play with the 'friends' its judicial/judicious parents chose.

While the infant metaphor is instructive to understanding these cases, the analogy I wish to consider concerns that of the 'monstrous feminine'.[102] According to Rosi Braidotti:

Woman as a sign of difference is monstrous. If we define the monster as a bodily entity that is anomalous and deviant vis à vis the norm, then we can

---

100 Cotterrell's two conceptions of community meet in relation to exclusion. The exclusions the courts perceive local government as pursuing, and which they, in turn, are 'correcting', are not the exclusions identified within feminist theory – based on gender, race, class, sexuality and disability; here it is the liberal rightsholder who faces marginalisation or expulsion. Yet, to the extent that community is defined as a relation of imperium, is exclusion undesirable? One way of understanding the tension is to see the courts' imagining of community as threefold: (a) the socially/politically marginal who have taken control (or whose interests dominate local government's agenda); (b) the submissive majority; and (c) the expelled – fascists, hunters, animal exporters, and apartheid visitors – who comprise the judicial flagwavers of freedom.

101 This last is particularly vivid in *R v Coventry City Council ex p Phoenix Aviation and Others* [1995] 3 All ER 37.

102 See *op cit*, fn 17, Braidotti, p 81; and *op cit*, fn 17, Thomson, p 402. The 'monstrous feminine' intersects with the metaphor of childhood in several ways, including through the equation of women with immaturity, nature and excess.

argue that the female body shares with the monster the privilege of bringing out a unique blend of *fascination* and *horror*.[103]

Drawing on Braidotti, in an innovative analysis, Michael Thomson uses the metaphor of the 'monstrous feminine' to explore attitudes and discourses relating to women's reproduction outside of conventional heterosexual intercourse, within the context of the British Conservative Government's reproductive policy of the 1980s.[104] Here, the metaphor of women reproducing autonomously, in ways deemed both horrifying and (potentially) beyond male control, is an effective one. To what extent, though, can the 'monstrous feminine' illuminate the seemingly more remote terrain of judicial review?

So far, in this chapter, I have discussed the gendering of local government as a question of authority and role. The courts masculinised local government in their idealisation of a commercial paradigm,[105] while, at the same time, feminising councils by limiting their power.[106] Yet, as well as portraying local government as the lowly, administrative Other, following Parliament's statutory and normative lead – thus, as 'a figure of abjection'[107] – the courts also rendered councils monstrous in their inability to behave appropriately – transgressing and transcending established norms.[108]

Within judicial discourse, municipal impropriety took two primary forms. First, local government placed inappropriate demands upon others: what could be said; with whom they could associate. Within this paradigm of familial domesticisation, civil society constituted the infant membership governed over by an authoritarian municipal head.[109] Claiming to act on behalf of the entire household unit, the municipal head displaced the collective interest with a 'frolic of her own', denouncing the independent

---

103 *Op cit*, fn 17, Braidotti, p 81.

104 *Op cit*, fn 17, Thomson, p 401.

105 And, paradoxically, in their emphasis on political ideology – thanks to Sue Millns and Noel Whitty for this point.

106 Interpreting local government through gender metaphors, as I have done in this chapter, does not mean that men and women are intrinsically linked to particular gender characteristics. Rather, analysis of gender discourse highlights the parallels and articulations between the way men and women are socially constructed and perceived, and the way other phenomena – in this case, local government – are identified within dominant discourses. The social contingency of this approach is crucial; without it, this kind of analysis – particularly its articulation of feminine to devalued qualities – can work to reinforce rather than destabilise women's culturally subordinate status.

107 *Op cit*, fn 17, Braidotti, pp 81–82.

108 *Op cit*, fn 17, Braidotti, pp 81–83. See, also, *op cit*, fn 46, Cooper, ch 5.

109 The courts however portray local government in a way that parallels how they see local government as treating civil society – namely, as an irresponsible body that requires domestication. For instance, in *Webster v Southwark London Borough Council* [1983] 1 QB 698, Forbes J describes the council as having 'forfeited all rights to be regarded as a responsible authority' for ignoring the court's declaration that the National Front were entitled to a meeting hall.

expression of aberrant opinions by other members as acts of disloyalty and insubordination. One might argue that, in terms of gender, this constructs local government as an out of control patriarch. However, the 'monstrous *feminine*' is apparent in the judicial imagining of councils as unable to maintain ordered, consistent boundaries in the allocation of power, responsibilities, and autonomy.

Secondly, echoes of the 'monstrous feminine' are apparent in judicial depictions of local government as violating principles of proper punishment. Norms of appropriate conduct are explored by Kathleen Jones in her excellent paper on authority.[110] She argues that the 'sphere of justice is ... structured in opposition to the sphere of personal, intimate, caring relations'.[111] From a judicial perspective, local government has transgressed the division between the two by punishing according to feminised, domestic sphere norms. In contrast to liberal justice rhetoric with its celebration of impartiality, dispassionate objectivity, and rationality,[112] local government punitive action demonstrates, so the courts claim, insufficient detachment, due process, proportionality[113] and fairness. Within the judicial imagination, councils overreact; they act out of emotion and partisan feelings rather than reason. As Swinton Thomas LJ declared in *Fewings*, 'the [council] debate was in fact fuelled to a substantial extent by antipathy to the hunters as opposed to a perceived cruelty to the deer'.[114] This is the justice shown to the 'unfavoured child' – a justice that is marked as symbolically female and primitive. In other words, as too irrational[115] for the modern public realm.[116]

On this reading, local government's failing is to reconstitute public practice according to private, domestic norms.[117] While councils have been criticised more generally for imposing public, political values on private, commercial and normative practice, the attack also works in reverse. In other

---

110 Jones, K, 'What is authority's gender?', in *op cit*, fn 47, Hirschmann and Di Stefano.

111 *Ibid*, p 83.

112 See *op cit*, fn 50, Naffine.

113 See *op cit*, fn 30, Boyron.

114 [1995] 3 All ER 20, p 35.

115 See, for instance, *R v Ealing London Borough Council* (1986) 85 LGR 316, p 329, *per* Watkins LJ, who declares 'no rational local authority' would have imposed a ban. See, also, *Council of Civil Service Unions v Minister for Civil Service* [1985] AC 374, p 410, *per* Lord Diplock, where he defines irrationality as a decision 'so outrageous in its defiance of logic or of accepted moral standards that no sensible person who had applied his [sic] mind to the question to be decided could have arrived at it'.

116 For discussion generally on this point, see Hudson, B, *Understanding Justice*, 1996, Buckingham: OU Press, p 91.

117 If domestic norms are politically inappropriate, how does this relate to classical theories that see the state and public life as replicating familial and domestic relations on a macro-scale? Perhaps, these theories simply do not apply to modern, liberal societies. Alternately, it may depend on how the private is identified. Thus, the reproduction within state practice of patriarchal familial norms is more judicially acceptable than culturally-defined feminine ones.

words, local government is censured for bringing the *wrong* private norms into the public domain. In this sense, we can see the courts as juxtaposing two models of private activity: the affective, feminised practices of the domestic realm, and the controlled, disciplined, masculine environment of commercial organisations. Local government is supposed to resemble the latter. In the cases I have discussed, however, it comes too – dangerously – close to the former.

CONCLUSION

This chapter has explored judicial discourse in a series of cases concerning local government's deployment of 'private' transactional powers to achieve ideological, symbolic and ethical objectives. In doing so, my aim has been to analyse the courts' understanding of punishment, freedom and community to comprehend more fully their hostility to local government action in this area. My starting point was to destabilise the taken for granted assumption within judicial discourse and much public law scholarship that councils acted punitively in withdrawing contracts, licences or grants for political or moral reasons. At the same time, I asked: what power does the rhetoric of 'punishment' have in this context? In contrast to its usual role of delegitimising those subjected to it, here, the language of punishment functioned to invalidate its deployers.

But to say that the trope of punishment proved rhetorically effective does not alone explain the courts' desire to portray local government so negatively. In this chapter, I have explored four possible explanations: the courts' belief in negative freedoms and traditional civil society; their desire to maintain a boundary between spheres of activity, in particular, between economics and politics; opposition to local government using 'private' contractual techniques to achieve political, moral and ideological goals; and judicial reluctance to give much value to community concerns other than those revolving around the conservative, property owning male of law's imagination.

Identifying these rationale as underlying judicial decision making is not remarkable. What this chapter, however, has done is to show how these motivations were played out in a particular series of cases which have to date received little attention as a group. My other aim has been to explore the connections between judicial review and feminist theory. Given their subject matter, these cases were not obvious candidates for a feminist reading; nevertheless, this chapter explores some of the ways in which feminist theory can help elucidate them. It highlights parallels (and discrepancies) between judicial reasoning and feminist writing, as well the ways in which the courts' own analysis can be seen as gendered. Judicial images of local government, constituted around subordination and excess, bring to mind the 'monstrous feminine' – a metaphor of danger, transgression, inadequacy and fascination.

The final section of this chapter uses this metaphor to explore how the municipal body of the judicial imagination is the body of the domestic realm. I want to finish here with the suggestion that judicial horror does not only relate to the threat a radical, expansionist local government poses, infecting and destabilising other spheres of life. It also concerns the fear felt within contemporary 'masculinity' that an uncontrollable domestic realm will infect both body-politic and civil society with specifically 'feminised' norms and values.

BIBLIOGRAPHY

Abel, R, *Politics by Other Means: Law in the Struggle Against Apartheid 1980–1994*, 1995, London: Routledge.

Adjei, C, 'Human rights theory and the Bill of Rights debate' (1995) 58 MLR 17.

Alder, J, *Constitutional and Administrative Law*, 1994, London: Macmillan.

Alexy, R, 'Basic rights and democracy in Jürgen Habermas's procedural paradigm of law' (1994) 7 Ratio Juris 227.

Alibhai-Brown, Y, 'Nations under a groove' (1998) *Marxism Today*, Nov/Dec.

Aliotta, J, 'Justice O'Connor and the equal protection clause: a feminine voice?' (1995) 78 Judicature 232.

Allan, J, 'Bills of Rights and judicial power – a liberal's quandary' (1996) 16 OJLS 337.

Allan, T, 'Pragmatism and theory in public law' (1988) 104 LQR 422.

Allan, T, 'Racial harmony, public policy and freedom of speech' (1986) 49 MLR 121.

Allan, T, 'Rugby, recreation grounds and race relations: punishment for silence' (1985) 48 MLR 448.

Allan, T, *Law, Liberty and Justice: The Legal Foundation of British Constitutionalism*, 1993, Oxford: Clarendon.

Allison, J, 'Theoretical and institutional underpinnings of a separate administrative law', in Taggart, M (ed), *The Province of Administrative Law*, 1997, Oxford: Hart.

Allott, P, 'The crisis of European constitutionalism: reflections on the revolution in Europe' (1997) 34 CMLR 439.

Alston, P and Weiler, J, 'An "ever closer union" in need of a human rights policy: the European Union and human rights' (1999) Jean Monnet Papers (http://www.law.harvard.edu/Programs/JeanMonnet/).

Amnesty International, *Europe: The Need for Minimum Standards in Asylum Procedures*, June 1994.

Amnesty International, *Slamming the Door: The Demolition of the Right to Seek Asylum in the UK*, April 1996.

Amnesty International, *Cell Culture: The Detention and Imprisonment of Asylum-Seekers in the UK*, December 1996.

Anker, D, 'Rape in the community as a basis for asylum: the treatment of women refugees' claims to protection in Canada and the United States 1997: Part I' (1997) 12 Bender's Immigration Bulletin 476 .

Anker, D, Gilbert, L and Kelly, N, 'Women whose governments are unable or unwilling to provide reasonable protection from domestic violence may qualify as refugees under United States asylum law' (1997) 11 Georgetown Immigration LJ 709.

Armstrong, K and Bulmer, S, *The Governance of the Single Market*, 1998, Manchester: MUP.

Armstrong, K and Shaw, J (eds), 'Integrating law' (1998) 36 Journal of Common Market Studies (Special Edition).

Arriola, E, 'Sexual identity and the constitution: homosexual persons as discrete and insular minorities' (1992) 14 Women's Rights Law Reporter 263.

Arrowsmith, S, 'Judicial review and the contractual powers of public authorities' (1990) 106 LQR 277.

Assiter, A, *Enlightened Women*, 1996, London and New York: Routledge.

Atkins, S and Hogget, B, *Women and the Law*, 1984, Oxford: Blackwells.

Australian Department of Immigration and Multi-Cultural Affairs, Guidelines on Gender Issues for Decision-Makers, July 1996.

Bagehot, W, *The English Constitution*, 1963, London: Fontana.

Bakan, J, *Just Words: Constitutional Rights and Social Wrongs*, 1997, Toronto: Toronto UP.

Baldwin, R, *Rules and Government*, 1997, Oxford: Clarendon.

Barendt, E, 'Libel and freedom of speech in English law' [1993] PL 449.

Barnes, J, *England, England*, 1998, London: Jonathan Cape.

Barnett, A (ed), *Power and the Throne: The Monarchy Debate*, 1994, London: Vintage.

Barnett, H, *Constitutional and Administrative Law*, 2nd edn, 1998, London: Cavendish Publishing.

Barrett, M and Phillips, A (eds), *Destabilising Theory: Contemporary Feminist Debates*, 1992, Cambridge: Polity.

Barrett, M, *Women's Oppression Today: The Marxist/Feminist Encounter*, 1990, London: Verso.

Barron, A and Scott, C, 'The citizen's charter programme' (1992) 55 MLR 535.

Barron, CM and Sutton, AF (eds), *Medieval London Widows*, 1994, London: Hambledon.

Barry, B, *Political Argument*, 1964, London: Routledge and Kegan Paul.

Barton, JL, 'The story of marital rape' (1992) 108 LQR 260.

Basit, T, '"I want more freedom, but not too much": British Muslim girls and the dynamism of family values' (1997) 9 Gender and Education 425.

Baudrillard, J, *Symbolic Exchange And Death*, 1993, London: Sage.

Baudrillard, J, *Simulacra and Simulation*, 1994, Ann Arbor: Michigan UP.

Bean, D (ed), *Law Reform for All*, London: Blackstone.

Beaston, J, Forsyth, C and Hare, I (eds), *Constitutional Reform in the United Kingdom: Practice and Principles*, 1998, Oxford: Hart.

Bell, C, Buss, D, Mansell, W, Millns, S and Whitty, N, *Teaching Human Rights*, 1999, Warwick: National Centre for Legal Education.

Bell, V, *Interrogating Incest: Feminism, Foucault and the Law*, 1993, London: Routledge.

Benhabib, S, *Situating the Self: Gender, Community and Postmodernism in Contemporary Ethics*, 1992, Cambridge: Polity.

Benhabib, S, (ed), *Democracy and Difference: Contesting the Boundaries of the Political*, 1996, Princeton, NJ: Princeton UP.

Benhabib, S and Cornell, D (eds), *Feminism as Critique: Essays on the Politics of Gender in Late Capitalist Societies*, 1987, Cambridge: Polity.

Berlin, I, *Four Essays on Liberty*, 1969, New York: OUP.

Bernier, C, 'The IRB Guidelines on Women Refugee Claimants Fearing Gender-Related Persecution' (1997) International Journal of Refugee Law (Special Issue) 167.

Berry, D, 'Conflicts between minority women and traditional structures: international law, rights and culture' (1998) 7 SLS 55.

Beveridge, F and Mullally, S, 'International human rights and body politics', in Bridgeman, J and Millns, S (eds), *Law and Body Politics: Regulating the Female Body*, 1995, Aldershot: Dartmouth.

Beyleveld, D, 'The concept of a human right and incorporation of the European Convention on Human Rights' [1995] PL 577.

Bhabha, J and Shutter, S, *Women's Movement. Women Under Immigration, Nationality and Refugee Law*, 1994, Stoke-on-Trent: Trentham.

Bingham, TH, 'The European Convention on Human Rights: time to incorporate' (1993) 109 LQR 390.

Birkinshaw, P, *Freedom of Information: The Law, the Practice and the Ideal*, 2nd edn, 1996, London: Butterworths.

Black, A, *Guilds and Civil Society in European Political Thought from the Twelfth Century to the Present*, 1984, London: Methuen.

Black, J, 'Regulation as facilitation: negotiating the genetic revolution' (1998) 61 MLR 621.

Black, J, *Rules and Regulators*, 1997, Oxford: Clarendon.

Blackburn, R (ed), *Rights of Citizenship*, 1993, London: Mansell.

Bock, G and James, S (eds), *Beyond Equality and Difference*, 1992, London: Routledge.

Boddy, M, and Fudge, C (eds), *Local Socialism?*, 1984, London: Macmillan.

Bogart, W, *Courts and Country: The Limits of Litigation and the Political and Social Life of Canada*, 1994, Toronto: OUP.

Bogdanor, V, *The Monarchy and the Constitution* 1995, Oxford: OUP.

Borrie, G, 'The regulation of public and private power' [1989] PL 552.

Bottomley, A (ed), *Feminist Perspectives on the Foundational Subjects of Law*, 1996, London: Cavendish Publishing.

Bottomley, A and Conaghan, J (eds), *Feminist Theory and Legal Strategy*, 1993, Oxford: Blackwells.

Bowlby, R, 'Flight reservations' (1998) Oxford Literary Review 61.

Boyron, S, 'Proportionality in English administrative law: a faulty translation?' (1992) 12 OJLS 237.

Bradley, AW and Ewing, KD, *Constitutional and Administrative Law*, 1997, 12th edn, Harlow: Longman.

Braidotti, R, *Nomadic Subjects*, 1994, New York: Columbia UP.

Breitenbach, E, Brown, A and Myers, F, 'Understanding women in Scotland' (1998) 58 Feminist Review 44.

Bridgeman, J, 'Skeletal frames and labouring women: the impact of the female body upon medical treatment decision-making' (conference paper), *Gender, Sexuality and Law: Reflections; New Directions*, International Conference, Keele University, 19–21 June 1998.

Bridgeman, J and Millns, S, *Law and Body Politics: Regulating the Female Body*, 1995, Aldershot: Dartmouth.

Bridgeman, J and Millns, S, *Feminist Perspectives on Law: Law's Engagement with the Female Body*, 1998, London: Sweet & Maxwell.

Brooks, A, *Postmodernisms: Feminism, Cultural Theory and Cultural Forms*, 1997, London: Routledge.

Brophy, J and Smart, C (eds), *Women in Law: Explorations in Law, Family and Sexuality*, 1985, London: Routledge and Kegan Paul.

Brown, W, 'Finding the man in the state' (1992) 18 Feminist Studies 7.

Brown, W, *States of Inquiry: Power and Freedom in Late Modernity*, 1995, Princeton, NJ: Princeton UP.

Brownmiller, S, *Against Our Will: Men, Women and Rape*, 1975, New York: Simon and Schuster.

Bulbeck, C, '"His and hers Australias": national genders' (1996) 47 Journal of Australian Studies 43.

Bunch, C, 'Women's rights as human rights: toward a re-vision of human rights' (1990) 12 HRQ 486.

Buss, DE, 'Women at the borders: rape and nationalism in international law' (1998) 6 FLS 171.

Butler, J, *Gender Trouble*, 1990, New York: Routledge.

Butler, J, *Bodies that Matter*, 1993, New York: Routledge.

Butler, J, *Excitable Speech*, 1997, New York: Routledge.

Butler, J and Scott, J (eds), *Feminists Theorize the Political*, 1992, New York: Routledge.

Cameron, D, 'A gilded cage' (1997–98) Trouble & Strife, Winter, p 70.

Campbell, B, *Diana Princess of Wales: How Sexual Politics Shook the Monarchy*, 1998, London: The Women's Press.

Campbell, T (ed), *Law and Enlightenment in Britain*, 1990, Aberdeen: Aberdeen UP.

Canadian Immigration and Refugee Board, Guidelines on Women Refugee Claimants Fearing Gender-Related Persecution, 9 March 1993 (updated November 1996).

Carter, S and Kinloch, I, 'Local authorities and moral judgments' (1994) 144 NLJ 1474.

Castel, JR, 'Rape, sexual assault and the meaning of persecution' (1992) 4 International Journal of Refugee Law 39.

Chambers, S, *Reasonable Democracy: Jürgen Habermas and the Politics of Discourse*, 1996, London: Cornell UP.

Charlesworth, H, Chinkin, C and Wright, S, 'Feminist approaches to international law' (1991) 85 AJIL 613.

Clapham, C, *Human Rights in the Private Sphere*, 1993, Oxford: OUP.

Clark, T, 'Human rights and expulsion: giving content to the concept of expulsion' (1989) 1 International Journal of Refugee Law 155.

Clarke, J and Newman, J, *The Managerial State*, 1997, London: Sage.

Clements, L and Young, J (eds), 'Human rights: changing the culture' (1999) 26 JLS (Special Edition).

Cole, GDH, *Social Theory*, 1920, London: Methuen.

Coliver, S (ed), *The Right to Know: Human Rights and Access to Reproductive Health Information*, 1995, Pennsylvania, NJ: Pennsylvania UP.

Colley, L, *Britons: Forging the Nation 1707–1837*, 1992, London: Yale UP.

Collier, R, *Masculinity, Law and the Family*, 1995, London: Routledge.

Colombo, S, 'The legal battle for the city: anti-pornography municipal ordinances and radical feminism' (1994) 2 FLS 29.

Conaghan, J, 'Gendered harms and the law of tort: remedying (sexual) harassment' (1996) 16 OJLS 407.

Conaghan, J, 'Tort litigation in the context of intra-familial abuse' (1998) 61 MLR 132.

Connolly, W, 'Modern authority and ambiguity', 1984, Amherst: University of Massachusetts, unpublished manuscript.

Cooke, M, *Language and Reason: A Study of Habermas's Pragmatics*, 1994, London: MIT.

Cooper, D, 'The citizen's charter and radical democracy: empowerment and exclusion within citizenship discourse' (1993) 2 SLS 149.

Cooper, D, *Sexing the City: Lesbian and Gay Politics within the Activist State*, 1994, London: Rivers Oram.

Cooper, D, *Power in Struggle: Feminism, Sexuality and the State*, 1995, Buckingham: OU Press.

Cooper, D, *Governing Out of Order: Space, Law and the Political Belonging*, 1998, London: Rivers Oram.

Cooper, D, 'Regard between strangers: diversity, equality and the reconstruction of public space' (1998) 18 CSP 465.

Cornell, D, *Beyond Accommodation*, 1991, London: Routledge.

Cornell, D, *The Philosophy of the Limit*, 1992, London: Routledge.

Cotterrell, R, 'Must legal ideas be interpreted sociologically?' (1998) 25 JLS 171.

Cotterrell, R, 'A legal concept of community' (1997) 12 Canadian Journal of Law and Society 75.

Cotterrell, R, *Law's Community: Legal Theory in Sociological Perspective*, 1995, Oxford: Clarendon.

Cowley, P, 'Daleks? Labour's rebels are alive and kicking' (1999) Parliamentary Brief, March, p 48.

Craig, P, *Public Law and Democracy in the United Kingdom and the United States of America*, 1990, Oxford: Clarendon.

Craig, P, 'Sovereignty of the United Kingdom Parliament after *Factortame*' (1991) 11 YBEL 221.

Cram, I, 'Public authorities, political protest and judicial review' 1995 24 SLT 213.

Crawley, H, *Women as Asylum Seekers: A Legal Handbook*, 1997, London: ILPA and Refugee Action.

Crick, B, 'Essay on Britishness' (1993) 2 Scottish Affairs 71.

Daintith, T, 'Regulation by contract: the new prerogative' (1979) 32 CLP 41.

Dalton, H, 'The clouded prism' (1987) 22 Harvard Civil-Rights Civil-Liberties L Rev 435.

Davies, M, *Asking the Law Question*, 1994, Sydney: Law Book.

Davies, M, *Delimiting the Law*, 1996, London: Pluto.

De Beauvoir, S, *The Second Sex*, 1953, Parshley, HM (trans), London: Penguin.

De Smith, S and Brazier, R, *Constitutional and Administrative Law*, 1994, London: Penguin.

De Sousa Santos, B, *Toward a New Common Sense: Law, Science and Politics in the Paradigmatic Transition*, 1995, London: Routledge.

Dean, J (ed), *Feminism and the New Democracy*, 1997, London: Sage.

Deflem, M (ed), *Habermas, Modernity and Law*, 1996, London: Sage.

Derrida, J, *The Other Heading, Reflections on Today's Europe*, 1992, Bloomington and Indianapolis: Indiana UP.

Detmold, M, 'Provocation to murder: sovereignty and multiculture' (1997) 19 Sydney L Rev 5.

Dewey, J, *Liberalism and Social Action*, 1935, New York: GP Putnam.

Dewey, J, *Reconstruction in Philosophy*, 1957, Boston: Beacon.

Dews, P, *Logics of Disintegration: Post-Structuralist Thought and the Claims of Critical Theory*, 1987, London: Verso.

Diamond, I and Quinby, L, *Feminism and Foucault: Reflections on Resistance*, 1988, Boston, MA: Northeastern UP.

Dicey, AV, *An Introduction to the Study of the Law of the Constitution*, 10th edn, 1967, London: MacMillan.

Dicey, *Law and Public Opinion,* 2nd edn, 1963, London: Macmillan.

Dietz, M, 'Citizenship with a feminist face: the problem with maternal thinking' (1985) 12 Political Theory 19

Dignan, J, 'Policy-making, local authorities and the courts: the "GLC Fares" case' (1983) 99 LQR 605.

Dixon, D, *Law in Policing: Legal Regulation and Police Practices,* 1997, Oxford: Clarendon.

Dore, E (ed), *Gender Politics in Latin America,* 1997, New York: Monthly Review.

Doyle, T, 'The conservative mythology of monarchy: impacts upon Australian Republicanism' (1993) 28 Australian Journal of Political Science 121.

Duncan, S, '"Disrupting the surface of order and innoncence": towards a theory of sexuality and the law' (1994) 2 FLS 3.

Duxbury, N, *Patterns of American Jurisprudence,* 1995, Oxford: Clarendon.

Dworkin, R, *Taking Rights Seriously,* 1977, Mass, MA: Harvard UP.

Dyzenhaus, D, 'The legitimacy of legality' (1997) XLVI Toronto ULJ 129.

Dyzenhaus, D, *Legality and Legitimacy: Carl Schmitt, Hans Kelsen and Hermann Heller in Weimar,* 1997, Oxford: Clarendon.

Easton, SM, *The Problem of Pornography: Regulation and the Right to Free Speech,* 1994, London: Routledge.

Edelman, B, 'La dignité de la personne humaine, un concept nouveau' (1997) Dalloz, chron, p 185.

Edge, S, "Women are trouble, did you know that Fergus?": Neil Jordan's *The Crying Game'* (1995) 50 Feminist Review 173.

Eisenstein, Z, *The Radical Future of Liberal Democracy,* 1986, Boston: Northwestern UP.

Erler, M and Kowaleski, M (eds), *Women and Power in the Middle Ages,* 1988, Athens: Georgia UP.

Ewing, K, 'The Human Rights Act and parliamentary democracy' (1999) 62 MLR 79.

Ewing, K and Gearty, C, 'Terminating abortion rights?' (1992) NLJ 1696.

Feldman, D, 'Public law values in the House of Lords' (1990) 106 LQR 246.

Feldman, D, *Civil Liberties and Human Rights in England and Wales,* 1993, Oxford: Clarendon.

Feldman, D, 'Secrecy, dignity, or autonomy? Views of privacy as a civil liberty' (1994) 47 CLP 41.

Ferguson, K, *The Feminist Case Against Bureaucracy*, 1984, Philadelphia: Temple UP.

Feria, M, 'Commentaries on the Social Security Persons from Abroad (Miscellaneous Amendments) Regulations 1996' (1996) 10 Immigration and Nationality Law and Practice 91.

Figgis, JN, *Churches in the Modern State*, 1913, London: Longman.

Fineman, MA, and Thomadsen, NS (eds) *At the Boundaries of Law: Feminism and Legal Theory*, 1991, New York: Routledge.

Fitzpatrick, J, 'Revitalising the 1951 Convention' (1996) 9 Harvard Human Rights Journal 228.

Fitzpatrick, P, *The Mythology of Modern Law*, 1992, London: Routledge,.

Fitzpatrick, P (ed), *Nationalism, Racism and the Rule of Law*, 1995, Aldershot: Darmouth.

Foster, R, *Modern Ireland: 1600–1972*, 1988, London: Penguin.

Foster, R, *Paddy and Mr Punch: Connections in Irish and English History*, 1993, London: Penguin.

Foucault, M, *Discipline and Punish: The Birth of the Prison*, 1979, New York: Vintage.

Foucault, M, *Power/Knowledge: Selected Interviews and Other Writings, 1972–1977*, Gordon, C (ed), 1980, New York: Pantheon.

Foucault, M, *The History of Sexuality:Volume 1*, 1990, London: Penguin.

Fout, J and Tantillo, MS (eds), *American Sexual Politics: Sex, Gender and Race since the Civil War*, 1993, Chicago, IL: Chicago UP.

Frank, L and Smith, P (eds), *Madonnarama: Essays on Sex and Popular Culture*, 1993, Pittsburgh, PA: Cleis.

Franzway, S, Court, D and Connell, RW, *Staking a Claim: Feminism, Bureaucracy and the State*, 1989, Cambridge: Polity.

Fraser, N, *Justice Interruptus: Critical Reflections on the 'Postsocialist Condition'*, 1997, London: Routledge.

Fraser, N, 'What's critical about critical theory?', in Meehan, J (ed), *Feminists Read Habermas: Gendering the Subject of Discourse*, 1995, London: Routledge.

Fraser, N, *Unruly Practices: Power, Discourse and Gender in Contemporary Social Theory*, 1989, London: Polity.

Frazer, E, and Lacey, N, *The Politics of Community: A Feminist Critique of the Liberal-Communitarian Debate*, 1993, Hemel Hempstead: Harvester Wheatsheaf.

Fredman, S and Morris, G, 'The costs of exclusivity: public and private re-examined' [1994] PL 69.

Freeman, MDA and Halson, R (eds), *Current Legal Problems 48*, 1995, Oxford: OUP.

Freye, J, 'Women litigators in search of a care-orientated judicial system' (1995) 4 Journal of Gender and the Law 199.

Frug, MJ, 'A postmodern feminist legal manifesto (an unfinished draft)' (1992) 105 Harv L Rev 1045.

Fudge, J, 'Evaluation rights litigation as a form of transformative politics' (1992) 7 Canadian Journal of Law and Society 153.

Fukuyama, F, *The End of History and the Last Man*, 1992, New York: The Free Press.

Galligan, DJ (ed), *A Reader on Administrative Law*, 1996, Oxford: OUP.

Galligan, DJ, *Due Process and Fair Procedures: A Study of Administrative Procedures*, 1997, Oxford: Clarendon.

Gibson, S, 'The discourse of sex/war: thoughts on Catharine MacKinnon's 1993 Oxford Amnesty Lecture' (1993) 1 FLS 179.

Giddens, A, *The Transformation of Intimacy*, 1992, Cambridge: Polity.

Gilligan, C, *In a Different Voice*, 1982, Cambridge, MA: Harvard UP.

Gilroy, R, *There Ain't No Black in the Union Jack: The Cultural Politics of Race and Nation*, 1987, London: Hutchinson.

Ginsburg, R, 'Remarks for California women lawyers' (1994) 22 Pepperdine L Rev 1.

Ginsburg, R and Brill, L, 'Women in the Federal judiciary' (1995) 64 Fordham L Rev 281.

Goetz, AM, 'No more heroes? Feminism and the state in Australia' (1994) Social Politics 341.

Goodrich, P, *Languages of Law: From Logics of Memory to Nomadic Masks*, 1990, London: Weidenfeld and Nicolson.

Goodrich, P, *Oedipus Lex*, 1995, Berkeley: California UP.

Goodrich, P, *Law in the Courts of Love*, 1996, London: Routledge.

Goodwin-Gill, G, *The Refugee in International Law*, 1996, 2nd edn, Oxford: Clarendon.

Graham, C and Prosser, T, *Privatising Public Enterprises: Constitutions, The State and Regulation in Comparative Perspective*, 1991, Oxford: Clarendon.

Graycar, R and Morgan, J, *The Hidden Gender of Law*, 1990, Annandale, NSW: Federation.

Greatbatch, J, 'The gender difference: feminist critiques of refugee discourse' (1989) 1 International Journal of Refugee Law 518.

Griffith, JAG, 'The political constitution' (1979) 42 MLR 1.

Griffith, JAG, *The Politics of the Judiciary*, 1997, London: Fontana.

Guinier, L, 'Of gentlemen and role models' (1990–91) 6 Berkeley Women's LJ 93.

Gyford, J, *The Politics of Local Socialism*, 1985, London: Allen & Unwin.

Habermas, J, *The Philosophical Discourse of Modernity*, 1987, Cambridge: Polity.

Habermas, J, *Moral Consciousness and Communicative Action*, 1990, Cambridge: Polity.

Habermas, J, *The Structural Transformation of the Public Sphere* 1989, London: Polity.

Habermas, J, *Between Facts and Norms: Contributions to a Discourse Theory of Law and Democracy*, 1996, Cambridge: Polity.

Hague, W, 'Identity and the British way', 1999, London: Conservative Party Headquarters (http://www.conservative.org.uk).

Hames, T and Leonard, M, *Modernising the Monarchy*, 1998, London: Demos.

Hansard Society, *Women at the Top*, 1989, London: Hansard Society.

Harden, I, *The Contracting State*, 1992, Buckingham: OU Press.

Harden, I, 'The constitution of the European Union' [1995] PL 609.

Harden, I and Lewis, N, *The Noble Lie: The British Constitution and the Rule of Law*, 1986, London: Hutchinson.

Harlow, C and Rawlings, R, *Law and Administration*, 1997, 2nd edn, London: Butterworths.

Harlow, C, 'Changing the Mindset: the place of theory in English administrative law' (1994) 14 OJLS 419.

Harlow, C, 'Back to basics: reinventing administrative law' [1997] PL 245.

Harrington, M, *Women Lawyers – Rewriting the Rules*, 1993, London: Plume-Penguin.

Harris, A, 'Race and essentialism in feminist legal theory' (1990) 42 Stan LR 581.

Harris, B, 'The "third" source of authority' (1992) 109 LQR 626.

Harris, D, O'Boyle, M and Warbrick, C, *Law of the European Convention on Human Rights*, 1995, London: Butterworths.

Harvey, C, 'The right to seek asylum in the UK and "safe countries" [1996] PL 196.

Harvey, C, 'Expulsion, national security and the European Convention' (1997) 22 EL Rev 626.

Harvey, C, 'Restructuring asylum: recent trends in UK Law and policy' (1997) 9 International Journal of Refugee Law 60.

Harvey, C, 'The procedural paradigm of law and democracy' [1997] PL 692.

Harvey, C, 'Mainstreaming gender in the refugee protection process' (1999) 149 NLJ 534.

Hathaway, JC, *The Law of Refugee Status*, 1991, Toronto: Butterworths.

Hayes, J, 'Appointment by invitation' (1997) 147 NLJ 520.

Hegel, GWF, *Philosophy Of Right*, Knox, TM (trans), 1967, Oxford: OUP.

Hegel, GWF, 'The difference between Greek imagination and positive Christian religion', in *Early Theological Writings*, Knox, TM (trans), 1971, Philadelphia: Pennsylvania.

Held, D, *Democracy and the Global Order: From the Modern State to Cosmopolitan Governance*, 1995, Cambridge: Polity.

Held, D, 'Globalisation: the timid tendency' (1998) *Marxism Today*, Nov/Dec.

Herman, D, 'Beyond the rights debate' (1993) 2 SLS 25.

Herman, D, 'The Good, the bad, and the smugly: sexual orientation and perspectives on the charter' (1994) 14 OJLS 589.

Herman, D, *Rights of Passage: Struggles for Lesbian and Gay Equality*, 1994, Toronto: Toronto UP.

Herman, D, *The Antigay Agenda: Orthodox Vision and the Christian Right*, 1997, Chicago, IL: Chicago UP.

Herman, D and Cooper, D, 'Anarchic Armadas, Brussels Bureaucrats and the valiant maple leaf: sexuality, governance and the construction of British nationhood through the Canada-Spain Fish War' (1997) 17 LS 415.

Hervey, TK and O'Keeffe, D (eds), *Sex Equality in the European Union*, 1996, Chichester: John Wiley.

Hervey, TK, 'Buy baby: the European Union and regulation of human reproduction' (1998) 18 OJLS 207.

Heuston, R, *Essays in Constitutional Law*, 1964, London: Stevens.

Hewson, B, 'You've a long way to go, baby' (1996) 146 NLJ 565.

Hewson, R, 'New definitions, new directions', *Re-Inventing Britain Conference*, 1997, London: The British Council.

Hindess, B, 'Divide and rule: the international character of modern citizenship' (1998) 1(1) EJST 57.

Hinshelwood, G, 'Interviewing female asylum-seekers' (1997) International Journal of Refugee Law (Special Issue) 159.

Hirchsmann, NJ and Di Stefano, C (eds), *Revisioning the Political: Feminist Reconstructions of Traditional Concepts in Western Political Theory*, 1996, Boulder, CO: Westview.

Hitchens, C, *The Monarchy*, 1990, London: Chatto & Windus.

Honneth, A, 'The Other of justice: Habermas and the ethical challenge of postmodernism', in White, S (ed), *The Recent Work of Jürgen Habermas: Reason Justice and Modernity*, 1988, Cambridge: CUP.

Hood Phillips, O and Jackson, P, *Constitutional and Administrative Law*, 1987, 7th edn, London: Sweet & Maxwell.

Hudson, B, *Understanding Justice*, 1996, Buckingham: OU Press.

Hughes, S, *The Circuit Bench – A Woman's Place?*, 1991, London: The Law Society.

Humm, M, *Feminisms: A Reader*, 1992, Hemel Hempstead: Harvester Wheatsheaf.

Hunt, A, 'Foucault's expulsion of law: towards a retrieval' (1992) 17 Law and Social Inquiry 1.

Hunt, A and Wickham, G, *Foucault and Law: Towards a Sociology of Law as Governance*, 1994, London: Pluto.

Hunt, M, *Using Human Rights Law in English Courts*, 1997, Oxford: Hart.

Hunt, M, 'The "horizontal effect" of the Human Rights Act' [1998] PL 423.

Hutchinson, AC and Green, LJM (eds), *Law and the Community: The End of Individualism?*, 1989, Toronto: Carswell.

Hutton, W, 'Britain is changing' (1998) The Observer, 30 August.

Hyppolite, J, *Genesis and Structure of Hegel's Phenomenology of Spirit*, Cherniak, Sand Heckman, J (trans), 1974, Evanston: Northwestern UP.

Indra, D, *Engendering Forced Migration: Theory and Practice*, 1998, New York: Berghahn.

Institute for Public Policy Research, *The Constitution of the United Kingdom*, 1991, London: IPPR.

Institute for Public Policy Research, *A British Bill of Rights*, 1996, London: IPPR.

Irigaray, L, *Je, tu, nous*, 1996, London: Routledge.

Irvine, D, 'The development of human rights in Britain under an incorporated convention on human rights' [1998] PL 221.

Irving, H, 'The republic is a feminist issue' (1996) 52 FR 87.

Jackson, E, 'Catharine MacKinnon and feminist jurisprudence: a critical reappraisal'(1993) 19 JLS 195.

Jackson, E, 'The problem with pornography: a critical survey of the current debate' (1995) 3 FLS 49.

Jacob, J, *The Republican Crown: Lawyers and the Making of the State in Twentieth Century Britain*, 1996, Aldershot: Dartmouth.

Jacobson, J, 'Perceptions of Britishness' (1997) 3 Nations and Nationalism 181.

Jacques, M, 'Good to be back' (1998) *Marxism Today*, Nov/Dec.

Jagger, A, *Feminist Politics and Human Nature*, 1988, New Jersey: Rowan and Littlefield.

Janis, M, Kay, R and Bradley, A, *European Human Rights Law: Text and Materials*, 1995, Oxford: OUP.

Jennings, I, *The British Constitution*, 1966, 5th edn, Cambridge: CUP.

Johnson, C, 'Negotiating the politics of inclusion: women and Labor governments 1983–95' (1996) 53 Feminist Review 102.

Johnsson, AB, 'The international protection of women refugees' (1989) 1 International Journal of Refugee Law 221.

Jowell, J and Oliver, D (eds), *The Changing Constitution*, 3rd edn, 1994, Oxford: Clarendon.

Jowell, J and Lester, A, 'Beyond *Wednesbury*: substantive principles of administrative law' [1987] PL 368.

Juss, S, *Discretion and Deviation in the Administration of Immigration Control*, 1997, London: Sweet & Maxwell.

Justice, *The Judiciary in England and Wales*, 1992, London: Justice.

Kant, I, *Critique of Pure Reason*, Smith, NK (trans), 1929, London: Macmillan.

Kantorowicz, E, *The King's Two Bodies: A Study in Medieval Political Theory*, 1957, Princeton, NJ: Princeton UP.

Karvonen, L and Selle, P, *Women in Nordic Politics: Closing the Gap*, 1995, Aldershot: Dartmouth.

Keller, P, 'Rethinking ethical and cultural rights in Europe' (1998) 18 OJLS 29.

Kelley, K, *The Royals*, 1997, New York: Time Warner.

Kelly, DR, *The Human Measure*, 1990, Cambridg, MA: Harvard UP.

Kelly, L, 'Including others' (1997–98) Trouble & Strife, Winter, p 68.

Kemp, S and Squires, J, *Feminisms*, 1997, Oxford: OUP.

Kennedy, H, *Eve was Framed*, 1992, London: Chatto & Windus.

Kiberd, D, *Inventing Ireland: The Literature of the Modern Nation*, 1995, London: Jonathan Cape.

Kingdom, E, 'Feminism and political priorities', Working Paper No 10, in Department of Politics, *The Transition to Socialism*, 1982, Liverpool: University of Liverpool.

Kingdom, E, 'Legal recognition of a woman's right to choose', in Brophy, J and Smart, C (eds), *Women in Law: Explorations in Law, Family and Sexuality*, 1985, London: Routledge and Kegan Paul.

Kingdom, E, *What's Wrong with Rights? Problems for Feminist Politics of Law*, 1991, Edinburgh: Edinburgh UP.

Kingdom, E, 'Transforming rights: feminist political heuristics' (1996) II Res Publica 73.

Kingdom, J, *Government and Politics in Britain*, 1991, Cambridge: Polity.

Klapisch-Zuber, C (ed), *A History of Women*, 1992, Cambridge, MA: Belknap.

Klug, F and Starmer, K, 'Incorporation through the back door?' [1997] PL 223.

Knights, E, 'The women's point of view', Working Paper No 2, in Feminist Legal Research Unit (University of Liverpool), *'For Richer or Poorer?' Feminist Perspectives on Women and the Distribution of Wealth*, 1995, Liverpool: University of Liverpool.

KPMG Peat Marwick, *Review of Asylum Appeals Procedure*, 1994, London: Home Office/Lord Chancellor's Department.

Kristeva, J, 'Women's time', in Moi, T (ed), *The Kristeva Reader*, 1986, Oxford: Basil Blackwell.

Kuhn, A and Wolpe, AM (eds), *Feminism and Materialism*, 1978, London: Rouleldge and Kegan Paul.

Kymlicka, W, *Multicultural Citizenship*, 1996, Oxford: OUP.

Labour Research, 'Judging from on high' (1997) 86(7) Labour Research 13.

Lacey, N, 'From individual to group', in Hepple, B and Szyszcak, E (eds), *Discrimination: The Limits of Law*, 1992, London: Mansell.

Lacey, N, 'Theory into practice? Pornography and the public/private dichotomy', in Bottomley, A and Conaghan, J (eds), *Feminist Theory and Legal Strategy*, 1993, Oxford: Basil Blackwell.

Lacey, N, 'Normative reconstruction in socio-legal theory' (1996) 5 SLS 131.

Lacey, N, *Unspeakable Subjects: Feminist Essays in Legal and Social Theory*, 1998, Oxford: Hart.

Lacey, N, 'Feminist perspectives on ethical positivism', in Campbell, T (ed), *Reorienting Legal Positivism*, 1999, Aldershot: Dartmouth.

Lacey, N, and Wells, C, *Reconstructing Criminal Law*, 1998, London: Butterworths.

Lardy, H, 'Citizenship and the right to vote' (1997) 17 OJLS 75.

Laski, HJ, *The Foundations of Sovereignty and other Essays*, 1921, London: Allen & Unwin.

Laws, J, 'Is the High Court the guardian of fundamental constitutional rights?' [1993] PL 59.

Le Sueur, A and Sunkin, M, *Public Law*, 1997, London: Longman.

Lee, J, *Ireland 1912–1985*, 1989, Cambridge: CUP.

Lees, S, *Ruling Passions: Sexual Violence, Reputation and the Law*, 1997, Buckingham: OU Press.

Leonard, M, *Britain, TM: Renewing Our Identity*, 1998, London: Demos.

Lester, A, 'Fundamental rights: the United Kingdom isolated' [1984] PL 46.

Lewis, JL, *Mary Queen of Scots: Romance and Nation*, 1998, London: Routledge.

Lewis, N, 'Public law and legal theory', in Twining, W (ed), *Legal Theory and Common Law*, 1986, Oxford: Basil Blackwell.

Lewis, N, *Choice and the Legal Order: Rising Above Politics*, 1996, London: Butterworths.

Leyland, P and Woods, T (eds), *Administrative Law Facing the Future: Old Constraints and New Horizons*, 1997, London: Blackstone.

Liberty, *A People's Charter: Liberty's Bill of Rights*, 1991, London: Liberty.

Lister, R, 'Dilemmas in Engendering Democracy' (1995) 24 Economy and Society 1.

Lister, R, *Citizenship: Feminist Perspectives*, 1997, London: Macmillan.

Lister, R, 'Citizenship and difference: towards a differentiated universalism' (1998) 1(1) European Journal of Social Theory 71.

Lloyd, D and Freeman, MDA, *Introduction to Jurisprudence*, 5th edn, 1985, London: Stevens.

Logie, J, 'Party policy and the law' (1988) 138 NLJ 307.

Loughlin, M, *Public Law and Political Theory*, 1992, Oxford: Clarendon.

Loughlin, M, 'The pathways of public law scholarship', in Wilson, GP (ed), *Frontiers of Legal Scholarship*, 1995, Chicester: John Wiley.

Loughlin, M, *Legality and Locality*, 1996, Oxford: Clarendon.

Loughlin, M, *Rights Discourse and Public Law thought in the UK*, 1997, Warwick: University of Warwick Legal Research Institute.

Loughlin, M and Scott, C, 'The regulatory state', in Dunleavy, P, Gamble, A, Holliday, I and Peele, G (eds), *Developments in British Politics*, 1997, London: Macmillan.

Lovenduski, J, 'Toward the emasculation of political science', in Spender, D (ed), *Men's Studies Modified*, 1981, Oxford: Pergamon.

Lovenduski, J and Norris, P (eds), *Women in Politics*, 1996, Oxford: OUP.

Lovenduski, J and Randall, V, *Contemporary Feminist Politics: Women and Power in Britain*, 1993, Oxford: OUP.

Luping, D, 'Women's rights' (1998) *Liberty*, Autumn, p 4.

Lyotard, J, *The Postmodern Condition*, 1984, Manchester: MUP.

MacCormick, N, 'Beyond the sovereign state' (1993) 56 MLR 1.

MacCormick, N, 'The ideal and the actual of law and society', in Tasioulas, J, *Law, Values and Social Practices*, 1997, Aldershot: Dartmouth.

MacCormick, N, 'Democracy, subsidiarity, and citizenship in the "European Commonwealth"' (1997) 16 Law and Philosophy 331.

MacCormick, N, 'Risking constitutional collision in Europe?' (1998) 18 MLR 517.

Macdonald, IA and Blake, NJ, *Macdonald's Immigration Law and Practice*, 1995, 4th edn, London: Butterworths.

MacKinnon, CA, 'Feminism, Marxism, method, and the state: an agenda for theory' (1981–82) 7 Signs 515.

MacKinnon, CA, *Feminism Unmodified: Discourses on Life and Law*, 1987, Harvard: Harvard UP.

MacKinnon, CA, *Toward a Feminist Theory of the State*, 1989, Cambridge, MA: Harvard UP.

MacKinnon, CA, *Only Words*, 1993, Cambridge, MA: Harvard UP.

Macklin, A, 'Refugee women and the imperative of categories' (1995) 17 HRQ 213.

Maguire, M, Morgan, R and Reiner, R (eds), *The Oxford Handbook of Criminology*, 1997, Oxford: Clarendon.

Malleson, K, 'The use of Judicial Appointments Commissions: a review of the US and Canadian models', 1997, Research Series No 6/97, London: LCD.

Marcus, I and Spiegelman, PG (moderators), DuBois, EC, Dunlap, MC, Gilligan, CJ, MacKinnon, CA and Menkel-Meadow, CJ (conversants), 'Feminist discourse, moral values and the law – a conversation' (1985) 34 Buffalo L Rev 11.

Marshall, BL, *Engendered Modernity: Feminism, Social Theory and Social Change*, 1994, Cambridge: Polity.

Marshall, T, *Citizenship and Social Class*, 1950, Cambridge: CUP.

Martin, D, 'Have women judges really made a difference?' (1986) 6 Lawyers Weekly 5.

Martin, S and Mahoney, K (eds), *Equality and Judicial Neutrality*, 1987, Toronto: Carswell.

Matas, T and Aiken, S, 'International human rights law and legal remedies in expulsion: progress and some remaining problems with special reference to Canada' (1997) 15 Netherlands Quarterly of Human Rights 429.

Mathieu, B, 'La dignité de la personne humaine: quel droit? Quel titulaire?' (1996) Dalloz, chron, p 282

McAuslan, P, 'Public choice and public law' (1988) 51 MLR 687.

McCollum, H, 'Surviving in public' (1997–98) Trouble & Strife, Winter, p 65.

McCormick, JP, 'Habermas' discourse theory of law: bridging the gap between Anglo-American and Continental legal traditions?' (1997) 60 MLR 734.

McCrudden, C and Chambers, G (eds), *Individual Rights and the Law in Britain*, 1994, Oxford: Clarendon.

McDowell, L and Pringle, R (eds), *Defining Women: Social Institutions and Gender Divisions*, 1992, Cambridge: Polity in association with The Open University.

McEldowney, J, *Public Law*, 1998, London: Sweet & Maxwell.

McGlynn, C, *The Woman Lawyer – Making the Difference*, 1998, London: Butterworths.

McIntosh, M, 'The state and the oppression of women', in Kuhn, A and Wolpe, A (eds), *Feminism and Materialism*, 1978, London: Routledge.

McKibbin, R, *Classes and Cultures: England 1918–1951*, 1998, Oxford: OUP.

McLennan, G, 'Feminism, episemology and postmodernism' (1995) 29 Sociology 403.

McNay, L, *Foucault and Feminism: Power, Gender and the Self*, 1992, Cambridge: Polity.

McRobbie, A, *Postmodernism and Popular Culture*, 1994, London: Routledge.

Means, R, and Smith, R, *Community Care: Policy and Practice*, 1994, London: Macmillan.

Meehan, E, *Citizenship and the European Community*, 1993, London: Sage.

Menkel-Meadow, C, 'Portia in a different voice: speculating on women's lawyering process' (1987) 1 Berkeley Women's LJ 39.

Meyers, DT (eds), *Feminist Social Thought: A Reader*, 1997, London: Routledge.

Mill, JS, *On Liberty*, 1974, London: Penguin.

Millbank, J, *Theology and Social Theory: Beyond Secular Reason*, 1990, Oxford: Blackwells.

Miller, D and Walzer, M (eds), *Pluralism, Justice and Equality*, 1995, Oxford: OUP.

Millns, S, 'Dwarf-throwing and human dignity: a French perspective' (1996) 18 JSWFL 375.

Millns, S and Sheldon, S, 'Delivering democracy to abortion politics: *Bowman v The United Kingdom* (1999) 7 FLS (forthcoming).

Mitchell, J, 'The causes and effects of the absence of a system of public law in the United Kingdom' [1965] PL 95.

Mole, N, *Problems Raised by Certain Aspects of the Present Situation of Refugees from the Standpoint of the European Convention on Human Rights*, 1997, Council of Europe, Human Rights Files, No 9.

Morgan, D and Lee, RG, *Blackstone's Guide to the Human Fertilisation and Embryology Act 1990*, 1991, London: Blackstone.

Morgan, D and Lee, RG, 'In the name of the father? *Ex parte Blood*: dealing with novelty and anomaly' (1997) 60 MLR 840.

Morison, J and Livingstone, S, *Reshaping Public Power: Northern Ireland and the British Constitutional Crisis*, 1995, London: Sweet & Maxwell.

Morison, J, 'The case against constitutional reform?' (1998) 25 JLS 510.

Morris, A and Nott, S, *Working Women and the Law: Equality and Discrimination in Theory and Practice*, 1991, London: Routledge.

Morris, A and O'Donnell, T (eds), *Feminist Perspectives on Employment Law*, 1999, London: Cavendish Publishing.

Mouffe, C (ed), *Dimensions of Radical Democracy: Pluralism, Citizenship, Community*, 1992, London: Verso.

Mouffe, C, *The Return of the Political*, 1993, London: Verso.

Mount, F, *The British Constitution Now*, 1992, London: Heinemann.

Munt, S, 'Sisters in exile: the lesbian nation', in Ainley, R (ed), *New Frontiers of Space, Bodies and Gender*, 1998, London: Routledge.

Naffine, N, *Law and the Sexes*, 1990, Sydney: Allen & Unwin.

Naffine, N and Owens, R (eds), *Sexing the Subject of Law*, 1997, Sydney: Law Book.

Nairn, T, *The Enchanted Glass: Britain and its Monarchy*, 1988, London: Hutchinson Radius.

Nairn, T, 'The departed spirit' (1997) LRB, 30 October, p 6.

Nairn, T, 'Breaking up is hard to do' (1998) *Marxism Today*, Nov/Dec.

Nardell, G, 'The Quantock hounds and the Trojan Horse' (1995) PL 27.

Naylor, B, 'Pregnant tribunals' (1989) 14 Legal Service Bulletin 41.

Nedelsky, J, 'Law, boundaries and the bounded self' (1990) 30 Representations 162.

Negt, O and Kluge, A, *Public Sphere and Experience*, 1993, Minneapolis: Minnesota UP.

Nelken, D, 'Blinding insights? The limits of a reflexive sociology of law' (1998) 25 JLS 407.

Neumann, F, *The Democratic and the Authoritarian State: Essays in Political and Legal Theory*, 1957, New York: The Free Press.

Nicholson, L (ed), *Feminism/Postmodernism*, 1990, London: Routledge.

Nicolson, F and Twomey, P (eds), *Current Issues in UK Asylum Law*, 1998, Aldershot: Ashgate.

Nygren, A, *Agape and Eros: A Study of the Christian Idea of Love*, 1930, London: SPCM.

O'Connor, S, 'Portia's Progress' (1991) 66 New York UL Rev 1546.

O'Donovan, K, *Sexual Divisions in Law*, 1985, London: Weidenfeld and Nicolson.

O'Donovan, K, 'Engendering justice: women's perspectives and the rule of law' (1989) 39 Toronto ULJ 127.

O'Donovan, K, *Family Law Matters*, 1993, London: Pluto.

O'Donovan, K, 'A new settlement between the sexes? Constitutional law and the citizenship of women', in Bottomley, A (ed), *Feminist Perspectives on the Foundational Subjects of Law*, 1996, London: Cavendish Publishing.

O'Donovan, K and Szyszczak, E, *Equality and Sex Discrimination Law*, 1988, Oxford: Basil Blackwell.

Okin, S, *Justice, Gender and the Family*, 1989, London: HarperCollins.

O'Leary, B, 'What should public lawyers do?' (1992) 12 OJLS 304.

O'Leary, B, 'The conservative stewardship of Northern Ireland, 1979–97: sound-bottomed contradictions or slow learning?' (1997) XLV Political Studies 663.

Oliver, D, 'Is the *ultra vires* rule the basis for judicial review?' [1987] PL 543.

Oliver, D, 'State property and individual rights' (1988) 25 Coexistence 103.

Oliver, D, 'Common values in public and private law and the public/private divide' [1997] PL 630.

Oliver, D and Drewry, G (eds), *The Law and Parliament*, 1998, London: Butterworths.

Oliver, P, Douglas Scott, S and Tadros, V, *Faith in Law*, 1999, Oxford: Hart.

Olsen, F, 'The family and the market: a study of ideology and legal reform' (1983) 96 Harv L Rev 1497.

Olsen, F, 'The myth of state intervention in the family' (1985) 18 Michigan Journal of Law Reform 835.

Oosterveld, VL, 'The Canadian guidelines on gender-related persecution: an evaluation' (1996) 8 International Journal of Refugee Law 569.

Paglia, C, *Vamps and Tramps: New Essays*, 1994, New York: Vintage.

Palmer, S, 'Rape in marriage and the European Convention on Human Rights: *CR v UK, SW v UK*' (1997) 5 FLS 91.

Pannick, D, 'Who is subject to judicial review and in respect of what?' [1992] PL 1.

Parker, S and Sampford, C (eds), *Legal Ethics and Legal Practice: Contemporary Issues*, 1995, Oxford: Clarendon.

Patel, KP, 'Recognizing the rape of Bosnian women as gender-based persecution' (1994) 60 Brooklyn L Rev 929.

Pateman, C, *Participation and Democratic Theory*, 1970, Cambridge: CUP.

Pateman, C, *The Sexual Contract*, 1988, Stanford: Stanford UP.

Pateman, C, *The Disorder of Women*, 1990, Cambridge: Polity.

Paxman, J, *The English: A Portrait of a People*, 1998, London: Michael Joseph.

Pennock, JR and Chapman, J (eds), *Authority Revisited*, 1987, London: New York UP.

Petchesky, R, 'Foetal images: the power of visual culture in the politics of reproduction', in Stanworth, M (ed), *Reproductive Technologies: Gender, Motherhood and Medicine*, 1997, London: Polity.

Phillips, A, *Democracy and Difference*, 1993, Cambridge: Polity.

Phillips, A, *The Politics of Presence*, 1995, Oxford: Clarendon.

Phillips, A (ed), *Oxford Readings in Feminism: Feminism and Politics*, 1998, Oxford: OUP.

Phillips, A, 'From inequality to difference: a severe case of displacement' (1998) 224 NLR 143.

Pringle, R and Watson, S, '"Women's interests" and the poststructuralist state', in Phillips, A (ed), *Feminism and Politics*, 1998, Oxford: OUP.

Prosser, T, 'Towards a critical theory of public law' (1982) 9 JLS 1.

Prosser, T, 'Journey without maps' [1993] PL 346.

Prosser, T, *Law and the Regulators*, 1997, Oxford: Clarendon.

Radford, M, and Kerr, A, 'Acquiring rights – losing power: a case study in ministerial resistance to the impact of European Community law' (1997) 60 MLR 23.

Ramazanoglu, C, *Up Against Foucault: Explorations of Some Tensions Between Foucault and Feminism*, 1993, London: Routledge.

Rawls, J, 'Justice as fairness: political not metaphysical' (1985) 14 Philosophy and Public Affairs 223.

Rawls, J, 'The idea of an overlapping consensus' (1987) 7 OJLS 1.

Rawls, J, *Political Liberalism*, 1993, New York: Columbia UP

Raz, J, *The Morality of Freedom*, 1986, Oxford: Clarendon.

Razack, S, *Canadian Feminism and the Law: The Women's Legal Education and Action Fund and the Pursuit of Equality*, 1991, Toronto: Second Story.

Richardson, G and Genn, H, *Administrative Law and Government Action. The Courts and Alternative Mechanisms of Review*, 1994, Oxford: Clarendon.

Rivero, J and Waline, R, *Droit Administratif*, 17th edn, 1998, Paris: Dalloz.

Robson, R, *Sappho Goes to Law School: Fragments in Lesbian Legal Theory*, 1998, New York: Columbia UP.

Rorty, R, *Contingency, Irony and Solidarity*, 1989, Cambridge: CUP.

Rose, G, *The Broken Middle*, 1992, Oxford: Blackwells.

Rosenfeld, M, 'Law as discourse: bridging the gap between democracy and rights' (1996) 108 Harv L Rev 1163.

Rosenfeld, M, *Just Interpretations: Law Between Ethics and Politics*, 1998, Berkeley: California UP.

Sachs, A and Hoff Wilson, J, *Sexism and the Law – A Study of Male Beliefs and Judicial Bias*, 1978, Oxford: Martin Robertson.

Saint-James, V, 'Réflexions sur la dignité de l'être humain en tant que concept juridique du droit français' (1997) Dalloz, chron, p 61.

Salecl, R, *The Spoils of Freedom*, 1994, London: Routledge.

Salter, M, 'Habermas's new contribution to legal scholarship' (1997) 24 JLS 285.

Sandel, M, 'The procedural republic and the unencumbered self' (1986) 12 Political Theory 81.

Sandland, R, 'Between "truth" and "difference": poststructuralism, law and the power of feminism' (1995) 3 FLS 4.

Scanlon, J, 'The horrors of heterosexuality' (1997–98) Trouble & Strife, Winter, p 72.

Scheuerman, W, *Between the Norm and the Exception: The Frankfurt School and the Rule of Law*, 1994, Cambridge, MA: MIT.

Schmitt, C, *Political Theology: Four Chapters on the Concept of Sovereignty*, 1985, Cambridge, MA: MIT.

Schmitt, C, *The Crisis of Parliamentary Democracy*, 1988, Cambridge, MA: MIT.

Schor, N and Weed, E (eds), *The Essential Difference*, 1994, Bloomington: Indiana UP.

Sebestyen, A, 'Tendencies in the movement: then and now', in Sebestyen, A (ed), *Feminist Practice: Notes From the Tenth Year*, 1979, London: In Theory.

Sedley, S, 'The sound of silence: constitutional law without a constitution' (1994) 110 LQR 270.

Sedley, S, 'Human rights: a twenty first century agenda' [1995] PL 386.

Shah, P, 'Quarterly legal update' (1997) 11 Immigration and Nationality Law and Practice 95.

Shaw, J, 'European Union legal studies in crisis? Towards a new dynamic' (1996) 16 OJLS 321.

Shaw, J, ' The interpretation of European Union citizenship' (1998) 61 MLR 293.

Shaw, J and More, G (eds), *New Legal Dynamics of European Union*, 1995, Oxford: Clarendon.

Sheldon, S, *Beyond Control: Medical Power and Abortion Law*, 1997, London: Pluto.

Sheldon, S and Thomson, M (eds), *Feminist Perspectives on Health Care Law*, 1998, London: Cavendish Publishing.

Sheridan, S, *Wife and Widow*, 1993, Anne Arbor: Michigan UP.

Sherry, S, 'Civil virtue and the feminine voice of constitutional adjudication' (1986) 72 Vanderbilt L Rev 543.

Showstack Sassoon, A (ed), *Women and the State*, 1987, London: Hutchinson.

Shute, S and Hurley, S (eds), *On Human Rights: The Oxford Amnesty Lectures 1993*, 1993, New York: Basic Books.

Simons, J, *Foucault and the Political*, 1995, London: Routledge.

Smart, C, 'Feminism and law: some problems of analysis and strategy' (1986) 14 International Journal of the Sociology of Law 109.

Smart, C, *Feminism and the Power of Law*, 1989, London: Routledge.

Smart, C (ed), *Regulating Womanhood: Historical Essays on Marriage, Motherhood and Sexuality*, 1992, London: Routledge.

Smart, C, *Law, Crime and Sexuality*, 1995, London: Sage.

Smith, A, *New Right Discourse on Race and Sexuality*, 1994, Cambridge: CUP.

Smith, D, 'Bagehot, the Crown and the Canadian Constitution' (1995) 28 Canadian Journal of Political Science 619.

Smith, J, *Different for Girls: How Culture Creates Women*, 1997, London: Chatto & Windus.

Snider, L, 'Feminism, punishment and the potential of empowerment' (1994) 9 Canadian Journal of Law and Society 75.

Somers, M, 'Rights, relationality, and membership: rethinking the making and meaning of citizenship' (1994) 19 Law and Social Theory 63.

Spijkerboer, T, 'Woman and refugus status: beyond the public/private divide' (1995) 7 International Journal of Refugee Law 756.

Stanworth, M, (ed), *Reproductive Technologies: Gender, Motherhood and Medicine*, 1987, Cambridge: Polity.

Steiner, H and Alston, P, *International Human Rights in Context: Law, Politics, Morals,* 1996, Oxford: Clarendon.

Sterrett, S, *Creating Constitutionalism? The Politics of Legal Expertise and Administrative Law in England and Wales,* 1997, Ann Arbor: Michigan UP.

Stevens, D, 'The Asylum and Immigration Act 1996: erosion of the right to seek asylum' (1998) 61 MLR 207.

Storey, H, 'Country reports: UK' (1997) International Journal of Refugee Law (Special Issue) 71.

Story, A, 'Owning Diana: from people's princess to private property' [1998] 5 Web JCLI (http://www.webjcli.ncl.ac.uk/).

Straw, J and Boateng, P, *Bringing Rights Home: Labour's Plans to Incorporate the European Convention on Human Rights into United Kingdom Law,* 1996, Labour Party Consultation Paper, December.

Stychin, C, *Law's Desire: Sexuality and the Limits of Justice,* 1995, London: Routledge.

Stychin, C, *A Nation by Rights: National Cultures, Sexual Identity Politics and the Discourse of Rights,* 1998, Philadelphia: Temple UP.

Sugarman, D, 'Legal theory, the common law mind and the making of the textbook tradition', in Twining, W (ed), *Legal Theory and Common Law,* 1986, Oxford: Basil Blackwell.

Taggart, M (ed), *The Province of Administrative Law,* 1997, Oxford: Hart.

Taylor, C, *The Sources of the Self: The Making of Modern Identity,* 1989, Cambridge: CUP.

Taylor, C, *Philosophy and the Human Sciences: Philosophical Papers 2,* 1985, Cambridge: CUP.

Thomas D and Beasley, M, 'Domestic violence as a human rights issue' (1993) 15 HRQ 36.

Thompson, D, *Queen Victoria: Gender and Power,* 1990, London: Virago.

Thomson, M, 'Woman, medicine and abortion in the 19th century' (1995) 3 FLS 159.

Thomson, M, 'Legislating for the monstrous: access to reproductive services and the monstrous feminine' (1997) 6 SLS 401.

Thornton, M, *Public and Private: Feminist Legal Debates,* 1996, Oxford: OUP.

Tobias, C, 'Closing the gender gap on the federal courts' (1993) 61 Cincinnati L Rev 1237.

Tong, R, *Feminist Thought: A Comprehensive Introduction*, 1989, London: Unwin Hyam.

Toulmin Smith, J, Toulmin Smith, L and Brenato, L (eds), *English Guilds. The Original Ordinances of More than One Hundred Early English Guilds*, 1870 (reprinted 1963), os 40, London: Early English Text Society.

Townsend, S, *The Queen and I*, 1993, London: Mandarin.

Trend, D (ed), *Radical Democratic Politics: Identity, Citizenship and the State*, 1995, Routledge: London.

Tuitt, P, *False Images: The Law's Construction of the Refugee*, 1996, London: Pluto.

Turner, BS (ed), *Citizenship and Social Theory*, 1993, London: Sage.

Turpin, C, *British Government and the Constitution: Text, Cases and Materials*, 1995, London: Butterworths.

Twigg, J, 'Integrating carers into the service system: six strategic responses' (1993) 13 Ageing and Society 141.

Unger, RM, *Passion*, 1984, New York: The Free Press.

Unger, RM, *False Necessity; Anti-Necessitarian Social Theory in the Service of Radical Democracy*, 1987, Cambridge: CUP.

UNHCR, *Handbook on Procedures and Criteria for Determining Refugee Status under the 1951 Convention and the 1967 Protocol Relating to the Status of Refugees* (re-edited Geneva, January 1992).

UNHCR, Guidelines on Preventing and Responding to Sexual Violence Against Refugees, 1995.

UNHCR, Interviewing Applicants for Refugee Status: Training Module, 1995.

UNHCR, Division of International Protection, 'Gender-related persecution: an analysis of recent trends' (1997) International Journal of Refugee Law (Special Issue) 79

van Dijk, P, and van Hoof, G, *Theory and Practice of the European Convention on Human Rights*, 2nd edn, 1990, Deventer: Kluwer.

Varikas, E, 'The burden of our time' (1998) *Radical Philosophy*, Nov/Dec, p 92

Vincenzi, C, *Crown Powers, Subjects and Citizens*, 1998, London: Pinter.

Visek, RC, 'Creating the ethnic electorate through legal restorationism' (1997) 38 Harv Int L Rev 315.

Wade, H, 'What has happened to the sovereignty of Parliament?' (1991) 107 LQR 1.

Wadham, J, 'Bringing rights home: Labour's plans to incorporate the European Convention on Human Rights into UK law' [1997] PL 75.

Wadham, J and Mountfield, H, *Blackstone's Guide to the Human Rights Act 1998*, 1999, London: Blackstone.

Walby, S, 'Is citizenship gendered?' (1994) 28 Sociology 379.

Wallace, R, 'Making the Refugee Convention gender sensitive: the Canadian Guidelines' (1996) 45 ICLQ 702.

Walzer, M, 'Liberalism and the art of separation' (1984) 12 Political Theory 315.

Ward, I, *A Critical Introduction to European Law*, 1996, London: Butterworths.

Warner, M, *Monuments and Maidens: The Allegory of the Female Form*, 1985, London: Picador.

Waters, M, *Modern Sociological Theory*, 1994, London: Sage.

Watson, CW, 'Born a lady, became a princess, died a saint' (1997) 13 Anthropology Today 3.

Watson, S (ed), *Playing the State: Australian Feminist Interventions*, 1990, London: Verso.

Watts, C, 'Time and the working mother' (1998) *Radical Philosophy*, Sept/Oct, p 91.

Weeks, J, *Invented Moralities: Sexual Values in an Age of Uncertainty*, 1995, Cambridge: Polity.

Weiler, J, *The Constitution of Europe*, 1999, Cambridge: CUP.

Wells, C, 'Abortion counselling as vice activity: the free speech implications of *Rust v Sullivan* and *Planned Parenthood v Casey*' (1995) 95 Columbia L Rev 1724.

Welstead, M, 'A hunting we will go' (1994) The Conveyancer 416.

West, R, 'Women's hedonic lives: a phenomenological critique of feminist legal theory' (1987) 3 Wisconsin Women's LJ 81.

West, R, 'Jurisprudence and gender' (1988) 55 Chicago UL Rev 1.

White, S, *The Recent Work of Jürgen Habermas: Reason, Justice and Modernity*, 1988, Cambridge: CUP.

Whittle, S, 'An association for as noble a purpose as any' (1996) 146 NLR 336.

Whitty, N, 'Law and the regulation of reproduction in Ireland: 1922–92' (1993) 43 Toronto ULJ 851.

Whitty, N, 'The mind, the body and reproductive health information' (1996) 18 HRQ 224.

Whitty, N, Murphy, T and Livingstone, S, *Civil Liberties Law*, 1999, London: Butterworths.

Willets, D, *Who Do We Think We Are*? 1988, London: Centre for Policy Studies (http://www.cps.org.uk/willetts.htm).

Williams, GL, *Learning the Law*, 1st edn, 1945, London: Stevens.

Williams, P, *The Alchemy of Race and Rights*, 1991, Cambridge, MA: Harvard UP.

Wilson, E, 'The unbearable lightness of Diana' (1998) 224 NLR 136.

Wilson, B, 'Will women judges really make a difference?' (1990) 28 Osgoode Hall LJ 507.

Wilson, E, *The Myth of British Monarchy*, 1989, London: Journeyman.

Woolf, H, 'Public law – private law: why the divide? A personal view' [1986] PL 220.

Wright, J, 'Local authorities, the duty of care and the European Convention on Human Rights' (1998) 18 OJLS 1.

Yeatman, A, *Bureaucrats, Technocrats, Femocrats: Essays on the Contemporary Australian State,* 1990, Sydney: Allen & Unwin.

Yeatman, A, *Postmodern Revisionings of the Political*, 1994, New York: Routledge.

Young, H, *This Blessed Plot: Britain and Europe from Churchill to Blair*, 1998, London: Macmillan.

Young, IM, 'Polity and group difference: a critique of the ideal of universal citizenship' (1989) 99 Ethics 250.

Young, IM, *Justice and the Politics of Difference*, 1990, Oxford: Princeton UP.

Yuval-Davies, N, *Gender and Nation*, 1997, London: Sage.

Yuval-Davis, N, 'Women, citizenship and difference' (1997) 57 FR 4.

Zander, M, *A Bill of Rights*, 4th edn, 1997, London: Sweet & Maxwell.

INDEX